THE BOOK OF SHOOTING FOR SPORT AND SKILL

THE BOOK OF
SHOOTING
FOR SPORT AND SKILL

Edited by
FREDERICK WILKINSON

A HERBERT MICHELMAN BOOK

CROWN PUBLISHERS, INC. NEW YORK

First published in the U.S.A. in 1980
by Crown Publishers, Inc., New York
First published in Great Britain in 1980 by
Frederick Muller, Ltd, Victoria Works,
Edgware Road, London NW2 6LE

Created, designed and produced by
Trewin Copplestone Publishing Ltd, London

ISBN 0-517-541777
Library of Congress Catalog Card Number: 80-50322

Editor: Pamela Tubby
Designer: Michael Robinson
Diagrams: Jim Wilkinson

Phototypeset by Tradespools Ltd, Frome
Printed in the U.S.A.

CONTENTS

CONTRIBUTORS

Principal advisers
Frederick Wilkinson (UK)
Vice-President, Arms and Armour Society;
Vice-President, Historical Breechloading
Small-arms Association

Jan Stevenson (USA)
Imperial War Museum, London

Contributors
Dr Lazlo Antal
British National Air Pistol Coach

DeWitt Bailey
Firearms Historian

John and Margot Bell
Officers of the Muzzle-loading Association
of Great Britain

Kenneth Brechin
Scottish National Fullbore Rifle Coach

John Chandler
Chief British National Smallbore and Fullbore
Pistol Coach

Sgt James E. Collins
Alabama State Police; National Police Combat
Pistol Champion; Firearms Instructor

Malcolm Cooper
World Three Position Shooting Champion

Norman F. Cooper
Clay Pigeon Shooting Coach; International
Judge; Gunsmith

Roy F. Dunlap
Gunsmith; Champion Metallic Silhouette
Rifle Shooter

Dr Alonso Garcelon
Director, National Rifle Association of America;
Past President, National Bench-rest Rifle
Shooters Association

Elgin Gates
Director, International Handgun Metallic
Silhouette Association; Editor, *The Silhouette*

Major R. Greenwood, R.A.
British Board of Ordnance

Nigel Hinton
International Practical Pistol Shooter

Carey Keates
Archivist, Holland and Holland

Brian D. Kett
Architect with a special interest in shooting
range design

Lee and Marilynn La Combe
Champion BB Gun Shooters

David Penn
Keeper of Weapons, Imperial War Museum,
London

Matthew Pumfrey
Legal Adviser to The Scottish Landowners
Federation

Derek Robinson
British National Air Rifle Coach

Stuart Williams
Former Shooting Editor, *Field and Stream*

David Winks
Gunmaker, Holland and Holland

INTRODUCTION

One of the great attractions of shooting is that it is a pastime of endless variety. Once the basic skills have been learnt, there are many directions in which one can develop. All aptitudes and abilities are catered for. There are shooters of the .22 rifle and pistol who are happy to put up a reasonable score, while others are perfectionists who use weapons that have almost ceased to be firearms and have become more like projectile machines. These free pistols, as they are known, can be electronically operated, counter-balanced, and fitted with a grip so complex that it can only be described as being put on rather than held. Other shooters prefer practical or combat shooting, which offers simulated situations that make very different mental and physical demands from formal target shooting. This form of shooting measures a shooter's ability to react to a situation quickly, coolly, safely and accurately. Shooters of black powder guns, originals or replicas, recreate historical adventure in a flourishing contemporary sport.

Typical 'free pistol' with all-round grip which ensures a steady hold, however, its use is restricted to certain competitions.

There are some who prefer long range target shooting where very different skills and judgements are called for. Not only does the weapon have to be aimed, but weather conditions, including the direction and force of wind, have to be considered together with the trajectory and ballistics of the cartridge being used – all play a very important part. For those who seek the excitement of a moving target there are skeet and clay pigeon shooting, fast growing sports, and running boar targets.

Hunting and game shooting remain as popular as ever, but few today would condone the old attitude towards hunting which was prevalent until the nineteenth century. All that mattered then was the size of the 'bag', the number of birds, rabbits, deer, lions, elephants or tigers, brought down in a single day. Today, the hunter is generally a far more responsible person, for he knows that his actions are going to affect the balance of nature. He is more than ever likely to be concerned with all aspects of the shoot – wood and field craft, knowledge of the game and its habits, tracking and methods of travel, concealment and survival in the terrain where game is found. Both his gun and his ammunition will be selected with care to suit the prey. Whether the prey are varmints – squirrel, rabbit and groundhog – or grouse, pheasant, partridge, duck, deer or larger game like elk, there is plenty to be found in this book for novice shot and experienced hunter alike.

Shooting is a hobby full of challenge – it is both satisfying and infuriating. Any shooter will tell you that with the same weapon, the same ammunition, the same weather conditions, the same range, the variation in performance can be shattering. It is a sport in which concentration is vital. Every target shooter has had the experience of putting a sequence of shots in a group centred comfortably on the ten ring and then with apparently the same stance and all conditions being the same, has put the next through the five ring.

Shooting is a hard taskmaster, for, all other things being equal, the bullet goes where it is sent. There are those who discuss the play of a barrel, the wear, the variations in muzzle velocity, the effects of different bullets and powders, but basically, a gun sends the bullet where you point it and poor results can seldom be blamed on anyone but the shooter. Knowing this, the satisfaction of achieving a good score is very real and rewarding. One soon comes to know, almost before the bullet has hit the target, that the shot is a good one. Shooting is a sport where one can compete happily against a previous score, seeking always for improvement.

In this volume the reader can find the experience, advice, suggestions and accumulated knowledge of more than twenty experts active in all fields of the shooting sports. The authors include national and international champions, national coaches, top gunmakers – all leading shooters with a wealth of knowledge to pass on to their fellow sportsmen.

Enthusiasts of the North South Skirmish Association regularly recreate the battles of the Civil War.

1 THE EVOLUTION OF THE GUN

FROM CHINA TO EUROPE

A superb quality, double-barrelled shotgun by a famous firm such as Holland and Holland and the intricate, electronically operated free pistol of the present-day Olympic marksman have an ancestry that stretches back some six or seven centuries. The story of the modern gun begins somewhere in China during the eleventh century, but its origins are by no means clear. Gunpowder, an explosive mixture of sulphur, charcoal and salt-petre, was first compounded in China during the eleventh century, but the evidence suggests that it was used not as a propellent, but primarily as a means of distracting and frightening an enemy. The bright flash, the cloud of smoke and a very loud report would certainly have made any attacker fear the worst. Later, the Chinese de-veloped the idea and produced very simple firearms. The *huo ch'iang* consisted of a hollowed out bamboo tube, blocked at one end and prob-ably strengthened at appropriate points. A measure of the powder was poured down the tube, followed by a clay or metal ball. If the powder was then ignited, the confined explosion blew out the projectile, albeit in a very haphazard fashion. Strangely, the Chinese seem not to have developed the concept further, but retained this old matchlock system.

Probably because of their trading contacts, the Arabs learned the secret of gunpowder and it is likely that the knowledge reached Europe by way of the Islamic traders.

Evidence of its first use in Europe is vague and confusing. It is claimed by many that Roger Bacon, a learned cleric of the thirteenth century, knew of its existence and gave details of its manu-facture in a coded passage in one of his works. This evidence is somewhat suspect, as it is not certain that the relevant passage was included in his original work. The earliest known edition con-taining it dates from much later than the thirteenth century.

The first really firm evidence dates from the fourteenth century. In 1326 Walter de Milemete, chaplain to King Edward III, produced copies of books intended for the guidance of his royal master. The manuscripts have survived and they contain two coloured marginal inserts. They clearly show an armoured knight of the early fourteenth century firing what is thought to be the earliest representation of a firearm. The vase-shaped gun is shown lying on a wooden trestle table while the knight holds a hooked rod with which he is apparently touching the vase; from the open end of the vase-shaped gun the point of an arrow protrudes. The gun, for such it must certainly be, is unfortunately, not mentioned in the text. However, one of the earliest surviving handguns found in Sweden has a form similar to that illustrated in the Milemete manuscript. This bronze gun is only some 12 inches long and has a small hole drilled through the wall of the chamber. It was into this hole that the tip of the rod held by the knight would have been inserted. The end may have been heated or it may have held a piece of burning moss or a glowing ember, which would have ignited the gunpowder to blast out the arrow or metal projectile. This date of 1326 is coinci-dentally confirmed from the records of the Italian city of Florence, where the entries for that year contain references to men whose job it was to supply guns and ammunition.

Left: A musketeer with matchlock and rest. From 'Maniement des Armes' by Jacob de Gheyn.
Below: The Milemete manuscript, showing the earliest European firearms.

THE MATCHLOCK

From the beginning of the fourteenth century there were gradual improvements in the design of firearms, but at first they were concerned with artillery. To the military engineers of the period gunpowder must have seemed the answer to their problems, for by then fortifications were extremely strong and capable of resisting the older means of attack. Cannon of various sizes were produced. However, the idea of using gunpowder to propel a projectile was naturally extended and soon smaller versions, known as handguns, were available. They consisted of a metal barrel with a socket at the rear into which a wooden pole could be fitted. Some were fashioned entirely from metal with the rod extending from the breech end. When the weapon was fired, the rod or wooden stock was tucked under the arm or held against the chest. Aiming, apart from pointing the weapon in the general direction of the enemy, was virtually impossible.

One greatly limiting feature of these firearms was the problem of ignition. The earliest references do not elaborate on the details. If the powder was ignited by a heated iron, there were obvious problems since the shooter must, of necessity, have stayed somewhere near a fire, for the rod would have cooled rapidly. If a glowing ember was used, similar problems existed, so that some improved device was needed. The answer, produced late in the fourteenth century, was the match. This was a length of cord that was soaked in a very strong solution of potassium nitrate and then dried. Once lit, this match burned very slowly and the glowing end could be used to ignite the charge of powder. Obviously, there were practical problems in handling this match and, probably early in the fifteenth century, a mechanical system was devised. An S-shaped metal arm was fitted on the right side of the wooden stock, which by now had been shortened so that it could be more readily tucked under the arm. The match was fitted to the top arm of the S-shaped serpentine and positioned so that when the lower end, which projected beneath the wooden stock, was pressed, the top end swung forward and placed the tip of the match into the touch-hole to fire the weapon. In a later develop-

Prime your Pan.

Return your scouring stick.

ment of this idea the touch-hole was moved from the top of the barrel to the side to simplify construction and a small metal pan was fitted level with it. A pinch of fine-grained powder was placed into this pan and the serpentine was so positioned that when operated the end holding the match was pressed into the pan. As the powder in the pan, the priming, flashed, the flame passed through the touch-hole to the breech and ignited the main charge of powder.

The serpentine mechanism was improved; in place of the simple pivoted arm, a spring-operated mechanism was developed. Pressure on a trigger or bar would make the arm swing forward into the priming powder. During the sixteenth century the wooden stock was also improved. Two basic shapes were commonly in use. The French shape had an acutely curved butt, which was held against the chest. The Spanish stock was much straighter and had a widened butt with a concave end to fit comfortably against the shoulder. Both shapes are illustrated in the guns shown on page 15. By the latter part of the sixteenth century a form of musket, or smooth-bored firearm, was in common use by most of the armies of Europe.

The seventeenth century saw the increasing dominance of firearms on both the field of sport and battle, as the matchlock musket was cheap to produce and simple to use. It had a metal barrel about 48 inches long, blocked at one end and with an internal diameter of about $\frac{3}{4}$ inch. The plain walnut stock was almost invariably made in the Spanish style, which practical experience had shown to be the most useful, and it had a simple serpentine mechanism fitted on the right-hand side at the breech. The trigger was more commonly used than the lever, and to reduce the chance of it being knocked, a flat metal guard was fitted around it.

Engravings from a book of instruction for musketeers. The musketeer is shown with all his accoutrements and each step in the firing of a matchlock musket is carefully illustrated.

Cock your match.

Give fire

The charge of powder was poured down the barrel from a powder horn or from small metal or horn containers, each of which held one measured charge. The lead bullet was fairly loose fitting so that it could be dropped down the barrel quite easily. It was rammed down firmly on top of the charge of powder by means of a long, thin, wooden stick. This rod was known as the scouring stick in the seventeenth century, and later as the ramrod.

The touch-hole was now invariably on the right-hand side of the breech and the pan had been fitted with a pivoted cover so that the priming could be held in place more safely. The length and weight of the musket made it difficult to manage and the musketeers of the first part of the seventeenth century were equipped with a wooden stick, the rest, which was used to support the weight of the barrel when firing.

The matchlock musket was simple, generally reliable, but certainly limited in its use. The greatest handicap was the match because without it the weapon was useless. It had to be kept constantly alight, and wind and rain could render a musketeer totally helpless. In order to reduce the chance of this happening it was usual for both ends of the match to be lit. This was a good idea, but it made the musket even more inconvenient and difficult to handle, as the musketeer now had to make sure that both ends of the match were in no danger of causing an accidental explosion. The match was continually being consumed, which meant that the musketeer had to carry a supply of spare lengths. Besides his musket and match, he had to carry a bag of bullets and containers to hold his powder, so he soon became festooned with accoutrements.

Another limitation of the matchlock was that it could hardly be used on horseback because it really needed both hands to operate it. Trying to cope with a plunging horse and a matchlock weapon was just too difficult. It was also rather inconvenient to use a matchlock for hunting because the glowing tip betrayed the hunter, and moving through woods and grassland with a piece of lighted match was not easy. Matchlocks were used by hunters and continued in use for many years after they had been superseded by more efficient means of ignition simply because they were cheap and easy to manufacture and maintain in good working order.

1, 2 and 3. Matchlock muskets with crook-shaped butts.
4. A late sixteenth century matchlock. The ramrod is housed beneath the barrel.
5. A late sixteenth century French matchlock with the typical down-curving butt.
6. Sixteenth century Italian matchlock arquebus with walnut stock inlaid with engraved staghorn. Below it, an arquebus rest made in Germany.

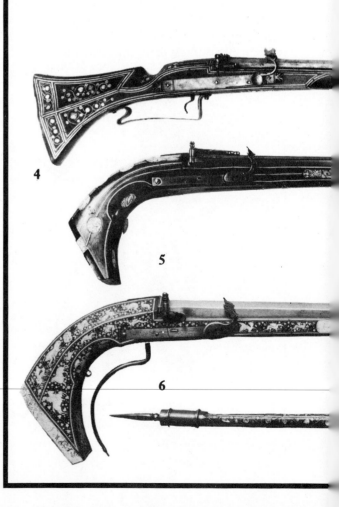

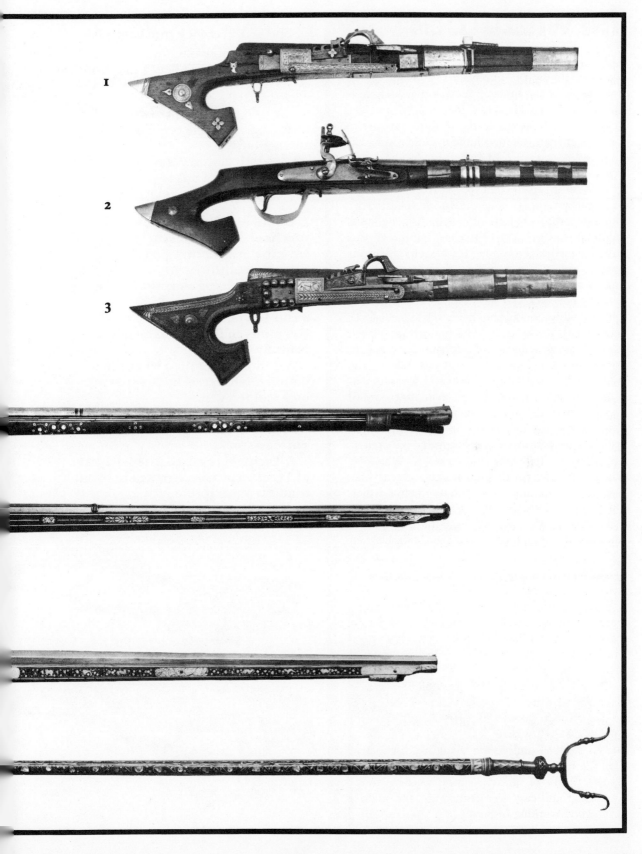

THE WHEEL-LOCK

Other, and less restricting, methods of ignition were sought by the gunmakers, and one of the earliest practical alternatives was that known as the wheel-lock. The basic idea was to produce sparks that dropped into the priming powder to fire the charge. The available evidence suggests that it was probably an Italian invention dating from the early sixteenth century. By the middle of the century an efficient spark-producing device had been developed. The wheel-lock consisted of a thick steel disc, the edge of which was roughened by deep cuts. A piece of pyrites, a mineral, was pressed against the edge of the wheel, which was spun round. The resulting friction produced small, incandescent sparks. The wheel was rotated by means of a strong V-spring and, although the mechanical details might vary, all wheel-locks had first to be spanned. The spring was placed under tension by means of a spanner, or wrench, which was fitted over the squared axle of the wheel and then rotated. The wheel was connected, by means of a short linked chain, to the tip of the V-spring so that as the wheel was rotated the spring was compressed. At a certain point a small spring-activated, metal arm engaged with a recess on the side of the wheel and locked it. When the trigger was pressed this metal arm, or sear, was withdrawn from the wheel, and the spring, which was under tension, caused the wheel to rotate. The pyrites was held between the jaws of an angular metal arm known as the dog's head or

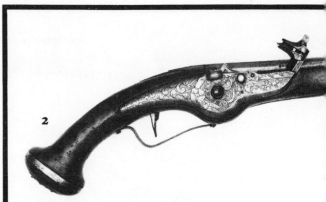

1. Detail of the wheel-lock mechanism from an early seventeenth century pistol.
2. Seventeenth century wheel-lock pistol of the type commonly used by cavalry.
3 and 4. Wheel-lock pistols made in Germany in the late sixteenth century.
5. A double-barrelled wheel-lock pistol. Each barrel has a separate lock and trigger.
6. A seventeenth century German wheel-lock rifle with carved and painted stock.
7. A Tschinke, named after the town of Teschen or Cieszyn, where it was made around 1630.

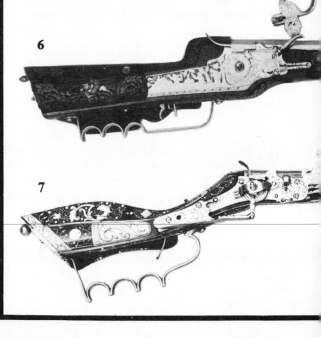

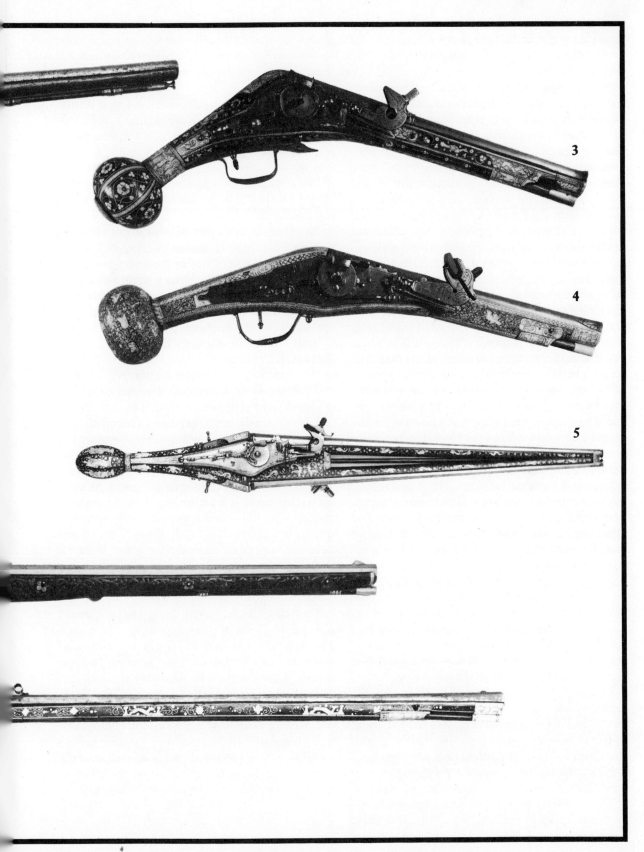

cock. The wheel was positioned so that the edge projected through the base of the pan next to the touch-hole and the sparks dropped directly into the priming.

The wheel-lock offered considerable advantages over the older matchlock. It was less at the mercy of the elements, as there was no glowing tip to be extinguished, although rain could still dampen the priming and prevent ignition. Another tremendous advantage of the system was that the weapon could be loaded, primed, spanned and then left ready for instant use – something impossible with the matchlock except for very brief periods. The arm could be swung clear of the pan so that the weapon was safe and, when required, the arm could be pushed down and the weapon was ready to fire. When the trigger was pressed, the pan cover was automatically withdrawn, allowing the pyrites to make contact with the rotating wheel and the sparks to fall into the priming.

Another great advantage of the wheel-lock was that it could be made in any size. For the first time easily portable firearms could be produced. These are known as pistols, a name probably derived from Pistoia, a town in Italy. Pistols introduced a new threat to the rulers of Europe, for the assassin now had a firearm that could be easily concealed on the body. It is from this period that the legislation controlling the use and carrying of firearms can be dated.

The wheel-lock was not without its drawbacks. The mechanism was, in comparison with the matchlock, quite complicated and consequently more prone to jamming, breakage and malfunction. The complexity of the mechanism also meant that it was expensive to produce and consequently the issue of wheel-lock pistols was limited to some cavalry units and to chosen bodyguards. Later on, in the seventeenth century, when production methods and design were simplified and improved, more wheel-lock pistols were used, but they were never issued to all the troops.

However, the matter of expense did not inhibit demand, and the rich huntsmen of the late sixteenth and seventeenth centuries relished these new and reliable weapons. The nobles at the European courts could afford the very best and some of the hunting weapons produced in this period are works of art. The stock, normally of walnut, was frequently inlaid with engraved horn, mother-of-pearl or chiselled steel. The lock itself might be engraved with classical scenes or military motifs, and the cock was often fashioned into grotesque shapes. Similar decoration was applied to the barrel and the entire weapon represented the combined efforts of a whole range of different craftsmen.

Since cost was not a problem, the rich hunter of this period could afford the accuracy offered by a rifled barrel. The majority of these wheel-lock hunting rifles had a very short butt, and the weapon was fired, not from the shoulder, but with the butt pressed against the side of the face. The thick, heavy barrel helped reduce the recoil to a minimum.

Pistols of the latter part of the sixteenth century were frequently decorated with inlay and chiselling in much the same way as the wheel-lock rifles. One feature of the wheel-lock pistols was a large ball pommel on the butt. This was intended not for use as a club, but to offer a convenient grip for the hand when drawing the pistol from the holster, which was normally fitted at the front of the saddle.

During this period there were numerous efforts to overcome a limitation of all these early firearms, for they were only single shot weapons. Some pistols were produced that had two barrels and two locks fitted to a single stock. By one means or another, first one barrel and then the other could be fired. Other more ingenious methods were tried whereby two charges could be fired from the same barrel using a superimposed charge. The pistol had a special barrel with two spaced touch-holes and either two locks or one lock that could be moved along the stock. A charge of powder and ball was rammed home, followed by a tight-fitting wad of felt or card on top of the ball. A second charge of powder and ball was then placed in position in front of the wad and this was held in place by another thick wad. The lock fired the front charge first and the wad prevented any flash-back from igniting the rear charge. This was fired by adjusting the lock to a position appropriate to the rear touch-hole.

By the middle of the seventeenth century wheel-lock pistols were out of fashion. The wheel-lock rifle, with its lines of beauty and superb decoration, was produced and used well into the century and in some areas seems to have remained in use well into the eighteenth century.

THE FLINTLOCK

Although the wheel-lock offered a greatly improved performance when compared with the old matchlock, it was nevertheless subject to limitations, expense and complexity being the most important. However, the basic concept of combustion by mechanical means was one that the firearms designer could exploit. Various mechanisms were produced that utilized not pyrites, but an even commoner mineral, flint. A piece of flint, by one means or another, was struck against a steel plate and the result was a shower of small, incandescent sparks. One of the earliest forms of such a mechanism seems to have been the Baltic lock, so called from its area of first development. In Italy and southern Europe the snaphaunce enjoyed a spell of popularity. The snaphaunce lock consisted of a cock with adjustable jaws, set to grip a wedged-shaped piece of flint. The cock moved through an arc of some 60°, and during its travel scraped down a vertical steel plate situated above the pan. The resulting sparks dropped directly into the priming to ignite the charge. The flint's momentum pushed the steel plate, which was pivoted, clear, allowing the cock to complete its arc. One of the problems with the snaphaunce was that the priming pan had to be protected by a small cover and by some means, either manual or mechanical, this cover had to be pushed clear before the sparks could fall into the priming.

During the first decade of the seventeenth century a French gunmaker, Marin Le Bourgeoys, took features from several types of flint locks and produced what was to become the standard form of flintlock, the French lock. Although details varied, one main feature of this lock was that the pan cover and steel were united in the form of an L-shaped piece of metal, generally known as the frizzen. The pan was primed and the frizzen was closed so that the steel plate stood vertically at the rear of the pan. The cock, which held the flint, had two positions; when vertical it was locked into place by means of a small metal arm, the sear, and in this position the trigger could not activate the mechanism. The weapon could be loaded, primed and the cock set to this safety, or half-cock, position. The weapon could be carried in this position with reasonable safety, although a mistake or malfunction might discharge the weapon. To prepare it for firing the cock was pulled back a further 10° or 20°. This disengaged the sear from its original position and engaged it in a second position, which could be activated by the trigger. When the trigger was pressed, the arm swung forward, the flint scraped down the steel face of the frizzen and produced sparks. At the same time the force of the cock and flint striking the plate tilted the frizzen forward to uncover the priming and allow the sparks to fall directly into it.

Despite its many advantages, this form of lock was not immediately adopted by all gunmakers and enjoyed only limited popularity until the second half of the seventeenth century. It does not appear to have been used outside Paris, where Le Bourgeoys lived, until after 1630 and for the next ten years, was not seen outside France, although after that its use spread and a few were used in the English Civil Wars. However, once its many advantages became apparent, it was to continue in use for the next two centuries and was not really made obsolete until the mid-nineteenth century. Although produced in several forms that differed in detail, all operated on the same basic principle. Spanish, Italian and other Mediterranean gunmakers favoured a form known as the miquelet. The main difference was in the mechanism of the half and full cock positions. The main spring was usually fitted on the outside of the lock and the cock was locked in position by a sear that passed through the lock plate. Other features on many of these locks are the square, grooved frizzen and the rather squat, straight cock.

In western Europe and America the French lock continued as the commonest means of ignition, and by the early eighteenth century it had acquired its basic form. At various times the mechanism was modified by the addition of little improvements, such as the detent. This ensured that when the trigger was pressed with the mechanism set at full cock, the sear would not snag in the half-cock slot and so prevent the weapon from firing. Small metal bearings were also set at certain points to reduce friction and speed up the action. Flintlocks were fitted to all types of firearms from tiny pistols carried in a lady's bag or gentleman's pocket to large cannon. Some of the best were reserved for duelling pistols, which, for their purpose, had to offer reliability and accuracy.

Hunters welcomed the flintlock, for it gave them greater freedom than they had previously known. It meant simpler mechanical handling and quicker operation. In addition, there was no longer a need to carry a spanner. From the middle of the eighteenth century onwards a great range of sporting guns was produced, many of superb craftsmanship. The double-barrelled shotgun was developed and much effort went into the production of top quality barrels. The best were reckoned to be those known as Damascus barrels. These were made by a system of interleaving layers of various grades of steel and iron and beating them out to give a very hard-wearing and consistent barrel. The method of production resulted in a series of distinctive patterns on the metal surface.

London, Paris and Vienna became main centres for the production of quality arms although they were by no means the only ones. In America, following the War of Independence (1775–1781), magazines or arsenals were set up at Harpers Ferry, Virginia (1796) and Springfield, Massachusetts (1797). The towns of Suhl and Berlin in Germany, Vienna in Austria, Madrid and Barcelona in Spain, Liège in Belgium and St Etienne and Charleville in France, and Birmingham in England established themselves as centres of firearms production.

The quality of workmanship varied enormously. From the middle of the nineteenth century Birmingham and Liège maintained a high rate of output of cheap and rather nasty pistols and trade muskets, but both towns also produced weapons of the highest quality.

Although the principles of rifling were known from the fifteenth century, the technical problems involved in mass producing rifled barrels were not overcome until the mid-nineteenth century, and the majority of pistols, sporting guns and military weapons were smooth bore until this period. Consequently, accuracy was never of a very high order. Another problem that was not really solved until the mid-nineteenth century was that of producing multi-shot weapons. The flintlock mechanism was not readily adaptable to multi-barrel or multi-chambered weapons, although a number of quite reliable repeating weapons was produced.

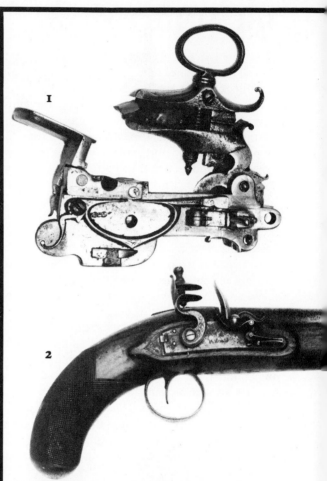

1. A snaphaunce lock made in Italy, mid-seventeenth century.
2. One of a pair of officers' flintlock pistols made in London, mid-nineteenth century.
3. One of a pair of flintlock pistols made in Dublin around 1770.
4. A tap action box-lock flintlock pistol. The selector ring for priming each barrel is below the frizzen.
5. A French military flintlock pistol, dated 1777.
6. A fowling piece once owned by Louis XIII of France and fitted with one of the earliest recorded flintlocks. Made by Pierre Le Bourgeoys, brother of Marin.
7. A Pennsylvanian flintlock, or Kentucky rifle, with the typical long barrel and patch box set in the butt. Dated 1809 on the lock plate.

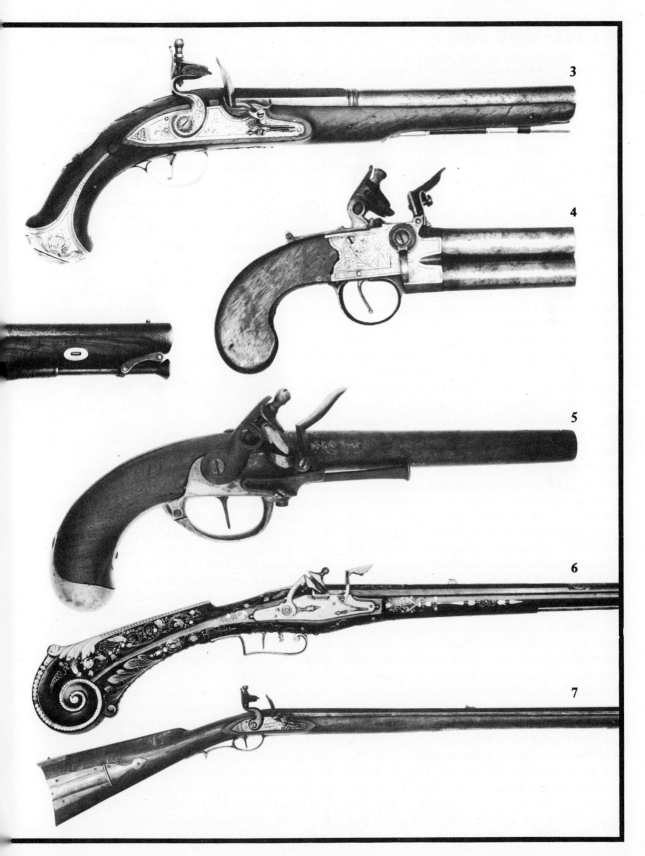

3

4

5

6

7

HANGFIRE AND THE PERCUSSION CAP

Although the flintlock lasted for a very long time, it was not without its problems. The piece of flint was reckoned to be reliable for about thirty shots, although quality varied considerably. Some would not spark after considerably less than thirty strikes, and others would continue sparking happily for fifty or sixty shots. Spare flints were therefore a necessity for all shooters. The main centre of production for this vital commodity was in Suffolk, England.

The priming in the pan was, as always, at the risk of wind and weather and another serious inconvenience to the hunter was the hangfire. Every action of the flintlock movement occupied a small, but nevertheless appreciable, time lapse. As the trigger was pressed, the cock moved forward and took time to scrape the face of the steel. More time elapsed as the sparks fell into the priming and there was a minute delay while it flared up and the flame passed through the touch-hole. The main charge then had to burn. The total of all these periods resulted in a small delay between the pressing of the trigger and the actual discharge of the shot. When volley fire was employed by the army and several hundred muskets were pointed in the general direction of the enemy, this hangfire was of no great consequence. For the hunter, particularly if he was aiming at a moving target, it was an annoying complication for which he had to make allowance in aiming. The solution was developed by an obscure Scottish cleric, Alexander Forsyth, who coupled with his calling an interest in shooting and chemistry.

Forsyth was familiar with the qualities of chemicals known as fulminates, which were so unstable that a knock was sufficient to make them explode. Forsyth experimented with fulminates, replacing or supplementing the normal gunpowder, hoping that this would speed up the rate of discharge. He was unsuccessful and the combination proved to be extremely dangerous. He was, however, clear-sighted enough to see that the principle might be adapted. Instead of the fulminate forming the main charge, he experimented by using it as the priming charge and found that this largely eliminated hangfires and also reduced the number of misfires.

Eventually, in 1807 he had a system that was practical enough to be patented. His patent was a little complex and comprised a small metal container, the shape of which earned it the name 'scent bottle'. This held grains of fulminate and was pivoted around a metal tube leading to the touch-hole. The scent bottle was inverted and this allowed a few grains of fulminate to fall into the channel directly adjacent to the touch-hole. The scent bottle was then returned to its original position and this brought into place, above the grains of fulminate, a spring-loaded rod. The flint cock had been removed and a solid-nosed hammer substituted, the internal mechanism remaining unchanged. When the trigger was pressed, the hammer flew forward, striking against the spring-operated plunger, banging it down on the grains of fulminate. These exploded and the flash passed through the touch-hole and exploded the main charge. This percussion system was to revolutionize the whole history of firearms.

Forsyth had patented his system, but there were numerous attempts to circumvent the patent. Various methods of inserting the fulminate into the touch-hole were attempted. The fulminate was enclosed in small quills, paper or metal foil caps, or supplied as small pellets bound together with an adhesive. All these systems proved to be somewhat defective. The solution that proved to be the most effective was the copper percussion cap. This consisted of a small, copper thimble with a quantity of fulminate deposited inside at the top. The cap was placed over a small pillar, known as the nipple, which was drilled with a hole connecting directly to the touch-hole. The cap had corrugated sides to give a grip when pushed into place over the nipple. When the hammer fell, it pressed the cap against the top of the nipple, exploded the fulminate and so produced the requisite flash. The nose of the hammer was hollowed out so that a protective lip enclosed the whole of the cap and prevented any fragments flying into the face of the shooter. Who the inventor of the cap was has never been satisfactorily settled. A number of people laid claim to the idea, but all that can be said with certainty was that by the 1820s the copper percussion cap had been adopted universally.

The advent of the percussion cap opened the way to the solution of another problem for the gunmaker – the construction of multi-shot weapons.

A number of designs were used, including the pepperbox revolver, which had a cylinder of metal drilled with five or six bores, each of which was fitted with a nipple. Each bore was loaded and the nipple capped. A small hammer was so positioned that its head could strike each cap in turn as the cylinder was rotated. This action could be repeated manually or mechanically until all shots had been fired. The majority of pepperboxes were smooth-bored and inaccurate, and the solid metal cylinder made them very muzzle heavy.

1. A percussion rifled carbine, adopted by the British Army in May 1856. It fired a .577 bullet.
2. A pair of percussion duelling pistols in a case with all accessories, including a small mallet, bullet moulds, rods and powder flask. The complete beautifully decorated and finished set was made by Bartolomeus Joseph Kuchenreuter around 1850.

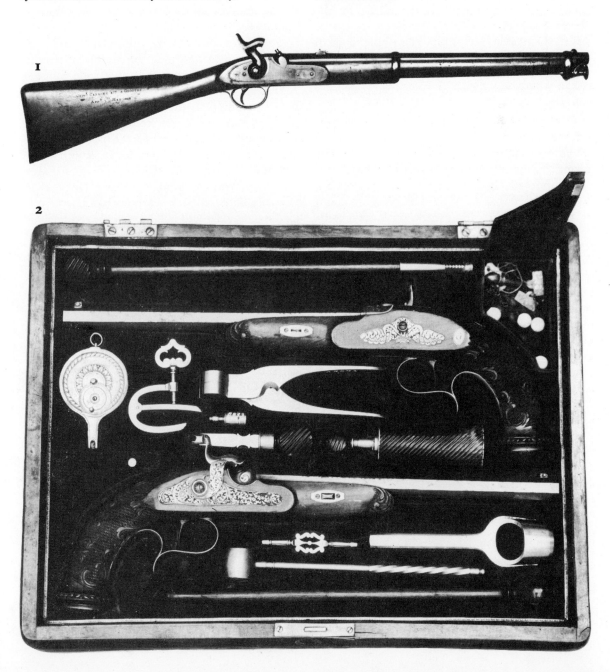

THE REVOLVER

Samuel Colt, an American with a very inquiring mind, had been considering the design for a revolver and tradition has it that the final idea came to him during a voyage to India. True or not, in 1836 he produced a patent for a percussion cap revolver that was to prove very effective. Despite its obvious advantages, the revolver did not achieve instant success and it was not until a number of his weapons were ordered by the Texas Rangers that Colt's revolvers began to sweep the market. He produced a whole range of weapons, including the famous .44 Dragoon, the .31 pocket pistol, and the .36 Navy and the .44 Army holster pistols, all of which used basically the same system.

Colt not only developed an efficient revolver, but was also one of the first to introduce modern manufacturing methods into the gun trade. His factories were organized in such a way that something approaching a production line was set up. It was claimed that any part of his weapons could be replaced by parts from stock. Each main component of a weapon carried the same number, but some of his early weapons now have parts bearing different numbers. This may well mean that a repair was made during its working life.

After a very successful display at the Great Exhibition of 1851 in London, Colt decided to establish a London factory to produce and market some of his revolvers. The pocket and Naval revolvers were made at the London factory, while other models were imported, and sold through a shop in Pall Mall in the centre of London. It was not an unqualified success and did not remain in operation for very long.

The gun trade took up Colt's ideas and from the 1850s onwards a plentiful supply of percussion revolvers was produced by a wide range of American, British and European makers. The next great step in the development of modern firearms came with the Rollin White patent of 1855, which paved the way for the breech-loading, metallic cartridge weapon of today. Rollin White patented the principle of loading the cartridges into the cylinder from the rear. Until then, virtually all percussion weapons had been front-loading; powder and ball or paper cartridges had

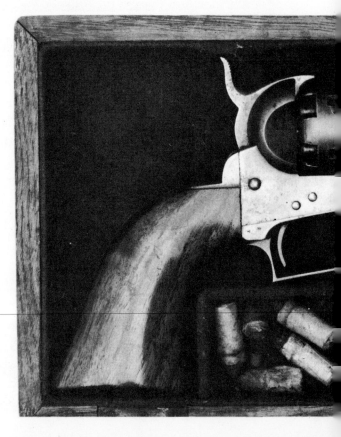

Above: Samuel Colt.
Right: A cased percussion Colt Navy 1851 .36 revolver, with square back trigger guard. Some of the original paper cartridges are in the bottom compartment of the case.

been inserted into the chamber from the front of the cylinder. Rollin White's idea was simple: he drilled each chamber right through the cylinder, so permitting a cartridge to be inserted from the rear. His patent was acquired by Smith & Wesson, who were also developing the concept of the metallic cartridge. This was not a new idea; it had been used in the pinfire weapons, whose cartridges held a pellet of fulminate, or explosive compound, in the base. Passing through the side of the case was a small, metal rod or pin, the tip of which was directly above the fulminate. When the hammer struck the pin, it was driven down onto the fulminate, which exploded and thus ignited the main charge.

Smith & Wesson took up the idea and deposited a small quantity of fulminate around the inside circumference of the metal flange. The nose of the hammer was fitted with a flat projecting striker. The cartridge was inserted in the rear of the cylinder so that the flange rested against the face. When the trigger was operated, the hammer fell forward and struck the rim of the cartridge, crushing it against the cylinder block. This detonated the fulminate and so initiated the ex-

plosion. This type of cartridge is known as rimfire.

The first of the Smith & Wesson cartridge loading weapons, the Model 1, or seven-shot, was produced in 1857. The advantages of the system were obvious, but there were practical limitations, for it was difficult to produce large calibre rimfire cartridges. The early Smith & Wesson's were only .22 calibre. However, cartridge loading obviously had great potential and many other manufacturers, including Colt, sought to develop the idea. Smith & Wesson held the master patent and, consequently, until it expired in 1869 their competitors were unable to circumvent the prohibition of manufacture.

In the meantime there had been improvements in cartridge design, and by 1866 the modern, centrefire cartridge had been developed. This comprised a metallic case with a small hole at the centre of the base, into which was fitted what was essentially a percussion cap. The firing pin on the hammer struck against the percussion cap, which detonated to ignite the main charge of powder. There were variations but two types, differing only in the priming design, became standard–the Boxer and the Berdan.

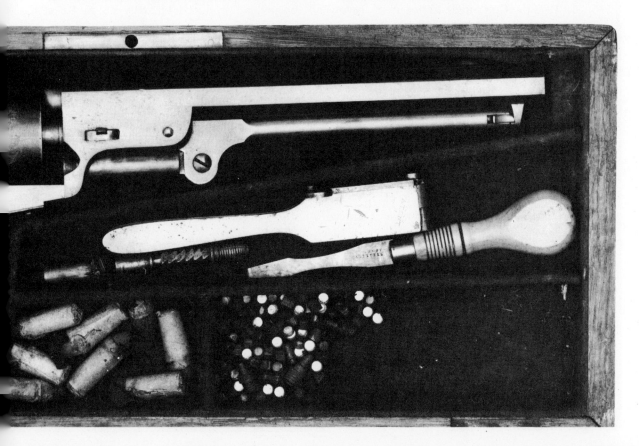

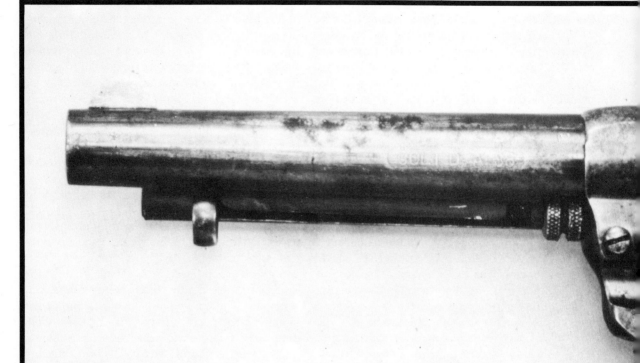

In 1873 the Colt Single Action Army revolver, one of the most successful and popular revolvers ever produced, first appeared on the market. Like the majority of contemporary Colt revolvers, it was single action, which meant that the hammer had to be cocked manually before each shot. A flood of cartridge weapons came onto the market and, as the centrefire cartridge was capable of great variation, they were made in many calibres. The most popular were probably .32, .38, .44 and .45. Larger sizes were produced, but for practical purposes the .45 proved to be the largest reliable and generally acceptable calibre.

In 1864 a Prussian artillery man produced a smokeless powder. The old gunpowder, or black powder, had always generated considerable quantities of smoke. In battle one of the commander's problems had been the obscuring of the battlefield by the immense clouds of gunsmoke that rolled backwards and forwards across the ground. Smokeless powder removed this problem, and better varieties were developed. In 1884 Paul Vieille, a Frenchman, produced one that was adopted by the French army and navy. The new

propellent produced virtually no smoke at all. Chemical engineering had also developed and propellents were better and far more consistent in quality. The better quality propellent ensured greater consistency and accuracy, and target shooting, always a popular pastime, became even more widespread.

From the 1850s mechanical engineering was capable of manufacturing rifled barrels in quantity at reasonable prices. Virtually every army in the world equipped its troops with rifles while the officers carried a revolver in addition to a largely superfluous sword.

The Colt Lightning revolver, barrel length 4½ inches.

SELF LOADING REVOLVERS AND PISTOLS

Most revolvers were six-shot, and the majority were double action and could be cocked either manually or by means of the trigger. However, one disadvantage of the revolver was the necessity to rock the hammer back prior to each shot. No matter which system of cocking was used, the pressure involved tended to throw the weapon off aim as well as slowing the rate of fire. Gun-makers sought to produce a weapon that would cock the hammer, remove the empty case and insert a fresh cartridge into the breech all in one movement. It fell to Hugo Borchardt to produce one of the first really practical self-loading systems. The idea was developed by Georg Luger; his pistol, with its toggle breech and angled butt, was to remain one of the world's most popular automatics. The Luger Parabellum pistol was not the only successful design, and other systems were equally good.

These pistols are described as automatic, but this is, strictly speaking, incorrect; 'self-loading'

would be a more accurate title. Most utilized the recoil of the weapon to operate the mechanism. As the bullet leaves the cartridge case it is travelling forward at high velocity, driven by the expanding gases. The cartridge case is driven in the opposite direction with equal force. This force may simply be absorbed by the frame of the revolver and transmitted to the shooter's arm to produce the recoil, or kick, but it can also be utilized to operate a mechanism. Although there are variations, most self-loading pistols use a spring that is compressed as some section of the mechanism moves under the impact of the recoil. This reverse movement is used to withdraw the empty cartridge case from the breech and, by means of a deflecting arm, eject it through a hole in the slide. The rearward movement drives the metal block, or slide, over the top of a metal box, known as a magazine, which holds a number of cartridges and, at the same time, compresses the spring. As the slide moves, it operates the mechanism that cocks the action ready for a second shot. When the force of the recoil is spent, the spring is under tension and so drives the slide forward. As the slide moves forward, it engages the top cartridge and slides it from the magazine into the breech. At this point the slide is usually locked into position ready for the next shot.

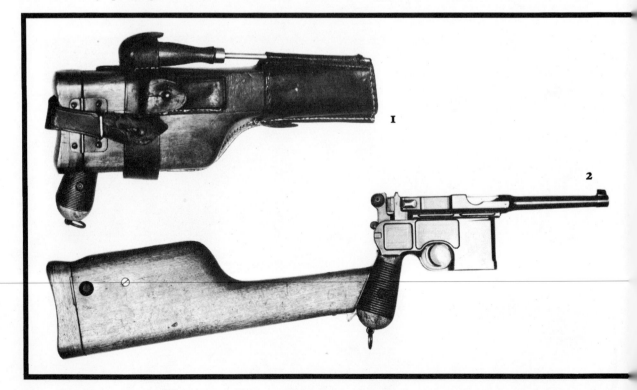

1

2

Pressure on the trigger allows the firing pin to fly forward and strike the cap to fire the shot and so recommence the same sequence of events. This means that once a full magazine has been inserted, all that is required to discharge each shot, after the initial cocking has been done, is simple pressure on the trigger.

At the beginning of this century a range of names well-known in the gun trade began to produce self-loading pistols: Mauser, his popular Broom Handle pistol, Luger, Webley and Scott, Savage, Browning and many others. Colt entered this field and in 1911 produced their famous .45 automatic pistol, which, slightly modified, became the present 1911 A1. This sturdy, reliable handgun saw service throughout World War I and World War II and is still favoured by most practical pistol shooters today as one of the best combat handguns ever produced.

One further development in this field was yet to come: the double action self-loading pistol. On the majority of self-loading pistols the hammer had to be manually cocked before the first round could be fired. Pistols such as the Smith & Wesson Model 39 and the Mauser HSc incorporated mechanisms that eliminated the need for this first movement, the action being operated by means of pressure on the trigger.

Military rifles of this century were, until recently, mostly manually operated, bolt action magazine weapons. A full magazine was inserted into the weapon. By one means or another, a bolt or metal arm was moved backwards or forwards to extract a cartridge from the magazine and push it into the breech; this movement also cocked the firing mechanism. The bolt was then locked into position for firing. When the bolt was pulled back, the empty cartridge case was withdrawn from the breech and ejected; as the bolt was pushed forward, the next cartridge was loaded. With this system it was possible to maintain a high rate of fire, which was, of course, limited by the manual dexterity of the soldier.

Although this was the most common military system, there were others, including the Henry/ Winchester system, which carried out the same action by means of a pivoted lever operated by by the fingers of the firing hand. Lever action weapons were, generally speaking, thought not suitable for military use and were primarily absorbed by the civilian market.

1 and 2. Mauser self-loading pistol with combined wooden holster and stock. The carrying harness is attached to the first pistol complete with cleaning rod and compartment for the spare magazine spring.
3. The Winchester lever action in the open position. The saddle ring means that this is a carbine version.
4. A 1967 version of the Winchester lever action rifle.

2 GUNS FOR THE SHOOTING SPORTS

There are hundreds of guns available to the shooter and new developments and innovations arrive continually to join classic guns that have proved their worth over the years. To the brand new gun the shooter can add all manner of improvements.

Regarding guns, there are as many opinions as there are shooters; but in the end a good gun is one that, in combination with the shooter, produces the desired results. Here is a collection, by no means complete, of some of the guns that shooters are using today.

Special Frontiersman edition of the popular Winchester model 94 lever action rifle in calibre .38–55.

GAME RIFLES

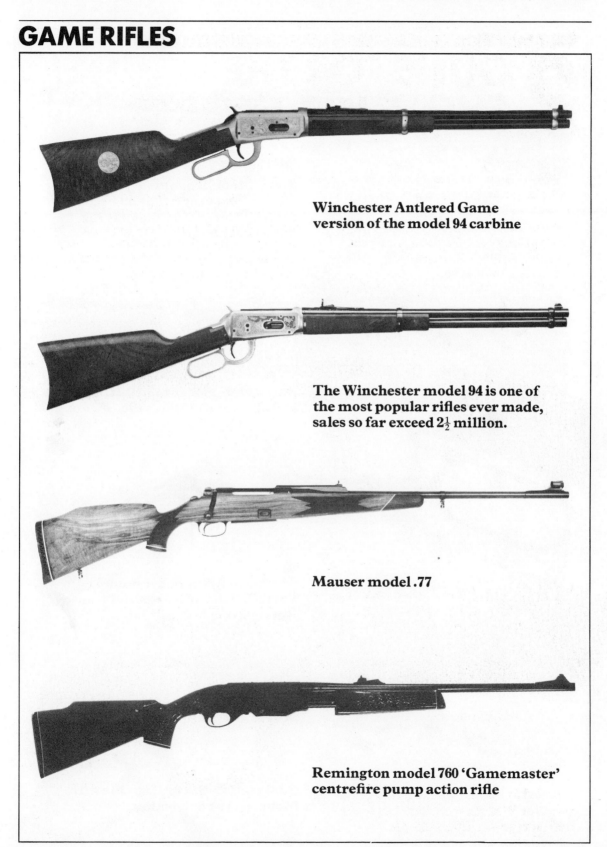

Winchester Antlered Game version of the model 94 carbine

The Winchester model 94 is one of the most popular rifles ever made, sales so far exceed 2½ million.

Mauser model .77

Remington model 760 'Gamemaster' centrefire pump action rifle

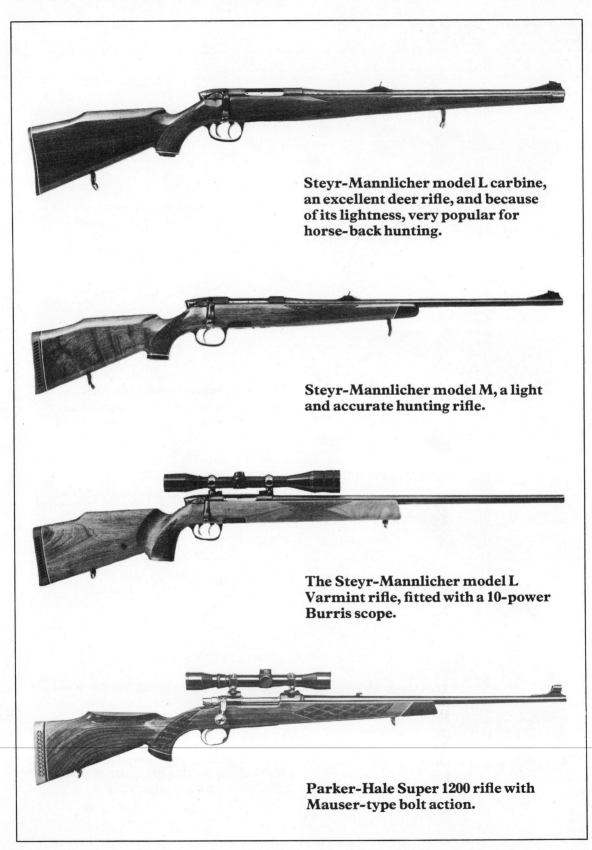

Steyr-Mannlicher model L carbine, an excellent deer rifle, and because of its lightness, very popular for horse-back hunting.

Steyr-Mannlicher model M, a light and accurate hunting rifle.

The Steyr-Mannlicher model L Varmint rifle, fitted with a 10-power Burris scope.

Parker-Hale Super 1200 rifle with Mauser-type bolt action.

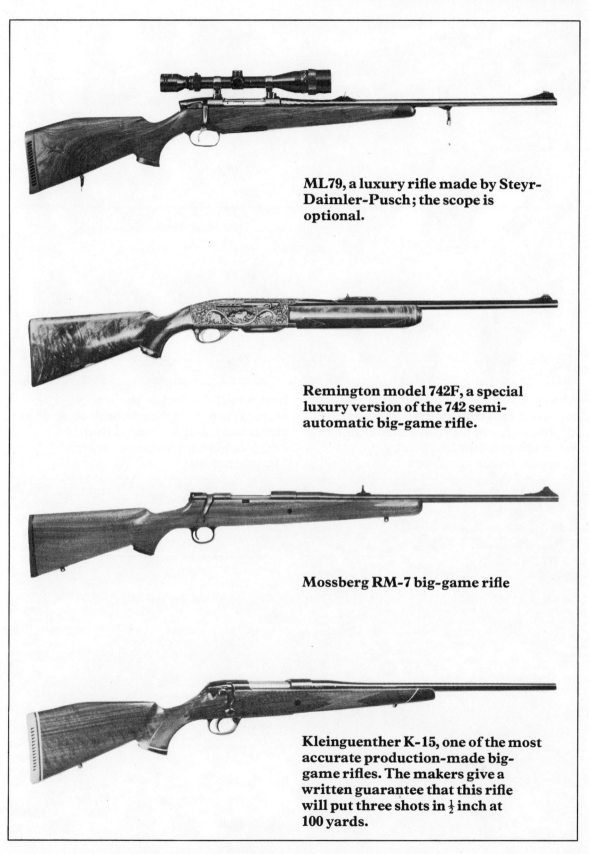

ML79, a luxury rifle made by Steyr-Daimler-Pusch; the scope is optional.

Remington model 742F, a special luxury version of the 742 semi-automatic big-game rifle.

Mossberg RM-7 big-game rifle

Kleinguenther K-15, one of the most accurate production-made big-game rifles. The makers give a written guarantee that this rifle will put three shots in $\frac{1}{2}$ inch at 100 yards.

Above: Exquisite customized rifles; top, built on a reworked 98 Mauser action; bottom, built on a model 70 Winchester action. Scopes by Leupold, stocks of walnut.

Below: Rifles stocked in rare walnut; top, 257 Roberts built on a reworked short Mauser action; bottom, built on a square-bridge Mauser action.

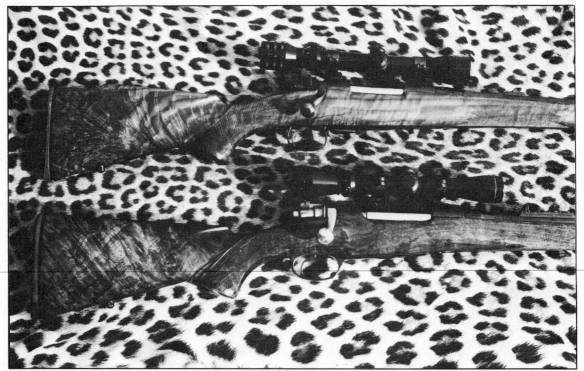

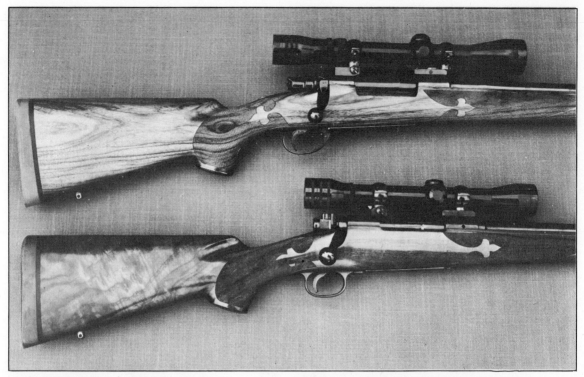

Above: Classic styling in custom rifles; top, built around an FN Mauser action; bottom, built around a model 70 Winchester action, both scopes by Redfield.

Below: Ruger Number One single shot rifle restocked in classic style with feather-crotch American black walnut. The scope is manufactured by Leupold.

TARGET RIFLES

The growing popularity of target rifle shooting has led to rapid changes in the style of rifles designed specially for the target sports; although many favourite models are used off-range for game shooting also.

Standard target shooting rifles in big bore and small bore. The top rifle is an air rifle.

Semi-automatic .22, model 2117L made by Voere of Austria; scope by Bushnell of Pasadena, California.

Remington Nylon 66, a .22 calibre autoloader

Remington model 572 'Fieldmaster' slide action .22 rifle

Remington model 700 bolt action centrefire rifle

Remington 700 BDL, custom deluxe version

Remington model 552 'Speedmaster' autoloading .22 rimfire rifle

Remington model 40X 'Rangemaster' .22 centrefire rifle

P14 fullbore target rifle with walnut stock

Musgrave 7.62 millimetre fullbore rifle

Musgrave fullbore rifle with Anschutz stock

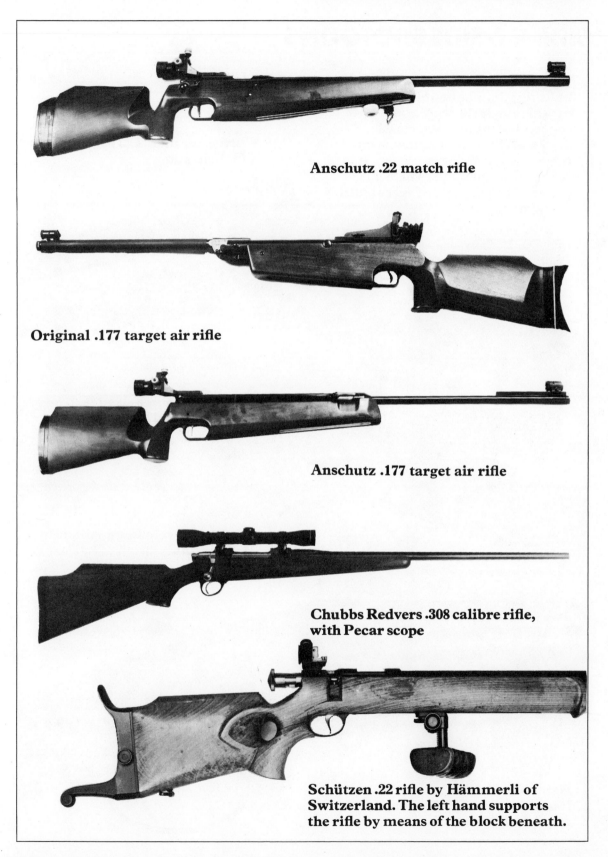

Anschutz .22 match rifle

Original .177 target air rifle

Anschutz .177 target air rifle

Chubbs Redvers .308 calibre rifle, with Pecar scope

Schützen .22 rifle by Hämmerli of Switzerland. The left hand supports the rifle by means of the block beneath.

SIDE-BY-SIDE SHOTGUNS

The shotgun is the most widely used hunting gun. The double barrel side-by-side gun is the traditional style, continuing the original classic design of the first shotguns, twin-tubed models firing two shots. It is really two guns, with twin lock systems, usually two triggers and a single stock.

Winchester model 23 Pigeon grade XTR field gun

Double-barrel shotgun made by W. Griffiths.

Gamba model Ambassador Executive side-by-side gun, exquisitely engraved.

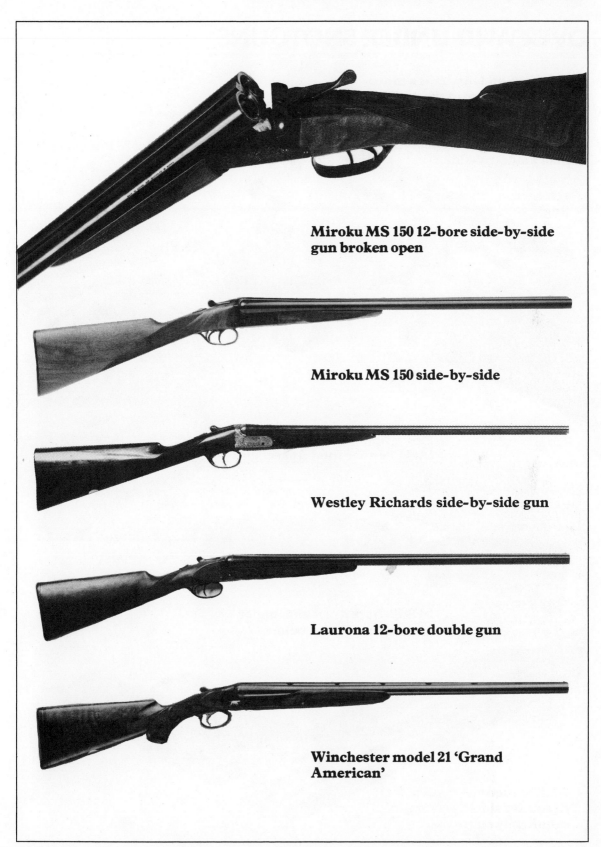

Miroku MS 150 12-bore side-by-side gun broken open

Miroku MS 150 side-by-side

Westley Richards side-by-side gun

Laurona 12-bore double gun

Winchester model 21 'Grand American'

OVER-AND-UNDER SHOTGUNS

The over-and-under is a more modern version of the double gun; its advantage is a single sighting plane along the top barrel, less confusing to some shooters than a side-by-side.

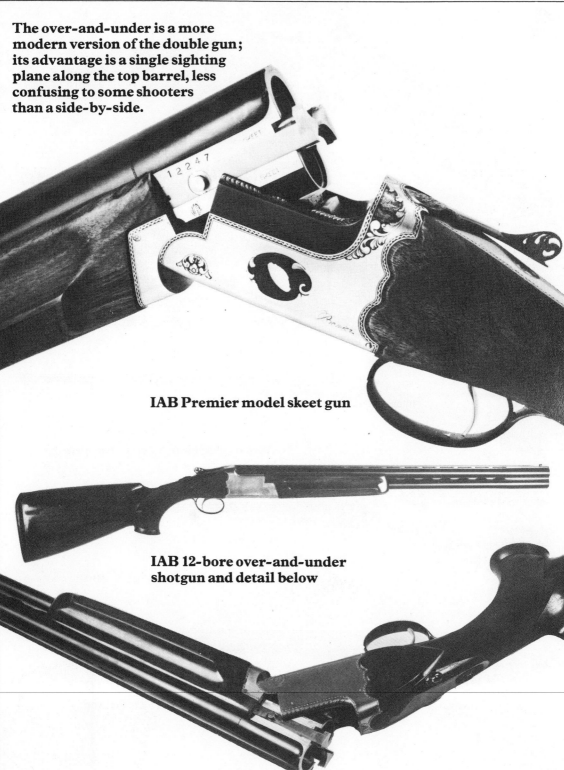

IAB Premier model skeet gun

IAB 12-bore over-and-under shotgun and detail below

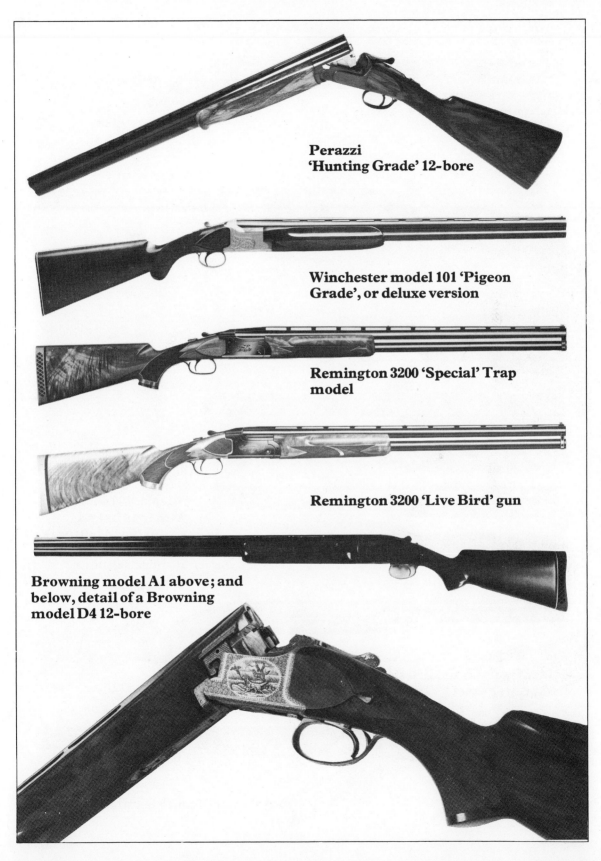

Perazzi
'Hunting Grade' 12-bore

Winchester model 101 'Pigeon
Grade', or deluxe version

Remington 3200 'Special' Trap
model

Remington 3200 'Live Bird' gun

Browning model A1 above; and
below, detail of a Browning
model D4 12-bore

Miroku 3800SW

Miroku 800

Miroku 800 shotgun with four barrels; (from top to bottom) 410, 12-bore, 16-bore, 20-bore.

Golden Eagle Grade II designed for field, trap or skeet

Mannlicher-Renato Gamba, model Icaro

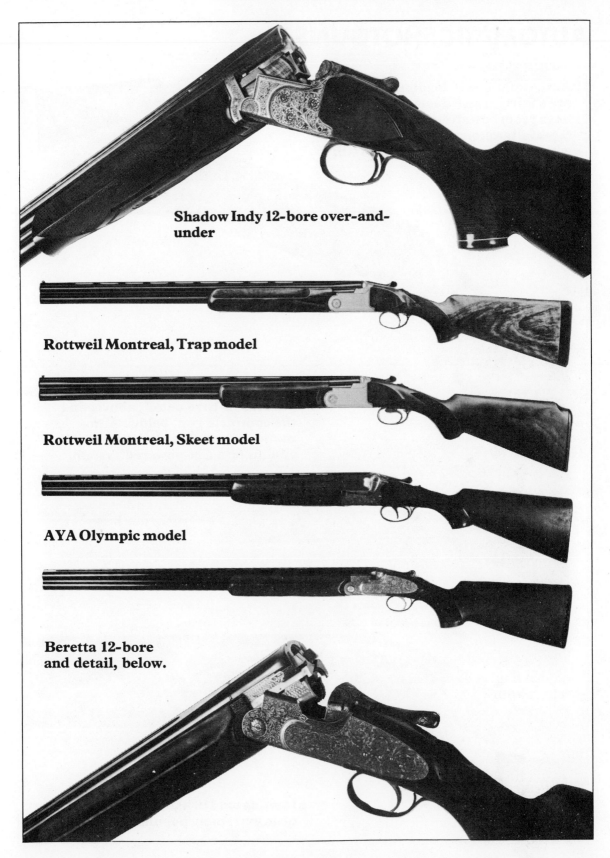

Shadow Indy 12-bore over-and-under

Rottweil Montreal, Trap model

Rottweil Montreal, Skeet model

AYA Olympic model

Beretta 12-bore and detail, below.

AUTOMATIC SHOTGUNS

Automatic or self-loading shotguns are a fairly recent development and have yet to be universally accepted, especially among live bird shooters where traditional side-by-sides still hold sway.

Beretta 12-bore detail, above, and the complete gun, below. Automatics can work either on a recoil system or a gas-powered system.

Remington 1100F, the deluxe version of an extremely popular gun.

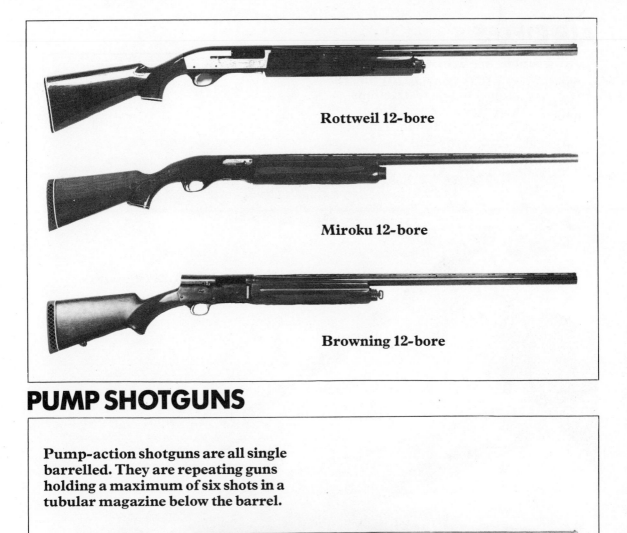

Rottweil 12-bore

Miroku 12-bore

Browning 12-bore

PUMP SHOTGUNS

Pump-action shotguns are all single barrelled. They are repeating guns holding a maximum of six shots in a tubular magazine below the barrel.

Remington model 870F pump gun, has sold well over a million. This is the deluxe Premier Grade with gold inlay.

Mossberg 12-bore pump gun

AIR RIFLES

Air weapons are lightweight, accurate and precise. In many places they are subject to few restrictions making them ideal for practice or varmint shooting, or for demanding target shooting competitions.

Anschutz model 250 .22 rifle with a side lever loading action.

Anschutz .22 rifle with underlever tab action.

Anschutz rifle with break-barrel loading mechanism.

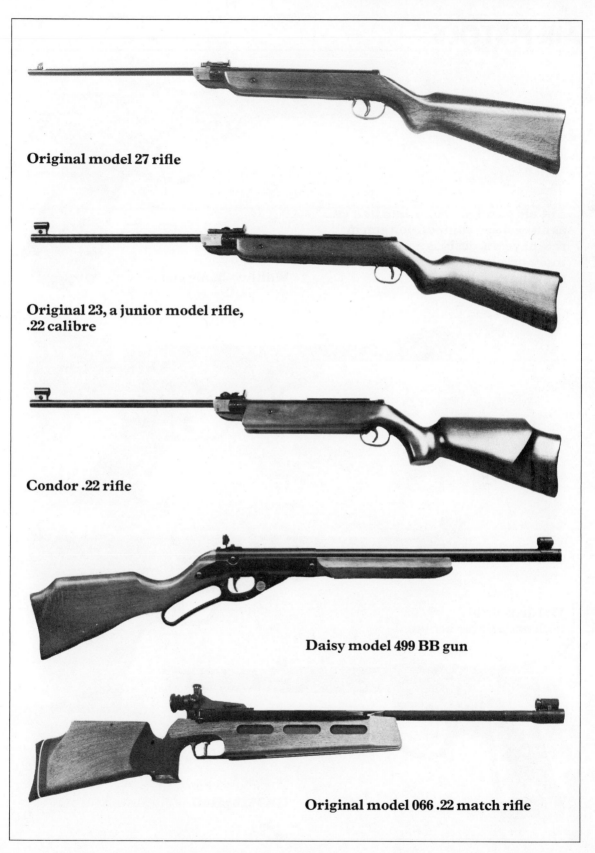

Original model 27 rifle

Original 23, a junior model rifle, .22 calibre

Condor .22 rifle

Daisy model 499 BB gun

Original model 066 .22 match rifle

AIR PISTOLS

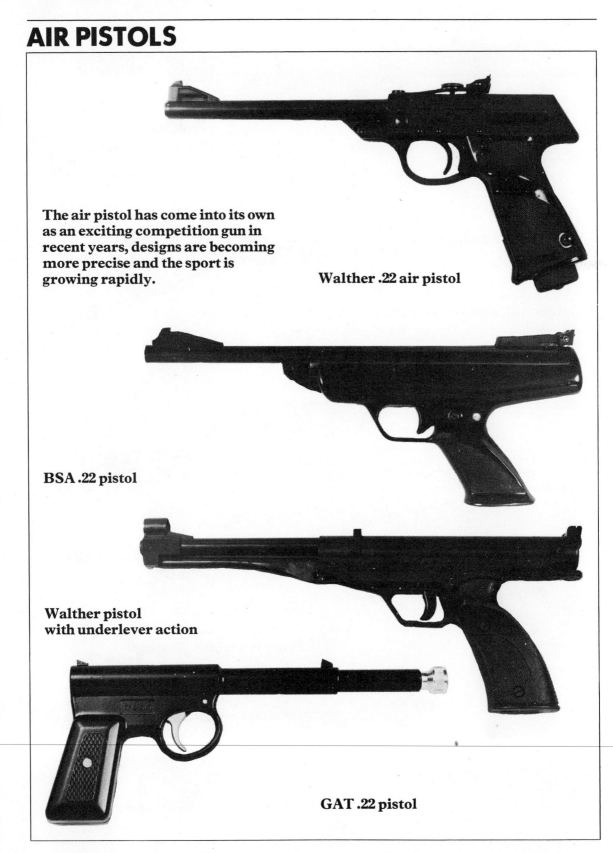

The air pistol has come into its own as an exciting competition gun in recent years, designs are becoming more precise and the sport is growing rapidly.

Walther .22 air pistol

BSA .22 pistol

Walther pistol with underlever action

GAT .22 pistol

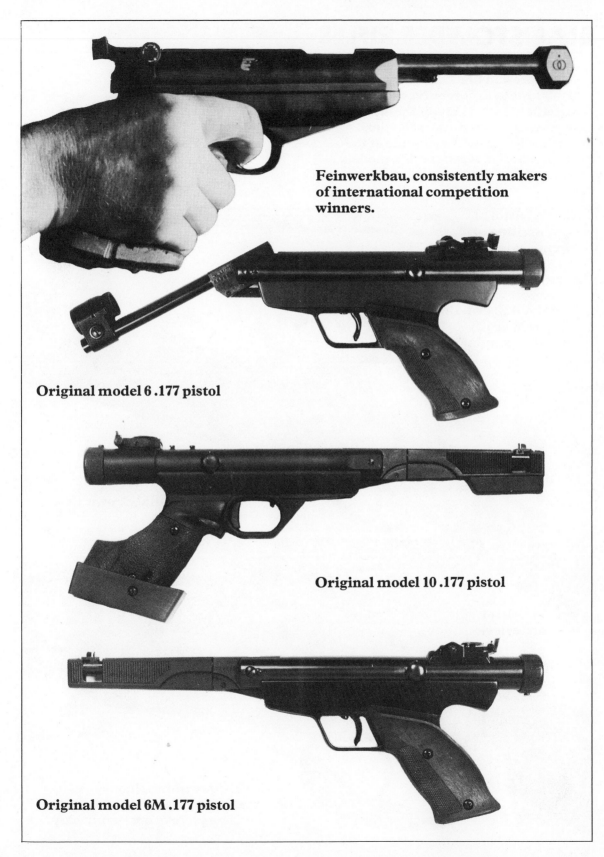

Feinwerkbau, consistently makers of international competition winners.

Original model 6 .177 pistol

Original model 10 .177 pistol

Original model 6M .177 pistol

BLACK POWDER RIFLES

An interest in black powder guns
draws many different types of people
together – historians and collectors
as well as shooters and reloaders.
Both original guns and some of the
most popular reproduction models
are shown.

Pedersoli Brown Bess,
replica of one of
the most popular flintlocks.

Original 'India' Brown Bess.

20-bore muzzleloader
made by Gameson of London,
a fine piece of craftsmanship.

Enfield carbine made around 1860 by Parker Field of London, this model is a P61 short rifle.

Lee Enfield black powder gun

Parker Hale 1861 Enfield carbine replica

Enfield 1861 carbine, the original made by BSA in 1865 (below), and the replica, made by Parker Hale.

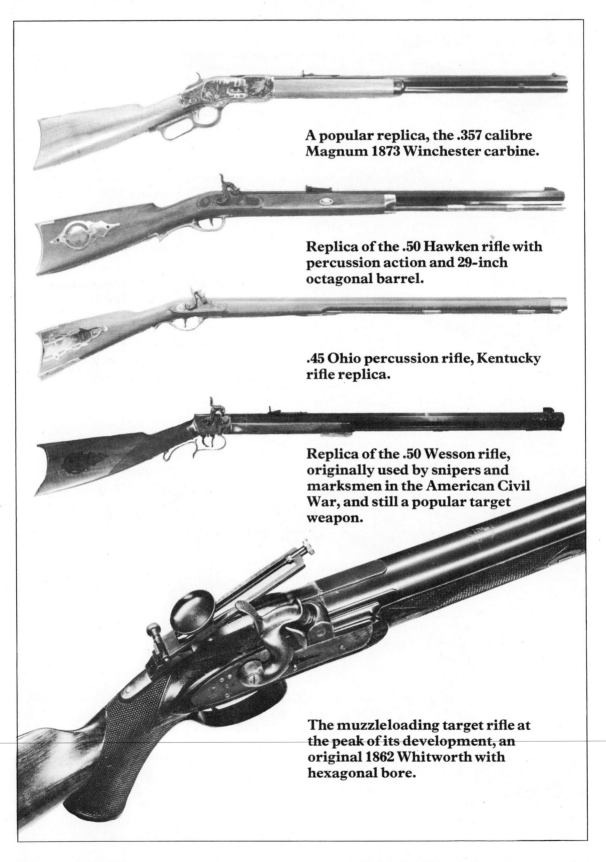

A popular replica, the .357 calibre Magnum 1873 Winchester carbine.

Replica of the .50 Hawken rifle with percussion action and 29-inch octagonal barrel.

.45 Ohio percussion rifle, Kentucky rifle replica.

Replica of the .50 Wesson rifle, originally used by snipers and marksmen in the American Civil War, and still a popular target weapon.

The muzzleloading target rifle at the peak of its development, an original 1862 Whitworth with hexagonal bore.

BLACK POWDER HANDGUNS

Black powder handguns offer as
many exciting possibilities as long
guns to collectors and shooters
with a lively sense of history.

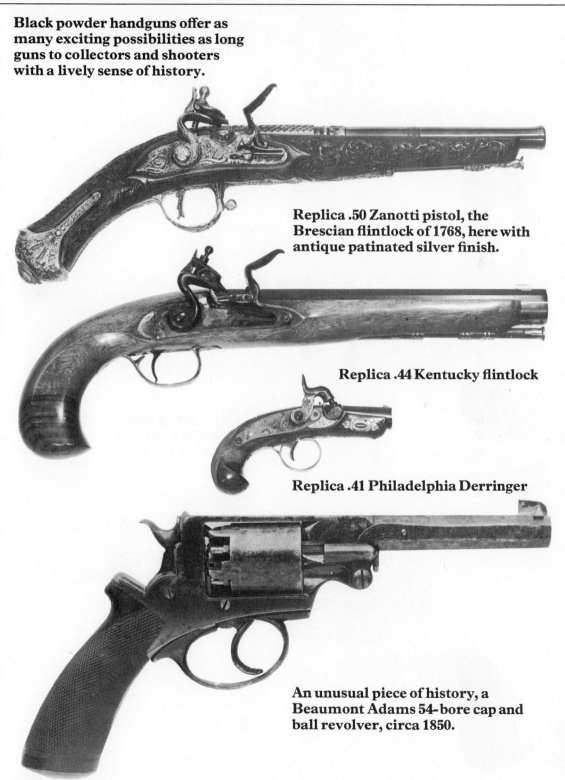

Replica .50 Zanotti pistol, the
Brescian flintlock of 1768, here with
antique patinated silver finish.

Replica .44 Kentucky flintlock

Replica .41 Philadelphia Derringer

An unusual piece of history, a
Beaumont Adams 54-bore cap and
ball revolver, circa 1850.

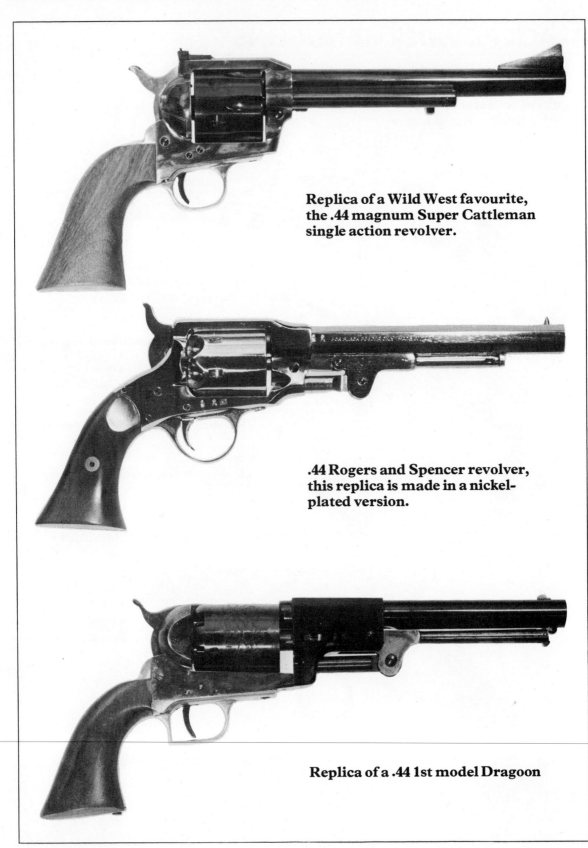

Replica of a Wild West favourite, the .44 magnum Super Cattleman single action revolver.

.44 Rogers and Spencer revolver, this replica is made in a nickel-plated version.

Replica of a .44 1st model Dragoon

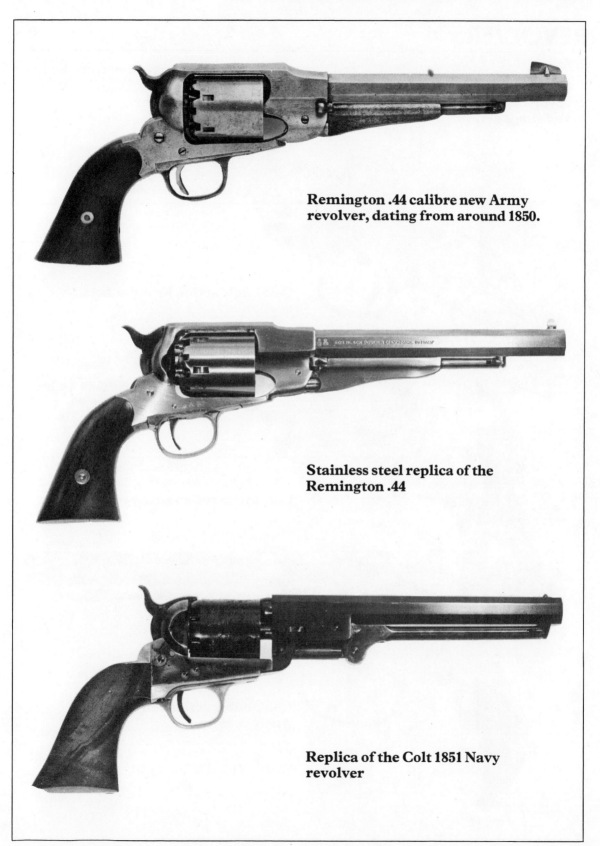

Remington .44 calibre new Army revolver, dating from around 1850.

Stainless steel replica of the Remington .44

Replica of the Colt 1851 Navy revolver

REVOLVERS

Reliable and strongly constructed, revolvers are available with double and single actions.

Colt single action Frontier Scout

Colt single action Army revolver

Colt double action self-cocking Army revolver

Colt New Service revolver chambered for the .455 Eley cartridge. This target model differs slightly from the standard service issue in production from 1898 until 1944.

Smith & Wesson K38 Masterpiece model 14, first supplied in 1947. One of the most popular .38s for target shooting.

Smith & Wesson K38 Combat Masterpiece, first supplied in 1950 to meet the demands of law enforcement officers for a short barrel version.

Smith & Wesson .38 Chief Special model 36 with 2-inch barrel.

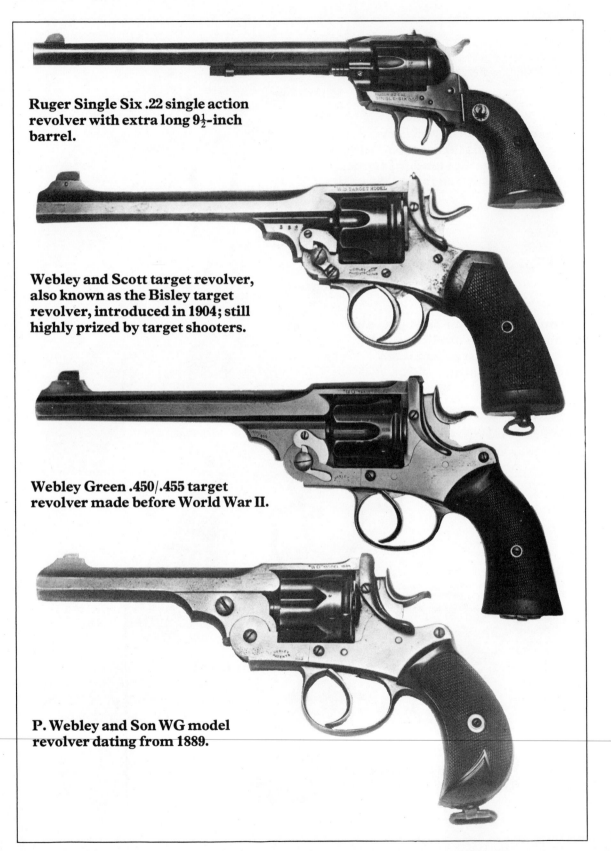

Ruger Single Six .22 single action revolver with extra long 9½-inch barrel.

Webley and Scott target revolver, also known as the Bisley target revolver, introduced in 1904; still highly prized by target shooters.

Webley Green .450/.455 target revolver made before World War II.

P. Webley and Son WG model revolver dating from 1889.

Webley RIC revolver, .450 calibre

Webley pocket revolver, .38 S&W calibre

British Government Enfield revolver, standard issue for the British Army from 1927 until 1957.

AUTOMATIC HANDGUNS

The automatic pistol is lighter and more compact than the revolver, making it easy to carry and conceal. Its great advantage is its capacity for rapid fire, however, because of its more complex construction, it can easily go wrong – improper loading or a faulty magazine can cause jamming or misfiring.

Swiss-made SIG P 210-6 9 millimetre pistol, one of the most accurate of all self-loading pistols, with cartridges and magazine.

**P.08 Luger semi-automatic
9 millimetre pistol with bolt
detached and shown in plan.**

**Beretta .22 automatics in large and
small models.**

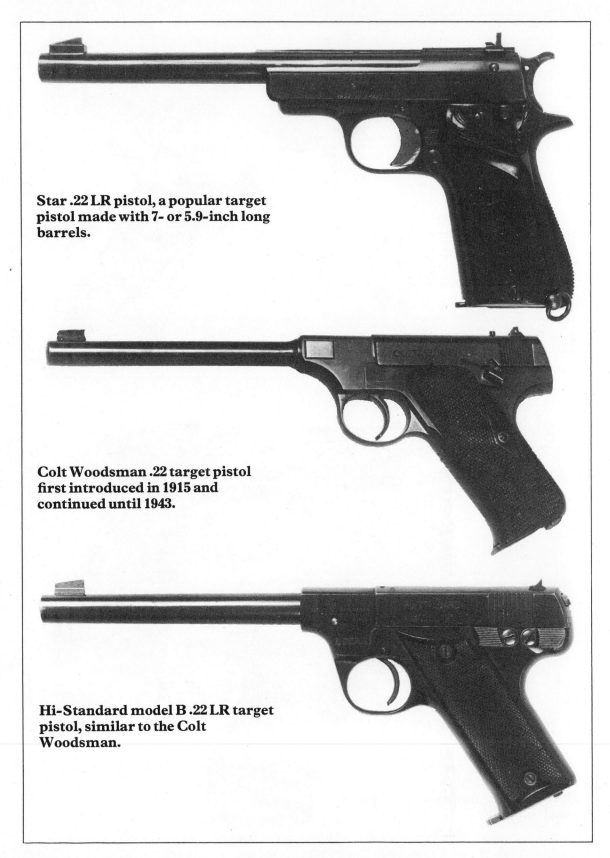

Star .22 LR pistol, a popular target pistol made with 7- or 5.9-inch long barrels.

Colt Woodsman .22 target pistol first introduced in 1915 and continued until 1943.

Hi-Standard model B .22 LR target pistol, similar to the Colt Woodsman.

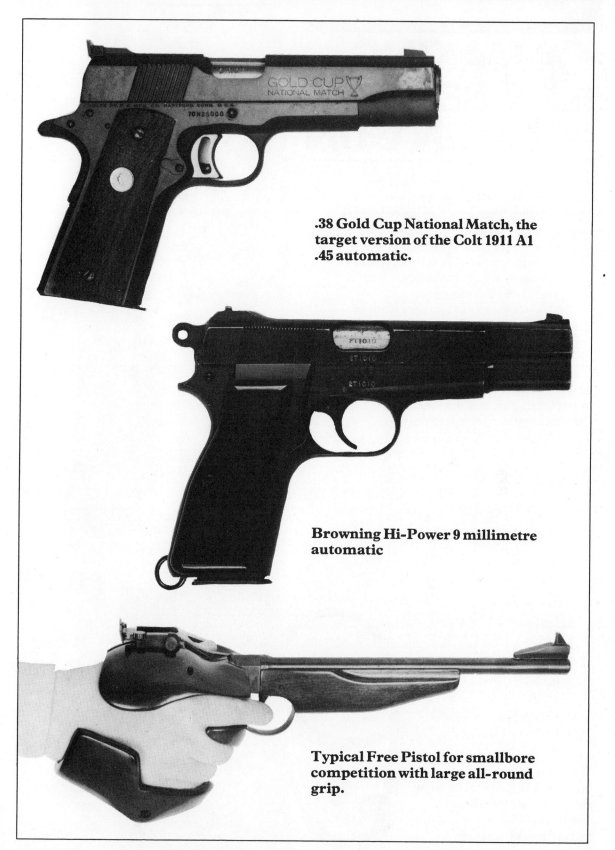

.38 Gold Cup National Match, the target version of the Colt 1911 A1 .45 automatic.

Browning Hi-Power 9 millimetre automatic

Typical Free Pistol for smallbore competition with large all-round grip.

3 MAKING A BEST LONDON GUN

Many people do not realize how busy the sporting gun world is today. The modern gunmaker must keep pace with the times in all respects, and is always on the lookout for ways and means – be it a man, a machine, or a new process – to try to reduce, or at least prevent from increasing, the enormous costs involved in the manufacture of a fine gun.

The gun trade cannot find enough skilled gunmakers to keep pace with the full order books, and there is no quick and easy way to produce a best gun. A part of the action can be machined to within thousandths of an inch of its final dimension, but then a skilled man must pick up a file, and it is the last cut of a file that requires the most judgement.

The last .600-bore double big game rifle to be made by Holland and Holland. The barrels were made by the author.

FROM ORDER TO ACTION

There are many stages in the production of a best gun. First, of course, there is the initial order, which involves discussions with the client as to the bore required, chokes, chamber lengths, weight, single or double triggers. The client will examine the engraving pattern books to select an engraving. He will also be asked to select the walnut stock blank to his liking, and then visit the range with a qualified instructor to determine the stock measurements. The order is placed with the factory and in due course production starts.

The barrels, made of chopper lump tubes, are brazed together at the breech end. This is a simple brazing process using silver solder. The two tubes are placed on a jig so that they are lying perfectly parallel. They are then clipped together at the muzzle and a clamp is placed on the lump portion so the barrels will not slip. Binding wire is carefully wrapped round the lumps, and flux is applied. The barrels are again checked for parallel, then placed in a thermostatically controlled furnace. Silver solder is applied when the correct temperature is attained, and then you have a pair of brazed tubes. The next operations are filing the breech end to the correct size, fitting the loop for the fore-end catch, and filing and fitting the top and bottom ribs, which are soft soldered on with pure tin fluxed with rosin. Some European countries braze the ribs on, but the heat required in that operation can distort the barrels to a considerable degree. The barrels are then struck up – in plain terms, made good to look at – and the lump and flats of the barrels are machined to within approximately ten-thousandths of an inch of finished size.

The action of the gun also starts as a forging, and there are numerous machining operations before it is given to the action shop for fitting the barrels. A spark erosion machine is a great asset in the preparation of the action, as it is capable of cutting the slots in the action to virtually finished size to receive the cocking limbs, bolt and spindle. The action shop is responsible for fitting the barrels into the action and all the mechanical working parts, i.e., ejectors, triggers, cocking parts, safety mechanism and, of course, the exterior shape of the action. It always gives me great

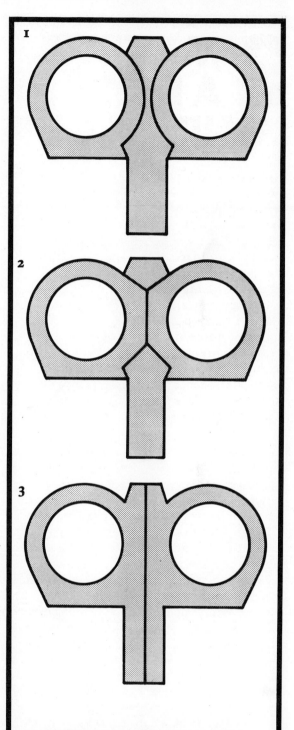

**1 and 2. The two different methods of constructing dovetail barrels.
3. Chopper lump barrels, made with a single join. Each entire barrel tube half is machined from a drop-forging.**

pleasure to see an actioner cutting the intricate shape of the action, using a hammer and chisels.

The action shop is the foundation of the gun. If the action is poorly made, that gun will never function at its best, and no amount of rework will correct it. If it is actioned correctly, the gun will last generations. Anyone who knows guns can open and shut the gun once and instinctively know whether it has been actioned correctly or not.

STOCKING

We have now reached a position where the gun is at a stage called 'in the white', in other words, it is a bright metal colour. It is in full working order, it cocks, fires and ejects the cartridges, and is ready for stocking to the client's measurements with the piece of walnut selected. A typical stock measurement might be:

Length $15\frac{1}{8} \times 15 \times 15\frac{3}{8}$ inches
Bend $1\frac{1}{2} \times 2\frac{3}{8}$ inches
Cast-off $\frac{1}{4} \times \frac{1}{8} \times \frac{1}{4} \times \frac{5}{16}$ inches

The first stock length measurement is from the centre of the trigger (i.e., where your finger rests) to the heel of the stock. The second figure is the measurement from the trigger to the centre of the stock, and the last figure is the measurement from the trigger to the toe of the stock.

The bend (also called the drop) is a measurement taken from the comb of the stock to an imaginary line extending from the length of the barrels over the stock, and from the bump of the stock to the same line. Clients usually have some idea of their stock length and cast-off measurements, but it is seldom one takes an interest in the bend or drop, although in some shooting instructors' opinion it can be a much more important dimension to get exactly correct for his client. Bend measurements vary with the type of shooting taking place, as competitive 'down-the-line' clay pigeon trapshooting is far removed from the grouse moor. It is quite common to see a bend measurement of three inches plus at the heel on some European guns, particularly from East European areas. The standard American measurements differ slightly from the British.

The last group of figures is cast-off, or, if you are left-handed, cast-on. As the name suggests, it is a bending to the right or left of the stock at the wrist. This bending can be to a very excessive

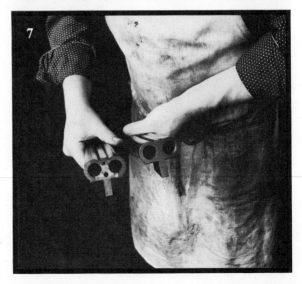

1. Lapping out – removing metal from the internal bore of the barrel.
2. A deep hole drilling machine. Oil is forced up the hollow shaft under pressure to clear away the swarf that can be seen in the tray beneath.
3. The final grinding of a 12-bore tube. The operator checks the diameter every 3 inches.
4. Straightening a chopper lump tube. With the large fly wheel press it is possible to bend a tube by as little as 1/1000 inch.
5. The chopper lump tubes have been brazed together and the breech end of the barrels are being filed to receive the top rib.
6. Pure tin with resin flux is being used to solder the ribs to the barrels.
7. The breech ends of two pairs of 12-bore barrels. The extractors have been removed from the barrels on the left.

degree. For example, a stock can be cut to fit the right shoulder, but when the gun is mounted into the right shoulder, the barrels line up with the left eye. This degree of cast off is called a cross-eyed stock, and is required by a shooter who is blind in the right eye but cannot use the gun from his left shoulder. I have seen a flintlock fowling piece dating back to the early nineteenth century that had a two-inch cast-off, so you see, customized stock dimensions are not a new idea. The idea of cast-off is that the touch of the cheek upon the stock should ensure the correct position of the eye in respect to the line of the rib, or of the rib in respect to the eye. As the strength of eyes and human frames differ, so do degrees of cast-off.

The actual stocking of the gun itself needs little explanation. The tools required have not changed much over hundreds of years; the wood chisel in varying forms still reigns supreme. What is required is a very skilled man who can not only achieve the perfect wood-to-metal fit, but also put into his work the correct feel of the stock so that anybody who mounts the gun to the shoulder instinctively feels 'I can't miss with this gun'.

PROOFING

Now the gun has been built, but it should not be fired until it is subjected to the nitro proof test, which is compulsory. The bores of the barrels are opened up to an internal diameter of .729 inch. At the same time the constriction in the last inch of the muzzles, i.e., the choke, is set to the customer's requirements. Choke is very important in a gun barrel, as it regulates the spread of shot. I am pleased to see that clients are asking for lesser degrees of choke constriction than in the past, as I believe that improved cylinder and quarter choke are perfect for the game gun. The gun is submitted to the proof house stripped down to just barrels and action. It is placed in a proof testing jig in an enclosed room and the gun is fired from outside. It is the duty of the proofmaster to examine the barrels and action for any defect. If the gun passes inspection, the flats of the barrels are marked with the acceptance marks of the London Proof House, which will show the year of proof, the bore size, chamber length, and the proof pressure (measured in tons per square inch). It will also have the provisional and definitive proof mark of the London Proof House.

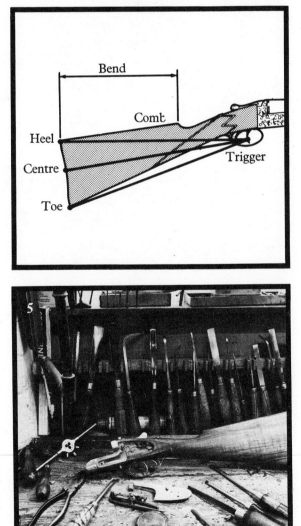

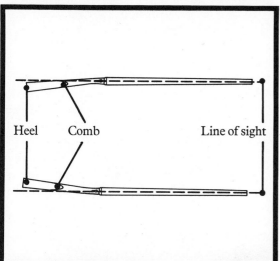

Heel   Comb   Line of sight

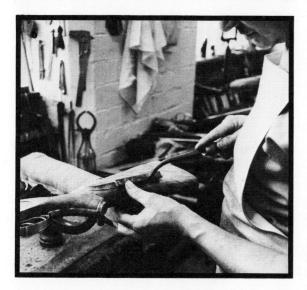

1. Shaping the action with a hammer
and chisel – work that requires a high
degree of skill.
2. The foreman of the repair shop
working on a Dickson Round
Action gun.
3. Close up of the Dickson action,
showing the mechanism on the
trigger plate.
4. A selection of walnut stock blanks.
It is becoming increasingly difficult
to find wood of this quality.
5. A stocker's bench showing the
gauges and chisels used.
6. Shaping the cheek piece on the
stock of a double-barrelled rifle.

FINISHING

The gun has now reached the finisher. He must prepare the surfaces to be engraved by hand polishing them with fine emery papers, ensuring that the crisp corners of the fences chiselled by the actioner are not rounded over. He sends the barrels to the barrel shop for the final polish to the exterior. The barrelmaker must remove every scratch from the barrels, working along the barrels, going down through various grades of emery cloth until he produces an almost chrome-like finish. This process takes up to eight hours and is thoroughly checked by the foreman on completion.

The finisher must oil the stock, which has already been chequered. This process can take up to two months. The stock oil is applied and left to soak into the wood. It is then rubbed in with 'rotten stone', which is a fine flour-like powder. This operation takes place twice a day, first thing in the morning and last thing at night, and is continued until all the grain of the wood is filled and a fine, smooth, weather-resistant finish is produced. All the mechanical internal parts must be mirror finish and, if requested by the client, gold plated, which acts as a rust preventative. Meanwhile, the engraver is applying his expert skill to the action, barrels, locks and furniture, cutting the required design with a diamond-shaped engraving tool approximately three inches long, fitted with a mushroom-like handle that fits into the palm of the hand. This simple tool in the hands of an expert can transform bare metal into a work of art. Outside the gun trade gun engravers are unknown and their work is, in my opinion, an unrecognized art form. I hope the day will come when the best gun engravers receive the recognition they deserve.

Our best London gun is now near completion. The barrels are being blued at Johnsons, the barrel browners (the correct term), who are unequalled anywhere in the world. The action, fore-end, trigger plate and locks are colour-hardened by being immersed in bone meal and heated to 800°C, and then plunged into cold water. This treatment gives the metal parts a mixture of blue and brown colours in various shades and, what is more important, gives the outer parts a hardened protective skin that will last the gun's lifetime.

Our best London gun is now assembled and the original order received from the showroom is examined to see if all the client's instructions and specifications have been followed in every detail, which will include checking the trigger pulls to see if they are the correct weight; if the balance of the gun, the stock measurements, and the overall weight of the gun are correct; if the safety catch flies back to safe immediately when the top lever is pushed to the open position; if the chambers and bores or barrels are polished to mirror finish; and if the blows of the tumblers are heavy enough to hit the strikers so that they detonate the cartridge. Then the outward appearance of the gun is checked: is the grain of the wood completely filled in; are there any wood diamonds; is the chequering to the stock fore-end and butt missing or chipped; is the gun too tight to open (a complaint from some clients who do not realize that a new gun is like a new automobile engine, it needs 500 cartridges to ease it in just as a car requires running in)?

When all the tests and examinations have been carried out, the gun is sent to the showroom, where it is again carefully examined by the senior sales staff. This will not be a mechanical inspection, as the salesman is viewing the gun from a different point of view than that of a factory craftsman. He will know his client's likes, dislikes and personality. He must judge the gun from his client's point of view and be satisfied that on handing over the best London gun, the client will realize that his patience and his money have rewarded him with one of the finest hand-built products this country can produce.

The author wishes to acknowledge the craftsmen of Holland and Holland shown in the photographs, and in particular:
Mr Sidney Harvey – Machine Shop Foreman.
Mr Keith Pennell – Action Shop Foreman.
Mr Angel Rego – Stocking Shop Foreman.
Mr Frederick Brown – Finisher.
Mr Ernest Touboulic – Foreman Finisher.
Mr John Bakall – Workshop.
Mr Peter Wenman – Workshop Foreman.

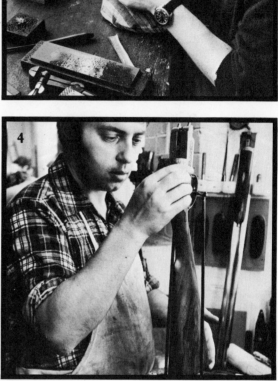

1. Boiling linseed oil is poured over the hand of the stock to create movement in the wood and alter the cast-off. The stock is left in the jig overnight to set.
2. A young apprentice engraver.
3. Checking the timing of the ejecting mechanism. The gun is opened very slowly to ensure that both ejector kickers come forward to hit the extractors together.
4. Checking trigger weights.
5. The foreman of the finishing shop with a pair of Holland and Holland 'Royal' model shotguns.

4 CARE AND MAINTENANCE

**An ivory-gripped Smith & Wesson
.44 Magnum revolver. The cylinder
is open and the ejector push rod is
clearly defined.**

CARE

Every pleasure has its price and shooting is no exception. The price the shooter pays is the rather tiresome chore of cleaning the guns after use. For the shooter who wishes to keep his weapons in first-class condition, cleaning after every firing is an absolute necessity – the longer it is delayed, the less effective it becomes. Each weapon usually has some special features but generally the manufacturer's instruction sheets give these details. There are, however, certain features which are common to virtually all firearms.

The first step must *always* be to prove the weapon, which simply means that the weapon must be checked to make sure that it is completely safe, without rounds in magazines or chambers. This should be done *every time* a firearm is picked up even if the previous handler has just done it. So many accidents involving firearms are caused by 'empty' weapons!

With a magazine-fed weapon, the magazine must be withdrawn and the breech checked to ensure that it is empty. In the case of a pistol this is done by pulling back the slide and looking into the breech. In a bolt action rifle the bolt must be withdrawn, and with a shotgun the breech should be broken or the action opened.

While proving the weapon the finger should be kept well clear of the trigger and the muzzle must be pointed in a safe direction.

CLEANING

When, and only when, the gun is known to be completely safe the cleaning can begin. The purpose is to remove any deposits left behind by the burning powder and to remove any lead deposits left in the barrel. The basic requirements are:

1. phosphor-bronze brushes
2. jags
3. rods
4. solvents
5. oils
6. cleaning patches.

For cleaning purposes it is not necessary to do more than field strip the weapons, which means that only the basic parts are removed from the frame. Weapons can be stripped to their com-

ponent parts, but this is seldom necessary or even desirable. Instruction manuals detail the steps to be followed, but the shooter would, unless very competent, be well advised to leave this job to the gunsmith.

It is possible to clean the inner mechanism without having to strip the whole weapon. Remove the grips and place the frame of the pistol inside a plastic bag or other similar container, then pour in some carbon tetrachloride or similar cleansing fluid, and gently agitate. The amount of dirt and deposit that is washed out will probably surprise the most fastidious of shooters. The weapon must then be thoroughly dried, cleaned and oiled. Care is necessary when handling these cleaners, as the fumes from some can be harmful, make sure the room is well-ventilated and the container well-sealed.

MUZZLE LOADING WEAPONS

These weapons are the most vulnerable to the effects of corrosion and rust, and prompt cleaning is absolutely vital. The deposits left by burning black powder are particularly active and can damage the bore of the weapon in a very short time. If there is some compelling reason to leave the weapon uncleaned, various proprietary solvents can be applied to delay the effects, but there is really no substitute for a proper clean.

In order to avoid any possibility of damage the barrel should be removed from the wooden stock. If there is any doubt as to how this is done, refer to the appropriate manual or ask an experienced shooter or gunsmith. When the barrel has been removed it should be given a few rubs with an appropriate sized phosphor-bronze brush to loosen the deposits. The touch-hole or nipple should be checked to make sure that it is clear and, if in doubt, a piece of appropriate sized wire should be gently worked through. Needles are not advised because they are rather brittle and if they break in the nipple, the nipple has to be unscrewed and it may prove difficult to get the broken piece of needle out.

Prepare a bucket of hot, nearly boiling, soapy water and immerse the breech. Water can be poured down the barrel; a funnel will prove very useful. Some people advocate the use of a pumplike action, using a cleaning rod with cleaning patches wrapped around the tip. If the rod is pumped slowly up and down, the suction will force water in and out of the bore.

The lock can also be removed from the stock and soaked in the soapy water.

When the bore has been thoroughly scoured, the barrel and lock should be rinsed in clean, hot water. Some shooters like to warm them to ensure that they are thoroughly dry. If this is impractical, then a very thorough wipe to remove all moisture is necessary, followed by an application of an anti-rust oil. It is essential that this drying be done very carefully and every part of the surface covered, or rust will certainly attack the metal. If the barrel has not been removed from the stock, great care is necessary to ensure that there is no seepage of water onto the wood or under the barrel where it cannot be removed.

Damp and detergents can also remove the polish from a stock, so careful drying is important. After drying, an appropriate polish can be applied.

With some black powder revolvers and pistols the barrel and cylinder can be removed from the frame or stock. This makes for very simple cleaning, for the metal parts can be left to soak.

The chapter which deals with the shooting of muzzle loading guns also contains information on their care and maintenance.

FULLBORE CARTRIDGE WEAPONS

Although modern primers and powders are non-corrosive and produce remarkably little fouling, the weapon still needs a thorough cleaning. A phosphor-bronze brush of the *correct diameter* should be pushed through the barrel several times, preferably from the breech to the muzzle but, of course, with revolvers this is usually impossible and it is necessary to work from muzzle to breech. The chambers of a revolver must also be scrubbed with the phosphor-bronze brush and one of the proprietary solvent oils should be wiped over the centre frame and inside the barrel. Particular attention should be paid to the areas around the cylinder housing and the breech end of the barrel where it joins the frame. An old toothbrush—thoroughly cleaned of all traces of

paste or powder—is a useful tool for reaching awkward places. After a while the solvent should be wiped off and an anti-rust and moisture oil should be wiped over. During the cleansing with the solvent the bore needs special attention. The cleaning patches should be wrapped around the metal jag and pushed through the barrel several times and, if necessary, several clean patches should be used in turn until they show no sign of soiling at all. The pistol should then be wrapped in a protective covering and kept in a secure, dry place. It is a good idea to remove the cylinder of the revolver occasionally so that the crane and axis can be thoroughly cleaned.

Basically the same technique is used for rifles, but extra care is necessary to see that the cleaning rod does not rub against the muzzle. Some shooters like to use a guideplug when cleaning the barrel, which prevents any contact between rod and muzzle.

SMALLBORE WEAPONS

Smallbore .22 weapons do not need quite such a thorough cleaning. Some people say that these weapons need no cleaning, but oil, wax, grease and grime accumulate and the weapon should be given a fairly good cleaning every so often. The routine is the same as for fullbore weapons, although the phosphor-bronze brush should be used sparingly.

AIR WEAPONS

These require less cleaning than cartridge weapons, but much greater care in their lubrication. Occasionally, the bore needs a clean with a brush, and patches and special rods are available for this purpose. Another way of achieving similar results is to use quick cleaning pellets made of felt and moistened with any one of various proprietary compounds. They are fired through the weapon in exactly the same way as an ordinary pellet to clean the bore.

The use of oil on an air gun requires considerable care, or an explosion can result. What happens is that, under certain conditions, the air gun acts rather like the cylinder in a diesel engine. The

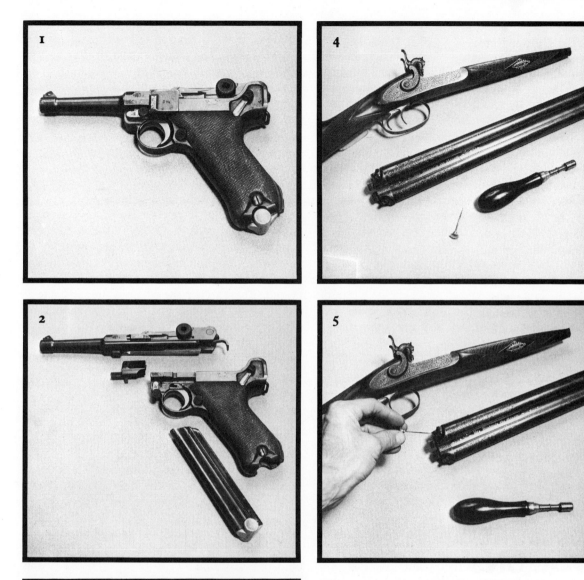

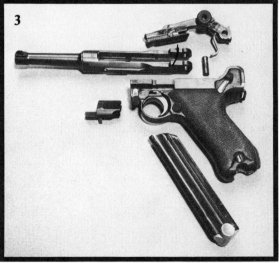

1. A 9 millimetre Luger Parabellum pistol.
2 and 3. The Luger pistol stripped to its basic parts ready for cleaning.
4 and 5. A rare 14-bore muzzle-loading percussion shotgun, made in the 1840s for His Highness The Nizam of Hyderabad by Thomas Elsworth Mortimer. The photographs show the barrels removed from the stock with the nipple key, used for cleaning the nipples, and the pricker being used to clean out the hole of the percussion nipple.

oil may be vaporized under pressure and explode. If the conditions should be just right, the explosion can be severe enough to damage the weapon and the shooter. Thus the oils used must be ones that will not flash at the temperature and pressure encountered in a modern air weapon. Manufacturers now offer a range of such oils, these are silicone-based oils; mineral oils should never be used as they are the most likely to result in dieselling. Dieselling is also explained in the chapter on air weapon shooting.

Lubrication points vary slightly from weapon to weapon, but generally the compression chamber, trigger and links joining various parts will need oiling. A variety of oils, each designed for a specific task, is available from gunshops and the manufacturer's instructions should be followed exactly. The latest type of recoilless air weapons require less oiling than the piston type and reference should be made to the manufacturer's instructions.

particularly automatics, but they all require some degree of major alteration to the firearm. As the cost of weapons continues to soar, it is as well to think very carefully before undertaking such work yourself. The cost of handing over the somewhat mutilated parts to a professional gunmaker to restore can be high. This caution applies to all major repairs, and the more complex and expensive the weapon, the greater should be the caution exercised.

Most weapons today have the external parts treated to give them a blue or black surface. This protects the metal from rust. Inevitably, constant handling eventually wears the surface, and the occasional scratch occurs. There are a number of proprietary 'cold blues', so called because, unlike genuine bluing or blacking, the metal is not heated. These are, on the whole, quite satisfactory for small retouching jobs, but they should be applied with great care, following the maker's instructions.

MAINTENANCE AND REPAIRS

While cleaning any weapon it should become second nature to look closely at the various parts for any signs of wear or damage. On flintlocks there is always a danger of the cock cracking, and a close eye to the neck of the cock may well spot the first sign of a hairline crack. Wear on the frizzen can get so bad that the flint will not strike sparks, and this is another point to watch. On percussion weapons the hammer is vulnerable and the nipple is also liable to damage.

Modern weapons are normally very durable, but even so they do develop cracks at vulnerable points – extractors, firing pins, springs and hammers are probably the most likely to crack and break. Fortunately, it is usually possible to obtain replacement parts from the manufacturers without too much difficulty.

The heavy loads of some cartridges inflict strain on the weapon and over a period the recoil may loosen screws, so a check on the tightness of all visible screws is wise. It is most important to ensure that the correct size of screwdriver is used for each screw, or the tool may well slip and gouge the surface or burr the head.

There are methods of 'accurizing' weapons,

SECURITY AND STORAGE

Firearms are only as safe as the person who handles them, and it is most important that every effort be made to ensure that they do not fall into the wrong hands. When not in use, weapons should be empty and safe: for an automatic this means magazine out and slide back for a revolver, empty and, if possible, with the cylinder swung out from the frame. For storage purposes a strong security box, cabinet, or a safe bolted to the floor or wall is essential. Special plastic-covered chains are available to pass through trigger guards so that the weapon can be secured to the case itself. Small trigger locks can be fitted into the trigger guard so that it is impossible to fire the weapon.

Loss of any weapon must be notified to the appropriate authority and a note of all numbers and identifying marks given. It is also very wise to store ammunition separately from the weapons.

The cost of replacement today is high and it is certainly worth considering insuring all weapons and equipment. The premiums are not excessive and represent a wise investment.

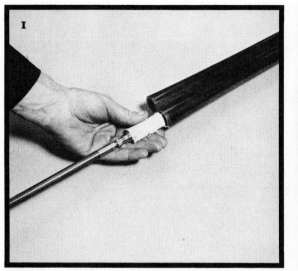

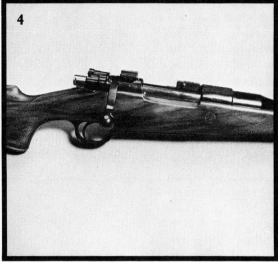

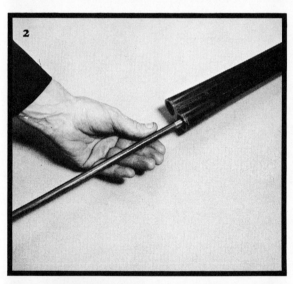

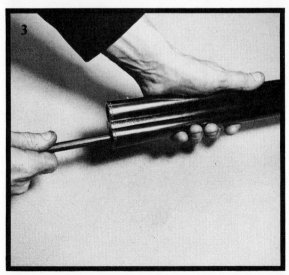

1, 2 and 3. Cleaning the barrels of a modern 12-bore shotgun with a cloth patch wrapped around a brass jag.
4 and 5. The Mauser action of a high powered fullbore sporting rifle in the .375 Holland and Holland magnum calibre.

5 AMMUNITION, BALLISTICS AND RELOADING

Left to right: Sako .38 Special bullet;
Martini-Henry rifle bullet; Kynoch
360 Nitro Express bullet and
Holland and Holland magnum
express for big game.

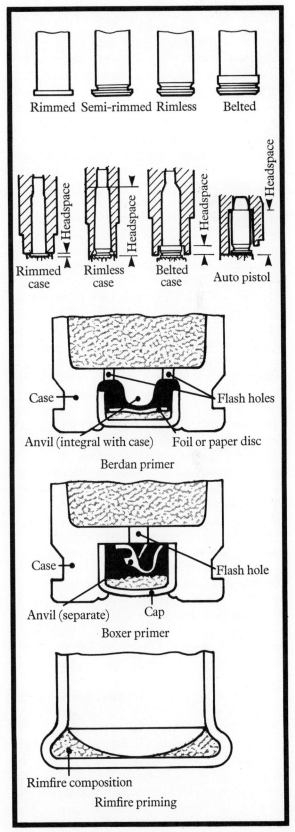

CLASSIFICATION AND DEVELOPMENT

Modern ammunition is the result of selective development of the most successful of the many types of self-obturating cartridges introduced during the middle decades of the nineteenth century. Rimfire cartridges have changed very little in concept since then, but have been refined and improved in detail. Centrefire cartridges still use the methods of ignition attributed to Colonels Boxer and Berdan, but modern versions of their designs have been modified to meet the considerable increase in working pressures that occurred after the introduction of smokeless propellents. Although cartridges made a century ago resemble those manufactured today, better materials and improved design and methods of manufacture make the modern product safer, more efficient, and more convenient to use.

Sporting cartridges are classified as metallic, for use in rifles and pistols, or of composite construction for shotguns. Metallic cartridges have cases made entirely of metal; shotgun cases have plastic or paper tubes supported by metal heads or bases and are usually loaded with a charge of small shot instead of a single bullet.

Caseless ammunition has shown promise in experimental military firearms, but the design features necessary to ensure obturation of the breech add to the cost and complexity of the system. It is unlikely to come into use for sporting purposes in the forseeable future. Some of the characteristics of the main types of cartridge are illustrated here.

CARTRIDGE CASE DESIGN

The cartridge case is more than a convenient package for projectile, propellent, and means of ignition. On discharge its primary function is to act as an obturator, preventing the rearward escape of gases produced by the combustion of the charge. In this capacity it becomes effectively a part of the firearm. The gas pressure in shotguns is of the order of 3 tons per square inch, and composite cases can resist it very satisfactorily.

Rimmed   Semi-rimmed   Rimless   Belted

Rimmed case   Rimless case   Belted case   Auto pistol

Headspace

Case   Flash holes
Anvil (integral with case)   Foil or paper disc
Berdan primer

Case   Flash hole
Anvil (separate)   Cap
Boxer primer

Rimfire composition
Rimfire priming

High velocity rifles have breech pressures of up to 23 tons per square inch, which is beyond the strength of the metals commonly used in cartridge case manufacture. To withstand the high pressures generated, cases must be solidly supported by the breech mechanism of the firearm. Even so, rimfire cases in which the detonating compound is distributed around the edge, are limited by their thin construction to quite low pressures. Centrefire cases, in which the detonating compound is located at the centre of the base, are thicker and are treated in manufacture to make the head of the case hard and strong while the mouth is left softer and more ductile so that it can grip the bullet firmly. Cases that have been overheated and in which the granular structure of the metal has been altered are dangerous and likely to fail if fired.

Metallic cases are nearly all made from 'Alpha' 70/30 cartridge brass of high purity. As the name indicates, it is composed of 70 percent copper and 30 percent zinc, is easy to fabricate and machine, and can be hardened by cold-working or annealed to give the required characteristics. Steel is sometimes used as a substitute for brass (particularly when copper is scarce) because it is cheaper, but it is more difficult and expensive to process. Cases made of steel are light and strong, and have satisfactory resistance to corrosion if treated against it in manufacture. They are often copper-washed to facilitate extraction. Nearly all the military ammunition manufactured by the Soviet bloc is loaded into steel cases. Cases made entirely of aluminium have not been very successful until comparatively recent times. Gas escaping from an alloy case tends to set it on fire, producing a phenomenon known as 'burn-through', which sometimes has catastrophic results. Cases made of ultra-high strength alloys fitted with flexible internal linings of a plastic material have overcome the problem, but they have not been used other than experimentally in shoulder-fired weapons.

The extraction of cases after firing is facilitated by machining a rim or a cannelure around the head of the case. The original design was the rimmed version; while it is strong and suitable for the task, it is not thought to feed as well as the rimless type in repeating and semi-automatic arms. The semi-rim is an attempt to combine the virtues of the rimmed and rimless designs. The belted style was introduced for high pressure cartridges; modern cases of any of the rim types shown are capable of containing very high pressures if properly made. Headspace is the longitudinal clearance of the cartridge in the chamber, and is controlled in the ways illustrated here.

BULLETS

The bullet is the means by which the user of a firearm inflicts damage upon his target. Accuracy of delivery, retention of the energy imparted to it by the gun, and behaviour after impact are considerations that must be taken into account when designing a bullet for a particular purpose. In early times bullets were round, or approximately so. Experimenters soon discovered that an elongated bullet was better, but only when kept point-on by being spun around its longer axis. The behaviour of high velocity projectiles was explored experimentally in the late 1800s and various air resistance laws deduced, but a fuller understanding of the principles involved only followed the development of aerodynamics as a science.

Two important characteristics of a bullet, which determine its ability to overcome the resistance of the air, are its sectional density and its shape. Sectional density relates weight to cross-sectional area. It is found by evaluating the expression:

$$\frac{W}{d^2},$$

where W is the weight of the bullet in pounds and d is its unfired diameter in inches. It is an approximation, since bullets are round and not square as the formula would indicate, but it provides a useful guide to the 'carrying power' of bullets of different calibres.

The shape of a bullet plays a major part in determining the characteristics of its trajectory; pointed bullets suffer far less retardation at high velocities than those with blunt noses. At subsonic velocities a streamlined or 'boat tail' base causes least resistance. Military bullets, which are designed to be effective at extended ranges, are sharply pointed and usually have boat tails as well. This type of bullet is more difficult to stabilize than one of the same weight that has a round nose and a flat base. To relate the shape of bullets to that of the standard projectile used to derive a particular air resistance law a factor of shape is determined, and written as 'i', 'n', or 'K' (Kappa) depending on the law in use. By combining this factor with the sectional density, the ballistic coefficient C may be obtained, thus:

$$C = \frac{W}{id^2}.$$

The larger the ballistic coefficient, the better the performance of the bullet.

When gunpowder (black powder) was the only propellent in use, bullets were made of lead, sometimes alloyed with tin or antimony to harden them. A few were fitted with paper patches, which engaged the rifling of the barrel and partially insulated them from the hot gases of combustion and from barrel friction. The greater temperatures of combustion of smokeless powders, and the higher velocities they made possible, forced the introduction of jacketed bullets. The first generation of compound bullets had fairly soft lead cores covered with thin jackets of cupro-nickel or soft steel. As development continued, cores got harder and jackets became thicker, so that modern bullets are stronger for a given purpose than those made before about 1910. Cupro-nickel was found to produce metal fouling in the barrel and has been replaced by gilding metal, an alloy of copper with between 5 percent and 10 percent zinc. Steel is still used, usually plated with gilding metal. Most cores are made from lead antimony alloys, but soft steel has been used for the cores of some modern military ball bullets, using the production techniques developed for the manufacture of armour-piercing ammunition. The cores of military bullets are inserted from the rear to comply with international conventions, which outlaw the use of expanding or explosive small-arms bullets for warlike purposes.

Bullets intended for game shooting are designed to expand after impact, except those used against thick-skinned animals such as elephants and rhinoceros, where depth of penetration is the most important consideration. Expansion is usually controlled by the design of the bullet jacket. The aim is to produce a large wound channel and deep penetration over as wide a range of impact velocities as possible, without allowing the bullet to break up completely. The shape of hunting bullets depends on the type of target and the expected range of engagement; round nose bullets hold their original course well, while

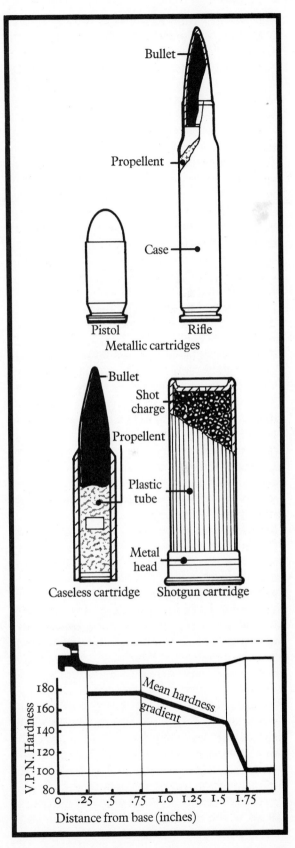

Bullet

Propellent

Case

Pistol   Rifle

Metallic cartridges

Bullet

Shot charge

Propellent

Plastic tube

Metal head

Caseless cartridge   Shotgun cartridge

Mean hardness gradient

V.P.N. Hardness

180
160
140
120
100
80

0   .25   .5   .75   1.0   1.25   1.5   1.75

Distance from base (inches)

pointed bullets tend to glance or turn over when entering a medium denser than air but retain their velocity better.

Pistol bullets are constructed on the same principles as rifle bullets, but are less stiff, as velocities are lower. At one time revolvers used lead bullets and semi-automatic pistols had jacketed bullets to ensure jam-free operation, but the introduction of high velocity revolver cartridges such as the .357 and .44 Smith & Wesson magnums has necessitated the use of compound bullets with jacketed bearing surfaces in some revolvers. Pistol bullets designed to expand will not do so reliably if loaded in low velocity cartridges.

PRIMING ARRANGEMENTS

Small-arms cartridges are initiated by primers sensitive to the blow of a firing pin, which crushes the explosive compound they contain. Primers for centrefire cartridges are of two types: the Boxer, which has a separate anvil and central flash hole, and the Berdan, in which the anvil is part of the case and there are multiple flash holes. In rimfire cases the priming compound is distributed round the hollow rim, which is crushed by the nose of the firing pin against the base of the barrel or cylinder.

The Boxer primer is loaded into almost all the centrefire ammunition of all types made in America, and is also used in the majority of shotgun cartridges manufactured elsewhere in the world. It is slowly gaining acceptance for metallic ammunition loaded in Europe. It was originally introduced in 1867 as part of the coiled brass Boxer case for the Snider conversion of the .577 muzzleloading Enfield rifle. The Berdan primer was developed in America during the 1870s, and is fitted to most of the metallic ammunition manufactured in Britain and the rest of Europe. Both types have been developed to the point at which there is little to choose between them for reliability and performance. The Boxer case is much easier to decap and reprime than the Berdan, making it a better choice for reloading.

Primers are filled with explosive compounds that are sensitive to sudden crushing and impact. These compounds burn to detonation within a very short space of time (0.0003 second approximately). The result of the detonation is that an intensely hot jet of gas ignites the propellent on all its surfaces simultaneously. Priming mixtures used to contain chlorates, which caused severe barrel corrosion if not washed out after firing, and fulminate of mercury, which attacked and weakened brass cases. Modern priming compositions are non-mercuric and non-corrosive.

PROPELLENT CHARACTERISTICS

The original propellent used in all weapons was gunpowder, also called black powder. It was a mixture of approximately 75 percent saltpetre (potassium nitrate), 15 percent charcoal and 10 percent sulphur. Early gunpowders contained many impurities, and the proportions of the constituents varied with the whim of the maker. By the beginning of the nineteenth century purer materials and better manufacturing techniques had improved the quality of black powder. Further research aimed at controlling its rather rapid combustion by making it into dense 'grains' of suitable size increased its utility. Black powder technology reached its zenith in the last quarter of the nineteenth century, just before the widespread use of smokeless powders. Gunpowder is very easy to ignite if dry, but quickly absorbs moisture from the air. Its combustion is practically unaffected by confinement or atmospheric temperature. It produces a large amount of soot and smoke when it explodes.

Nitrocellulose, the basis of all modern smokeless propellents, was discovered by Schonbein in 1845. Attempts to use it as a propellent were hampered by its very rapid combustion, and by the extremely dangerous manufacturing process. In the late 1860s and early 1870s smokeless shotgun powders made from nitrated wood granules were introduced, but were too quick-burning for use in rifles. In 1884 Vieille prepared a colloidal form of nitrocellulose, using solvents that were subsequently driven off. When cut into small flakes, this material formed the basis of Poudre 'B', which was adopted by the French for their service cartridge. The process had been described and brought into use in Austria ten years earlier, but had been supressed by the authorities. In

1888 Alfred Nobel produced 'ballistite' by gelatinizing nitrocellulose with nitroglycerine by applying heat and pressure. Shortly afterwards Sir Frederick Abel patented a method of manufacture using nitroglycerine and solvents such as acetone. The propellent he produced, called 'cordite' after the thin cord-like rods it was pressed into during manufacture, was adopted for the British forces in 1890.

Nitrocellulose, once gelatinized, is a hard, horn-like substance impermeable to gases. It burns only at exposed surfaces at a rate that varies directly with pressure and temperature. The rapidity of combustion of smokeless propellents is controlled by varying the area of surface exposed to flame by pressing it into tubes, cords, flakes, or strips of a suitable size. The rather small size of the individual propellent 'grains' produced in this way probably gives rise to the popular appellation 'powder'. Powders based on nitrocellulose alone are classified as single-based, and those containing a proportion of nitroglycerine are described as double-based. Some artillery propellents contain large quantities of other organic compounds as a substitute for a part of the nitrocellulose; they are described as triple-based, and are seldom used for small-arms.

Most smokeless powders for rifle cartridges have the basic propellent that forms the powder granules treated with surface moderants, also called deterrent coatings. These substances are oxygen-deficient organic compounds that retard the combustion process in its initial stages, making the powder more progressive in action. The most recently developed method of powder manufacture is that used to produce ball powders. It was developed in America before World War II and is easier, cheaper, and much quicker than the original methods, and requires much less equipment. The nitrocellulose is made into a lacquer, which is emulsified and treated with nitroglycerine. The powder grains are formed when the droplets of lacquer solidify, and are round, or nearly so. They are sometimes flattened to alter their characteristics, and are subsequently coated with a surface moderant to improve their otherwise degressive rate of burning. Ball powders measure well volumetrically, and are relatively dense; they often give better performance in cases of limited capacity than extruded powders and are reputed to cause less barrel erosion.

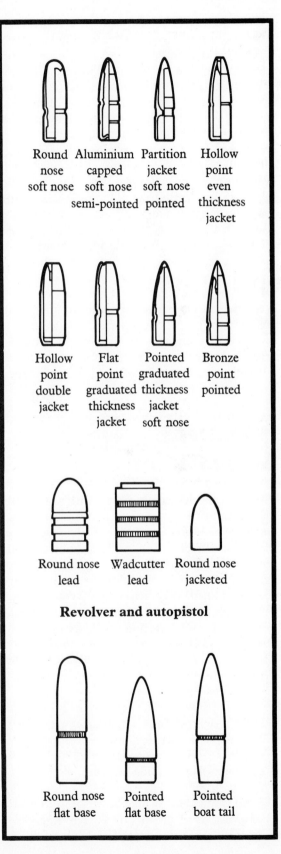

Round nose soft nose

Aluminium capped soft nose semi-pointed

Partition jacket soft nose pointed

Hollow point even thickness jacket

Hollow point double jacket

Flat point graduated thickness jacket

Pointed graduated thickness jacket soft nose

Bronze point pointed

Round nose lead

Wadcutter lead

Round nose jacketed

Revolver and autopistol

Round nose flat base

Pointed flat base

Pointed boat tail

The products of combustion of smokeless powders burnt at high pressure are almost entirely gaseous, and such 'smoke' as is visible is composed mainly of water vapour. The calorific value of propellents is much lower than that of common hydro-carbon fuel liquids, as the propellent must contain the oxygen for its combustion reaction. The principles of guns using liquid propellents are known, and research towards practical applications is continuing; it seems very unlikely that liquid propellents will replace conventional solid materials for small-arms ammunition. Existing propellents are made from substances that are also high explosives. It is possible to detonate them, whereupon the molecules of explosive rearrange themselves and release heat, the reaction taking place as a wave of detonation at a velocity of up to 26,000 feet per second. However, the shock necessary to make the small quantities of propellent in a cartridge detonate is several orders higher than that provided by the primer. Modern powders can be relied on to burn in an orderly and predictable way after they have been ignited.

INTERNAL BALLISTICS

Internal ballistics is concerned with the events that occur between the impact of the firing pin on the primer and the time at which the bullet leaves the muzzle. Methods of ignition and the way in which propellents burn, together with methods by which combustion is regulated, have been examined. The selection of components, particularly the powder, to meet a requirement depends on the interaction of a large number of variables, which may be grouped conveniently under two main headings—cartridge characteristics and weapon factors. The most important cartridge characteristics are:

- bullet weight, stiffness, and bearing area;
- capacity of the cartridge case;
- weight and type of propellent;
- efficiency of the ignition process.

The loading density may be deduced from the second and third points above. The important weapon factors are:

- restrictiveness of the barrel (form, depth, and surface finish of the rifling);
- bore diameter and length of the barrel;
- dimensions of the barrel leed (throat), in particular, free travel of the bullet.

These variables affect the confinement of the charge, so that identical cartridges may show a wide variation in performance when fired in two nominally similar firearms.

To make useful comparisons between different cartridges or calibres two ratios must be obtained: the ratio of charge weight to bullet weight (CWR), found by dividing charge by bullet weight, and the expansion ratio (ER), which relates the volume of chamber to the volume of barrel and chamber combined. Both can be used to assess the efficiency of a cartridge or load, and at a given level of maximum pressure can be used to predict the performance of a cartridge within narrow limits, provided that the correct powder is chosen.

It is not possible to exceed a muzzle velocity (MV) of more than about 6,500 feet per second (fps) with conventional propellents. As the charge is increased, more and more of it is required to accelerate the gases themselves, until the limit is reached. The practical limit is about 4,500 fps, which requires a CWR of more than one. The CWR is increased by the use of a larger powder charge, by reducing bullet weight, or both. A typical example is illustrated below. The ER points to the efficiency likely to be obtained from a weapon/cartridge combination; when it is numerically large, a greater expansion of the propellent gases takes place within the barrel. For this reason long barrels increase the MV, except in the case of the .22 rimfire, where the expansion ratio is so large that the bullet attains its maximum velocity after between 16 and 20 inches of travel; in longer barrels it eventually starts to decelerate slowly. Rechambering a firearm for a larger cartridge reduces the ER, and also the efficiency, although it may result in an increase in performance. A hypothetical example demonstrates this. An 8 pound rifle with a 24 inch barrel is chambered for the .308 Winchester (7.62 millimetre NATO) cartridge. The owner, feeling that it is underpowered, decides to investigate the advisability of rechambering it for the larger .308 magnum cartridge. He intends to use the same 180 grain bullet as before and assumes that the maximum pressure level will remain constant. The main ballistic differences, with their immediate effects are below.

Cartridge	ER	CWR	MV
.308 Winchester	9.2	0.24	2,575 fps
.308 Magnum	5.8	0.41	2,950 fps

Muzzle energy	Recoil energy	Efficiency
2,650 foot/pounds	17.2 foot/pounds	35 percent
3,480 foot/pounds	33.2 foot/pounds	26 percent

It is worth noting that the effective range against deer-sized animals would be increased from about 300 yards to about 425 yards. The larger cartridge would have superior kinetic energy at the longer range, but difficulties of estimating the true range and elevation required limit the theoretical gain. The extra performance has been bought by a 9 percent reduction in efficiency and a 93 percent increase in recoil energy, accompanied by an increase in muzzle blast. The barrel life to be expected would fall from approximately 5,000 to 1,500 rounds.

An examination of the sequence of events that takes place when a cartridge is fired is useful and instructive. After ignition by the primer, the propellent starts to evolve gas, and rising temperature and pressure rapidly accelerate the combustion process. At quite a low pressure the case expands to grip the walls of the chamber, and the bullet moves forward into the throat of the barrel. The bullet is forced into the rifling, which engraves it. The pressure rises steeply, and the bullet accelerates rapidly. After a short distance, the increasing volume of the bore behind the bullet causes the pressure to peak, and then start to fall. Shortly thereafter the propellent is completely consumed, and the gases expand adiabatically (with no addition or loss of heat) to the point at which the bullet is ejected from the muzzle. The bullet continues to accelerate during the expansion phase, but more slowly than at first. The illustration is a graphical representation of the process. The area under the pressure/space curve is indicative of the work performed. By using progressive powders that burn slowly and locate 'all-burnt' nearer the muzzle, the whole curve can be raised without increasing the maximum pressure, but, unfortunately, this reduces the regularity of ballistics and causes large variations in the MV, with a consequent loss of accuracy.

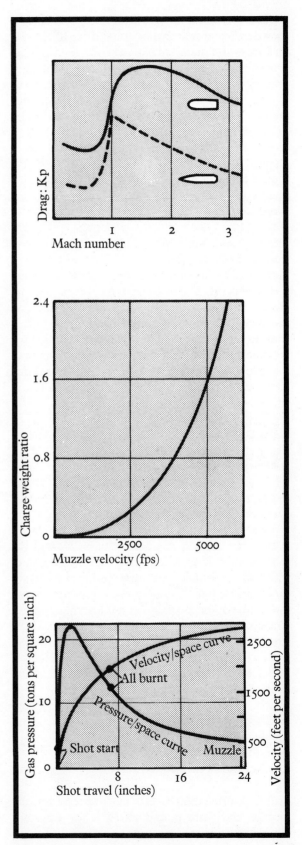

Pistols have quite respectable values of ER because the volume of their cases is small, which compensates for the short barrels. It is necessary to load quick-burning powders in pistol ammunition, as the time during which the bullet travels up the barrel is extremely short. With a few exceptions, pistol pressures are much lower than those employed in centrefire rifles.

EXTERNAL BALLISTICS

External ballistics deals with the flight of projectiles from the gun to the target, and is important in that it plays a major part in determining the accuracy and effectiveness of a weapon at any but the shortest distances. The effect of sectional density and shape on the ranging power of a bullet, and the determination of the ballistic coefficient C have been discussed previously. It was assumed that the bullet remained point foremost during its flight. To ensure that this happens, bullets are spun rapidly about their longest axes to produce a gyroscopic force that overcomes the tendency to yaw and tumble exhibited by an unspun bullet. The rates of spin given to bullets are extraordinarily great; up to 24,000 revolutions per minute is not uncommon.

The ratio of gyroscopic stabilizing force to the overturning forces is called the 'S' factor; it must be greater than unity if stability is to be achieved. If the value of S is too great, the bullet will be reluctant to follow the curve of the trajectory and will drift in the direction of the rifling twist to an excessive degree. Under normal circumstances the drift of a .308 Winchester round is about 12 inches at 1,000 yards. Values of S between 1.5 and 2 are favoured when designing a projectile and the barrel with which to fire it, but an S factor of 3 is not excessive when an existing barrel must be used. A simple method of checking if the twist of a barrel is suitable for a particular bullet is given by Greenhill's rule:

$$\text{pitch of rifling (in calibres)} = \frac{150}{\text{length of bullet (in calibres)}}.$$

Although originated for use with lead bullets of specific gravity 10.9, it works well for jacketed bullets.

The rapid rotation of bullets makes them very sensitive to minute imperfections of symmetry or dynamic balance. These are the result of careless manufacture, or damage caused by firing. A mismatch in size between bullet and barrel, a badly worn bore, or a bullet insufficiently strong to resist the firing stresses (including accelerations of up to 200,000 times the force of gravity), can result in yawing movements inside the bore, and erratic behaviour in flight. Modern rifling with narrow lands and wide, shallow grooves gives best results with bullets that are within 0.0005 inch of groove diameter; those larger than the groove diameter but within the tolerance provide a slightly better gas seal. The optimum depth of rifling for accuracy is the shallowest that can rotate the bullet correctly, which is about 0.0015 inch. A compromise with acceptably long barrel life dictates a depth of about 0.003 or 0.004 inch for sporting and target weapons, although military small-arms have rifling of greater depth; up to 0.010 inch in calibres of less than 8 millimetres. Most barrels have from four to six grooves; but some manufacturers make barrels with 16 or more grooves only 0.002 inch deep, which are claimed to reduce bullet distortion.

When the bullet leaves the gun, it starts to fall to earth under the influence of gravity. The distance it falls in any space of time is given by $\frac{1}{2}gt^2$, where g is the acceleration due to gravity and t is the time of flight. If a high velocity gun and a low velocity gun are fired horizontally at the same instant, the bullets will reach the ground at exactly the same time provided they were the same height above it at the moment of discharge. The high velocity projectile will be further from the gun than the bullet from the low velocity weapon; the former will have seemed to shoot flatter; and to have a longer 'point blank' range. High velocity weapons are easier to hit with at longer ranges because their flatter trajectory reduces the errors caused by incorrect range estimation.

Wind deflection of a bullet is proportional to the period of time described as the 'delay' over the range. Delay is defined as the difference between the actual time of flight and what the time of flight to the same range would be in a vacuum. When multiplied by the cross-component of the wind speed it gives the deflection, thus:

$$\text{deflection (in inches)} = 12w(t-T)$$

where w is the cross-wind in fps, t is the time of flight, and T is the vacuum time of flight, which is easily obtained from:

$$\frac{\text{range in feet}}{\text{MV in fps}}.$$

The way to reduce the wind deflection of a cartridge or load is to decrease the total time of flight by increasing the MV, or more effectively, by using a bullet with less drag. If bullets with a poor ballistic coefficient are fired at high velocity, they can show a longer delay than a bullet of better C fired over the same distance but at a lower MV, due to their high drag and rapid deceleration. The drag characteristics of two rifle bullets are shown in the illustration, which plots the drag coefficient against Mach number. (Mach 1, the speed of sound, is approximately 1,120 fps at normal atmospheric temperature and pressure.)

WOUNDING POWER OF BULLETS

The wounding capacity of a bullet depends primarily on the energy it has at impact, and how efficiently it transfers that energy to the target. The influence on the size of the wound channel and on the rate of energy transfer exercised by the design and construction of the bullet has been explained earlier. The nature of the tissues in the area of the wound, in particular their fluid content, is also an important factor. Kinetic energy is the usual yardstick for comparison of bullet effectiveness at the target. A simple way of calculating it when velocity is known is:

$$\text{kinetic energy} = \frac{WV^2}{45{,}0240};$$

W being the bullet weight in grains and V its velocity at the point in question. Since kinetic energy varies as the square of the velocity, the energy of some small calibre weapons is flattered at ranges at which the striking velocity is unusually high. When dealing with animals that are thick skinned or not susceptible to shock, it is sometimes useful to look at the momentum of a bullet:

$$\frac{\text{bullet weight in grains} \times \text{MV}}{7{,}000} \text{ in pounds/feet.}$$

When selecting a bullet for a particular quarry, it it is important to consider the nature of the target in relation to the bullet's construction; those designed for rapid expansion on small animals at long range are unlikely to be suitable for hunting buffalo at close quarters. Jacketed military bullets have greater wounding power than their non-expansive construction might suggest, as they often tumble when penetrating a target. In doing so they make a larger wound channel than if they had remained point-on, dissipating their energy more quickly. They are unreliable for shooting game, as they frequently veer off course after impact, and it is not unknown for them to menace the firer after hitting an animal shot at short range. Bullets with high striking velocities set up a hydrodynamic wave in the tissues around their track, particularly if the tissues have a high fluid content; the area of damage is greatly extended, and the effect of the shot enhanced. All bullets that hit bone tend to produce secondary missiles in the shape of splinters of bone. These missiles cause extensive additional damage to the tissues around the bullet path; the blow to the skeleton of the target adds to the overall effect.

RELOADING AMMUNITION

The reloading of factory ammunition after it has been fired, or the assembly of new components purchased separately is widespread in America, and is gaining in popularity in Britain. Born of necessity in the last century, it supports a considerable industry of component manufacturers today. The mechanics of reloading are deceptively simple: the case must be deprimed, resized, and reprimed; a charge of powder put into it and the bullet seated with the aid of a suitable tool. All the component manufacturers publish loading manuals with very detailed instructions covering the use of loading tools and the selection and assembly of components. One of these manuals should be the first tool the aspiring reloader purchases, as his safety may depend on how carefully he follows the advice therein. Enough has been said in earlier sections about the many variables that can affect the way propellents behave; if the wrong powder is used by a reloader, the result could be disastrous. Case condition is also vital and cases that have been overstressed or heated should not be used.

Having emphasized the dangers. it is only fair to describe the advantages to be gained by reloading. The most important of these is the flexibility conferred by the almost limitless choice of components. Factory ammunition must function safely and satisfactorily in all weapons adapted to fire it, while the reloader can prepare ammunition that exactly matches his firearm and purpose. He can spend as much time as he likes in ensuring uniformity, often achieving a higher standard than is possible within the limits of commercial production costing. Ammunition for rare and obsolete weapons can be made, and the versatility of the firearms owned by the reloader greatly increased. Considerable cost savings are possible, as the case, the most expensive component of a cartridge, can be used several times. Shotgun and pistol reloading show the greatest saving; users of these weapons tend to use large quantities of ammunition, so the financial advantages of reloading become even more attractive. Finally, it adds a new dimension of interest and understanding to the shooting activities of those who reload; it can even be called fun!

EQUIPMENT

Certain items of reloading equipment are essential and there are a number of 'extras' that, although not vital, help to simplify the whole operation.

The first essential is a press, which can be anything from a small, hand-held device to an electrically operated, multi-purpose monster. For general use a lever-operated model, secured to a bench or table, is quite adequate.

The next basic items are a set of dies and a shell holder for each calibre to be reloaded. Various brands of dies are available and, although more expensive, those with a tungsten carbide resizing die are best. Tungsten resizing dies require little or no case lubrication.

An accurate set of scales is most important and it should be capable of weighing small amounts of powder, say, 0 to 10 grains and bullets of up to 300 or 400 grains. It is perfectly acceptable to weigh each charge of powder individually, but this is time consuming and a powder measure which can be set to dispense a charge by a turn

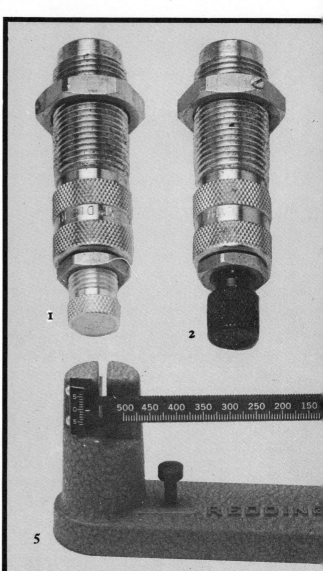

1, 2 and 3. A three-die set for reloading .32 cartridges.
1. Widens the neck of the case to accept the bullet.
2. The seating die which pushes the bullet into the case.
3. The decapping die which pushes out the exploded primer.
4. Key for adjusting the dies.
5. Powder measure with magnetic damping.
6. Accurate powder dispenser.
7 and 8. Small pistol primers and box, suitable for most calibres up to .38.
9. Automatic primer dispenser.

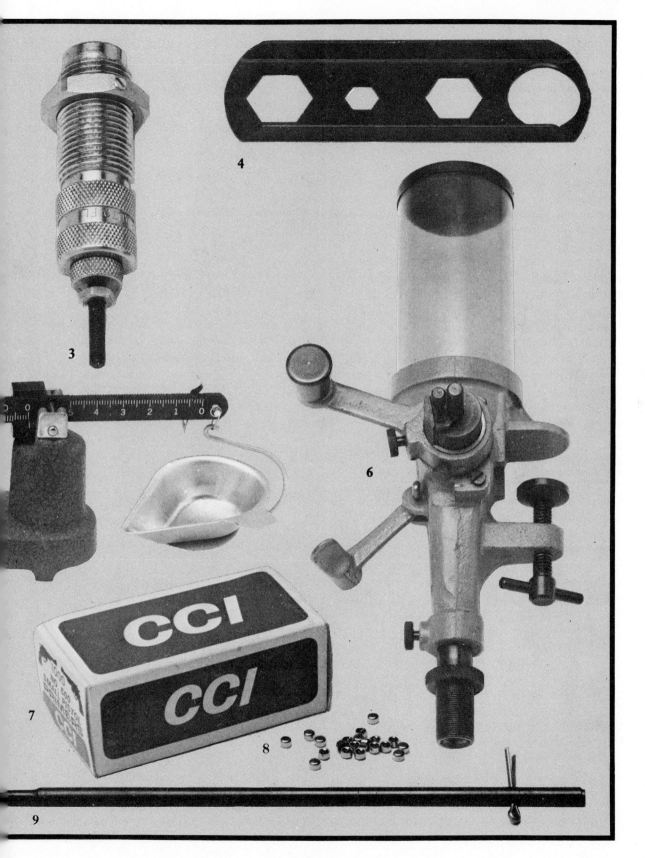

of a handle is always a great time and labour saver.

A recessed tray capable of holding the cases upright with reasonable security is desirable. This can be easily made with no more than a drill and two pieces of wood.

SAFETY

Although it appears to be quite complicated, reloading is a straightforward and simple task. However, it cannot be stressed too strongly that safety is of paramount importance. Modern materials are very safe, but every precaution must be taken to ensure that the risk of accident is kept to an absolute minimum. It is also advisable to wear safety glasses during the operation.

COST

The saving achieved by reloading is very considerable and even if commercial bullets are used the overall cost will be cut by around 50 percent. The larger the number of cartridges loaded the sooner the initial cost can be recouped.

PRELIMINARIES

The first step is to examine the empty cases for any splitting or distortion. The neck (open end) of the case is usually the first part to split, but the entire case needs to be examined carefully.

For the very best results the cases should then be sorted so that all those with similar head stamps are in one group.

The cases should be cleaned thoroughly, although many reloaders simply wipe them over with an oily rag.

With the cases cleaned and checked, it is now possible to commence the loading.

DECAPPING AND RE-SIZING

First the old, fired primer must be removed from the base of the case. There are two common types of primer – Boxer and Berdan. It is quite simple to identify them by looking into the mouth of the

A general view of a well-equipped loader's bench with powder dispenser and six-station turret press (left); a shotgun cartridge press (centre back); and a lubricator/sizer for cast rifle and pistol bullets (right).

case while holding it under a light, so that the base may be seen: the cartridge with a Boxer primer has only a single hole in the base, while one with a Berdan primer has two small holes side by side in the base. Boxer primers are the easiest to remove and for this reason are most often used.

The sequence for decapping a Boxer primer begins when the appropriate die and shell holder are fixed into the press and the case placed in the holder. When the lever is operated, the cartridge is forced into the die and a small metal rod pushes out the primer, which then falls away from the case.

Sometimes the full-length resizing and decapping operations are done separately, although both operations may be incorporated in a single die. In this case the die would not only remove the primer, but also force the case back to the correct size. This is necessary because when the powder burns, the pressure of the gases causes the case to expand slightly and this expansion has to be corrected. Unless a tungsten carbide die is being used the outside of the case must be slightly lubricated.

CAPPING

The resizing and decapping die is now removed and a second expanding die is fitted into the press. The turret press shown is especially convenient. Below the shell-holder is a small, pivoted arm, on the tip of which is an ingenious, spring-loaded tube, and into this goes a primer.

The lever action forces the case down onto the priming arm and this action pushes the primer into the central hole. It is possible to fit an automatic device that speeds up the action. It consists of a long, narrow tube filled with primers, which can be fed quickly and simply into the priming arm.

The next die expands the neck of the case slightly in order to facilitate later seating of the bullet. If full-length resizing is done in a separate die, mouth expanding may be done simultaneously with decapping. Which operations are done separately and which in combination depends on the brand of the dies, for various manufacturers have different ideas on the subject, as, indeed, do reloaders themselves.

CHARGING

The cases are now ready to be charged with powder. Several brands of powder are available in different grades. Reference to the manufacturers' tables and other literature will provide the necessary details as to quantities and grade of powder best suited to any particular cartridge. Most tables indicate a recommended and a maximum charge. The recommended charge is an average one and may not prove ideal for every weapon, and this calls for some controlled experimentation. Starting with a charge slightly less than the recommended charge, a small number, say six cases, should be loaded; the charge can then be increased by a small amount and another six charged. This can be done until perhaps a near maximum charge is reached. These groups of cartridges can then be fired to decide on the optimum charge. This checking is usually more important with self-loading weapons, for the charge needs to be sufficient to operate the self-loading mechanism as well as to deliver an accurate shot.

1. The first stage of reloading. A cartridge case is in the press beneath the decapping and resizing die. The case length trimmer is the horizontal tool beside the press. Notice that both the rifle and shotgun presses have been bolted to a thick wooden beam so that they are secure and steady in use.
2. The decapping needle has been lowered to reveal the neck expander button which carries the needle.
3. The case is about to be lowered (from the neck expanding die) onto the priming arm. It is thus recapped on the up-stroke of the press lever, having been neck-expanded on the down-stroke. The die shown is the optional third die for rifle cartridge loading, it will give the case neck a slight bell-mouth, useful when using cast bullets as there is no need then to shave the lead.
4. The case in the process of being primed by the priming arm.

As maximum recommended charge is approached, one should proceed in movements of no more than $\frac{1}{10}$ grain per batch of test cartridges. It is never wise to exceed the maximum recommended charge.

When the correct charge has been decided the powder measure can then be set to dispense this amount. A few sample charges should be thrown and weighed to check for correctness. Each case is now placed beneath the drop tube and one charge deposited therein and the filled case is placed on the tray. In the interests of accuracy every tenth charge should be checked on the scales and any necessary adjustments made.

When all the cases are charged, a visual inspection should be carried out to ensure that each has a correct amount of powder. The bullet can then be placed in the neck, and the case, with bullet, is placed into the shell holder. The seating die is now placed in the press and the lever operated. This action forces the bullet into the case; obviously, the die has to be adjusted to give the correct seating. This die can also be set so that the neck of the case is crimped – that is, gently pinched in to hold the bullet more securely. Crimping is only necessary with heavy recoil loads. For milder loads, i.e. for target use, uncrimped loads usually give better accuracy.

The cartridge is now ready for firing and should be stored in an appropriate container. The box should be labelled with details of primer, charge, bullet weight and date of preparation.

When the loading is completed the equipment should be cleaned and a check made to ensure that no powder or primers are left lying around.

BULLETS

Bullets can be purchased in bulk or they can be cast at home, a cheaper but time-consuming occupation. The metal, usually an alloy of lead, tin and antimony, is melted and poured into a mould. When it sets, the mould is opened and the bullet removed. These bullets now have to be passed through a sizer, a press that ensures that the bullet is exactly the right diameter, and also deposits lubricant around the bullet.

There are many bullets of various designs and weight and these are factors that affect the flight

and impact. For target work the wad-cutter—a flat-ended bullet—is most popular, for it makes a clear-cut hole in the target.

CASE LIFE

With normal care and use each case can be loaded many times, but it is difficult to give an exact figure. Some cases will last only four or five reloads while others will easily survive twenty or more. For safety's sake each case should be examined before it is used and any suspect ones discarded.

SUMMARY

This brief outline has given only the general principles of reloading, and there is much more to be learned before the best results are obtained. It will prove extremely useful if the guidance of an experienced reloader is sought for it is so much easier to learn from example than from written instructions.

5. The powder dispenser has been fitted to the top of the press. The cartridge case is beneath the drop-tube and a measured, charge of powder is being dropped. The powder dispenser can be fitted to the press as shown here to save time, or it can be separately mounted.
6 and 7. The bullet is about to be seated in the cartridge with the seating and crimping die. The advantage of a multi-station press is well illustrated here. Both dies and the powder dispenser can be brought into use simply by turning the handle of the press, instead of having to fit each one and then remove it from the press for each cartridge. Other cartridges are beside the press, with bullets poised in the necks, awaiting the same operation.
8. The final bullet seating and case crimping operation with finished cartridges beside the press.

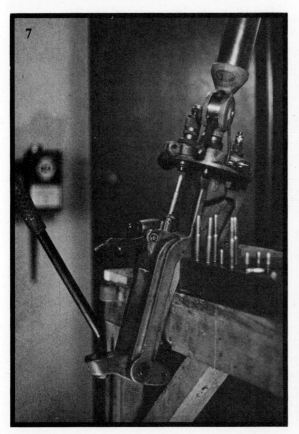

6 GEAR: EQUIPMENT AND ACCESSORIES

Shooting requires much more than a gun and a box of cartridges – there is a vast range of accessories for shooters. Some, like basic cleaning materials, are essential, others depend on the shooter's commitment to the sport.

HOLSTERS

The standard belt holster for a 3½-inch barrel revolver with safety retaining strap.

A high-seated holster custom moulded for a short barrel revolver. The screw is for adjusting grip.

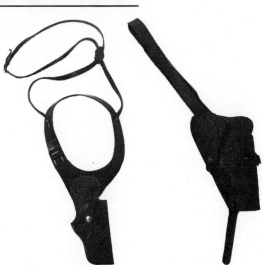

Left: Shoulder holster. The cross-over straps, which pass over the left shoulder, can be adjusted for fit. Right: Military shoulder holster for the Colt 1911 A1, adopted by the US Forces in October 1942 and designed for use by parachutists and air crew.

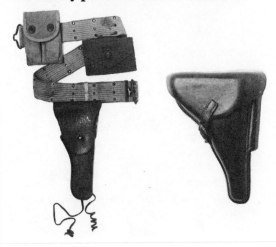

Left: Full rig for the Colt 1911 A1 automatic with pouches for spare magazines and first aid equipment. Right: Holster for the 9 millimetre Luger Parabellum. A spare magazine is kept in the front section.

CARTRIDGE BELTS

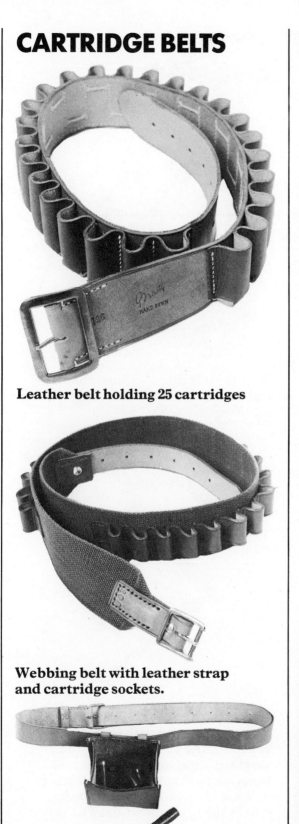

Leather belt holding 25 cartridges

Webbing belt with leather strap and cartridge sockets.

Leather belt with cartridge pouch

RIFLE SLINGS

Plaited leather sling with stud and buckle fastening.

Webbing sling, 2 inches wide, the maximum NRA permitted width for service rifles.

Leather target rifle sling; shown below in use on an indoor range.

GUN CASES

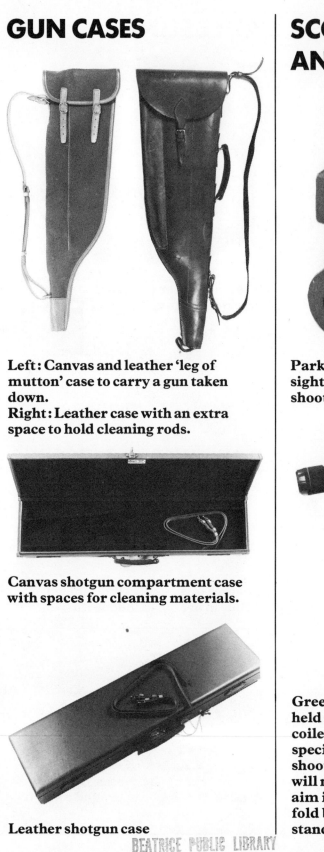

Left: Canvas and leather 'leg of mutton' case to carry a gun taken down.
Right: Leather case with an extra space to hold cleaning rods.

Canvas shotgun compartment case with spaces for cleaning materials.

Leather shotgun case

SCOPES AND SIGHTS

Parker Hale micro-adjustable rear sight for long-range target rifle shooting.

Greenkat prismatic spotting scope held on the stand with scratchless coiled spring clamps. The stand is specially designed for target shooting so that the shooter's elbow will not foul the legs when taking aim in the prone position. The legs fold back against the pillar so the stand can be packed away.

Top: BSA scope with a versatile variable power range of $4\times-15\times$ for anything from varmints to big-game and long-range target shooting.

Centre: Redfield $3\times-9\times$ variable power scope for spotting and shooting.
Bottom: Weaver scope with interchangeable reticule.

A Nikko 4×32 scope mounted low on a Czechoslovakian B.R.N.O. $\times22$ sporting rifle. Notice that the bolt handle has been ground away to clear the scope.

TARGETS

CLUB ACCESSORIES

Recoil pad provides a non-slip surface against the shoulder.

Selection of air pistol targets and a portable metal target holder.

Field   Trap   Skeet

Different pads suit different ways of shooting.

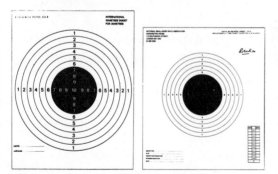

Pistol target and competition smallbore rifle target.

Cartridge box for competitions holds 50 shots, sufficient for five 10-shot series, but exposes only 10 rounds at a time.

Pellets are caught in the back of the holder, making it useful for practice.

Plastic and home-made cartridge holders

CLOTHING

Lightweight trap and skeet vest

Another lightweight summer vest for clay shooters, with quilted leather butt pad. Elastic under-arm straps can be adjusted and roomy pockets hold spare cartridges.

Rifleman's coat with butt pad

Quilted leather rifleman's jacket

Fully equipped international rifle shooter in action.

PROTECTIVE DEVICES

Leather gloves leave trigger finger free

Cotton fingerless mitts

Padded earphone hearing protectors

Shooting glasses and case

Custom shooting glasses made for a rifleman around the turn of the century are specially designed so they cannot slip down the wearer's nose.

Rubber ear plugs are smaller and cheaper than full size earphones and slip into a pocket when not in use.

BAGS

Canvas cartridge bag

Larger bag with extra pockets

Rubber-lined game shooting bag with net front pocket.

DECOYS

Pigeon decoy has a ring to suspend it over a perch.

Rubber pigeon decoy

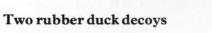

Two rubber duck decoys

CLAYS AND TRAPS

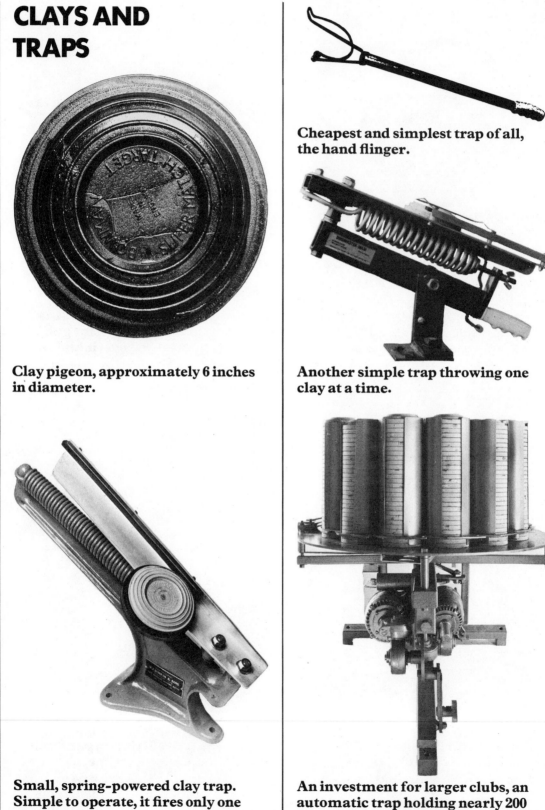

Clay pigeon, approximately 6 inches in diameter.

Cheapest and simplest trap of all, the hand flinger.

Another simple trap throwing one clay at a time.

Small, spring-powered clay trap. Simple to operate, it fires only one clay at a time.

An investment for larger clubs, an automatic trap holding nearly 200 clays, perfect for competitions.

CLEANING AND CARE

Left to right: Gun blue for touching up scratches on the metal parts; handy bluing stick for instant touch-up on the range or in the field; gun sight black ensures matt black, non-reflective sights.

Left to right: Spray lubricant is quick and clean to use; spray cleaner and rust preventative also contains a powder solvent for gun cleaning; gun oil and rust inhibitor.

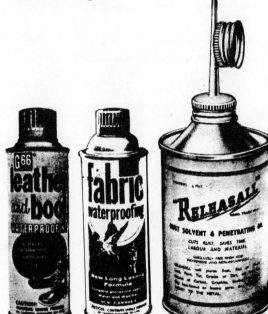

Left to right: For the hunter, game shooter and outdoor range shooter, leather and fabric waterproofing solutions in spray cans; 'Releasall' rust solvent and oil maintains its popularity amongst many newer products.

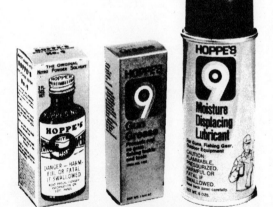

Left to right: Nitro powder solvent removes the deposits formed each time a gun is fired; when a gun is put away for any length of time, it should be thoroughly greased or sprayed with a moisture displacing lubricant.

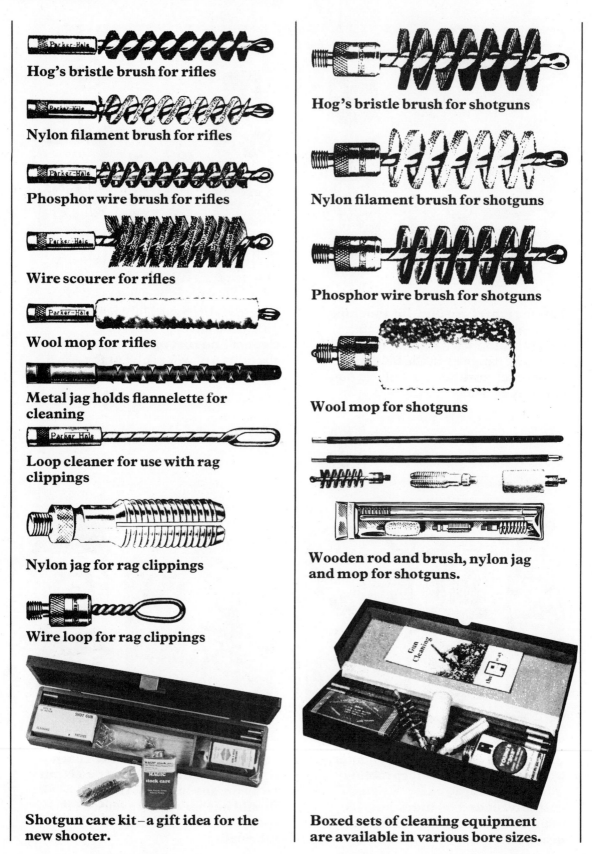

Hog's bristle brush for rifles

Nylon filament brush for rifles

Phosphor wire brush for rifles

Wire scourer for rifles

Wool mop for rifles

Metal jag holds flannelette for cleaning

Loop cleaner for use with rag clippings

Nylon jag for rag clippings

Wire loop for rag clippings

Shotgun care kit – a gift idea for the new shooter.

Hog's bristle brush for shotguns

Nylon filament brush for shotguns

Phosphor wire brush for shotguns

Wool mop for shotguns

Wooden rod and brush, nylon jag and mop for shotguns.

Boxed sets of cleaning equipment are available in various bore sizes.

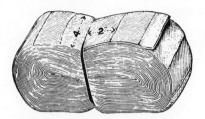

Roll of 'Forbytoo' flannelette for cleaning gun barrels.

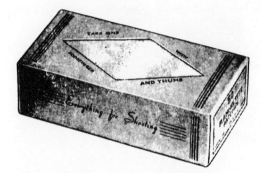

Cleaning patches for use with jags when cleaning barrels.

Pullthrough consisting of cord and weight, for .303 calibre rifles.

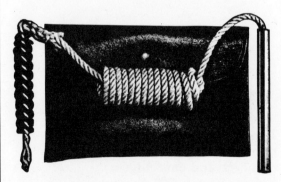

Rifle pullthrough with bristle brush, made to suit various calibres.

RIFLE ACCESSORIES

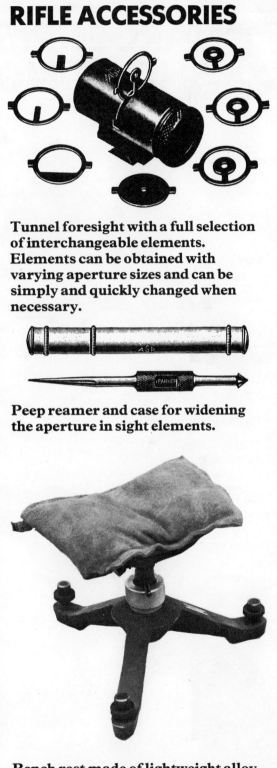

Tunnel foresight with a full selection of interchangeable elements. Elements can be obtained with varying aperture sizes and can be simply and quickly changed when necessary.

Peep reamer and case for widening the aperture in sight elements.

Bench rest made of lightweight alloy cast metal with leather bench-rest bag; height can be extended from $5\frac{3}{4}$ to $8\frac{1}{4}$ inches.

7 TARGET PISTOL SHOOTING

Top: A Smith and Wesson .357 magnum Highway Patrolman revolver and cartridges.
Below: Ruger .357 magnum Blackhawk single action revolver, modelled on the Colt single action.

FROM CLUB TO OLYMPICS

Target pistol shooting is a fast-growing modern sport demanding great skill, dedication and concentration from its participants. It is a sport included in the Olympic Games, which accepts only the best from the world's best. It relates in all ways to other sports, with different 'games' to be played – matches or disciplines to the initiated – and, of course, many differing levels of performance. The higher the level of the shooter's performance, the more he has to lean towards another activity, that of physical fitness – in other words, he has to train to become an athlete as well as a shooter.

The sport of pistol shooting usually starts with the club shooter. In the club a person will start by learning safety, the most important factor of all, for although he may never be the greatest shot in the sport, he must certainly be safe, and master of his pistol. He will learn that in all circumstances he must be seen to be safe and that his pistol must at all times be 'proved' and safe.

SAFETY IN THE CLUBHOUSE

Never ever point a pistol at anyone.

Always carry a pistol in an open condition. A semi-automatic must have the slide locked back and the magazine out, while a revolver must be 'broken', or have the cylinder swung out.

The pistol must remain open until it is put away.

On picking up a pistol, handing it to someone else, or receiving it, 'prove' it, in other words, spin it and check that it is empty.

Never handle a pistol without permission from the owner.

Never release the trigger without permission from the owner.

When firing an unloaded pistol, point it at something safe – there's many a slip and it's always an unloaded pistol.

Do not load magazines or cylinders in the club room – our memories are short.

SAFETY ON THE FIRING POINT

Do not handle a pistol for any reason while people are forward of the firing line.

When not actually firing a shot, but holding the pistol, keep it pointing down range at all times.

If someone has to go forward of the firing point after 'load' has been given, unload, put the pistol down and stand back.

After firing, check that the breech is empty, remove the magazine, put the pistol down, stand back and await the range officer's orders.

In Britain if ammunition is bought on the range, it must not be taken away from the range unless a record of sale is entered in the personal Firearm Certificate of the purchaser. Any breach of this regulation constitutes a criminal offence and the club committees accept no responsibility for those persons who fail to comply.

EQUIPMENT

The novice will soon begin to assemble a shooting kit – equipment that he will need before, during and after a match. The more dedicated he becomes, the more elaborate his shooting kit becomes. An ideal set of equipment should comprise:
● a substantial shooting box for transporting it all
● a telescope in order that he may see where his shots are going, and to allow him to correct faults
● ear defenders to protect his ears from the sound of the pistol firing, and to aid concentration
● glasses to protect the eyes, filter the light, and aid the in-focus relationship of the sights
● peaked cap to cut off reflective light, side distractions and flying empty cartridge cases
● stop watch for personal discipline
● tools to regulate sights, balance weights, or adjust grips
● match regulations, rule book, score book and pen; target fasteners
● sight blacking material, candle, carbide lamp

Setting up the equipment should be as important to the shooter as the match itself, for if anything at all should not be quite right during the shoot – sight adjustment, blacking, or palm-shelf working loose, for example – the shooter *must* know exactly where everything is at the time when it is wanted. Not being able to find something in a hurry in order to make an essential adjustment can destroy confidence, undermine concentration and disturb the sense of 'match tranquility' that the shooter has worked hard to obtain. It is easy to avoid this problem: make the setting up of equipment a learned habit – a place for everything and everything in its place. The foregoing holds true for all disciplines, and should be practised with great care during the initial stages of learning.

Having learnt how to shoot safely but perhaps with only a small degree of accuracy, we have to progress to the fundamental principles and elements of technique necessary for the production of a good shooter. These principles are the same for any form of pistol shooting although the method of application differs to suit the particular discipline being shot.

THE CONTROL FACTORS: STANCE

Stance is the posture of the body required to produce the greatest stability and balance in the body/weapon system, facilitating the delivery of a shot or series of shots without any strain or discomfort. It is the upright and erect position of the head that will allow for vision out of the eye centre throughout the sighting and aiming process. Since the entire performance is closely related to stance, every effort must be taken to ensure that it is maintained exactly for every shot fired. The position of feet and the 'free' hand are most important, and the shooter needs to experiment to find his own stable and comfortable posture. The free hand must not be allowed to move because this movement might well put the pistol off-target.

BODY POSITION

Body position is the relationship of the body and the stance to the target. It is insufficient merely to assume a comfortable and stable stance. The shooter must be able to aim at the target in a natural and consistent manner, without muscular strain, and be able to obtain an identical position throughout the complete period of shooting. Improper positioning will affect the ability to hold in the centre of the aiming area. Any feeling of discomfort or fatigue, or a need to correct the body's orientation with the target during the shoot will undoubtedly break concentration from the release of an accurate shot.

GRIP

Grip should provide the shooter with the maximum uniform control of the pistol, so that he can maintain a natural sight alignment and allow a constant rearward pressure to be applied to the trigger with the least possible movement, at the same time producing no tremor through strain or undue muscular tension. It should be set up to give the same uniform position and pressure for each shot fired.

BREATH CONTROL

Breathing is also a control factor. The whole upper torso moves during breathing. If this movement occurs at the moment of the release of the shot, the shot will be a bad one. Breathing rhythm or control is important because there should be:
● no bodily movement at the time of firing a shot;
● the maximum amount of oxygen in the blood when on aim;
● a reserve of oxygen in the lungs at the time of firing.

A plentiful supply of oxygen is needed to keep muscles, nerves and brain working at maximum efficiency, to combat fatigue and to help coordination. Breath control should allow the shooter to restrain his breathing comfortably, without strain or tension, long enough to fire a shot or series of shots, and without affecting his ability to hold still in the aiming area or concentrate on sight alignment. Obviously, the act of breathing must be halted for the time taken to aim and fire. In shooting at turning targets, breath control is used to 'count time' and to help anticipate the target's turning. Being an automatic action, the shooter is able to learn this easily.

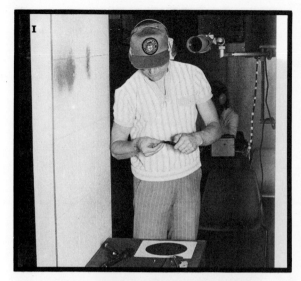

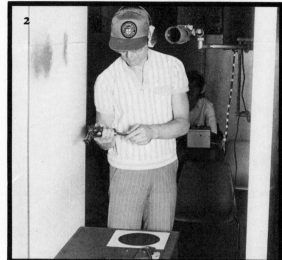

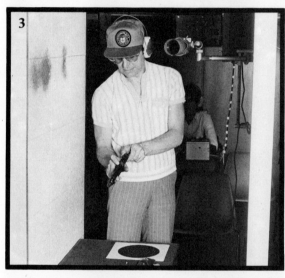

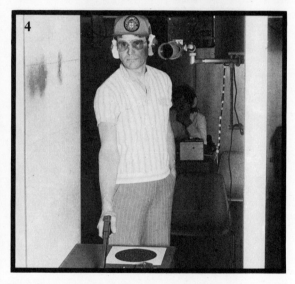

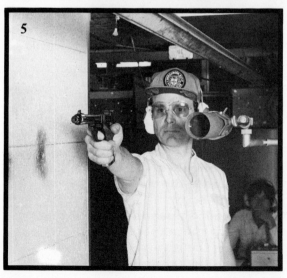

Loading and firing the smallbore pistol.
1. Loading the magazine. The pistol lies safely on the bench, the barrel pointing up range and slide back.
2. The full magazine is inserted and gently pushed home. In the rear the Range Warden checks that the shooter is observing safety rules.
3. The pistol is set for the first shot by moving the slide forward to feed the first cartridge into the breech.
4. Concentrating on the target before bringing the pistol up.
5. The shooter concentrates his attention on the fore sight not the target.

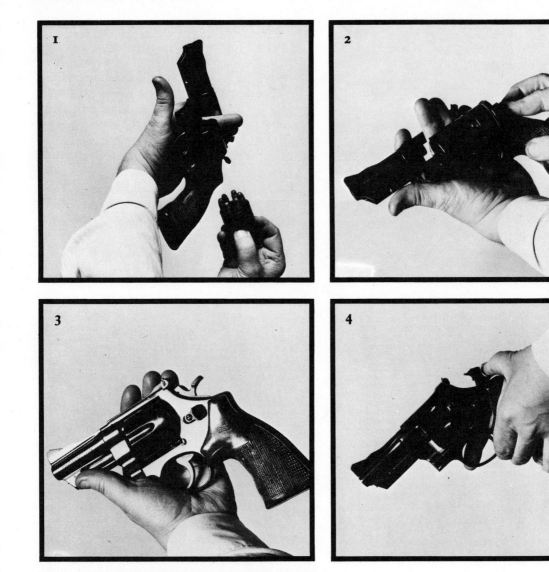

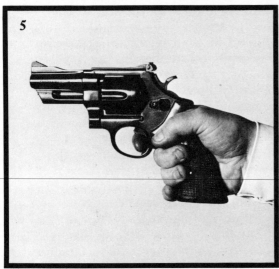

Loading and firing the full bore revolver.

1. Loading the gun, a Smith and Wesson, with a 6-cartridge quick loader.

2. Pushing the release on the quick loader. Notice that the shooter's fingers under the chamber prevent it slipping home.

3. The loaded weapon ready to fire.

4. Cocking the revolver.

5. Aiming the revolver and slowly squeezing the trigger.

SIGHT PICTURE AND AIM

Sight picture and aim are extremely important factors in firing an accurate shot or series. Almost all conscious effort should be directed towards maintaining sight alignment while holding in the aiming area during the release of the shot. When in this position, the top of the front sight should be level with the top of the rear sight, with an equal light space on either side of the front sight. With this sight picture, the eye focus should be on the front sight and the target should appear blurred and out of focus. However, unless the shooter is acutely aware of the in-focus relationship of the rear sight to the clearly defined front sight – still with the out-of-focus target – vertical and horizontal undulations will occur, causing a shift of group. It would appear to be easy to line up the two sights, maintain a minimum arc of movement in the aiming area and apply pressure to the trigger at the same time. However, the difficulty lies in maintaining the two sights in precise alignment and in focus relationship without looking forward at the target.

There are two suggested sight pictures:

The 6 o'clock hold: the top of the front sight is positioned just underneath the black aiming mark, without letting the sight merge with the mark.

Area aiming: the point of aim is between one-third and one-half of the distance from the bottom of the aiming mark to the bottom of the target. This method is used by most shooters, as it has many advantages over the 6 o'clock hold. If the shooter makes his aiming area the 'white' well below the aiming mark and focuses on the sights, the wobble of the sight picture seems to decrease. The silhouetted sights are easier to concentrate on and keep in focus, and show the faults in 'pushing' and 'pulling' the trigger.

TRIGGER CONTROL

All the effort and concentration that has been put into obtaining the correct stance, position, grip, breath control and sight alignment in order to keep the pistol as steady as possible while in the aiming position, can be wasted by faulty trigger control. In order to release a shot a physical movement has to be made by the trigger finger. If this movement is incorrect, it can move the pistol at the moment when optimum conditions exist for firing the shot. The finger must apply direct, even pressure on the trigger so that it moves directly in line with the barrel, keeping well away from any other part of the pistol. Once the shooter has perfected this exacting trigger pressure and finger movement, it must become a completely reflex action so that he can channel all concentration into sight alignment and focus. A shooter has only sufficient ability to concentrate on one specific factor at a time.

WEAPON SELECTION

An additional problem that faces all shooters, novices and top shots alike, is the selection of a target pistol. The desire within all of us to achieve perfection in everything in which we are really interested is reflected in the equipment we use. Consequently, few shooters are really completely satisfied with the pistols they use regularly, and readily succumb to new models as they come on the market. These masterpieces of engineering precision may offer such niceties as low recoil characteristics, two-stage triggers, roll off triggers, dual qualities built into the trigger, low barrel line, perfect sights and orthopaedic grips – all guaranteed to fit in the UIT weapon controller's box.

What is the best target pistol for competitive shooting? Ask a dozen different shooters and you will get a dozen different answers. Add to this all the inexpert advice that is available on the ranges, and a lot of people end up with a pistol that is not suitable to them in any way. Below is a list of the features that are essential for any competition target pistol.

The pistol should meet the requirements of the disciplines in which the shooter competes.

The pistol should have a 'target load' available to 'feed' it. This applies more to centrefire than any other form of shooting.

The pistol should be a recognized 'accurate' target weapon.

The trigger feel should be a sharp clean break with imperceptible movement, no drag or grittiness. The trigger should be easy to adjust and to 'work on'. (This is more important to the ex-

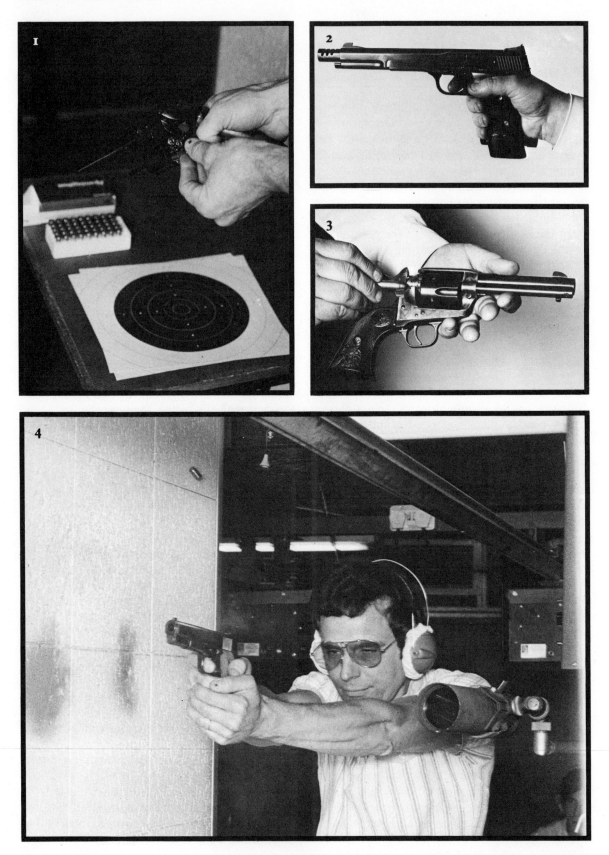

perienced shooter than the novice, but should not be overlooked.)

The trigger finger should be able to reach the trigger comfortably. If it cannot, consider whether the frame or grip can be modified.

Does the pistol 'sit' in the hand and come up well on the vertical raise? Does the grip fit and feel comfortable, and can it be modified to perfection? 'It's not me, it's the pistol', 'The grip is wrong', 'It points wrongly' are excuses for bad and indifferent shooting. Faulty weapon selection does not help the shooter in his search for perfection.

Weight, balance weights, two-stage triggers, and other refinements depend on one practical factor – the amount of money the shooter can afford to spend.

Buy from a reputable dealer who will have previously overhauled and adjusted the weapon, and who will provide an after-sales service. Take your time and choose carefully. Where strict police control is applied to possession of firearms, there is the added expense, time and trouble involved in changing a pistol.

CLUB SHOOTING

Since most people who indulge in pistol shooting belong to a club, it follows that there are many levels of performance within the club structure: county team members, national squad members, clubmen, and, of course, the novice. Whatever form of shooting people take part in outside the boundaries of the club, they will usually enter into competition with their own members and for their club against others. It may seem unfair to pit a top-class man against a person of lesser ability, but there is a classification system to cater for this so that all club members are at par.

Domestic shooting at this level is usually restricted to 'precision' shooting, and the form and the distance at which these matches are shot are dictated by the range facilities available to the club. Many ranges are limited to distances of 20 and 25 yards, the 25 yards being primarily for those long pistols called rifles. Of course, some clubs are the proud possessors of outdoor sites and boast the longest range at which club pistols are shot – 50 yards. In addition our sport is going metric, 25 metres and 50 metres being the range for the International disciplines. This difference

in the length of ranges produces difficulties in the sizes of the targets to be shot at, but this has been overcome by the introduction of related or scaled targets, i.e., the 25 metre target scaled down so that it can be shot at 20 yards and the 50 metre international precision target scaled for 20 yards. They are related in such a way that not only should the scores be the same, but the sight picture as well. Bull or 10 ring sizes for the 25 metre/ 20 yards scaled targets are 50 millimetres and 35 millimetres respectively, and for the 50 metre/ 20 yards they are 50 and 15 millimetres.

Precision shooting consists of firing 10 shots in 10 minutes (slow fire) at any one of the targets described. The pistol is usually a good quality semi-auto (self-loader), or a revolver or single shot weapon that complies with the rules and regulations laid down by the governing body of the sport. The salient points are the length of sight base and the weight required to release the trigger. The latter must not be less than 1 kilogramme (2.2 pounds). Pistols should be checked to see that they comply before the start of the match, and, if necessary, during and after. Some shooters still prefer to use single shot pistols and revolvers, but these have a limited application, are inferior to the semi-auto and are less suitable for general target shooting.

1. Loading a revolver with special .38 wadcutter cartridges. The weapon is held over the table so that any dropped cartridges will not fall on the floor.
2. A Smith and Wesson .22 pistol in the firing position.
3. Loading a Colt fullbore revolver by inserting one cartridge at a time in the chamber.
4. The double handed grip for an automatic. The shoulders are hunched forward as the pistol is punched towards the target. Notice the ejected case high on the left.

Postal leagues with teams of four shooters are run by the national body, county associations, and sometimes by clubs themselves. The teams shoot in divisions that compare favourably with the competing teams' individual averages, with points being awarded for a win, lose or draw. An Inter-County Postal Match has teams of ten shooters and is run only in the winter. It is backed up by a reserve team match, which gives clubmen who are not quite up to county 'A' standards a chance to compete against hard competition, perhaps bringing out the best in them and giving them a chance to try for county team membership.

For the individual club member a rating competition is run, and the competitor shoots against a series of standard scores in order to win a fixed award. For example, the shooter may fire forty shots – ten each at four targets – with a standard club pistol. The targets must be witnessed by an appointed witness, and signed and dated by the competitor and witness. The targets must be shot within two consecutive hours from the commencement of the shoot, and the stickers provided to qualify the targets must be placed behind the centre of the aiming mark. Qualifying scores (minimum) are listed below:

Master Shot 385 Average per target = 96.25

Expert	380	Average per target = 95
Class 'A'	365	Average per target = 91.25
Class 'B'	350	Average per target = 87.5
Class 'C'	335	Average per target = 83.75

The competitor may hold one award only for each year.

The National Rifle Association lays down similar standards for US pistol shooters. Qualifying scores, all over a minimum of 360 shots, are listed below:

Master	Average per target 95.00 and above
Expert	Average per target 90.00 to 94.99
Sharpshooter	Average per target 85.00 to 89.99
Marksman	Average per target below 85.00

This form of club competition stimulates people to shoot and is essential to keep the sport alive and healthy – pushing club members ever onwards to a better standard. Precision shooting, to a degree, is part of all disciplines except Rapid Fire, and it is the Precision Match that leads into the first UIT (Union Internationale de Tir, or International Shooters Union) event. The UIT, as its name implies, fosters compatibility between shooters of all nations. It has its own rules and regulations of shooting conduct and all International Matches are controlled by its governing committees.

UIT SHOOTING: FREE PISTOL MATCH

The Free Pistol Match is the longest match of all. It therefore requires the greatest amount of intense concentration, and that its participants be physically fit, with great stamina. It is said that the Free Pistol Match takes as much out of the competitor as does the 26 mile marathon, and training for this event is just as arduous. The Free Pistol shooter has to fire sixty shots plus fifteen sighting shots in $2\frac{1}{2}$ hours. This means at least 3 hours per training session. The name 'Free Pistol' is, of course, not derived from the price of the pistol! Because of its special nature and construction it is the most expensive target arm available, a balanced precision instrument, and a single purpose weapon that can be used only for this particular match. The name 'Free' relates to the lack of restriction imposed by the UIT on the pistol itself, i.e., length of barrel, distance between sights, weight, construction of the wooden grip, and the weight required to release the trigger, though it must be able to fire any 5.6 millimetre (.22 calibre) rimfire cartridge of lead or similar soft material. The International Precision Target is used for the Free Pistol Match. It has a 50 millimetre 10 ring, with the scoring rings going out to the 1 point, each 25 millimetres wide, and the black, or aiming mark going out to the 7 ring, 200 millimetres in diameter.

The match itself has to be shot on one day, with all competitors shooting at the same time so that the same conditions prevail for all. This poses quite a problem for the hosts because ranges with an excess of one hundred firing points have to be made available, and each firing point has to be provided with either automatic target changing equipment or pit marking. This is necessary because the regulations state that only five shots may be fired on any one target, and the match of sixty shots plus fifteen sighting shots must be completed within $2\frac{1}{2}$ hours with no competitors leaving the firing point without the Range Officer's permission – hence the shooter has everything done for him, unlike local matches where he changes targets himself.

Left: Custom made .22 pistol.
Below: Firing the .22 pistol.

STANDARD PISTOL MATCH

In this match the pistol must meet a set of 'standard' conditions in order to comply with the competition rules.
- the overall size must be such that it fits completely in a box 300 × 150 × 50 millimetres.
- the centre line of the barrel must pass above the upper part of the hand when in the firing position.
- the pistol weight must not exceed 1,400 grammes.
- the length of barrel must not exceed 153 millimetres.
- the sight radius must not exceed 220 millimetres.
- the trigger pull must be at least 1,000 grammes.
- the calibre must be 5.6 millimetres (.22). Any rimfire semi-automatic pistol or revolver that complies is acceptable.

The match is shot at 25 metres on the international precision target (the same as used for free pistol). The programme is sixty competition shots, divided into three courses of twenty shots each. Each course consists of four series of five shots fired as listed below:

First course in 150 seconds per series (precision);

Second course in 20 seconds per series (timed);

Third course in 10 seconds per series (rapid).

Before the competition begins, a series of five sighting shots may be fired in 150 seconds. While this match has a precision stage and relates to club and free shooting, it has been enhanced by the addition of two faster shooting stages, which make it more difficult as it progresses. The fundamental principles of shooting do not alter, only the methods of application – the elements of technique – differ to suit this particular competition. The three different speeds of shooting must be considered as being three different matches in one, requiring three differing techniques to perfect. For example, the precision stance and body position would be as already described, while for the timed and rapid stages the feet would need to be slightly farther apart, with slight pressure on the toes to produce a forward centre of gravity with equal weight distribution. The exact body position must be corrected in each case for the speed with which the shooter lifts the pistol into the aiming area, so that the five-shot group will be correct laterally. At the same time he must drop his shoulder and pistol as the lift is performed in order to lock his arm and prevent 'rocking shots', shots lifted vertically because of the recoil. The grip should be firmer and more positive to contain the effects of the five-shot recoil and to obtain a quick and correct sight alignment after recovery from recoil without correction of wrist, arm or head.

Breath control in this match provides the shooter with a method of counting time and, when related to the Range Officer's commands, gives him the ability to anticipate the exposure of the target for the time stage to commence. In the 20- and 10-second stages the shooter will have to hold his breath for a longer period than when shooting precision, and will, therefore, have to train for this sustained period of control. Eventually, breathing in this event becomes automatic and rhythmic, and the shooter does not have to think about doing it at all, releasing effort and concentration for the other factors.

Trigger release must be precise, because five shots have to be fired in quick succession, and a decided speeding up of the trigger action has to be made to coincide with the time for the series. The very nature of this quickened release lends itself to snatch, pull, push, and every other fault. As a composite discipline, this event leaves little room for the more common errors and requires a high degree of technique and self discipline for perfection.

INTERNATIONAL RAPID FIRE MATCH

This match, unlike the other UIT disciplines, has no precision stages. The match is for sixty competition shots, divided into two thirty-shot courses. Each course is subdivided into six series of five shots each, two in 8 seconds, two in 6 seconds, and two in 4 seconds. In each series one shot is fired on each of the five targets in the specified time limit. Before the start of each course, the competitor may fire one sighting series of five shots in 8, 6, or 4 seconds. The first half course of thirty shots must be completed by all competitors before the second course may commence. Any type of 5.6 millimetre (.22) pistol

may be used that complies with the following:
• the weight must not exceed 1,260 grammes.
• any 5.6 millimetre rimfire cartridge with soft lead projectile may be used.
• special grips are permitted.
• the overall size must be such that it fits completely in a box 300 × 150 × 50 millimetres. A tolerance of up to 5 percent in one dimension only is allowed.

No restriction is placed on the trigger release weight or on the length between the front and rear sights, and the pistol could be termed a 'free' automatic.

The techniques employed for this form of shooting differ radically from all other forms. They have to become rhythmic habits in order to meet the split-second timings required for a good score index. A perfect body position has to be achieved in order that the pistol is pointing exactly in the centre of the aiming area on completion of the vertical raise, for there is no time at all to make any form of correction. If the first shot in the series is a bad one, then the others will follow suit. The body position has to be corrected for differing speeds of vertical raise, and the dropped shoulder method used to correct 'rocking shots'.

To give some idea of the shot timings required for this match, and the accurate 'speed' within which the shooter must strive for perfection, the approximate times in seconds for the various actions for the three time stages are listed below.

Time for shot	3.0 seconds
Arm lift from 45° to aiming area (vertical raise)	1.2 seconds
Time for shot	1.6 seconds

The International Rapid Fire Target is used for this match. It is 160 centimetres high, 45 centimetres wide, black and divided into ten scoring zones by white lines 1 millimetre thick. The 10 zone is formed by two vertical lines 5 centimetres long and 10 centimetres apart, joined at each end by semi-circles with a 5 centimetre radius (10 centimetres wide and 15 centimetres high). The zones from 9 to 1 are similarly shaped, their width being successively increased by 10 centimetres (5 centimetres on either side), and their height by 15 centimetres (7.5 centimetres top and bottom).

Checking the scores on International Rapid Fire targets at the NRA range at Bisley.

INTERNATIONAL CENTREFIRE AND LADIES MATCH

The final two disciplines are an amalgamation of precision shooting and a form of rapid fire. They are two disciplines in name only. One is the Ladies' Match and is shot in .22 calibre. The rules for the pistol are the same as for the standard pistol. The other event is the Centrefire Pistol Match, shot in calibres from 7.62 millimetres (.30) to 9.65 millimetres (.38) with the following conditions applying.

Any centrefire pistol or revolver within the above calibre range.

Weight with all accessories must not exceed 1,400 grammes.

Barrel length must not exceed 152 millimetres (6 inches).

Distance between front and rear sights must not exceed 220 millimetres.

Muzzle brakes are not allowed.

Trigger pull must be at least 1,360 grammes (3 pounds).

No specialized grips are allowed.

Any 7.62 to 9.65 millimetre centrefire cartridge is allowed, except magnums.

Both events are shot at 25 metres and have the same competition rules. The programme is for sixty competition shots, divided into two courses of thirty shots each. The first course is the Precision, and the second course is the Duelling. The precision stages must be completed by all competitors before the duelling course can commence.

It is shot on the International Precision Target, and consists of six series of five shots per series, the time limit for each series being 6 minutes. Before the course begins, a series of five sighting shots may be fired with a time limit of 8 minutes.

The Duelling Course is shot on the International Rapid Fire Target, and consists of six series of five shots per series. During each series the target is shown five times, each time for 3 seconds. The time between each appearance is 7 seconds in the edge-on position. One shot is fired during each appearance. Before the course begins, a series of five sighting shots may be fired according to the above described procedure.

Pistol shooting on the range at Bisley.

The Precision stages are quite easily understood. The competitor has ample time to fire ten shots, more time, in fact, than allowed in the course of normal club matches. Control factors are the same as for club Precision shooting, except that the shots are fired in strings of five, and the range control orders are accordingly varied. Centrefire shooters have to learn to control the higher recoil characteristics of their big bore pistols, and stance, body position, grip, recovery and follow-through have to be more positive, and perhaps exaggerated in certain cases to obtain greater stability for accuracy.

The Duelling course is very similar to the Rapid Fire shoot in that the target presents itself five times (once for each shot), instead of once for five shots (one each on five targets). This course relates very favourably to the first shot in the 8 seconds time stage, repeated five times in sequence. As in Rapid Fire, particular attention has to be paid to body position, speed of vertical raise, shot timing and rhythm; standard pistol breath control is used as a method of counting time to anticipate the exposure of the targets for each duelling shot. Participants in both matches have to train to contain the higher recoil of the centrefire and long rifle cartridges fired in this very fast half course. The pistols are not allowed any form of recoil reduction accessories. Shot timings for the duel are as follows.

Time for shot	3.0 seconds
Arm lift from 45° to aiming area (vertical raise)	1.2 seconds
Time for shot	1.6 seconds
Time for vertical raise and shot release	2.8 seconds
Safety factor	0.2 seconds

These individual times from the turning of the targets serve only as a guide towards the ultimate in rhythmic shooting.

Turning targets have been mentioned more than once in the course of this chapter, and an explanation of what they are and what they do is needed. Firstly, they are required for all 25 metres UIT events. They are furnished with a rotating mechanism, and are mounted to permit turning through 90°.

The time permitted for turning should not exceed 0.3 seconds. Targets are placed in groups of five, and must turn simultaneously. The automatic turning and timing device ensures the rotation of the targets from the edge-on position to the face position, and remains in this position for the specified time period, then returns to the edge-on position. Shots fired before the targets have faced and after they have edged will be scored as misses. Shots fired while the target is in motion will not be scored as hits unless the greatest horizontal dimension of the bullet hole measures not more than 7 millimetres in the 5.6 millimetre (.22) events or 11 millimetres in the centrefire event.

PRE-MATCH PREPARATION

Complete all pre-match preparations, leaving the 'setting up' on the firing point until last.

Carry out the following warm-up exercises.

Turn head right, then left; bend head right, then left; bend head forwards, then backwards; circle head right, then left. (4 times)

Push one leg at a time forward and stretch, pushing with toes, then bend knee and pull up to chest. Alternate legs. (4 times)

Stand with legs apart and swivel from waist, flinging relaxed arms round body as you do so. (20 times)

Sit with soles of feet together, push knees to try to make them reach the floor (20 times)

Loose shoulder rolling–both together–forwards and backwards. (20 times)

Stand with arms at sides and palms forward. Swing arms forwards and up to touch shoulders, clenching fists and rolling wrists as you do so. (15 times)

Stand with arms extended above your head. Grip hands, and swing arms forwards and backwards. (8 times)

Stand with feet apart. Stretch sideways, pulling clenched fist up under armpit while reaching for floor with other hand. Alternate. (10 times)

Stand with legs wide apart. Swing down and touch the floor with arms relaxed and shoulders wobbling. (6 times)

Stand with feet together. Swing arms forward from sides, up to waist, chest, and then above your head, rising on toes as you do so; hold position for 4 seconds. (6 times)

Stand with legs wide apart and swivel. (10 times)

Run on the spot for two minutes.

TRAINING

The sport of target pistol shooting is a very highly developed science requiring a great deal of instruction and dedication, as well as mental and physical training. Most important for the production of a top-level pistol shooter are:
- the shooter's inherent skills and abilities;
- the comprehensiveness and suitability of his/her equipment;
- the natural aptitude and willingness to accept training – dedication;
- physical fitness;
- mental discipline and control.

Participants in all forms of sports activities train to improve. Pistol shooters must also have a programme of training in order to increase their performance and score index. The shooter must be able to stand motionless in the same place, hold the pistol still, and shoot for a sustained match period without tiring. This calls for a great deal of lifting, holding and muscular control. Muscular tone and fitness are required for the best performance at all times, especially if the actions or movements are of a complicated nature, or if conscious thought is required to initiate them. Conscious initiation requires extra energy to fulfill the necessary stillness/movement patterns, energy that should be used in the total concentration required for the end product – the release of the shot.

For a normal person it is the ability to perform a task efficiently, without undue fatigue, and to recover quickly from the effort. For the pistol shooter, it is the degree of increased thought and movement, stamina and effort produced over and above any that had been produced before, with immediate recovery. Muscles that are little used tend to lose their tone, and become weak and flabby. Proper exercise will tone up the muscles, improve coordination, stimulate blood circulation and thus sharpen reactions and increase stamina.

Mental fitness provides the control necessary to maintain confidence, produce continued duplication of performance, and override any disturbing factors likely to disrupt tranquillity.

Inert or passive relaxation is intended as a pre-match build-up. The shooter should lie down comfortably on a couch. His coach can then 'talk him down' into a state of muscular and mental tranquility, opening his mind to thought sequences that relate to confidence, reducing anxiety and errors in the control factors required for a match. As the shooter becomes skilled in this form of training, he will be able to self-induce relaxation.

Concentration can be learned by the use of a simple object, such as a matchbox. Put the object on the table, look at it, and then concentrate on it to the exclusion of all else for just three seconds. It may seem impossible in the beginning, but gradually you will be able to increase the length of time. If you learn to concentrate on one thing, it becomes second nature to concentrate on another, such as sights on your weapon.

Movement relaxation is a condition you should be able to achieve at work or at play. It is produced by allowing the muscles not in use to relax and giving only the required degree of tension to those that are doing the work. A 'trigger' image is used to switch on the movement. The trigger in current use is a black sight picture. During the first few days' training you should look at it quite frequently and deliberately. Each time you do this, allow your stomach to sag and start to breathe slowly and gently, and gradually more shallowly. Let your bottom jaw sag and place your tongue in the bottom of your mouth. If you are standing up, make sure that your buttocks are also slack. It will not take long to train yourself to relax in this way as soon as you see a correct black sight picture.

To reduce pulse rate quickly, sit down. If your body dictates that you breathe quickly, then help it by doing just that – exaggerate. Carry out the movement relaxation routine as detailed above, stomach sagging, jaw sagging, breathing getting slower and more shallow. Let yourself become heavy and relaxed, and form a mental picture of the sight picture card as you do so. Do this for 10 minutes (or time by experiment) and you should feel your pulse drop to 10 below resting rate. To keep the pulse rate as low as possible during a match, practise movement relaxation during the match. Take every opportunity to sit down and relax between series; don't fiddle and fidget about. Look at something softly coloured and blink your eyes. This is as much a part of the match as the shooting of a match shot.

Top: Shooting with an automatic pistol. Notice the wooden all-round grip.
Bottom: Pistol shooting in the covered stands at Bisley.

8 PRACTICAL PISTOL SHOOTING

A NEW KIND OF SHOOTING

Practical pistol shooting is probably the most exciting of the shooting disciplines as well as being one of the most interesting for the spectator. It has all the ingredients that appeal to the spectator and participant: movement, speed, and various courses of fire. Although it is a sport, the techniques of Practical Pistol Shooting are also used in police training.

As a sport, Practical Pistol Shooting developed in the United States in the 1950s by a number of shooters who were bored with the monotony of conventional target shooting, just punching holes in pieces of paper at known distances in set times, until one became virtually an automaton if a high degree of proficiency was to be attained. The question was how could shooters get out of the rut? The first step was to throw aside all recognized preconceptions of target shooting. Why, for instance, do we always shoot a pistol standing? Why always one-handed? The philosophy behind Practical Pistol Shooting is that an 8-inch group in four seconds is better than 4-inch group in eight seconds. All the essential elements of target shooting still apply: a correct sight picture, surprise break of the trigger, controlled breathing and stance. On most occasions these factors are applied so rapidly that the uninitiated can be excused for thinking that the shooter is firing instinctively.

Jeff Cooper, a former US Marine colonel, who had pioneered many of these ideas, realised that there was an increasing international interest in the sport. Accordingly, a conference was convened at Columbia, Missouri in May 1976, which shooters from all over the world attended, including the world's top Practical Pistol Shooters, Thell Read, Ray Chapman, the first world champion, and Dave Westerhout. The purpose of the conference was to form a world governing body, to be called the International Practical Shooting Confererdation (IPSC). Great stress was put on having as few rules as possible commensurate with safety.

After the IPSC had been formed, the delegates were given the task of returning to their countries and developing the ideas that had been proposed. The reactions in the various countries showed the enthusiasm with which this form of shooting was being received. A number of recognized international UIT shooters attended matches as competitors, commenting that this gave new stimulus to their shooting. The varied courses gave a diverse challenge and added interest. The essential characteristics of Practical Pistol Shooting are:

- the use of a large calibre pistol. (The Colt .45 Government model is most commonly used.)
- the use of a stable firing platform.
- a quick draw.
- a quick sight picture.
- a quick surprise break.

BASIC RULES

Anybody wishing to take up this challenging new sport should approach their national association and then make contact with a local club. For those wishing to run a course of fire, there are a number of basic rules to follow.

Safety must never be prejudiced.

Encourage the use of the large pistol by giving scoring bonuses based on calibre.

All courses should have the score divided by time, or have a *tight* time schedule.

No restriction on loading the weapon, such as limiting magazine capacity, except extension magazines on reload only.

Enforced reloads are permissible, provided it is borne in mind that the principle is to promote dexterity in weapon handling and not to limit the number of rounds.

Avoid impractical situations, such as firing until the weapon is empty.

All pistols should compete on an equal basis, avoiding discrimination among various types of weapon.

No restriction should be placed on shooting position, although the use of barricades and similar artificial rests is permitted.

'No shoot' targets must be quickly identifiable.

Weapons should generally be reholstered during movement.

Multiple hits of targets should be avoided to encourage practicality. Essentially, we are trying to promote speed, power and accuracy. To quote Jeff Cooper, 'speed without accuracy is useless, but so is accuracy without speed, and both together may not suffice without power.'

CALIBRE

The rules of Practical Pistol Shooting require the use of a heavy calibre weapon shooting full-charge ammunition. It is only the heavy calibres that have proved to be consistent man-stoppers, and .44 and .45 are the ones preferred. The more recently introduced .41 magnum calibre is adequate in its police loading, the magnum loading having too much recoil and penetration. Fully loaded, the .357 cartridge can produce the energy required, but it does this at the expense of relatively high pressure, heavy recoil and pronounced muzzle blast. The majority of police departments in America arm their officers with revolvers chambered for the .38 Special. In Europe even smaller calibres, such as the .380 automatic or the .32 automatic, are very common. Some people may think that because the police have been armed in such a manner the most effective calibres have been chosen. In many cases the choice has been made by a political committee, often without knowledge of ballistics or firearms, and without giving due consideration to the uses to which the weapons will be put.

Attempts have been made to overcome the inherent deficiencies in the chosen cartridges by the use of hollow-point bullets that expand upon impact or by lightening the weight of bullets and stepping up their velocities. At best, the efficiency increase is marginal and in most cases the bullet is still not driven at a sufficiently high velocity to ensure expansion. This only leaves the choice of going back to the old concept of a large calibre, heavy projectile travelling at relatively low velocity. In the trenches of World War I men armed with the .45 pistol found that a shot from it would stop a man in a bayonet charge, and it would appear that the findings of the various early twentieth century ordnance boards are having to be resurrected.

DISTANCE

6 metres

A low bank makes an ideal backstop for an informal open air range.

CARTRIDGES

The IPSC decided that there should be two standards in a power-rating system comprising two categories: major, a cartridge delivering terminal momentum equivalent to the Government Issue .45 ACP ball ammunition; and minor, the equivalent of the 9 millimetre service issue loading, generally accepted as being the 125 grain bullet travelling at 1,100 feet per second. There was argument, particularly from European shooters, because in some areas the law prevents the ownership of any pistol larger than 7.65 millimetres. In the end, the IPSC decided that certain principles could not be sacrificed, and 9 millimetre Parabellum was adopted as the power floor. No round less powerful than that would qualify for competition.

As the regulation requires cartridges to be able to perform to a certain standard, it is necessary to be able to test loads. The IPSC recommends that a ballistic pendulum be used for the test to determine whether any cartridge is to be classed as major or minor.

POSITIONING

The pendulum is designed to be shot at from the prone position. Testers and others in the vicinity should wear shooting-glasses. You may wish to use a splatter shield or the shield of a grinding wheel, which fits round the firer's face. Lead can splash straight back and, although having insufficient velocity otherwise to do serious damage, it can cause eye injury.

READINGS

The basic load test is five rounds. Discount any impacts that hit well off-centre or at the juncture of the target disc and the splash shield. Shoot until three well-placed hits result.

Two shooters in competition in the Columbia Fumble. They sprint towards the tin can on the ground (left) which must be placed on the pole 5 metres away (right) before they can fire.

INTERPRETATION OF READINGS

Standardize the readings by shooting the pendulum with 9 millimetre and .45 hardball on the day the loads are to be tested and every time the pendulum is set up. Lead bullets do not transmit their energy in the same way as jacketed bullets; the readings for lead bullets are 95 percent of jacketed bullets.

CALIBRATION

Always use the shortest barrel available for test purposes. If, for example, a Star PD is being used by a competitor, ensure that calibration is done with this weapon and not with the longer barrelled Government Model. Do not adopt an attitude that bars loads that are a $\frac{1}{4}°$ out on the protractor. The idea is to ensure competitors enter with full-charge ammunition. The pendulum should swing in an arc of about 150°–155° with the major calibre; adding or subtracting weight to or from the target disc will ensure that this degree of swing is easily attained. To ensure accuracy of reading, the pendulum should be fitted with a good-quality protractor.

STANCE

One stable firing platform often adopted is usually referred to as the Weaver Stance, after an American deputy sheriff. In this position the left foot (for a right-handed person) points roughly in the direction of the target, and the right foot is placed slightly in excess of the width of the shoulders to the rear, pointing a little outwards. In this position the shooter can absorb the recoil of the heavy calibre and, more importantly, swivel through a firing arc of about 180°. The pistol is grasped in the right hand and thrust forward, the left hand comes up and grasps the fingers of the right hand, pulling back hard to diminish recoil further. The right hand does not rest in the left; it is a firm, conscious, pulling effort that goes to make up the grip. This aids recovery from recoil, allows fast follow-up shots and promotes greater accuracy. This stance has been proven continually

in competition. The time taken to assume this posture is so short that nothing is gained from the one-handed grip popular in cowboy films.

In addition to the more conventional stance, competitions call for shooting from behind barricades or from the prone position to simulate conditions likely to be met in the field. Most police pistol courses that call for shooting from behind a barricade stipulate that when shooting round the left side, the competitors should use the left hand. Very little of the body need be exposed if one fires with the right hand around the left side. The only other position likely to be needed is the prone, which has definite practical uses. For long-range shooting, the weapon has firm support as the butt rests on the palm of the weak hand. A very low-profile target is then presented to an opponent. For competition purposes it is more comfortable to place the body at a more oblique angle, as it prevents straining the neck. Some competitions call for shooting with the weak hand, a technique that most shooters have difficulty in mastering. If this is a problem, cant the piece over at an angle of about 45°. This seems to aid prevention of displacement of shots.

The use of quick-draw raises the greatest mental block in rifle or target shooters. The slow-fire marksmen have a completely different approach in their quest for the maximum accuracy, and although they are still shooters, they feel that drawing from the holster places one in the category of 'cowboy'.

Flinching is as much of a problem for the Practical Pistol Shooter as for the UIT shooter. The release of the trigger must come as a surprise or a displaced shot will result. One also has to avoid snatching, a very common error because of the speed of the shooting.

SIGHTS

The use of sights is most important. Shooters have been surprised to find that they have been unable to hit a target as close as 7 metres when shooting at speed. With practice, the sights can be picked up extremely quickly; the more perfect the sight alignment the better the shot placement. A number of variations of sights have been tried, but the standard Partridge variety has proved best, and some shooters prefer using contrasting colours for rear and front sights.

TARGETS

The IPSC adopted two targets to be used at the discretion of match organizers. The idea of multiple, meaningless scoring rings was rejected. The 'O', or Option target has two rings, 25 centimetres and 35 centimetres respectively, and a 10 centimetre circle in the head box. The 'I' or Item target has rectangular scoring areas, as vertical sight alignment is less important than horizontal hold. The illustrations on the target depict dimensions and values. To avoid the shooter being able to form definite aiming marks and to break up the outline of the silhouette, a mottled or camouflage effect is recommended.

Below: A selection of turning targets.
Right: The standard International Option target and, below it, the International Item target.
Both targets are a neutral shade, Not black, white nor any vivid colour. All scoring lines and lettering are pencil-thin and invisible at a distance.

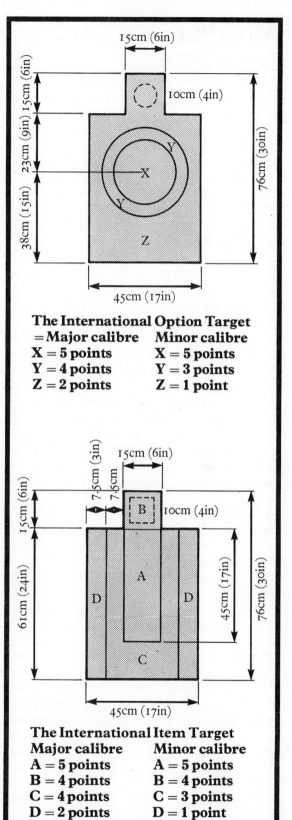

The International Option Target

= Major calibre	Minor calibre
X = 5 points	X = 5 points
Y = 4 points	Y = 3 points
Z = 2 points	Z = 1 point

The International Item Target

Major calibre	Minor calibre
A = 5 points	A = 5 points
B = 4 points	B = 4 points
C = 4 points	C = 3 points
D = 2 points	D = 1 point

HOLSTERS

Pistols were originally designed to be carried in pockets or holsters, so it seems a logical extension of the sport to require competition that calls for drawing a pistol from the holster. Naturally, a branch of the sport with relatively few restrictions promotes the quest for the ultimate in pistol, holster and ammunition to give every possible advantage on the firing line. For a short period, some outlandish contraptions were arriving on the range. They lacked all practicality and, without trying to stifle development and invention, regulations were introduced that emphasized a sense of reality.

When drawing from the holster, it is most important that one achieve a firing grip on first contact with the pistol, taking care to keep the index finger outside the trigger guard until the pistol clears the holster. The draw must be completed smoothly, the safety catch flicked off, the gun punched forward to snap into the left hand and the Weaver Stance assumed at the same time. This action takes place in about half a second. To achieve this it is quite obvious the holster needs to be well designed.

The delegates of the first IPSC conference spent a great deal of time trying to decide what should constitute a practical holster. Some favoured the idea that all holsters should be allowed as long as they were capable of retaining the weapon during violent movement, while others considered that only those holsters suitable for the political environment in which they would be worn could be considered truly practical. The regulations require that a holster be capable of holding the pistol when the wearer performs a 360° backward roll or a standing jump of 18 inches.

Holsters are very much a personal matter. General guidelines can be given but observation should be made of what the top-flight competitors are using. Quality is essential and the adage of getting what one pays for certainly applies with leatherwork. The first decision to be made is on the type of holster: cross draw, high-riding hip holster, or shoulder holster. The popular model on the firing lines is the hip holster worn on its own belt and riding a little lower than the trouser belt, at the preference of the shooter. To keep the holster securely anchored, a retaining strap around the leg is often used. It has to be borne in mind that the holster has to hold the pistol during violent movement and, consequently, some method must be used to retain the piece. There are two popular ways of doing this. One is to have a securing strap going between the hammer and slide with a quick-release button that is pushed by the thumb when drawing. This is very secure, and its only drawback is that there is an additional thought process at a time when the pistol is required at high speed. The other popular method is to use a tensioned welt bearing on the underside of the slide (of an automatic pistol), which provides friction during the first $\frac{1}{4}$ inch of the draw and then becomes completely free.

The correctly designed holster is made in such a manner that it is not possible to place the forefinger in the trigger-guard until the piece is clear of the holster. A style coming into vogue is to wear what would conventionally be thought of as a cross-draw holster, but worn just to the left of the centre-line of the body. This is advantageous, particularly where a course of fire calls for shooting from the sitting position. A number of shooters also wear this holster on the other side of the body over the appendix. Shoulder holsters, although very practical as a means of carrying a weapon, are not popular in competition, as considerable contortion is required during the draw. If this holster is the choice, it is almost universally accepted that the spring-tensioned method should be incorporated, whereby a leather-covered spring clamps round the cylinder of a revolver or the slide and trigger-guard of an automatic. Among the high-ride variety of holsters, by which we mean those worn high on the trouser belt, the so-called 'Summer Special' designed by top-flight American shooter, Bruce Nelson, is both practical and fast, and can be carried even in the hottest weather. It can be concealed by only a shirt worn outside the trousers. The holster is designed to be worn inside the trousers, attached to the trouser belt with the butt of the pistol sticking out of the top of the trousers and the muzzle going down inside. All the tension required is provided by the wearer's belt. In any competition requiring the pistol to be carried concealed, a very short jacket can be worn provided it reaches to the waist. As long as the jacket reaches the wearer's belt, the weapon will not be visible.

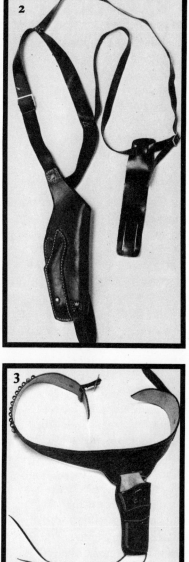

1. A spring-tensioned holster holding an automatic.
2. Shoulder holster for an automatic. The arm passes through the large loop and the elasticated section goes across the back. A retaining strip attaches to the waistband.
3. A Western-style holster for a quick draw.

THE NEW WEAPON

A certain amount of attention has to be paid to the pistol as it comes out of the box, assuming that it is a factory-new product. In today's high production technology there is very little time allowed for finishing; this is very readily apparent by comparing a pistol of contemporary manufacture with the same make made prior to the last war. So, although not vital, additional aesthetic appeal can be given to the weapon by time spent on the polishing and smoothing of the moving parts. For military weapons, when the most adverse conditions are likely to be encountered, tolerances are necessarily generous to enable the piece to function even if there is a considerable amount of foreign matter present. For the average Practical Pistol competitor this factor will not be of paramount importance. He will lavish considerably more attention on cleaning and will not normally be shooting in conditions where dust is an extreme hazard.

As many of the competitions call for shooting at ranges up to 150 metres, a weapon able to shoot extremely accurately is required. Top quality ammunition and a pistol that is capable of very tight grouping are needed. Most of the modifications made to the .45 will apply to other automatics. The .45 will generally be capable of grouping into 8 to 10 inches at 50 yards as it arrives from the factory. Some pistols will shoot better and some worse. It is generally agreed that the first requirement is to have a set of high-relief sights fitted; the factory sights are too small and slow to pick up. Either an $\frac{1}{8}$ inch or $\frac{1}{10}$ inch ramp front sight with a corresponding width rear sight are the ideal combination. Depending upon personal preference, the front sight can have a contrasting coloured insert, usually red or yellow. The rear sight is usually adjustable, although this is not mandatory if one retains the same load in the cartridge.

Adjustable sights are really required if one constantly changes loads and, of course, they are more fragile than fixed sights. In most makes of automatic pistol there is lateral and vertical play between the slide and the frame, which prevents the slide from returning to battery in exactly the same position and is detrimental to target accuracy. It is desirable to remove most of this play. The method of getting a closer fit of the rails

is to squeeze the rear end of the slide very gently where it mates with the frame, and also peen down the guide ribs on the frame. This has the effect of pulling the slide on to the frame. A lapping compound is then required to lap the two pieces until there is a smooth fit. This modification should not be attempted unless one has a certain amount of gunsmithing skill.

If the trigger pull is excessive, it should be lightened, but avoid taking the weight below about $3\frac{1}{2}$ pounds, or doubling may occur. The jar of the slide going into the battery after firing causes the hammer to jump the sear and so fire again.

It will be obvious from the courses described previously that a smooth reload is essential. When the weapon arrives from the factory, if it is a Colt, the magazine well has no chamfering at the base; bevelling makes for easier insertion of the magazine. The final modification is to have an oversize safety catch fitted. It is easier for the thumb to hit the safety on the draw, and also provides a rest on which to place the thumb when firing. In the United States these alterations have generated a minor industry, with companies being formed to carry out what has become known as 'accurizing'.

A number of courses of fire call for the shooter to start with the pistol underneath the jacket. When discussing concealed weapons, pistols such as the Smith & Wesson Chief's Special and Colt Cobra spring to mind. Yet, these are really quite bulky weapons with their bulbous cylinders and comparatively obtrusive grips. Most of the automatic's bulk is in its length, but this is the dimension most easily concealed. The barrel extends down inside the flank and the butt lies conveniently along the waist. By using the automatic, one has the convenience of higher fire power, a more powerful cartridge and a more rapid reload if required. If it is thought that there is too much bulk from the standard Government Model .45, there are options of using the Colt Commander or the Star PD. There are custom versions, usually modifications of the Colt, that can provide even less bulk, but the cartridge capacity often suffers as a consequence.

Drawing from beneath the jacket is aided if one has the pocket weighted with a small amount of loose change. The coat is flicked back with the right hand, the weight of the coins takes the jacket round the back and the draw is completed before the coat returns to the normal hanging position. At all stages of training one should develop the habit of changing magazines during convenient pauses in shooting, until the operation becomes reflexive. The idea is that there should always be a fully-loaded pistol in one's hand. This concept also applies to revolvers, with their smaller cartridge capacity. No matter how many rounds a particular course of fire requires, it is always a good practice to fill magazines to capacity.

Two courses of fire are given here. They can be treated as exercises upon which to assess a novice, but avoid the trap of shooting them to the exclusion of all others.

Right: A steady hold in the kneeling position. The gun is a .38 Webley pocket revolver.
Below: A Colt .45 automatic Government model.

EL PRESIDENTE

Three targets are set up 10 metres down range and spaced three metres apart, centre to centre. The shooter stands with his pistol loaded and holstered, his back to the targets and hands clasped at the centre line of the body. On the signal 'Go', the shooter turns, draws and fires two rounds on each target, reloads and fires a further two shots on each.

A stopwatch is started on the signal 'Go' and stopped when the shooter fires his twelfth round. The targets are then scored, the time taken is divided into the target score, and the total multiplied by ten. For example, shooter number one scores 4 fives on target 1, 4 fives on target 2, 3 fives and 1 four on target 3 for a total of 59 in 14.8 seconds. His final score is $59 \div 14.8 \times 10 = 39.86$.

Shooter number two scores 1 four and 3 twos on target number 1, 2 fives, 1 four and 1 two on target 2, and 1 five, 1 four and 2 twos on target 3 for a total of 39 in 8.7 seconds. His final score is $39 \div 8.7 \times 10 = 44.83$. The result is that, although the first shooter has scored higher numeri-

cally on the target, the second shooter fired his string at maximum speed (the whole concept of practical shooting) and maintained sufficient accuracy, and therefore, he wins. To ensure that people do not sacrifice accuracy, any misses are heavily penalised by deducting 10 points for each miss.

THE COLUMBIA FUMBLE

Three targets are placed at 5, 10 and 12 metres. The shooter starts, facing an impact target 15 metres down range (a timer gong or balloon make excellent targets, and add to spectator appeal). Five metres down range and 10 metres from the impact target, a pole 150 centimetres high, is set vertically in the ground; this marks the forward limit of the shooter's movement. Halfway between the start line and the pole a can, approximately 1 litre capacity and open at one end, is placed on the ground. One target is located at a 45° divergence 5 metres from the pole. Another target is located 12 metres from the pole 2 metres

beyond, and 1 metre to the side of, the impact target on the same side as the first target.

On the signal, the shooter sprints from the start line, picks up the can with his shooting hand and sets it on the pole, after which he draws and fires at target 1, then at target 2, reloads and hits the impact target to stop the clock. On this shoot, only hits in the 5 ring count. The shooter may fire as many rounds at each target as he wishes, but a maximum of 2 × 5 on each target will be scored. The time taken is divided into the score and the result multiplied by five.

In this course of fire a reload for an automatic consists of removing the magazine and inserting another. With a revolver, a reload consists of ejecting all cartridges or cases and inserting fresh ammunition. It is not necessary to fill all chambers. A shooter firing his pistol into the ground closer than 2 metres or dropping his weapon shall be disqualified. Failure of the shooter's equipment is his problem, but range equipment failure allows a re-shoot. The shooter starts on level ground, and toe-holds or chocks are not permitted. It is suggested that where people are inexperienced, the shooter starts facing the target with the pistol held at 45°. In the variation of the

Columbia Fumble instead of having the can 5 metres down range, the shooter has the pistol lying on the ground by the pole. He is then required to load his weapon, thus adding to the handicap but avoiding the problem of having to draw from the holster. These are only two of the courses that have been devised and are given as an example of how to use one's imagination.

Left: Running through the Columbia Fumble. The need for a holster which can hold the gun securely is quite clear from this sequence of photographs.
Below: The layout for the Columbia Fumble. After placing the can on the pole, competitors fire quickly at the three targets, ending with the impact target, usually a timer gong or large balloon, bringing the course to a spectacular close.

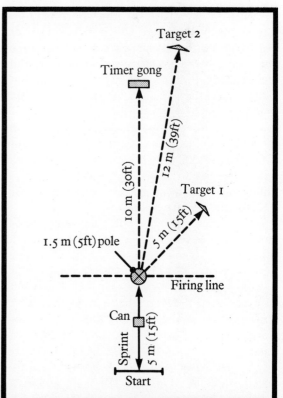

FITNESS

Physical condition plays a very important part in the make-up of the Practical Pistol Shooter. Not only does one need the coordination of the factors applicable in conventional target shooting, such as breath control and muscular reaction, but there is also the problem of violent movement. In the 1977 World Championships held in Rhodesia it was necessary for competitors to do a considerable amount of running over long distances and then place accurate shots on a target. As score was divided by time in nearly all contests, it needed a high degree of fitness to achieve a high position. This was proved by the winner, who was not only a first class shot, but also an athlete. Incidentally, he shot a Browning Hi-Power 9 millimetre. Provided one can place shots accurately, the use of a minor calibre need not prove an insurmountable handicap.

THE DEVELOPMENT OF THE SPORT

Growing in popularity is the sport of Long Range pistol shooting, which has very close associations with the Practical side. The accuracy potential inherent in the pistol is not generally appreciated. Provided the piece is properly tuned and the quality of the ammunition uniformly high, a pistol should be capable of grouping into 2 to 3 inches at 50 yards. By long range shooting we generally mean distances from 100 yards to 300 yards. Beyond that distance, unless one has an extremely good knowledge of bullet trajectory in most cases it would be considered impractical to shoot.

In America the sport of long-range handgunning has developed into shooting at metallic silhouettes of game animals. These silhouettes are constructed of heavy steel plate and require a good solid hit to knock them over. Silhouette shooting tends to favour the high velocity heavy bullet of large calibre, usually the .44 Magnum. Three weapons commonly available fit this criteria, the Smith & Wesson M29, the Ruger Super Blackhawk, and the more recently introduced .44 Auto Mag. The last is an automatic pistol shooting a cut-down .308 rifle case. The .357 Magnum revolvers need a heavy bullet to achieve a consistent knock-down of the targets.

In Britain the sport has developed a little differently, with courses being fired on conventional targets. At 100 yards the military silhouette is used, and the shooter fires two strings of five rounds in 30 seconds per string. At 200 and 300 yards the target changes to the conventional black 12 inch diameter aiming mark on a 48 inch × 48 inch white background, the shooter has ten minutes to fire ten rounds. There are four classes: All Comers, Free Pistol, Service Pistol, and Pocket Pistol. The last is restricted to pistols with barrels not longer than 3½ inches. Surprisingly good shooting can be done with these short-barrelled weapons, and groups in the order of 6 to 8 inches at 100 yards are not all uncommon. Because of the velocities obtained, the .357 Smith & Wesson and Colt revolvers are the most popular pistols on the firing lines, with relatively few automatics seen. Shooting with the Pocket Pistol is restricted to 100 yards. The All Comers class allows pistols with barrels up to 10 inches long and calibres up to .45; only iron sights are permitted. It is not unusual to see the leading shooters landing the majority of their shots in the central aiming area, even at distances of up to 300 yards. Because of its good wind-resisting qualities, the .44 Magnum is the favoured cartridge.

The Free Pistol class has few restrictions. The pistol bears little resemblance to the conventional handgun and is usually made from a rifle action and finishes up looking rather like the Remington XP 100 Fireball, but chambered in many cases for the .308 rifle cartridge. When the gun is fitted with one of the long eye-relief telescopic sights, extremely accurate shooting is possible. Rifle-size groups are the order of the day. Service Pistol class requires modified 9 millimetre Browning High Powers. Minimum target weight is 5 pounds.

The Colt .45 Government Model 1911 is ideal for virtually every Practical Pistol course. It has proved itself in live combat conditions, and the cartridge it fires is an undisputed man-stopper. Numerous exhaustive tests conducted by various ordnance boards have shown the reliability of the weapon, and yet there are still those who would say that it would be a better offensive weapon if it were thrown at the enemy.

It is more difficult to train a man to shoot a pistol than a rifle, but it is certainly far easier to train a man to shoot an automatic pistol than a revolver. Harder and more assiduous practice with the revolver will enable the enthusiast to reach standards comparable to an automatic, but even then it could be said that this extra time spent training could have been used to bring the proficiency with the .45 to an even higher level. It is recommended that any aspiring Practical Pistol shooter quickly take up the challenge of competition shooting. This will stimulate him to a higher level of competence and force him to shoot under some stress. Should the competitor still feel that he prefers to shoot a revolver, one of the heavier calibres such as the .44 or .45 are to be preferred. They are able to reach the velocity required and develop the energy for major calibre without the pressure and recoil associated with the .357 Magnum. Unless it is loaded downwards in velocity, the .44 Magnum is overpowered and does not warrant consideration as a practical weapon. For a man wanting to shoot a revolver, one of the most effective cartridges to shoot is probably the .44 Special – which will cover most contingencies.

Practical Pistol Shooting is a comparatively new sport and some clubs have not yet had time to sort out all the problems involved. Instruction for novices is somewhat patchy and this can lead to poor scores and subsequent discouragement. It is therefore most important to join a well-established club and so ensure good quality training. Once the basic skills have been mastered, it is a matter of constant practice if consistently good scores are to be achieved.

On the signal, the competitors sprint to the tin can and then to the firing line in the Columbia Fumble.

9 POLICE COMBAT PISTOL SHOOTING

THE POLICE TRAINING PROGRAMME

In the early 1960s, competitive shooting for police was declining in the United States. Then, in 1962, the National Rifle Association took charge of a programme which would eventually become the fastest growing shooting sport in America – Police combat competition. The NRA police programme was born with the understanding that competitive shooting and training go together. Shoulder to shoulder competition offers enjoyable recreation as well as providing a means of increasing an officer's ability to defend himself. As Robert C. Joerg, NRA Field Representative stated: 'Competitive shooting trains the officer in the proper techniques of marksmanship and handgun defence so when the moment of truth arises, he will survive.'

Many police departments across the United States had not emphasized a shooting programme, labelling it as 'unnecessary activity'. However, as the courts tended to become more liberal in the 1960s and a stricter view was taken of firearm misuse a more active approach was taken towards police firearm training. Each state began requiring higher standards in training, and basic marksmanship is now a priority. The NRA realizing the need for competent instructors, initiated a training programme for police. This programme has now trained thousands of officers.

Over 95 percent of police officers in the United States are armed with the revolver. It has become the classic handgun for many reasons; in America it is a familiar object to most people and it does not represent a threat. The revolver is looked upon as a means of protection rather than a warlike military instrument. It is easy to maintain, and when cared for properly, the weapon functions flawlessly. A revolver is not as expensive as most weapons, and under most circumstances is considered to be safer to use than the military semi-automatic pistol.

The author, Sergeant Jim Collins of the Alabama Police, twice National Police Combat Pistol Champion and police firearms instructor.

SHOOTING THE REVOLVER

The basics of marksmanship are the first instructions in weaponry given to a police recruit. Regardless of the circumstances or the target, accuracy will determine the final outcome in a shooting situation. In all shooting, basic marksmanship gives the recruit a solid foundation for the achievement of advanced marksmanship techniques. Delivery of an accurate shot can be taught to each individual – the element of speed comes with practice. Training on the bullseye target at 15 and 25 yards allows both the student and instructor to quickly see errors; with this knowledge, the errors can be corrected; the student can readily see his progress, and this can be a great confidence builder.

GRIP

A good shot starts with the grip the shooter has on the weapon. The single action firing method is used exclusively in this initial phase. The quickest way to teach a recruit the single action grip is by placing the weapon into the shooting hand with the weaker hand, so he can grip the weapon in the same way for each shot. He will learn to feel this positioning of the weapon

The correct shooting grip for the revolver with the barrel centred directly between thumb and forefinger.

in the same manner for each shot. Many new shooters have a strong tendency to grip the weapon too tightly causing the muscles to tire quickly, and they consequently fire a bad shot. The grip should be firm, but not to the point of causing muscle tremors. The correct position is one where the barrel of the weapon is centred directly in the middle of the natural V formed by the thumb and forefinger. Some people must vary their grip to a degree because their hand size does not permit them to reach the trigger with the index finger. Here trial and error will eventually allow the student to adopt the correct positioning of the trigger finger on the trigger.

STANCE

The feet should be about as wide apart as the shooter's shoulders with the feet firmly planted,

The classic off-hand standing position with the whole body firm and well-balanced, arm straight.

and the weight equally distributed. The legs must be straight, the body and the head held erect. The shooter must learn to become comfortable in this stance. The weapon should be held at eye level with the arm fully extended. The free hand should simply be placed in the pocket. The classic off-hand position is thus very simply achieved.

SIGHT ALIGNMENT AND SIGHT PICTURE

The proper understanding of this term is the key to the entire process of delivering an accurate shot. Sight alignment means that the top of the fore sight is even or level with the top of the rear sight, and an equal amount of light is visible between the fore sight and sides of the notch in the rear sight. Sight alignment does not include the target! When we speak of the sights being in alignment on the proper area of the target we are talking about sight picture. Since an individual can only focus on one object at a time, the shooter must concentrate primarily on the fore sight. With his secondary vision, he picks up the target. Good marksmanship can not be achieved unless each student understands the difference.

BREATH CONTROL

It stands to reason in precision shooting that an individual cannot be breathing normally through a shooting cycle. The body movement would make it almost impossible to maintain sight alignment. This is why the breathing must be controlled. Since we are all equipped with extra lung space to store extra oxygen for short periods of time, we simply hold this added breath for the time it takes to bring the weapon into alignment and fire. Do not hold the breath too long or the body will run out of oxygen, tremors will start, the sights will be difficult to see clearly, and a bad shot will result. When this happens, the student must start the complete cycle over again. During the period of breath control, the body will reach an optimum period of stillness. This is the desired moment you want the shot to break.

TRIGGER SQUEEZE

I prefer to use the term trigger control because the amount of pressure applied to the trigger during a firing cycle must be even and steady without any jerking. For the best results, the student must experience a surprise break at the instant the weapon fires. Sight alignment must not be disturbed. From the beginning, the student should be encouraged to think of the movement as one of squeezing the trigger smoothly straight to the rear of the weapon without any movement of the gun or the trigger finger to one side or the other.

STILLNESS

Many people associate being still with breath control; being still means absolutely no body movement whatsoever. The heart will continue to pump, but we can't stop that movement. Be aware of body movement.

FOLLOW-THROUGH

For every physical action there is a follow-through. The golf club must continue in the same arc after making contact with the ball. Mass which is in motion tends to continue in the direction it is travelling. In shooting, we mean a continuation of all elements in delivering a good shot for the period of time it takes for the bullet to leave the muzzle.

FLINCHING

Flinching is a common problem with a large number of new students. For some it is a physical reaction due to noise, and for others a mental reaction due to fear of the weapon, or in some cases, both. If the student, wants to stop flinching,

The two-handed grip gives extra stability, particularly for double action shooting, in many positions.

with help from his instructor, the problem can be solved. The sudden movement prior to firing can be noticed easily, and it will mean extra hours on the range to remove the anticipation and the problem.

DOUBLE ACTION SHOOTING

Previously we have discussed basic marksmanship and single action firing of the revolver. Double action shooting incorporates pulling the trigger completely through until the weapon fires. As the trigger is pulled through, the cylinder rotates, the hammer is forced back, falls forward, and the weapon fires as the hammer nose contacts the primer. Firing with this method requires several techniques different from single action

The two-handed grip seen from above with the fingers of the weak hand encircling the shooting hand.

shooting. Contrary to general belief, the weapon can be fired quite accurately in this way, even from great distances.

I advocate the two-handed grip because of added stability. The weapon can be fired from numerous different positions and the grip will remain the same. In double action shooting the grip should be higher on the weapon because the relationship of the thumb and hammer spur is no longer important, and this allows more finger to reach the trigger for better control. Double action shooting requires more control of the trigger because of the longer travel required to make the weapon fire.

The trigger finger is thrust further into the trigger guard so the trigger is in contact with the first joint of the index finger. This allows better control because the pull of the average double action revolver is around 9 to 11 pounds.

The thumb of the shooting hand should be thrust down for a good secure grip. The fingers of the weak hand should be placed around the lower fingers of the shooting hand. The thumb of the weak hand is placed over the rear portion of the shooting hand thumb. Not only is this a secure shooting grip, it prevents some culprit from taking the weapon away from the officer without the use of a wrecking bar. In combat, common-sense tells us that generally, the first and possibly the second shot will be fired immediately after the weapon clears the holster. The student must learn to have a strong one-handed grip with the weak hand coming into play for added support as quickly as possible.

WEAK HAND DOUBLE ACTION SHOOTING

Most young shooters will instantly tell you they cannot fire a weapon with their weak hand. This is simply because of a mental block, and the instructor must prove to the trainee that effective weak hand shooting can be attained. At this point, each student will be fairly confident of his strong hand shooting. Weak hand shooting, using the two handed grip, should be started at close range. The key here is to build confidence, quickly. The student must realize that the principles are the same and the instructor will continuously stress this to all students. There may be a physical problem with some new shooters, but this can be overcome by adjustments in the grip. The largest obstacle to overcome is the awkward feeling that weak hand shooting brings. Practice will change this feeling. I believe dry firing will speed up the process and help strengthen the weak hand. Exercises, such as squeezing a rubber ball, or grip exercisers will add strength to the hands, wrist, and forearm muscles.

COMBAT POSITIONS

The basic standing position is simply a position without cover. In most cases a shooter will not have time to think out a position or assume a particular position or thrust the weapon to shoulder level and fire. The method which allows the quickest most accurate shot possible is the most preferable. Here the weapon must be fired quickly and instinctively upon clearing the holster from the hip. At extremely close ranges, less than 20 feet, the average individual can develop a high degree of accuracy using only his God-given instinctive talents made better with practice. This is a method which allows the quickest shot possible, and with a high degree of accuracy. At distances greater than approximately 20 feet, and I know everyone won't have a yardstick to measure the target, a two-handed shoulder level position is desirable. There are some officers who have developed their in-

Classic variations on the standing combat positions, the two-handed and single-handed crouch and the two-handed standing position.

stinctive talents far beyond the rule of thumb 21-foot distance, but for the trainee shooter we must remain at the closer ranges. Quickness will naturally develop with practice. Extremely long distances of 25 yards and more, will require an extremely stable grip and position to retain accuracy, and quite naturally the sights must be used. However, the closer distances do not require the added time to aim, instead, the eyes are on the target, and secondary or peripheral vision picks up the weapon. When time, cover, and distance permit, use your sights.

BARRICADE POSITIONS

There are times when a supported position could be used, such as around a building, over the roof of a vehicle, etc. Much greater accuracy is

Correct use of the barricade, with minimum exposure.

The barricade position from the side, showing correct placing of the feet.

afforded both at close range and at longer ranges. Two hands should be used on the weapon, and the barricaded position used for support. The student should not depend on the barricade for added body support. He should only exert sufficient pressure to stabilize the body and maintain balance. As much body concealment as is available should be taught. This may be attained by placing the left foot forward (for right-handed shooting). The right foot is either behind or further to the left. When shooting left-handed the feet are reversed.

COMMON ERRORS

Many new shooters have a tendency to commit several errors. The most common one being that of breaking the wrist. They will either have the wrist bent up or down, right or left, and this will

be recognizable to the alert instructor. Once they are made aware of this and develop a proper feel, practice will help to correct the problem. Another common error is that students have a tendency to try and become fast and accurate too quickly. This can cause other errors such as not obtaining the proper grip, and violations of good safety measures. In a quest for speed, control of the weapon is lost. The instructor must insist on a deliberate, smooth operation until speed is achieved. There is no such thing as too many loading drills to attain speed loading. This is an important skill, and being able to load quickly under adverse conditions could save your life. Safety is the watchword on the range and off; the instructor will maintain rigid control to prevent unsafe habits from developing during the student's first weeks on the range.

THE NATIONAL CHAMPIONSHIPS

The National Police Revolver championships are held each year in the grounds of the Mississippi Law Enforcement Academy in Jackson, and they are the highlight of the shooting season for police. Over 900 top police marksmen from across the United States and Canada attend to represent their departments. These matches are made possible through the efforts of the National Rifle Association and the Mississippi Law Enforcement Academy. This tournament lasts four days and, upon completion, the National Police Revolver individual and team champions are named.

To fire the Police 1500 aggregate the officer must fire five individual matches. The first match, The Standing Match, is fired in two stages. The first stage is fired at the seven yard line, and the second stage is fired at the 15 yard line. As in all matches, the competitor is given the command to load and re-holster.

Upon the command to fire, the competitor draws and fires 12 rounds double action in 25 seconds. This includes time to reload his revolver. The 15 yard stage is fired in the same time limit. The possible score is 240 and 67 officers hold the record. This may seem like a large number, but it really is not since over 10,000 police officers hold a competitive classification.

Typical US police holster rig includes wide leather belt, pivoted holster and cartridge section, handcuff case, key ring and two types of bullet 'dumper' designed to drop six rounds into the hand.

The second match, the Kneeling and Standing Match, is fired in 90 seconds, and includes reloading time. The first six shots are fired kneeling and the remaining 12 shots are fired from behind a barricade with both weak and strong hand firing double action. Possible score is 180, five officers hold this record.

The third match, often referred to as the 50 Yard Match is a four-position match fired in two minutes and 45 seconds. Starting from a standing position, on the command to fire, the competitor assumes a sitting position and fires six shots. He must reload and take up a prone position and fire six shots prone. The remaining 12 shots are fired from a standing position with both weak and strong hand from behind a barricade. The possible score is 240, and two officers jointly hold this record.

The fourth match, sometimes called the Standing Without Support match is fired from 25 yards and is fired double action. Two strings of 12 shots must be fired in 35 seconds. A possible score of 240 points completes the match, and presently, three officers nationwide hold the record.

The National Police Revolver Course, the fifth match, consists of four stages. The first stage is fired at seven yards – 12 rounds are fired double action in 25 seconds. After this stage, the competitors move to the 25 yard line and fire 18 shots in the same manner as stated for the Kneeling and Standing Match. After this stage, the targets are changed for the third stage. This is the same as stated in the 50 Yard Match, but for this course, six shots are added. The competitor must return to the 25 yard line and fire six shots double action in 12 seconds standing without support. This match consists of a total of 60 shots, and the possible score of 600 is held by one officer.

An added attraction to the revolver championships is a shotgun course fired with the standard 20 inch police riot 12-gauge shotgun. The course consists of 25 rounds of skeet, ten rounds of buckshot, and five rounds of rifled slugs. This is a truly difficult match as no officer has ever fired a perfect score.

As the annual championship concludes, each officer returns to his duty station and his department filled with enthusiasm for the next year. Many lasting friendships are made, and useful police methods and ideas are exchanged. The National Rifle Association is to be commended for providing this programme for the police. Truly, a unique sport for the man behind the badge.

10 METALLIC SILHOUETTE PISTOL SHOOTING

A competitor raises a cloud of dust with a near miss at the Javelinas at 100 metres. The gun is a Smith & Wesson .44 magnum with 8 inch barrel. Notice the chickens in front of the shooter at 50 metres.

THE NEWEST SHOOTING GAME

Nothing has ever hit the handgun world with the dramatic impact of metallic silhouette shooting!

On past occasions, when firing at paper targets with big magnums, I've felt a sense of massive overkill. Even football-sized rocks on the side of a nearby hill seemed like flimsy targets for the smashing thunderbolts delivered from the .41 and .44 magnums, the .357 and .44 auto mags, and a few others.

The subject is academic now, because an exciting new game in town provides worthy opponents for big-bore handguns. It's a game called metallic silhouettes - the most interesting and exhilarating shooting sport that has appeared on the horizon in many a year.

Try it once and you will probably be hooked for good. Even minor success can bring instant gratification. On the other hand you may feel a sense of frustration and near impotence as you walk away from the firing line with the sudden realization that your big magnum isn't as powerful as you thought. You also may feel a bit ineffectual; at least thoughtful and subdued. And you can hardly wait to try it again! Furthermore, it opens up an entire new world of handgun ballistics that will add new pages to the loading manuals. Recently as much progress has been made in equipment, loads and techniques for long-range handgun shooting as has been made in the past 50 years!

Just what is this new game, and where did it come from? The sport originated in Mexico. No one knows exactly when or where. On fiesta day in the rancho country, we can picture a group of fun-loving vaqueros drinking tequila. There was talk about who was the best shot. To prove the point, a live steer or some other domestic animal was hobbled or tied to a stake with a length of rope at some distant point. Wagers were made and the vaqueros blazed away with their .30-30 saddle carbines or whatever other guns they had. First blood won the steer and/or the bets. Or perhaps it took a killing shot to win.

There were many variations. Sometimes it was a goat or sheep tethered so it could take evasive action when the bullets began to fly. Targets also included pigs, turkeys and chickens.

Twenty-four years ago I participated in one of those early matches while visiting the rancho of an old friend. A fiesta was in progress and livestock had been selected for a big feast. Rather than dispatch them in the usual manner, a shoot had been organized for the visiting guests. As I recall, chickens, sheep and two steers were tethered one at a time to stakes with lengths of rope, at distances of about 100 yards for the chickens to about 400 yards for the steers. Shooting was done from the veranda of the rancho. Most guests used the host's rifles, but a few had brought their own. Competition was fierce; some of the bets heavy. As the tequila flowed, so did the pesos.

In deference to the host I entered and got one of the chickens with a lucky shot the first time around. Then I stood back and became a spectator. I had done some big-game hunting, but shooting domestic animals tethered to stakes wasn't exactly my cup of tea.

TARGETS AND COURSES

Live animal shooting has virtually died out in Mexico, although occasionally such a shoot is still held. As a substitute, metal silhouettes of animals and birds were slowly developed into the present sport. *Sileutas Metalicas*, the Mexicans call it. Individual targets are: *Gallo*-rooster or chicken; *Javelina*- pig; *Guajalote*-turkey; *Borrego*-ram.

Shooting chickens watched by a coach/spotter. One spotter is allowed for each shooter.

Life-size targets of the chickens and javelinas are made of $\frac{1}{2}$ inch steel, the turkeys and rams of $\frac{3}{8}$ inch steel. All are painted flat black and set on stands or rails at the proper distances. For handgun shooting – and the targets are the same as used for rifle shooting – the chickens are set at 50 metres, javelinas at 100 metres, turkeys at 150 metres and the rams at 200 metres. In yards, the distances would be approximately 55, 110, 165 and 220.

The basic handgun match, as constituted by the International Handgun Metallic Silhouette Association (IHMSA), the sanctioning body for the handgun end of the game, consists of 40 rounds. Competitors shoot in relays, firing one shot at each target in a bank of five with a two-minute time limit for the five shots. Firing is free-style with no artificial rests or supports. Each competitor has his choice of the standing, kneeling, sitting or prone positions.

Each shooter fires at, say, the bank of five chickens. Then he may be moved to the next stage which will usually be javelinas, or he may, at the option of the sponsoring club, reload and fire his second five-shot string at the chickens again. In any event, he gets 10 shots at each of the four types of targets for a total of 40 rounds. For some state, regional and international matches, the course is refired a second time and the total score for the 80 shots decides the winners.

After the original introduction of metallic targets by the Mexicans, the sport, along with match terms, began to filter into the border states. *Listo* was the command to load or get ready; *Fuego* to fire; *Alto* to stop.

It wasn't long thereafter that somebody began to take pot-shots at silhouette targets with a handgun.

ORGANIZATIONS AND MATCHES

The first organized handgun match of any consequence was held in Tucson, Arizona on September 20 to 21, 1975 and was titled the First National Handgun Metallic Silhouette Championship. The event was pioneered by Lee Jurras, well known handgunner, founder of the Outstanding

American Handgunner Awards Foundation and former president of Super-Vel cartridge Corporation. At the time, Jurras had formed the Club de Auto Mag Internationale Inc., and it was with this name that the match was sponsored.

The 1976 national championships were held in El Paso, Texas on October 1, 2 and 3, 1976. Six matches, ranging from the National Two-man Team Championship to the aggregate of two 40-shot matches for the National Individual Championships, were held. As an example of the phenomenal growth of the sport, 57 shooters competed at El Paso. The 1977 International Championships, scheduled for October 22, 23 and 24 at the Angelus range in San Fernando, California, limited the entry to 300 competitors although at least 500 were expected to enter if range facilities would permit.

During the 1976 championships at El Paso, the IHMSA was formed by the competing shooters. Rules were formulated based on the two previous national championship events. John Adams, of Manhattan Beach, California was elected Executive Director of IHMSA and several well-known handgunners were appointed to the advisory committee.

In less than 10 months, more than 750 dedicated

Competitors lining up at Fresno, California. A variety of positions are used for this freestyle match.

handgunners from every state in the union, several other countries and all manner of handgun clubs have joined IHMSA to participate in this fantastic new sport. New members are coming in at the rate of more than 100 per month. At least 50 sanctioned IHMSA matches were held in the first six months of 1977, including some in such faraway places as Canada and Alaska. It is estimated the several hundred sanctioned matches will be held in 1978.

Membership of the IHMSA brings the member a complete set of rules, scale templates from which targets can be made, a handsome badge, a subscription to the bi-monthly IHMSA newspaper, *The Silhouette*, and a membership card. A match schedule and all match results are published in the paper.

Ready-made targets are manufactured on the West Coast and several other places. Details on cost and shipping, as well as how to set up a range (any existing 200-yard rifle range can be used without interfering with its original use) can be found in each issue of *The Silhouette*.

An example of an unorthodox, but effective, freestyle position. The gun is a heavy barrel Ruger .44 magnum.

IHMSA has established two major types of competition. One is the Stock Production Gun category, with handguns being used as they come from the manufaturers. No changes other than replacement grips (if a standard catalogue item available to all shooters) and a touch of paint to outline the sights as a contrast against the black targets, are allowed. Shooters are classed by their averages in AA, A or B class.

The other category is Unlimited, with the only rules being a 15 inch sight radius and an overall weight limit of 4½ pounds.

Thus, there is room in IHMSA for all handgunners from the Saturday afternoon plinker with his stock production handgun, to the dedicated shooter who wants to develop long-range handgunning to its ultimate degree.

THE FUN OF THE GAME

But whatever the style or handgun, something about the metallic silhouette game appeals to whatever latent instinct there is inside a man who wants action whenever he pulls the trigger. Action is the name of the game. Punching holes in paper targets at short distances has heretofore been the accepted technique of handgun competition. Silhouette shooting adds a new dimension. As practice for actual hunting in the field, or for the man who doesn't hunt, but who likes the *machismo* of shooting big-bore handguns, it is the perfect game.

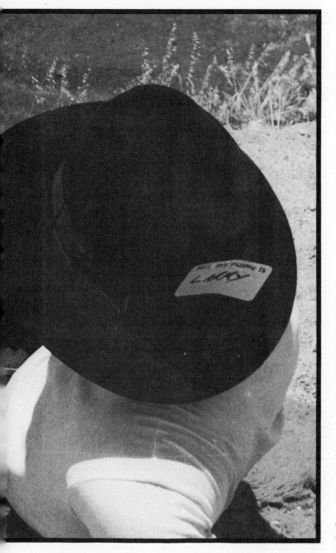

Then you are on the side of a valley shooting downhill at a row of life-size turkeys, 150 metres distant. More misses. Then you settle down, dig in and squeeze off a shot with tooth-gritting concentration. The chosen turkey turns slowly to one side from a front hit, then topples over slowly as the hit-clang comes floating back up the slope. How sweet it is!

Suddenly, it's your turn to shoot the rams – five of them. My God, you think, as you look at those tiny black silhouettes on the other side of the valley. They too are life-size. But shooting them at 200 metres? With a handgun? Nobody can hit one at that distance!

But they do. Maybe you miss the first five, the first 10, or maybe hit one on a leg. You get the satisfaction of a clang but the ram remains standing with regal contempt. Finally, with perseverance, skill, determination and luck, the moment comes when you tag a ram solidly. The distant silhouette seems to hang in suspended motion, then slowly, majestically, topples off the rail. I tell you pistoleros, there just isn't anything to equal it in artificial target shooting.

Spectator interest? Let any shooter blow down the first four silhouettes on any bank and you can bet that every eye will be watching as he buckles down – probably with the two-minute shooting limit coming to an end – to fire at the last target. There will be groans of sympathy if he misses, solid applause if he cleans the rack.

That's metallic silhouette shooting. It isn't the only handgun game in town, but for sheer, spine-tingling exhilaration, it's way ahead of whatever is in second place. It is, in one simple phrase, the epitome of long range handgunning.

For the uninitiated, here is a taste of what metallic silhouette shooting is all about. You level down on a $\frac{1}{2}$ inch steel plate chicken painted flat black at 50 metres with your favourite .357 magnum, .44 Special, auto mag, or whatever. A low hit will take the leg out from under the steel bird with a gratifying clang. A hit high on the back can tumble it end over end. A fore or aft hit can send it spinning wildly. A miss will likely send up a spurt of dirt – and you will miss a lot of them.

Next is the lifesize javelina silhouette at 100 metres, also of $\frac{1}{2}$ inch thick steel. Five of them are standing on a bank about 10 feet higher than the firing line. Miss, miss, miss. Then a satisfying clang from a solid hit that topples the pig off the rail.

FURTHER INFORMATION

All the rest of the details are covered in the rules as printed in *The Silhouette*. For further information, call or write the Executive Director of IHMSA, Box 1609, Idaho Falls, Idaho 83401, or call the National Headquarters Office 208-524-0880.

11 FULLBORE RIFLE SHOOTING

QUALITIES OF A MARKSMAN

The modern sport of fullbore target rifle shooting requires many attributes from the marksman: a keen eye, a steady hold, an acute sense of timing, and an ability to perceive the elements and assess and interpret their likely effects on the bullet's path. A steady temperament with a basic competitiveness is also an essential quality. While physical fitness is a useful adjunct to any sport, it is, perhaps, not quite so important in this one. People who are unfit or infirm are able to compete on equal terms with the most athletic. Similarly, age is relatively unimportant–some competitors graduate from smallbore shooting at perhaps nine or ten, or even younger, and continue until their late eighties or early nineties.

Eyesight is important, of course, but the prime function of the eyes is an ability to accommodate, or focus, satisfactorily. It is usual in early middle age that, due to the hardening of the lens and weakening of the eye muscles, the eye loses its ability to focus, particularly on nearby objects such as a front sight, and this condition is known as presbyopia. Long-sight, hypermetropia, and short-sight, myopia, are conditions that tend to become more pronounced with advancing years,

with a consequent diminishing power of accommodation. However, both conditions are easily rectified in shooting by the use of spectacles or corrective lenses that fit into the rear sight eyepiece. Convex (plus) lenses are employed to correct long-sight and concave (minus) lenses to correct short-sight.

One important factor that is sometimes forgotten in encouraging youngsters to shoot with fullbore rifles is that they should be physically robust enough to be able to cope with the size, weight and recoil of the modern fullbore rifle, otherwise they may be discouraged and possibly lose all interest in the sport. It is my opinion that the 'younger the better' principle should not be applied to fullbore shooting as it is to other sports, such as skiing or golf. Every encouragement should be given to young people to join in air rifle or smallbore shooting as soon as they are able, provided they are properly coached in the skills and the safety requirements. Thereafter they may graduate to the fullbore rifle with a good basic grounding in the general principles of marksmanship.

**Left: Weighing triggers at the start of a competition.
Below: Age is no bar to success in fullbore shooting; this rifleman started shooting in 1908.**

FEATURES OF THE RIFLE:

BOLT-OPERATED ACTIONS

There are two basic designs of bolt-operated rifles: forward- and rear-locking. The most commonly used forward-locking action is that of the German Mauser '98, which is a solidly constructed military design that has been adapted, modified, copied and employed with considerable success by many armies in the world. Forward-locking means that the locking lugs are at the front end of the bolt and lock into recesses in the action body together with a third rear lug at the other end of the bolt. It is generally accepted that this type of action is preferable for use at the shorter ranges, up to 600 yards. Its use can also be advantageous in adverse weather conditions, where there is a possibility of ammunition getting wet.

The most popular rear-locking action, which has proved itself readily adaptable to British NRA requirements, is the No. 4 Lee-Enfield action. This has two locking lugs about 4 inches behind the cartridge and, consequently, there is considerable stretch or spring in the action as it absorbs the pressures of recoil, producing an effect known as 'positive compensation'. This effect makes the rear-locking No. 4 action preferable at longer ranges, i.e. ranges in excess of 600 yards.

'Compensation' is the effect on bullet flight of barrel movement in the vertical plane, 'positive' describes the emergence of the bullet on an upward vibration of the barrel and 'negative', the departure of the bullet on a downwards vibration. When using ammunition of indifferent quality in terms of velocity and, perhaps, of differing friction within the barrel, the trajectories obviously vary. It also follows that high velocity bullets will have a flatter trajectory than low velocity bullets, and if these bullets are discharged on an upward movement of the barrel, as is inherent in the rear-locking or No. 4 action, then at some point distant from the weapon the paths of trajectory of the low, medium and high velocity bullets will coincide at what is termed the 'compensating range of

the rifle'. The grouping capacity of such a weapon will, therefore, be much better at this range, as the effects of variations in the velocity will be eliminated.

In a rifle that discharges its bullets during a downward movement (negative compensation), such as the Mauser, the paths of trajectory of the bullets of varying velocities move further apart and never cross; therefore, indifferent ammunition of varying velocities can have a marked negative effect on the weapon's grouping ability. A rifle that compensates will only do so at a particular range, and as the No. 4 action has pronounced positive compensation characteristics at longer range, it is preferable at distances over 600 yards.

In recent years an action has been developed purely for target shooting purposes rather than for service use. One such action is the SIN 71, which incorporates four forward-locking lugs in a strong bolt-operated action. It has proved itself to be of unquestionable accuracy, principally up to 600 yards, although some people have used it successfully at 900 yards.

STOCKS AND BARRELS

Rifle stocks have also changed in recent years. While the standard No. 4 or P14 stock is still used by many shooters, only slightly modified to suit the conversion to 7.62 millimetres, it is acknowledged that the specially designed match stocks with cheek piece and perhaps a handstop on the lines of smallbore target rifles make for more comfortable and accurate shooting.

Target rifle barrels should, ideally, be consistent in terms of vibratory behaviour from shot to shot. The bullets should leave the muzzle when it is in a neutral position, either at the top or bottom of its vibratory cycle, thus ensuring that possible errors due to variations in velocity will be reduced to a minimum, particularly at shorter range. The rifling of the barrel is also important: the slower the twist of the rifling, irrespective of the number of grooves in the bore, the better, particularly when a 145 grain bullet is being used. Opinions vary in this respect, but one complete twist of the rifling in each 14 inch length of barrel is thought by many to be best, certainly up to 600 yards.

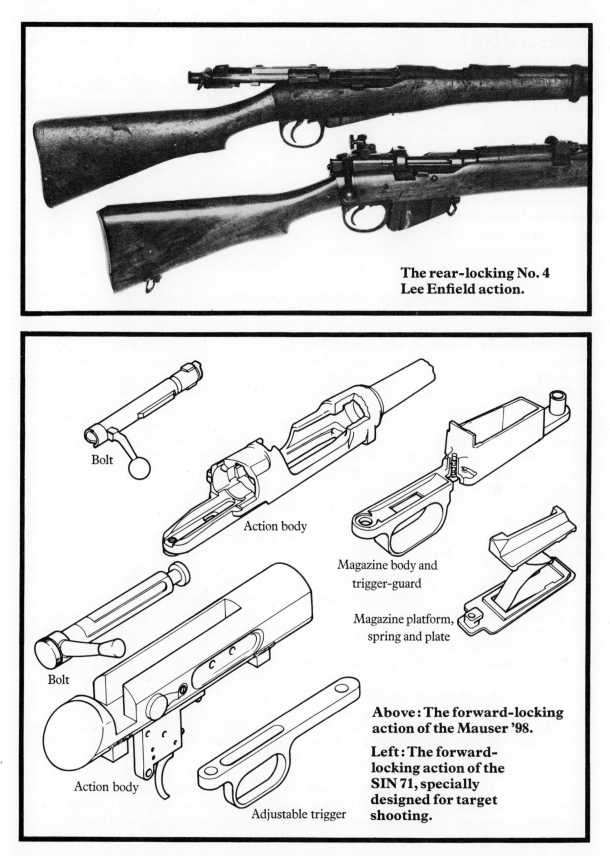

The rear-locking No. 4 Lee Enfield action.

Bolt

Action body

Magazine body and trigger-guard

Magazine platform, spring and plate

Bolt

Action body

Adjustable trigger

Above: The forward-locking action of the Mauser '98.

Left: The forward-locking action of the SIN 71, specially designed for target shooting.

APERTURE SIGHTS

The sophisticated aperture sights that are now used for fullbore target rifle shooting are constructed to fine tolerances and are adjustable to a quarter of a minute of angle, i.e. ¼ inch per 100 yards. To the uninitiated this may seem unduly fine, and it is true that while it is very seldom that only a quarter of a minute adjustment on its own is required, the facility for being able to adjust one's sights by perhaps three-quarters of a minute, or indeed one and a quarter minutes as circumstances dictate, seems to be most useful. It should be remembered that one minute of angle subtends a distance of approximately one inch at a hundred yards, therefore, at 600 yards, a quarter of a minute represents only one and a half inches on the target. While this may not seem much and no firer could hold to this fineness and no ammunition could group to this precision, it still permits the mean point of impact of the group to be centred with greater theoretical accuracy. And if such an adjustment allows a shot even to touch the bull line and score the higher value of five points, then no adjustment is too fine for the keen competitive marksman – every point counts!

Aperture sights are not new of course, and evidence exists of their use as early as 1675 on flintlock rifles. A rifle dated 1680 incorporated a multiple aperture rear sight, comprising a conventional type of rear-sight plate in which there are a series of four vertical holes, the firer using the correct aperture in relation to the required distance. It is doubtful that the inherent accuracy of the weapon justified this precision in sighting, but perhaps the same view was held by shooters of that time as we apply to the current facility of adjustment to a quarter of a minute of angle.

Front sights, their size and type, probably occupy more discussion time in fullbore shooting company than any other subject. It is generally accepted that ring front sights are preferable to blade front sights when a circular aiming mark is provided, but there are shooters who still use a blade successfully. One very successful shooter known to me uses a slightly tapered blade with a small 'v' formed in the top in which he balances the circular aiming mark. In common with many other aspects of fullbore shooting, there is no hard and fast rule about the type of front sight to use; personal preference resulting from trial and error inevitably produces the correct answer for the individual shooter.

SIGHT RESEARCH

It is my opinion that a front sight less than 3.2 millimetres is too small under any conditions, and a size of between 3.4 and 4 millimetres is recommended for normal fullbore use. It is a fallacy that the smaller the aperture, the easier the aiming mark is to centre; quite the reverse has been proved optically. Although beginners may find this hard to accept, they should be encouraged to use a ring size of about 3.6 millimetres at all distances, which will benefit them in the long term. One mistake to be avoided is that of making frequent changes of elements during a shoot or even between ranges. It should be noted that plastic elements are now allowable under NRA rules.

The Russians, who are unquestionably a nation of fine shots, have conducted extensive research to find the best combination of front and rear sight aperture, size and colour of filters, etc. Their findings suggest that although the Russian top shots have hitherto almost exclusively used blade fore sights, investigation into controlled squad experiments showed, not surprisingly in my view, that ring fore sights are superior both for accuracy and lessened fatigue. The ideal rear aperture size appears to be between 1.1 and 1.3 millimetres, but older shooters whose eyes have less accommodation are recommended to use one nearer the lower limit of 1.1 millimetres, provided this does not cause eye strain. The Russian investigation also proved conclusively that both eyes should be kept open during aiming and that optimum aiming time is between 4 and 8 seconds, which should be followed by about 30 seconds rest to allow visual acuity to return. A further recommendation is that the disengaged eye may be used for spotting, but that the telescope only be used for a fleeting check of the shot position and no attempt be made to determine score or whether or not doubtful shots were in or out.

Coaches, spotters, judges and spectators all make up a large and interested crowd at international rifle meets.

The effect of compensation on the trajectories of bullets of varying velocities.

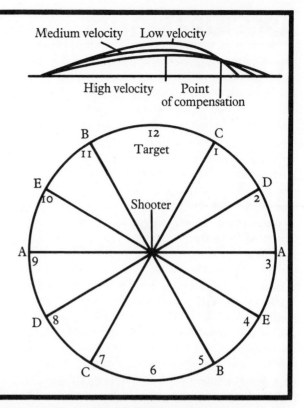

Using the clock face to assess wind direction. If the shooter is assumed to be standing in the centre and the target is at 12, then it is clear that a wind blowing from A to A will cause maximum deflection of the bullet. Winds blowing from B to B and from C to C will make about half as much impression on its path, while the effect of winds blowing from D to D and from E to E is about half again.
Wind changes in the sector B to C will have the most effect, while changes in the sector D to A to E will have relatively little effect on the bullet.

Experiments on front sight elements suggest that a pink or orange translucent disc with a plain hole, without a dark surrounding is preferable to the metal elements in common use. A pink disc used in conjunction with a light yellow filter in the rear sight produced the best results. The Russians found that any filter was better than none. On a relatively bright but cloudy summer day a blue filter produced the best results, and a yellow filter was most effective on a bright, sunny day.

USING THE SCORE BOOK

Corrected wind graphs in the score book, particularly at 900 and 1,000 yards, can be invaluable, because they let the shooter compare his sight adjustment to the location of the hit on the target. For example, a shot with the sights adjusted for, say, 8 minutes left windage, well-fired by the marksman, hits two minutes left of centre; the correct adjustment to hit the centre of the target should therefore have been 6 minutes. This process of comparison may be continued until a picture emerges indicating the mean windage for these particular conditions, alterations in strength and angle being related on a plus or minus basis to the emergent mean wind allowance.

The score book is an invaluable aid to the fullbore marksman, and, properly completed, apart from merely plotting the shots, it can provide complete records of all shoots, rifles used, ammunition fired, zeros, fore sights and filters for particular conditions and elevation graphs. The accumulation of old score sheets can also provide an accurate record of the precise number of rounds fired from a particular rifle, and this information is valuable when the question of re-barrelling the weapon is considered.

A fullbore competition in progress during an international rifle meet at Bisley.

WIND

Wind and weather in general are perhaps the principal factors that distinguish fullbore target rifle shooting from other forms of shooting sport. Wind presents the marksman with the more complex problems, due to its ever-changing nature in terms of force and direction. The computation of the speed of the wind, the angle from which it is blowing and the distance from the target all have to be decided by the firer or, in the case of a team match, by his coach. In judging the force of wind the firer has no measuring instruments at his disposal and must therefore rely on what can be seen and felt around him. Judgements based on this information are only estimates, of course, but the more experienced marksman can often judge with remarkable accuracy just what the effects will be. In arriving at his conclusion he may refer to his score book, where wind tables are set out for his information, and will naturally take great notice of how the wind flags are behaving. He may also take note of the gunsmoke from adjoining firers' rifles and perhaps refer to his telescope to see how other firers' spotting discs are distributed. Under certain circumstances he may use his telescope in an attempt to obtain an indication of how the mirage or hot air currents evident through a telescope on a warm day are performing. The shooter then relates all of this information to his position on the range and whether any physical undulations in the ground or any possible shelter from hedges or trees will affect the bullet's flight.

The effect of wind on a bullet is roughly proportional to distance; assuming the wind is equal in strength over the distance, whatever allowance is required at 300 yards may theoretically be doubled for 600 yards. This can be a useful, if very rough, additional guide if a mental picture can be established of wind effects at, say, 500 yards and relative adjustments made for 300 and 600 yards as appropriate. At 1,000 yards the allowance needed in minutes of angle is roughly the same as the speed of the wind in miles per hour when its direction is at right angles to the line of fire.

Aiming off to make allowances for wind can be successful in fast changing conditions, but it requires considerable skill to be effective and is

THE WIND FLAG

Up to 3 mph
Wind can barely be felt. Smoke shows direction.

About 4 mph
Gentle wind. Can be felt on the face; leaves show a slight movement.

About 8 mph
Moderate wind. The flag will be extended roughly by half.

About 12 mph
Fresh wind. Flag flies between half and full extension. Leaves and twigs in constant motion.

About 16 mph
Strong wind. It becomes more difficult to judge change in wind strength and direction.

About 20 mph
Very strong wind. Generally considered to be the strongest wind for which accurate calculations can be made.

not made easier with the use of a ring front sight. If it is to be attempted, it should be remembered, as stated previously, that one minute represents approximately one inch per 100 yards, therefore 3 minutes at 300 yards would require 9 inches of allowance on the target, 5 minutes at 500 yards would represent about 25 inches and 6 minutes at 600 yards, 36 inches.

ASSESSING WIND DIRECTION

The assessment of the direction of the wind is as important as determining its strength. It follows that a wind from 3 o'clock or 9 o'clock, that is directly across the bullets' path, will have maximum effect, that from 2, 4, 8 or 10 o'clock somewhat less (in fact, about $\frac{7}{8}$ of maximum), and that from 1, 5, 7 or 11 o'clock about half of the maximum for a right-angled wind. Directional changes in wind can sometimes be hard to detect on rifle ranges that are poorly equipped with wind flags.

Strength changes, however, can often be felt more readily by the firer. In general terms, changes in strength of wind are more significant from, say, the 2 o'clock to 4 o'clock directions, as virtually full allowance has to be made in such circumstances. Given a constant strength, the change of angle from 2 o'clock to 4 o'clock, or 60°, has a maximum difference of $\frac{1}{8}$ less than the full allowance and therefore can almost be ignored as far as the directional alteration is concerned. However, a change in strength in the same quadrant will have the maximum effect on the bullet's flight. Conversely, with a wind blowing from, say, the 11 o'clock to 1 o'clock quadrant, which requires about half the equivalent allowance at right angles for the same strength, a doubling in the wind's force would be about halved in terms of effective displacement of the line of fire. It is obvious that in this quadrant, or in the equivalent area between 5 and 7 o'clock, a full change in direction between 11 and 1 o'clock of even a light wind of perhaps 3 minutes at 600 yards would produce an error of 6 minutes or 36 inches on the target, which could be sufficient to provide a very wide shot indeed. The aspiring marksman should remember the following to aid him with wind judging.

Attempt to choose one or two flags to give an indication of strength and another one or two to guide on direction.

Flags nearer the firer are more significant than those further down the range, as the sooner a bullet's flight is deflected by the effects of wind, the larger will be the ultimate error on the target.

Use all available aids, e.g. wind tables, smoke from fellow competitors' rifles, other firers' spotting discs, etc.

Mirage can be most useful in light wind conditions. If the telescope can be focused one-third down the range, the movement of the warm air at this distance can provide invaluable information as to precisely what is happening to the air currents. This information may then be acted upon in preference to what the wind flags are indicating.

When an obvious change occurs, make appropriate allowance, but otherwise do not 'fiddle' with the sights. In making changes at long range, be bold; if an unmistakable change has occurred, it will probably require an alteration of not less than three or four minutes.

Fire shots quickly, particularly in fast changing conditions. Many well-judged shots have landed wide of the mark by taking too long in the aim because the conditions altered in the meantime. Slow shooting can also make the coaches' task even more difficult in team matches.

Do not put too much store on the wind allowance that you may overhear or may be mentioned to you by competitors of perhaps doubtful ability; know that your own wind gauge is accurately zeroed and rely on your own judgement whenever possible or take advice from others you know and trust.

Top left: A competitor in the International competition held at the NRA ranges at Bisley in Surrey.
Top right: Wind coaches, sub-coaches and spotters all assist the riflemen during fullbore competitions.
Bottom: Fullbore rifle shooting demands an intensity of concentration from both the rifleman and his coach.

WEATHER

Shooting in wet conditions is another facet of the sport that distinguishes it from smallbore shooting. Many are the times that fullbore shooters silently envy the covered and puddle-free firing points from which smallbore shooters compete. However, rarely do they complain, for, it is my belief, one of the great rewards of our branch of the sport of shooting is that we are totally exposed to the elements. Great is the satisfaction to be gained from competing success-fully against the wind and the rain. And, of course, as fellow shooters suffer similar adversity, this helps give rise to the unquestionable camaraderie of fullbore shooters.

Being properly dressed and equipped for inclement weather with adequate towels and leathers in the shooting box is important. A water-proof cover should also be provided for the telescope to avoid misting of the lenses.

In wet conditions it is not good practice to lie on a ground sheet, as it tends to collect water in puddles, which can be most uncomfortable. An old sack is much better–it tends to absorb the rain without causing puddles. In wet conditions it is of paramount importance in shooting to keep one's ammunition and rifle breech as dry as possible. A chamois leather or towel is most important; it can either be laid over the action between shots or used to dry the action or, indeed, the hands before touching the ammunition, which itself should be well-protected from water in the shooting box or, even better, in an inside pocket in the shooting jacket.

The reason for keeping ammunition as dry as possible is that when a round is fired the cartridge case expands as far as the chamber will allow and the force of sending the bullet up the barrel drives the cartridge case back on the bolt face. If the cartridge becomes wet, its friction on the chamber is reduced, it therefore places an increased force on the bolt and upsets the normal barrel vibrations and compensatory effects. In the case of the No. 4 action the effect is that dispersion of the shots is increased by about six minutes. It is known that the muzzle velocity remains unchanged, which leads to the conclusions that it is the rifle jump that is the sole cause of these differences in

performance. Although clearly it is not recommended to fire with wet rounds, which give rise to increased pressure and thus greater risk of a broken bolt, there is no significant increase in danger to the firer as long as the rifle body is in sound condition. Although the majority of forward-locking actions are relatively unaffected by water on the cartridge or in the chamber, there have been instances of recoil lugs fracturing on P14 rifles as a result of firing with wet ammunition.

SUMMARY

It is, of course, impossible to cover completely all facets and implications of the sport of fullbore target rifle shooting in a short article. I have attempted merely to provide a guide to the points that I consider particularly significant to this branch of the shooting art. The basic technique of shooting with regard to position and aiming, is the same as for smallbore shooting and is covered in the chapter on three position rifle shooting.

The attractions of fullbore shooting are hard to define and probably do not bear the most analytical investigation. However, suffice to say that one of the main attractions may be the satisfaction of competing with, and overcoming, the elements and in so doing attempting to achieve a good score. To many shooters the score itself may really be incidental to the stories and excuses for missed points and the outstanding camaraderie of the sport, which is world-wide. The successful competitive marksman can aspire to teams, involving meeting shooters in other parts of the world who, wherever they congregate with their friendly rivalry and sportsmanship, constitute the most congenial company. This, in my opinion, is what fullbore shooting is all about.

Left: Unlike other forms of competitive shooting, little has changed in fullbore shooting over the years, the rifles and the gear have remained much the same.

Below: Fullbore shooting requires a lot of open space. A low hill provides an excellent backstop.

12 THREE POSITION RIFLE SHOOTING

VARIATIONS ON THE SPORT

Throughout its history three position rifle shooting has been recognized as one of the most difficult types of sport shooting. It was the forerunner of all the modern shooting disciplines in terms of international standardization, and was one of the original sports entered in the reborn Olympic Games of 1896, and has been included ever since.

Originally, it was shot with a big-bore rifle at a distance of 300 metres. It survived in Olympic competition in its original form until the Montreal Olympics, when pressures – internal and external – precluded it. However, it is far from dead on the world scene, and is, in fact, currently enjoying an upsurge in popularity.

It has had a history of ups and downs, the downs mainly due to cost. Now it seems the attraction of competing in this match can be so strong that competitors will organize, finance and train themselves despite a frequent lack of support from official bodies. Perhaps, in the modern world of increased leisure and raised living standards, interest in this particular discipline will be revived sufficiently to warrant its return to the Olympics. In any case the original creators of the competition, the Scandinavian and central European countries, with Switzerland in the lead, have always unswervingly supported the competition during its difficult times, and will continue to do so.

While the original competition has led a fairly unstable life for one reason or another, there is no doubt that for the participants it is a great sport. Its popularity is confirmed by the many variations that have been developed over the years.

First there was the identical course, with identical rules, but shot with rimfire rifles at only 50 metres. Since then there have been half courses, with twenty shots at each of the three positions instead of forty. These were designed for ladies and junior competitors, and shot with a 'standard rifle'.

Lastly, there is the event that is proving to be an extremely popular and growing competition, the air rifle course. This course consists of forty shots in the standing position only, shot at a distance of 10 metres. It is similar to the standing section of the 'free rifle' match, but must be shot in 90 minutes instead of two hours. The beauty of this type of shooting is its use as a training aid as well as for enjoyment in its own right.

The English Match – sixty shots in the prone position – was originally conceived for the predominantly prone-shooting British Commonwealth as a separate and slightly more testing match than the forty shots in the prone section of the free rifle match. The three position shooters usually win this match too!

Clearly, with the 3 × 40 shot free rifle position match, the 60-shot English Match, and talk of the air rifle being included in the Olympics, the future of position rifle shooting is assured.

Left and below: Acknowledged as the most demanding form of target shooting, three position rifle shooting calls for the utmost in concentration and endurance from those who take part.

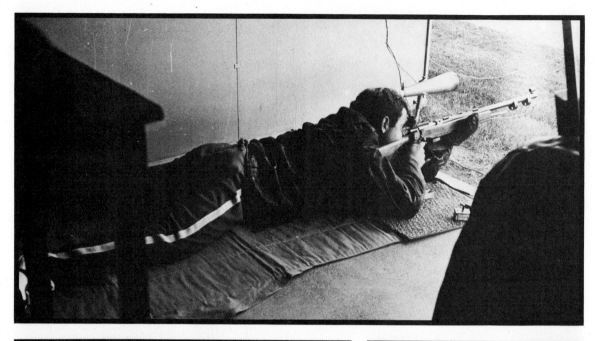

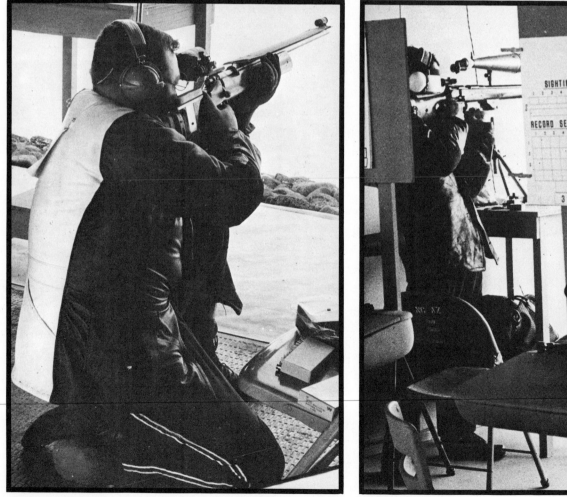

COMPETITION PROGRAMME AND PRIZES

The three position shoot consists of 120 match shots with a possible highest score of 1,200 points. The big-bore, 300 metre record is 1,159 and the smallbore record is 1,167. The total shooting time is 5¼ hours and the positions are shot as follows:

Prone: 90 minutes followed by a 15 minute break.

Standing: 2 hours followed by a 15 minute break.

Kneeling: 145 minutes.

A maximum of ten sighting shots is allowed for each position. They may be taken only before or between a 10-shot string, and are included in the total shooting time.

In the International Shooting Union (UIT) programme medals are given for all positions and for the aggregate in the big-bore event. In the smallbore event they are given for the standing and kneeling positions and the aggregate only, since there is a separate smallbore prone event and prize. In the Olympics the only prize given is for the aggregate, but scores gained in the separate positions do count for records. In the half course for ladies and juniors only the aggregate counts for prizes and records.

Although competitors in the ladies and juniors three position events use a special type of rifle, a standard rifle, they are still eligible to compete in the free rifle event. Some do, and win both! The rules for the half course are twenty shots in each position with no breaks in two and a half hours. Six sighting shots are allowed for each position.

Marksmen competing at the 41st World Championship held at Thun in Switzerland demonstrate the three positions of the sport and the use of the free rifle. The kneeling marksman has a thin band of steel fitted to the top of the barrel to eliminate mirages rising from the hot barrel and distorting the sighting image.

RANGES

Three position shooting as organized under the rules of the International Shooting Union takes place on ranges with specific basic characteristics. The shooting positions are protected from wind and rain in what are generally called 'shooting houses'. There is a place for each competitor to shoot. It is supplied with a mat, a table for his telescope and equipment used in the standing position, and a chair, on which he can place equipment, sit down if he feels the need to rest, or rest his rifle after firing a shot. Behind the firing position is a small space that runs the entire length of the range and is used by the range officials to supervise the proceedings. In a large match a scorer also sits in this space behind each shooter. His job is to change targets for the shooter, if necessary, and to show an estimated score to the spectators, who stand or sit in the third section of the range. Coaches and helpers of the shooters also sit in the spectator area, as they are not allowed to influence the shooter.

This arrangement is the best for both the shooter and the spectator. It can be very unnerving to be at a big international event for the first time and have to perform in front of a large crowd. This doesn't happen much in Commonwealth countries or America, but it is commonplace in Europe. The crowds naturally tend to gather behind the shooter whose estimated score is showing good prospects, and may become very enthusiastic when a record is in the offing. No harm is meant – in fact, the spectators are hoping that the record will be broken – but it becomes a severe test of concentration for the person behind whom they stand.

The Swiss, whose national sport is shooting, have the finest shooting ranges in the world. A typical Swiss range is a two-decked design of, say, 50 firing points. The lower deck is for 50 metres, with some points at 100 metres, and the upper deck is for 300 metres. Apart from the normal facilities at the firing line there are changing rooms, and restaurants and bars where spectators can sit and watch the proceedings in comfort.

The sport is recognized as being very difficult and having spectator interest, and ranges are built to provide an environment for records to be broken, as well as comfort for spectators.

GENERAL EQUIPMENT

Obviously, to be successful in competition, where high scores are required, attention needs to be paid to the general equipment, which can help to achieve a good performance. The competition is long and difficult and demands a high degree of physical effort and mental activity. Comfort facilitates this. The general equipment required for three position shooting is basically the same as for all target shooting, with the addition of a few special items: the kneeling roll, an extension for the spotting telescope, a pair of boots (not essential, but helpful), and a pair of specially padded trousers.

The kneeling roll is put under the instep of the foot on which one sits in the kneeling position. It greatly facilitates the shooter's stability by increasing the comfort and, consequently, the time that the shooter can remain in position.

The extension rod for the spotting telescope enables the firer to spot without breaking position on ranges where there are no tables or where the tables are not high enough. It can be used in both the standing and kneeling positions.

Boots can make the kneeling position a great deal more comfortable by supplying a stiff sole on which to sit. However, they are by no means essential. They are extensively used in standing to provide some support to the ankles, but mostly to provide a stiff, flat base on which to stand.

Special trousers with some padding sewn into the knees and the seat help to make the kneeling position more comfortable. The padding is usually only a sheet of very 'grippy' neoprene, which helps to stop the elbow slipping on the knee as well as increasing the comfort in this high pressure area.

Well-fitting leather shooting coats feel comfortable and help to minimize heartbeat pulses and muscle tremors. Leather is a material that gives to a certain extent under stress, but afterwards will return to its original shape.

A glove is a most beneficial comfort aid, as the rifle sling is used tight and for long periods. In the standing position gloves are usually worn when not using a palm rest.

An accurate and clear timepiece, hearing protectors (to help concentration and prevent

damage to hearing), and a notebook are essential. The notebook is used to record scores, data on ranges, positions of fittings on the rifle and so on. Rarely can one remember all that needs to be recalled.

RIFLES

The rifle is free from all restrictions except that it must not exceed a certain weight, it must have iron sights, and the hook and palm rest must not exceed a set of maximum dimensions. The 300-metre free rifle can be any calibre up to 8 millimetres, and the smallbore is, of course, .22 rimfire.

Most rifles have similar features, such as a thumbhole stock, adjustable butt length, twist rise, adjustable cheek pieces, and weight bars fitted to the fore end to alter weight or balance. In fact, the modern free rifle is almost infinitely variable. Shooters are allowed to use a palm rest in the standing position, and most do, as their arms are not long enough to assume the correct position without it. The palm rest is also variable. A hook can be used on the adjustable butt plate,

which helps greatly in the standing position when, for stability, the majority of the rifle weight is carried forward of the supporting hand.

Almost every rifle is unique to some degree, being altered to help the user achieve better and better performances. Many competitors enjoy altering and modifying the weapon as much as they do using the finished article, and are forever in their workshops making improvements or maintaining the arm's fine condition.

Left: Some of the equipment needed for competition shooting. As well as the correct clothing including mitts and a shooting hat (right), the rifleman needs a kneeling roll (left) and (bottom left, from top to bottom) an extension rod for the telescope, base for the scope stand, stopwatch, shooting glasses, bullet block, telescope and cleaning materials.
Below: Two typical free rifles in .22 and .308 calibres, together with their respective targets.

Many European shooters use the free rifle in the prone position quite successfully, but it has not been so popular in the Commonwealth and America for this position. Most of the modern rifles are quite heavy, between $12\frac{1}{2}$ and 17 pounds. Use of the mass to slow oscillations and dampen pulse beat is the main reason for this, although now there is a trend toward the lighter rifle, the tremors being overcome by muscle tension.

For ladies', juniors', big-bore standard rifle and air rifle events the rules governing the rifle are quite strict as regards dimensions and weight. There are none of the extras and adjustability of the free rifle.

AMMUNITION

Ammunition for the smallbore rifle is always factory-made. Champion shooters spend a great deal of time and effort matching ammunition to their rifles. Each rifle and each batch of ammunition has its own characteristics.

Big-bore has the advantage that matching can be done by handloading, and this is quite an extensive practice among big-bore 300 metre shooters. There are many components on the market, and superb accuracy can be achieved by hand selecting and loading. Factory loads, with their machining tolerances, are rarely able to match it.

It is quite common to take two different loads to a match, one, say, for light airs, and the other to smash through high winds should they arise. The advantage of using a heavier bullet to smash through wind has to be weighed against the extra pounding received by the firer due to the heavier loads and stronger recoil. In any case, big-bore free rifles can group inside $2\frac{1}{2}$ inches at 300 metres, with some notable exceptions lately which are approaching 1 inch or better. The advantage of these 'super-accuracy' capabilities are, that the user can afford a little more error in technique or misjudgment of conditions and still hit the 3.9 inch bull. There is also a delightful feeling when shot follows shot into what appears, through the spotting scope, to be one hole. Unfortunately, the smallbore is not in the same class as far as accuracy is concerned, but this factor is adequately compensated by the lesser recoil and noise. The difference in world record scores tends to illustrate this point.

COMPETITIVE MATCHES

In Britain position shooting competitions are available from postal leagues of the National Association, the County Associations and the British Free Rifle Club. There are organized shoulder-to-shoulder matches run by the counties and the BFRC through the year and finally there are the British Championships at the Bisley Meeting. Air rifle shooting follows a similar pattern and there are probably a greater number of shoulder-to-shoulder competitions to enter in this field, which is growing all the time.

Other competitions are available for those aspiring to greater things and wishing to enter national squads. Organization for these is the responsibility of the national body. Internationally, every major competition has position shooting in it. Most European countries and many others open their national championships for foreign competitors, or, often create an international match especially.

Generally, there is one major international competition each year in shooting. These include the Olympic Games and the World Championships, each held once every four years, and the European Championships in between, once every two years. The equivalent of the European Championships are the Pan American Games and the Championship of the Americas. The general idea of these matches, while being recognized as regional championships, is to give competitors and organizations a 'training run' for the World or Olympic competition in the following year. There are, in fact, many competitions, right up to regional level, so match practice at international level can be had if required.

The one exception to the format above is in air weapons. These are represented in the World Championships, but are not yet included in the Olympics. They have their own European Championships every year in February. Certainly, the expansion in this branch of our sport recently justifies all the matches organized for it.

Right: The standing position at the 41st World Championship.
Above: On the range at Bisley.

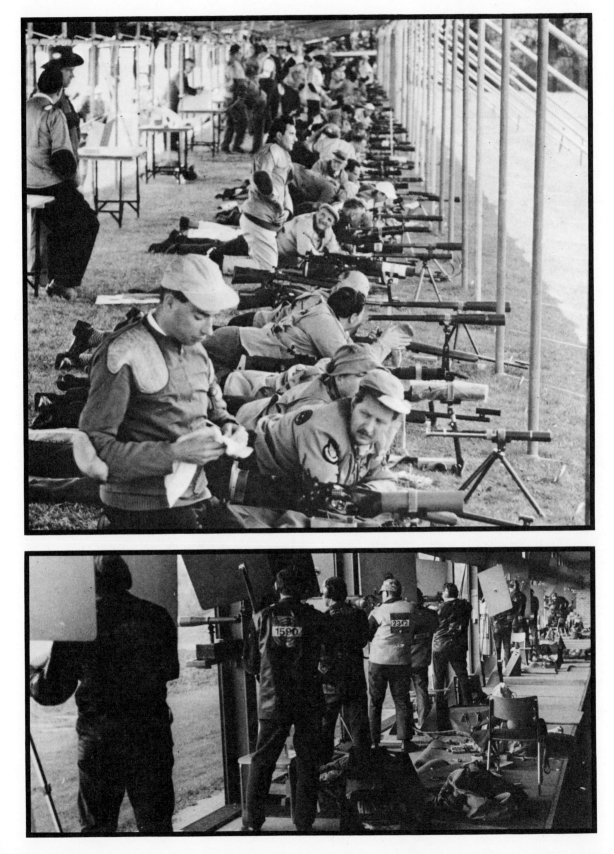

THE SERIOUS SPORTSMAN

Position shooting is fairly time-consuming if one takes it at all seriously, but there are ways in which it can be done, and done well if a little thought is given to the use and allocation of time. The serious shooter tries to take advantage of every situation to enhance his scores and, as in every sport, must sacrifice much.

The person who shoots the free rifle seriously has quite a difficult time problem. Most people work for eight hours, sleep for eight hours, travel to and from work for about two hours, leaving only six hours in which to complete all other things. The shooter must analyse his day and be determined to make best use of his time to carry out his training plan. There are moments and activities during the day that he can use to improve his skill with the rifle. For example, while watching television, the shooter can also be holding the rifle in position, aiming at a spot on the wall or a target in the garden, and in this way better use can be made of time available. Travelling long distances to a range for a short session is almost a waste of time, and dry-firing sessions at home can be more beneficial. Lunch hour at work can be used as a dry-firing session, or perhaps for jogging a few miles. A few spare minutes have to be put aside for keeping a shooting diary up to date and checking on the overall training plan. It is always worth putting a little time aside for checking equipment: it does marvels for the confidence on match day. All this is done outside of actual range practice, as most clubs have only one or two evenings a week available. Air rifle shooting and dry-firing with a telescopic sight on the .22 are two further training methods used.

The air rifle has the distinct advantage of requiring only the basic safety precautions, and therefore can be used anywhere, even in the home, on scaled-down targets if there is not room for a full 10 metres. Firing practice can thus be had at very little cost. Many of the shooting problems can be eliminated in the comfort and quiet of one's own home.

Another method of identifying faults and improving technique is to use a high-powered telescopic sight. A distant target can be chosen and training can be carried on throughout the winter from the comfort and warmth of the home. The telescope magnifies all movements and faults, giving real value in training time. Scores can be estimated with some accuracy, which makes training more interesting, as well as showing up improvements in performance.

A layman to shooting sports can only guess the limits to which top exponents of the sport go and what is felt when participating in intense competition that has been trained for over years rather than months. He cannot know the immense satisfaction in attaining the final goal, which seemed impossible at the outset.

DISCIPLINE CHARACTERISTICS

Prone shooting is the type of competition where the rifle and ammunition are capable of holding the ten-ring consistently. This means that the skill of the rifleman lies in his ability to make no mistakes throughout the course. Of course, bad weather alters matters, as it brings in a different type of skill. Prone is the position that can illustrate the incredible grouping capacity of modern equipment, and the extreme precision with which the body can be made to perform.

Standing, the most physically demanding and the most difficult position from which to achieve good results, can be equated roughly with the adage 'work in = results out'. As the rifle is held about five feet above the ground by bone and muscle, and you are expected to hit the same mark as in the prone position, the difficulty becomes clear. Funnily enough, it is this very difficulty that most free rifle shooters enjoy most. Perhaps it is because there is still so much to achieve, or perhaps because of the satisfaction obtained when one performs well. It really indicates achievement to be able to perform consistently in the standing position. There is a great thrill and sense of accomplishment when everything you desire of the mind and body is carried through, for to score highly and consistently, perfect control must be obtained over the body. Many of these controls are derived only by hours of practice and concentration, learning about the body's activities, how to isolate them and bring them under control. At the height of training the shooter commits all functions but his hold to his subconscious, which carries them through.

The kneeling position, too, has its own particular characteristics, and is second on the difficulty scale. Its main problem areas, enjoyable to some, are the setting out of the body conformation. Setting up the angles of arms and legs, the lean of the back, and distributing the weight to bearing areas, etc., can be an extremely absorbing problem when trying to achieve good results. An even more difficult problem is trying to repeat a good result at the next session, having got everything right at the last.

The main difficulty with the kneeling position is its instability when compared with the prone position. It takes only the minutest tremor or incorrect placement of a limb to start quite violent oscillations at the muzzle. Having achieved a balanced and technically perfect position, a mind not properly controlled and relaxed can also start up movement at the muzzle.

It is a position that takes hours of thought and analysis, followed by hours of training to enforce the new modification and character. It is a fairly uncomfortable position that demands time to acclimatize the body to the discomforts so that full concentration can be given to the hold and release. Many people seem to fall into a position that gives good results, but others try for years without being able to achieve results comparable to the other two positions. As in all shooting, when it is right and goes well, taking advantage of it is most satisfying.

There are obvious similarities between the three positions and yet each has completely different requirements if one is to perform well at all of them.

Prone requires a mentality that will enable as many repeat performances as are necessary, making few or no mistakes.

Standing requires a physical involvement, combined with stamina, coordination and patience in trying to achieve the perfect performance, over and over again.

Kneeling requires an analysing and careful mind, technical perfection, patience and an ability to perform well while enduring pain. The position comes at the end of the shoot, so the shooter requires reserves of concentration to enable him to undertake the tasks mentioned.

The full sequence of three position shooting is long and arduous, and sufficiently varied that if a mistake is made there always seems to be a chance of compensating before the end. Interest is sustained by the sense of achievement, and all the while one knows that one could do better. How many times does one hear after a shoot, 'If only I had controlled that eight', or 'If only I had rested after twenty instead of going right through'?

The sport always seems to provide a subject for shooters to discuss and research. It highlights, more than most, areas of human control about which little or nothing is known, not to mention the perpetual discussions into the perfection of equipment, ammunition, accuracy and human ability.

There seems to be something about the people who participate in it too! They share a sort of camaraderie that sometimes is not evident in other sports. It seems to spring from the fact that everyone appreciates the effort each person has made, and knows that the problems are not with the other competitors, but with oneself.

THE PERSONALITY

What type of person makes a successful free rifle shooter? He has to have patience, a willingness to learn, an acceptance of his own failings, ambition, drive and, most of all, the will to win. However, many of these attributes, which are so clearly seen in a champion, were not there in the first place, at least not to the same degree. The most important characteristics of the successful free rifle shooter are his ability to recognize his weaknesses and his determination to eliminate them. Many of the characteristics mentioned would be considered by most people as unchangeable. Not to the top marksman. Once it is noticed and accepted that one's character has in fact changed, the realization enhances confidence, since any further changes necessary to reach the objective can be made, knowing it is possible.

Why are people attracted to this type of competition? Perhaps it is because of the many challenges it offers:

● the challenge to achieve what no one has achieved before – a possible over the whole course has never been fired! All the masters will agree that the barriers are psychological, not physical, although the physical demands are great and to be successful requires a high degree of physical fitness and tone;

- the challenge of technical perfection, to have the most accurate ammunition and rifle tuned and tested, to find the most accurate equipment to assist one in obtaining and maintaining the hold required to keep the body and rifle system still, and to search for perfection in balancing the body system to enable the body to remain steady and still;
- the challenge to prove oneself the best on the firing line, to conquer the inhibitors of performance to a greater depth than other competitors, to prove that you can cope with the atmosphere and pressure better than anyone else.

Many people are also attracted to shooting by the pleasure of using a finely produced and tuned instrument, even though the results on the target do not always illustrate great skill or technique. To some, the individualism of this form of competition gives satisfaction. Each shooter must face and solve every problem alone and completely isolated on the firing line. To others, getting a good day's shooting in pleasant company is sufficient satisfaction.

THE PERFORMANCE

To an observer the perfect shot may appear simple and effortless, but it results from thousands of hours of training, conditioning and learning condensed into a perfectly coordinated act taking just 30 seconds.

In preparation for firing a shot the shooter's attention is focused on the *intention* to produce a good performance: this positive thinking itself is a learned condition. He picks up the rifle, fits it carefully to his shoulder and in his supporting hand. He settles his body down into a fixed and relaxed state, his mind searching for any unwanted muscle tensions and bad fit of the body/rifle system. He slowly settles the muzzle onto the target and feels that everything is firm, comfortable and under control: breathing is normal. As the muzzle drops in line with the target, the final signals come back from 'out-stations' in the body – the muscle tension in the legs, the fit and pressure of the cheek on the butt, the grip, placement and position of the hand that will operate the trigger, all are OK.

Now he focuses his attention on the sighting and alignment of the foresight and target. His senses pick up the natural body sways and pulsations that are preventing the foresight from staying on the target. He brings his will to bear on the problem areas, draws in the last deep relaxing breath, exhales, and concentrates his mind to stop all movement. Signals go out to all parts of the body 'Slow down! Slow down!' The heart slows down, and the pressure of the beat subsides from the inner ear. All is still, quiet and in a state of tranquility.

The will is now at full stretch to maintain this condition, while the highly trained subconscious mind automatically increases the pressure of the trigger finger on the trigger all the time that 'OK' signals are received from the now-accepted sight picture. The senses are now razor sharp. They perceive any likely disturbances and are geared to instant correction to a minute degree: the will is overriding failure signals and blocking doubts. The performance *will* be carried through and completed perfectly.

Through this state of intense alertness in the mind, and self-induced suspended animation in the body, the thud of ignition breaks only the stillness of the sights. The shooter holds his body in exactly the same state while rifle and body recoil naturally. The senses now note that the body has not influenced the natural recoil and, therefore, the original path of the bullet as it travels up the barrel. The sights and the feel of the movement of the rifle now indicate that the shot was good and the position of the strike on the target. Only when the hit is heard at the target, which seems ages later, does the shooter break the intense state of awareness, concentration and inner stillness. A feeling of elation and satisfaction follows the knowledge that you had the ultimate control over your mind and body, the proof of which is on the target. One doesn't have to look: the result is as certain as the original intention . . . to perform well.

It is easy to see that the rifle is just a vehicle to indicate the precision with which the human body can carry out a coordinate act. It performs as an extension to produce the result of the act on paper.

The feeling and sensations described, and the absolute sureness of the result, are really experienced only by the standing shooter. They are known to happen the same way in all forms of static shooting, but tend to be less pronounced and less recognizable in the more stable and sling-supported positions.

1. Shooting in the prone position. The left arm passes through the sling to ensure that pressure can be maintained to steady the barrel. The left hand is protected by a thickly padded shooting glove.
2. Loading the cartridge. Notice how the left hand passes between the sling and the barrel to maintain tension on the sling.
3. Ready to fire, with the eye close to the rear peep sight, the finger on the trigger and the rifle dead steady.

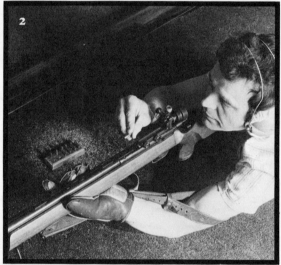

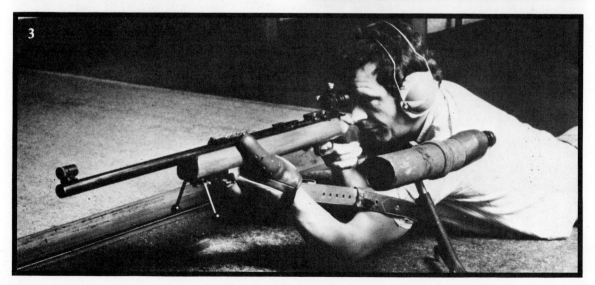

13 BB GUNS AND PLINKING

WINDMILLS AND THE DAISY GUN

The story of the BB Gun, first marketed in 1886 as a wooden air gun called 'The Chicago' by 'Captain' W. F. Markham of Plymouth, Michigan, could not be told without a short history of The Daisy Manufacturing Company . . . an integral part of the BB gun annals.

Daisy hasn't always been Daisy! In 1886, in Plymouth, Michigan, the company that is now internationally known as The Daisy Manufacturing Company was known as the Plymouth Iron Windmill Company. It was underwritten by $30,000 in subscriptions to its shares, eager to obtain a reasonable share of the then blossoming windmill business.

As early as 1885, it had become quite evident that the sale of iron windmills was proving much more difficult than previously supposed, with profits dwindling each year. In 1886, during this bleak period, a neighbouring plant, the Markham

Manufacturing Company, marketing a varied line of wooden products, produced a novelty item. It was a wooden airgun called 'The Chicago'. It resembled anything but a gun in looks or in accuracy, but did manage to fire a round lead ball, size BB shot which was about .004 inches larger than present-day air rifle shot. It brought Markham some sales and a patent on certain parts of the mechanism.

Meanwhile, as Markham climbed the ladder of success, the Plymouth Iron Windmill Company continued to sgruggle; and in 1888, a vote was taken to liquidate the company. One vote, that of Lewis Cass Hough, saved the company from the proposal and in effect, insured that Daisy air rifles would be a basic part of growing up for future generations.

Left: Young BB shooters competing in the 10 metre championships. Below: The original factory and the workers employed by the Plymouth Iron Windmill Company in Michigan.

Shortly after the decision against liquidation, a local inventor, Clarence J. Hamilton, stopped by the office of L. C. Hough, then general manager for the windmill company, to show him a device with a long barrel, trigger and a piece of wire shaped roughly like a gunstock. He cocked it, rolled a size BB lead ball down the muzzle and instructed Hough to shoot. After hearing the BB hit the bottom of the wastebasket where the scrap paper target had been, Hough decided to try it again . . . outside. He set up a shingle and when the BB penetrated it from a distance of 10 feet, turned to Hamilton and said, 'Boy, that's a daisy.'

By the time the board of directors met in July 1888, Hamilton had handmade several of his devices and it was agreed to offer one free to every farmer who bought a Plymouth Iron Windmill as a gimmick to increase sales. As salesmen roamed the countryside, armed with the model windmill and the crude, handmade air guns, time after time it was reported to the general manager of Plymouth Iron Windmills that 'the tail was wagging the dog'. Prospective windmill customers wanted to buy the air gun . . . which wasn't for sale.

In January 1889, the board of directors adopted the proposition that the Hamilton air rifle would be carried as a saleable item along with the windmills. By December 1890, the annual sales of the company were several times greater than had ever been with the iron windmills alone. With the evidence of a national market for air guns and steadily growing profits, the Plymouth Iron Windmill Company became the Daisy Manufacturing Company. Even though competitors were rapidly springing up along the way, Daisy was to emerge as the Number One producer of air rifles.

In 1958 Daisy left Plymouth, the town that had nurtured it for over 75 years and moved to Rogers, Arkansas and the beginning of a new era. Daisy's profits and reputation continued to climb both in the States and the international trade market, and with their success came the birth of a shooting education programme which continues to touch the lives of three million youngsters between the ages of eight and 14 each year. The inauguration of the programme came as the solution to a problem. More difficult to deal with than 'anti-gun' sentiment, was the fact that some youngsters using BB guns, had damaged property and accidentally destroyed the eyesight of others. Rather than ignore the misuse of their product, Daisy's Training Services Department began working to accomplish one ideal, to educate BB gun users in proper gun handling and to promote the gun as the excellent training tool that it is.

Right: One of Daisy's early advertisements.
Below: Captain W. F. Markham's wooden novelty gun 'The Chicago', with the original Daisy, the air rifle invented by Clarence J. Hamilton.

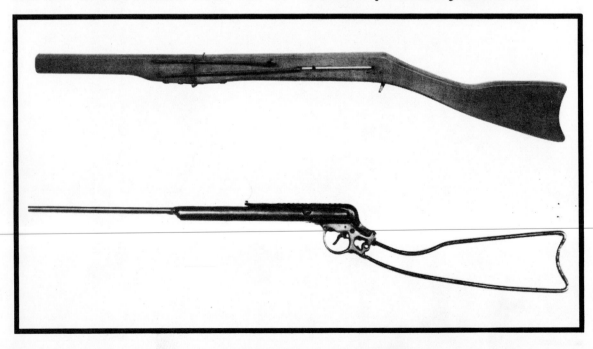

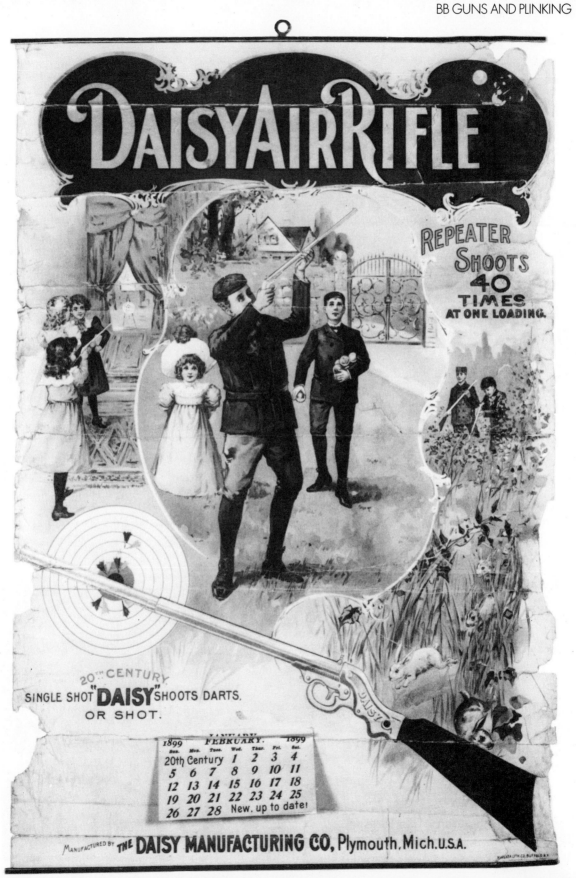

Soon schools began to have target shooting as part of their physical education programmes and in later years the Jaycee Shooting Education Programme was devised. Today, over 3,700 Jaycee chapters in all 50 states of the Union, and in Mexico, Canada, and West Germany, are helping boys and girls learn the fun of target shooting, while teaching them the most important lesson ... proper gun handling.

This unique programme, still jointly sponsored by the US Jaycees and Daisy, is the largest and most flourishing shooting education programme in the United States.

THE SHOOTING EDUCATION PROGRAMME

The four basic ingredients of this programme take the 'plinker' and teach him, or her, four things.

- education
- safety
- enjoyment
- competition

The shooting education programme introduces young boys and girls to a true lifetime of recreational activity: shooting is a sport that can be learned at a very young age and be continued to a very old age. It is a sport where girls and boys can compete on an equal footing. It is a sport that can be enjoyed outdoors through target shooting and hunting and indoors with air guns.

The programme has played a major role in making shooting not only fun, but safe. Most gun accidents involving eight to 14-year-olds are directly related to improper gun handling. Well-organized and concise instruction in proper gun handling and marksmanship is not only a community responsibility but a personal one. Safety is a necessary lesson in growing up with guns.

The first step in the programme is to teach a knowledge of the different types of guns and ammunition and rules for proper gun handling. Young shooters practise correct gun handling and learn the basic components of all guns ... from BB guns to 30–06's. They learn how to aim and they learn shooting positions for competitions.

After the basics, the next step in becoming a marksman is to find the 'master eye'. The dominant eye or master eye theory is based on the fact that one eye focuses directly on a given subject while the other eye focuses indirectly on the same subject.

Each person has a master eye. To excel in shooting, you must shoot from the same shoulder as the master eye. Find out which eye is dominant in this way: extend your arms in front of you, hands together and make a circle with your forefingers and thumbs. Look through the circle with both eyes and focus on an object. Now close the right eye. Open, and close the left eye. If the object moved when you closed the right eye, the right eye is the dominant eye and you should always shoot with the gun at your right shoulder; the reverse is true of a left dominant eye.

A problem occurs when a shooter has a left dominant eye and is naturally a right-shoulder shooter, or vice versa. It is impossible to be a successful shooter unless this situation can be corrected. If at all possible, train yourself to shoot from the same shoulder as the master eye. If it is impossible for you to change shoulders, you must learn to shoot with the master eye closed. This causes the shooter to shoot to the left of the master eye and sight alignment corrections must be made to achieve any amount of success.

All competitors must take a part in a 100 question quiz as part of the BB championship.

HOW BB GUNS WORK

BB shooting uses low-power weapons to discharge small diameter ball-bearings. Two main types of weapon shoot BB shot: spring-air compression and CO_2. As a simple and cheap introduction to learning some very rudimentary skills in the safe handling and shooting of firearms, there is a lot to be said for the BB gun. It must be stressed that, as with all firearms, these weapons are potentially dangerous and should never be used where there is any possibility of injury.

Probably the best known BB guns are those made by the Daisy Manufacturing Company. The usual form of Daisy air rifle or pistol is operated by means of one or more springs. To prepare the weapon, the spring is compressed; when the trigger is pressed, the spring is released and pushes a piston forward inside a cylinder. In the cylinder the air is compressed and escapes through the barrel and, in some air rifles, is sufficiently powerful to produce a muzzle velocity of up to 600 feet a second. The air pistols, of necessity, have a smaller cylinder and a smaller barrel and their power is considerably less. Many of the cheaper air rifles and pistols designed on this system fire a standard-shaped slug, but many others, such as the Daisy products, are chambered for BB shot that is .175 inches in diameter. The conventional BB shot is steel, and has a light, copper coating to prevent rusting, which might damage the inside bore of the weapon as well as causing possible jamming or clogging. Since the BB shot is spherical, it has one great advantage: it can be loaded into a magazine or other container and be fed into the breech or barrel with minimum difficulty, something that would be impossible if shaped shot were used.

The other popular type of BB weapon uses carbon dioxide – CO_2 – to provide the power. This type of weapon dates back to the 1880s, when Paul Giffard, who had patented a number of compressed air guns, developed the idea of using cylinders of compressed air for power, and designed a weapon that used a cylinder of liquid carbon dioxide. He was granted a patent in 1889. The cylinder was inserted at a convenient point on the weapon; pressure on the trigger opened the valve, allowing a small amount of the liquid carbon dioxide to vaporize and blast out the ball. Modern cylinders are much smaller than the original types and can hold sufficient propellent for a considerable number of charges. They generate considerable bullet velocity and, unfortunately for enthusiasts in many countries, may only be possessed by the person holding an appropriate authority. Their power is limited and so their effective range is short, but they are useful for cheap, indoor target work. There have been some attempts to produce units that could be fitted into the frame of a fullbore weapon to convert it into a CO_2 weapon, but the idea does not seem to have been exploited.

There are three points to look for in choosing the rifle that is the right size for you.
1. The reach to the trigger, the length of the forearm from the bend in the elbow to the first joint of the trigger finger.
2. Forearm reach.

3. Ease of sighting.
To check if a gun is the correct size for you, place the stock in your bent elbow so that the gun rests along your forearm. If the first section of the trigger finger can cover the trigger easily, then the stock is the right size.

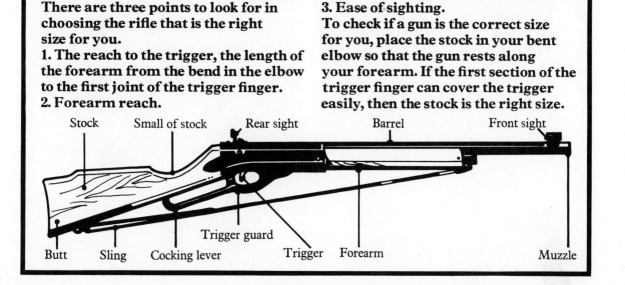

Stock   Small of stock   Rear sight   Barrel   Front sight

Trigger guard

Butt   Sling   Cocking lever   Trigger   Forearm   Muzzle

THE BASICS OF GUNMANSHIP
SHOULDERING THE GUN

To bring the gun to the correct position, for a right-shoulder shooter, bend the right arm at the elbow and touch the centre of your chest with your right hand. Raise your elbow so that it is level with your shoulder. This is known as making a 'chicken wing'. Without moving your right arm, take your left hand and find the pocket in your shoulder. The pocket is located between the shoulder muscle and the collar bone. Press hard on this shoulder pocket and make a mental note of its position.

Grip the gun at the forearm with your left hand, place the butt of the gun in your shoulder pocket. Place your right hand on the pistol grip and keep your fingers off the trigger. While the gun is pointed straight up in the air, place your cheek gently on the stock of the gun. With both eyes on the front sight, maintain this position and move your left foot forward about one foot and lean on it. Move the gun down to shoulder level, keeping the gun to your shoulder and your eyes on the sight.

LEARNING HOW TO SIGHT

You must learn correct sighting in order to shoot safely. If sighting is incorrect, you cannot hit the target. There are many types of sights and young shooters have no trouble understanding the 'lollipop' sighting method. Imagine that the post front sight is the lollipop stick. The rear peep sight is going to hold the lollipop. As soon as you find the lollipop stick in the rear peep sight, put the stick on the lollipop (the bullseye).

Using an aperture front sight (which may be thought of as a doughnut), put the doughnut in the centre of the rear peep sight and fill it with liquorice (the bullseye).

The lollipop stick must still be in full view and the top of the stick must be even with the top of the rear sight. Same as before, put the lollipop on the stick. As soon as the lollipop is on the stick . . . squeeze the trigger!

A chart showing the correct alignment and sighting pictures for the different types of front and rear rifle sights.

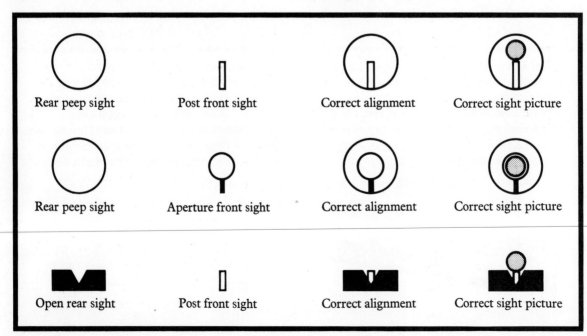

Rear peep sight	Post front sight	Correct alignment	Correct sight picture
Rear peep sight	Aperture front sight	Correct alignment	Correct sight picture
Open rear sight	Post front sight	Correct alignment	Correct sight picture

ADJUSTING THE SIGHT

If your picture of the stick on the lollipop is correct, most of your shots will be close together. This is called a 'group'. If you have a group of hits on the target and they are not in the centre of the bullseye, you need to adjust the sights on your gun.

Move the rear sight in the same direction you want the BB to go. To move the rear sight left or right, loosen the screw holding the sight to the gun; to move the sight up or down, loosen the sight and slide the peep sight. If you want the BB to hit further to the right, move the rear sight to the right, etc. No matter where you move the sights, you always want to 'put the stick on the lollipop'.

In recent international competitions, some shooters using Daisy's Model 499 match grade air gun, 'put the stick on the lollipop' and scored so many perfect scores that the competition is now held at a distance of 5 metres rather than 15 feet.

BREATH AND TRIGGER CONTROL

Trigger squeeze and breath control are two very significant aspects of good marksmanship. Trigger control is very important to obtain a good group. The trigger should be squeezed using the first joint of the first finger with a steady pull on the trigger, straight back towards the eye of the shooter. If the trigger is jerked or squeezed quickly, the shot will hit to the right of the bullseye.

Breath control, used in all except the prone position, enables a shooter to maintain more control over the release of the shot. The rule for correct breathing is to take a larger than normal breath, let half the breath out, sight, and squeeze the trigger while holding the remaining breath. With practice this control becomes automatic enabling you to consistently obtain good grouping. (The reason breath control is not used in the prone position is that the expansion of your chest will cause you to rise in your shooting position, creating another variable.)

BASIC POSITIONS
THE PRONE POSITIONS

In competitive shooting there are four basic positions – prone, sitting, kneeling and standing.

The prone position, lying on your belly, is probably the easiest for most shooters to master. In the regular prone position, the body lies at a 45 degree angle to the target. The spine is straight and legs are well spread. Both feet should be as flat to the ground as possible and the left elbow should be well under the gun. The rifle is gripped in a relaxed manner.

An alternate prone position is the bent-leg prone. The body lies at an angle of about 5 to 15 degrees with the line of aim. The spine is straight. The left leg is relaxed, parallel to the spine, with the toe pointed in. The left heel does not touch the ground. The right leg angles away from the spine, knee is bent and the body rolled on the left side. The left elbow is directly under the rifle.

THE SITTING POSITIONS

The two accepted sitting positions are 'open leg' and 'crossed leg'. In the open leg position, the right-hand shooter sits half-face to the right of the line of aim with feet well apart and heels dug in. The back of the shooter is leaned forward and elbows are rested on the inside of the knees.

In the crossed leg position, the body of the right-hand shooter faces 30 degrees to the right of the line of aim with the legs crossed. The outside of each foot rests on the ground and supports the knees. The elbows are placed on or near the knees and form triangles to support the rifle. The left elbow is directly under the rifle.

THE KNEELING POSITIONS

In the 'low kneeling' position, the right-hand shooter reaches a kneeling position by half facing

NRA approved firing positions.
1. **Prone position**
2. **Alternate prone position**
3. **'Open leg' sitting position**
4. **Crossed leg sitting position**
5. **High kneeling position**
6. **Low kneeling position**
7. **Army standing position**
8. **International standing position**

to the right of the line of aim and dropping to the right knee. The left foot is extended as far forward as is comfortable. The right leg is placed flat on the floor or ground. The shooter sits on the right foot which is flat on the ground, rotated inward. The right elbow is free and unsupported. The left knee supports the left elbow.

Some shooters will find it very difficult to sit on their foot and prefer the 'high kneeling' position. In the high kneeling position the right-hand shooter kneels half-face to the right of the line of aim. The shooter may sit on the right heel if necessary, or rest on the right knee which is well under the right arm. The left knee is bent so the lower leg is straight. The left arm is well under the gun and the left elbow rests on the left knee inside and in front of the kneecap.

THE STANDING POSITIONS

In the International Standing Position, the right-hand shooter stands facing to the right of the line of aim. The legs are straight, but the knees are not in a locked position. The left elbow is directly under the gun and the left hip is thrust forward to support the left elbow. The left hand is spread along the forearm of the gun supported by the fingers with the thumb supporting the trigger guard. The weight of the body is shifted to the left foot with the body moving away from the target.

In the Army Standing Position, the right-hand shooter stands half face to the right of the line of aim with feet spread from one to two feet apart. The body is erect and well balanced with the left elbow well under the gun. The forearm of the gun should rest in the palm of the left hand. The gun butt should be held firmly in the shoulder pocket. The right hand should grip the gun at the pistol grip with the thumb wrapped over the top of the grip. The right elbow should be at shoulder height.

These basic positions and techniques, used to train young air gun shooters, are invaluable as they graduate from the non-powder guns and ammunition to other types of gun usage. These are the accepted positions used in the Annual International BB Gun Championship which is now in its 14th year.

COMPETITIONS

BB compeition has become a fast growing sport. After learning the basics of gunmanship, shouldering, and sighting, many young marksmen pursue their new sport by entering the sponsored championship match, with the winning team progressing to the State Jaycee BB Gun Championships. From these matches, the winning teams move into the International Matches to determine the best individual and team shooters in 5 metre BB Gun Competition in the world.

In recognition of the rapid growth of interest in the Daisy training programme, the National Rifle Association of America established an official 5 metre BB gun shooting programme, complete with qualification medals, certificates and brassards for young shooters. In 1976 the NRA took a second step towards recognition of the programme. For the first time in its history, the NRA developed a 5 Metre Air Rifle Rules Book. They also established sanctioned 5 Metre Air Gun Matches to be conducted across the United States by any interested NRA member or affiliated NRA gun club.

The 1976 International BB Gun Championship was the first BB Gun Championship Match sanctioned by the NRA. Participants in that championship were the first to have 5 metre gun records established and recorded by the NRA, which is accepted as being the official record keeper of all shooting events in the United States.

Other programmes for 14- to 18-year-olds include the 10 Metre Precision Pellet Gun Championships, previously sponsored by Daisy, which are now under the tutelage of the National Rifle Association in co-operation with Daisy. This programme gives youngsters who are no longer eligible for BB gun programme a chance to continue their shooting education.

Daisy has recently developed a Running Boar Range which promises to open a new field to air gun training with its motorized 'rubot' which moves a target across a 10 metre area at variable speeds and can be equipped with a knock-down device for bullseye hits.

The first 10 Metre Running Boar National Competition was held in Rogers, Arkansas in 1978 in conjunction with the National Air Gun Match. National competition in this event has spread to the NRA/US Junior Olympic International Air Gun Match which will be an annual event held at the USOC centre in Colorado Springs, Colorado.

The .177 BB and the air gun have come a long way from 'plinking' and with continued research and development, along with avid young shooters like Lori Ann Kam from Hawaii who shot her way to a new world's record with a 100 plus 110 additional perfect bullseyes in prone position in 1978, will continue to be a fine training tool as well as a 'fun gun' for young and old.

Right: A competitor adopts the International standing position at the 10 metre precision pellet gun championships. Below: The Running Boar range can be used for practice at home and can be equipped with a knock-down device for bullseyes.

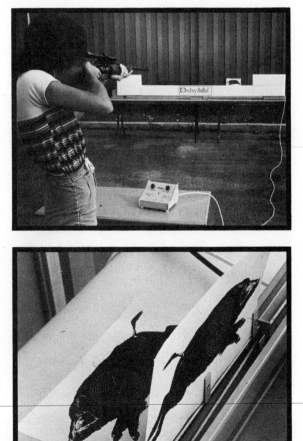

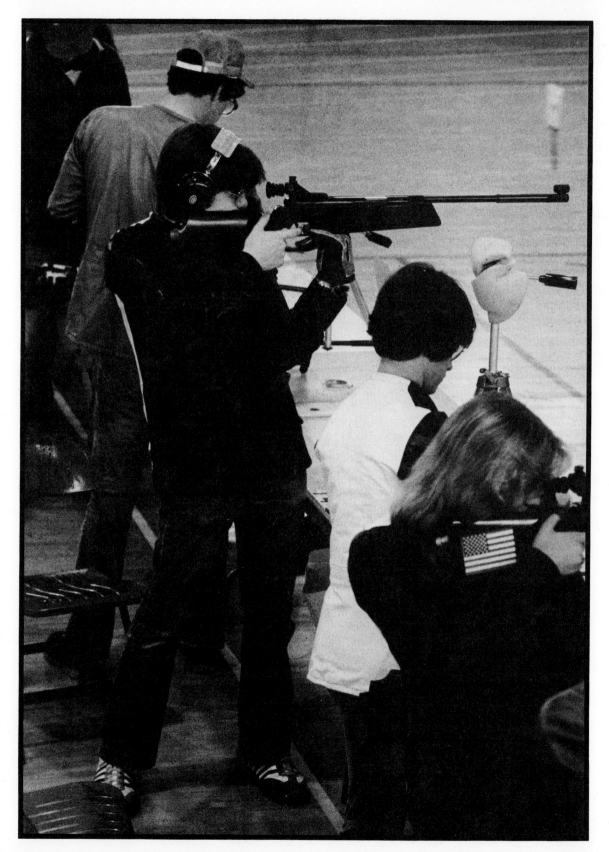

PLINKING

Plinking is a pleasure denied to shooters in many countries, although in the United States and other areas where there are large, open spaces, it enjoys tremendous popularity. Basically, plinking is firing at random targets, moving or stationary. The cost of ammunition tends to restrict it to .22 calibre weapons.

Although scorned by many serious shooters, plinking can be a very enjoyable pastime. The requirements are a reliable .22 weapon, usually a rifle, although it could equally well be a pistol and, of far greater importance, a safe place in which to plink. The backstop should be clear of rocks or large stones or there is a serious risk of the bullet ricochetting. A deep, dry river bed, an old quarry, in fact, anywhere where there is a good, high, solid backstop is recommended. Modern .22 ammunition is often regarded, even by some seasoned shooters, as smallbore and therefore small in terms of danger. In fact, its lethal range can be well in excess of a mile, and its use requires respect and care. Plinking is fun, but it can be dangerous unless care is taken to see that the backstop is of adequate dimensions and that the normal, basic safety rules of shooting are always observed with maximum care. It is essential that no one moves from the set firing positions while anybody is shooting or even handling a loaded weapon.

The targets can be virtually anything except bottles. Glass should be strictly taboo because it shatters, becomes impossible to clear up and is, of course, virtually indestructible, remaining a source of danger for a very long time. Whatever you use for a target, be sure to clear up when you leave. Drink cans would at first seem to be ideal targets, but, in fact, they suffer from one great disadvantage: being extremely light, they will absorb the shock of a .22 bullet passing through them almost without moving, so it is very easy to think that a shot has missed, when, in fact, it may be a dead-centre hit. If possible, the can should be filled with something that will give just a little body weight without too much solidity. Water is a possibility as other materials require the top of the can to be opened up. Clay pigeon targets are ideal in that they have a very satisfying shatter when hit. Empty ammunition boxes are also good. For slightly more elaborate plinking, targets cut from magazines and stuck on card offer an interesting variation.

Moving targets are not difficult to arrange. A can or box can be placed near the top of a slope and some loose earth packed underneath. An accurate shot to hit the ground just in front of the can will move the earth and start the can rolling; with luck, a few more shots will keep it spinning. Another form of moving target can easily be arranged by suspending a can on a piece of adhesive tape or string hung from a convenient branch or makeshift support.

In general it is better not to indulge in aerial shooting, that is, throwing up targets and shooting at them in the air, unless there is a very, very high backstop. A spent bullet travelling through the air can administer quite a nasty shock. It is always better to shoot down towards a target rather than up. However, if you are going to practise aerial plinking, then the safest ammunition is probably the BB cap. This is a small ball, usually .22 calibre, inserted in a very short case that usually contains no more than the primer or sometimes a very small charge. The range is very limited and therefore it is comparatively safe.

Obviously the standard of accuracy and effectiveness required of a good plinking .22 weapon is not the same as that demanded from a top target weapon. It is not worth spending a great deal of money to acquire a good-class weapon if it is to be used solely for plinking. Some of the more popular lever or pump action .22 rifles serve very well and a number of .22 self-loading, semi-automatic rifles are available. Plinking with hand guns obviously is more difficult, but it is also a sport enjoyed by many.

In some areas the legal authority specifies that the weapon may only be used on authorized ranges. Plinking is possible on a range, but obviously it is far less convenient and much more restricted than open-air shooting.

Plinking is an informal and pleasureable way of practising shooting, provided there is sufficient space. The gun is a .303 Enfield service rifle.

14 METALLIC SILHOUETTE RIFLE SHOOTING

In high winds targets may be nailed down. They are given a quick coat of spray paint and all bullet hits count.

FROM LIVE TARGETS TO SILHOUETTES

The sport of shooting at steel silhouettes of birds and animals developed in Mexico around 1950, to replace their hunters' older practice competitions using the live creatures as targets. (If your shot drew blood on a chicken, turkey, goat or sheep, you won it to take home and eat!) As the number of shooters increased and the cost and labour involved in shooting living targets rose, the metal silhouettes replaced them and the sport's popularity grew rapidly. By the 1960s all the northern Mexican towns had clubs; leagues for competition were formed and Americans were crossing the border to compete.

In 1966 the Tucson Rifle Club, of Tucson, Arizona, built the first competition silhouette range in the USA and I organized the first US silhouette match in April, 1969. By 1973 the NRA had recognized the sport and authorized a National Championship Match. Now, after just ten years this shooting sport covers the USA. and reaches further – Canada holds her first National Silhouette Championship in 1979. My first range had twenty silhouettes: the NRA range at Raton, New Mexico now the site of the US National Championships, has two hundred. Silhouette shooting now involves more people than does the established high-power target shooting game, with an estimated three thousand matches being held in 1979.

Metallic silhouette shooting is rapidly becoming the most popular shooting sport in the United States, not only in the main game, the high-power rifle, but in the offshoots such as .22 rifle, the hunter pistol, or short-range pistol, the long-range handgun and newest, the air rifle.

Metallic silhouette shooting is really the old shooting-gallery fun vastly enlarged and elaborated. The targets are visible to all. A hit registeres a 'clang' as the silhouette falls from its stand. This is really the only spectator shooting sport: the result of each shot fired can be seen with the naked eye by shooter, scorer and spectator.

A typical silhouette range in rough terrain, simulating the distances and conditions of actual hunting.

COURSES, TARGETS AND GUNS

Silhouette shooting is a difficult sport, based on the hunting concept that nothing easy is to be expected and that only hits count. All shooting is done from a standing position. Normal clothing for the weather is allowed, but no padded clothing, slings or artificial supports. A heavy jacket might be worn in cold weather, but would not be allowed in warm weather. The time limit is $2\frac{1}{2}$ minutes for five shots, one at each of five metallic silhouettes in a bank, or line, to be fired at in sequence, left to right. A hit out of sequence is a double miss . . . fired at wrong target, and then that target is gone when its turn comes. The silhouettes used are of chicken, javelina (the peccary, or small wild pig of Mexico and the southwestern USA) turkey, and ram, or sheep. This latter is a silhouette of the wild bighorn sheep with high and heavy curling horns.

With a high-power rifle (over 6mm calibre) the sizes of the silhouettes are: chicken, 13 inches long, fired at from a distance of 200 metres; the Javelina, or pig, 22 inches long, used at 300 metres; the turkey, 23 inches high and 19 inches long beak to tail, used at 385 metres; and the ram, 32 inches long, 27 inches high at the horns, shot at

500 metres. Rams and turkeys are made of $\frac{3}{8}$ inch steel alloys, and the shorter-range silhouettes of $\frac{1}{2}$ inch steel. Ranges are of the echelon type, with one firing line and target banks at their specified distances down range. 'Down range' may not always be the correct term – silhouette ranges may be laid out in almost any terrain, sheep can be high on the side of a mountain, other silhouette banks may be on the side of a hill or down a valley.

The same full-scale target silhouettes are used for the long-range handgun shooting, in which heavy calibre and high-powered handguns – revolvers, pistols and single-shot arms are used at 200 metres on sheep, and correspondingly shorter ranges for the other silhouettes, although lighter steels may be used.

The .22 rifle silhouettes are $\frac{1}{5}$ scale, and are used at 100 metres or 100 yards for sheep, shorter for others. They are made of $\frac{1}{4}$ inch steel for close ranges, $\frac{3}{16}$ inch for longer ranges for turkey and sheep. The short-range pistol, also fired at a maximum of 100 yards or metres, uses $\frac{1}{2}$-scale silhouettes. The air rifle uses $\frac{1}{10}$ scale; the maximum range for sheep is 50 metres, and shortest, for chicken, 20 metres. Yes, 50 metres, outdoors, for air rifles! Silhouette shooting is not meant to be easy. Only the best British and German air rifles are used although not the ultra-heavy elaborate international competition types.

Squads for the ordinary club or small league matches are made up on entry by lot. The match secretary puts the competitor number and relay on scorecards, places them face down on a table and mixes them up. Each competitor picks out one, fills in his name and class, and is then recorded on the entry list and scoreboard. Thus he may fire on any of the relays, and begin the match at any distance. Should he draw number 1, he would begin on chickens, and each time his relay was called to fire, would move up one, and finish on the rams. . . . Should he draw number 3, he would start on turkey, next fire on rams, then move down to short-range and would finish the day on pigs. Matches are seldom won until the last round is fired, which maintains interest. No sighting shots are allowed after a match commences, though informal and un-squadded practice is allowed before matches until the starting time, usually 10 am. Precise and reliable adjustments are needed on the telescopic sights used by nearly all shooters. The impact of this shooting sport is attested to by the fact that the top scope manufacturers have made great efforts to engineer sights primarily for the game, and some of these now rival the finest target equipment in all respects. Several US arms makers also now make rifles specifically suited to silhouette shooting and meeting NRA rules as to stocks and weight, etc.

All hits count the same, so when two or more competitors finish with tied winning scores they have a shoot-off to determine the winning and second places. Each fires one shot at the ram, if all hit or none hit, they move down to the turkey and each fires again, to repeat on down, and perhaps even start over again on rams, until the tie is broken. As all ties in all classes are shot off, several shooters may be on line, and spectator interest becomes very great, as everyone can see if a silhouette falls when a shot is fired. Since the rifle sight must be adjusted for each shot, the reliability of the adjustments becomes very evident.

HITS AND MISSES

This is a very challenging sport indeed. No one ever hits all his silhouettes in a match. . . . 50 percent of hits will win most club shoots! A miss does not carry the crushing defeat it can in other forms of rifle or pistol competition. For example: in the early 1970s I was in Mexico, shooting a season-end or other special shoot in which not only the normal match awards were provided, but also trophies for most individual silhouettes, and a club team match. I began on the javelina, shot over, under, before and behind . . . I missed all ten pigs, considered the easiest of all the silhouettes. At the end of the day, I had won the trophy for the most chickens hit, tied for and lost on the fourth shot in a shoot-off for the high turkey trophy, finished second in the overall match, and was high man on the winning team. I started the day with ten misses and took home three trophies!

In the US national championship I recently witnessed, the weather came up in the final rounds a bit. A champion competitor, very possibly the best all-round rifle shot in the world, including the international free rifle, won the match, hitting four of his ten rams in the final ten shots. The oldest man competing, 78 years old, hit four of his ten rams also.

Metallic silhouette shooting has a lure: no matter how you shoot, you are absolutely positive that if you can try again you will do far better. This habit-forming shooting game does not require the expensive specialized equipment demanded by most other forms of rifle competition. An accurate hunting-type rifle, comfortable to shoot standing, with reliable sights, telescopic or metallic (if the silhouettes are kept painted black or white or orange, to contrast with the backstop, metallic sights can be effective), enough ammunition for a match plus a few rounds for practice; this is enough to get into the sport. Ranges usually have two or three shooting tables or bench-rests to aid in sighting-in and testing loads. 'Gongs' – small sheets of steel – are placed with each bank of silhouettes for practice, and when kept painted, allow very excellent group-shooting for testing, the bullet-splashes being visible through any sort of spotting scope.

The competitor may have a coach during matches, as a hunter may have a guide. The coach stands close to his man so that he may be heard (he may not touch the shooter or his equipment during the firing time). He calls out or indicates with his hands where the bullets are hitting, high, low, between legs, etc. Using scope or binoculars very little practice is required to learn to see almost exactly where the bullets are going, by dust or impact on the earth backstop behind the silhouette. The coach can watch time, slow down a rusher, speed up a slow shooter.

While metallic silhouette shooting has become a rather stylized shooting sport in the past few years, with fine equipment and custom rifles the rule rather than the exception, the primary concept should remain true to field shooting. Rifles are quite heavy, weighing 10 pounds 2 ounces for either high-power or .22, with an extra $7\frac{1}{2}$ pound class in .22. This weight is due to the fact that when Mexican shooters first set up the rules, the only rifles made were well over 8 pounds in weight: add a scope and mount, and you end up with a rifle well over 10 pounds. Now, mostly light-weight rifles are made and a man shooting one is handicapped as the older and heavier rifle holds better standing . . . so, we put heavier barrels on the present-day featherweight sporters.

Normal safe range procedures are followed – rifles are kept in racks with bolts open when not in use, the bolt may not be closed until the rifle is on line and the loading command received. There is less formality than with conventional shooting. A relay is called to the line, the range officer looks up and down, decides that all are present and have scorers (usually the following relay, which ensures that they will be ready on line next) and calls 'ready' at which the shooters may pick up their rifles from the stands, dry-fire, load, aim. Fifteen seconds or so later, the range officer says 'fire', and time and shooting begin. At $2\frac{1}{2}$ minutes, the cease-fire is called or signalled. At the cease-fire command all rifles are laid on the stands and the competitors step back to check their score. The scorer has marked an X for each hit, an O for each miss. The remaining silhouettes down the range testify to the score. The target-setters are now called from their safe-houses and set up the fallen silhouettes then return to safety, at the side or behind a berm or backstop. The ready, fire and cease-fire are now in order for the second series of five shots, after which the relay retires from the line. Under no circumstances may a competitor touch his rifle while the target-setters are exposed. Shots fired after the 'ready' command and before 'fire' are misses and the rifle may be checked: a too-light trigger setting must be adjusted or a substitute rifle used to complete the match. The only trigger rule is that it be safe from accidental discharge. Except for this or any other malfunction, the same rifle must be used throughout the match.

A target setter puts rams back on the stands at the end of a relay. Targets must be knocked off the stand to score a point.

RANGES FOR SILHOUETTE SHOOTING

Range construction is not as difficult or expensive as for conventional target shooting. If a sufficiently large piece of land can be found, where bullet fall-out is allowable, a range can be laid out and in use within a short time. Requirements are flexible – firing can be in any direction, ranges can cross each other, distances can be a few metres short or long, pasture or woodland can continue services with the range existing in them, and members' ingenuity can do a great deal. Club members usually do 90 percent of the work themselves, having to hire a bulldozer or earth-moving equipment to make the firing line, throw up backstops behind the silhouette stand lines, perhaps make a safety berm or dig a drainage ditch. A welder is needed to cut the silhouettes out of steel plate and construct the stands.

The best material for the silhouette stands has been found to be used grader blades, the bar of tough alloy steel used to make the edge of road-grader blades. They are approximately 1 inch thick, 4 inches wide, and 7 or 8 feet long. Normally they can be bought at low cost from salvage yards. For smallbore stands, a long grader blade supported by angle-iron posts (V-edge forward) serves to hold five silhouettes at a time. The blades are cut to length for the stands, a short piece is cut off and welded to the top for each silhouette to stand on and the bottom set in cement in the ground. The NRA produces a booklet, the Silhouette Handbook, containing instructions on range-building, steels, rules for rifles, and templates for silhouettes. We do not really know how many clubs have built ranges, but estimate around 200. Firing points are at least 6 feet apart, each with a stand, a wood box on a pipe or post, notched to hold a rifle in a horizontal position, muzzle down-range, and usually with five holes drilled in it to act as a bullet block.

A feature of the silhouette range which makes it different from other ranges is the ramada, the roofed area behind the firing line. This can be extended over the line in rainy climates, of course. Under the ramada are benches for spectators and shooters, rifle racks, officials' tables, a large score-board or anything desired. Scores are posted after each 10-shot stage, so all may keep up with the match progress. At the end of the match, only three or four minutes are required to determine the winners and to rank award-winners. As an hour or more may intervene between a shooter's relays firing, there is ample time for visiting, eating or resting. Each relay fires only one stage at a time, and therefore goes on the line four times.

There are ranges limited to short distances, some are only 200 yards. They make reduced-size silhouettes, and do all firing at the 200 yard range. It is recommended that high-power rifles should not be used at shorter ranges because of the damage to silhouettes and the possible back-spatter should a bullet hit a steel stand squarely. Which brings us to the question invariably asked by those first hearing of silhouette shooting: 'Don't you have dangerous ricochets?' The answer is no. Ricochets almost never happen, even on rocky soil; as nearly all strike in the backstop area, or stop there. A bullet hitting a silhouette transmits practically all its energy to the steel target and falls, a misshapen fraction of its weight, to the ground. Incidentaly, a silhouette knocked down by a ricochet is a legal hit, providing it is hit in sequence.

CLASSES AND AWARDS

One of the best aspects of silhouette competition is that anyone who cares to can compete . . . men with weak hearts who cannot stand the exertion of hunting, old and young, handicapped persons who are allowed to rest one elbow on the arm of a wheelchair, amputees who rest a leg-stump on a folding chair to shoot standing. One quite competent shooter is paralyzed in all but his left arm due to a war wound. In the wheelchair, he holds his rifle with a rack around his neck, and can manipulate the bolt, load and fire with the left hand . . . and he hits a good many silhouettes.

Another advantage is that a person can enjoy silhouette shooting just by himself, alone on the range if need be. He can get immense satisfaction outwitting a wind on a bad day or running three or four straight on a good calm one, in testing a

Shooters setting up a range. Here, old railway sleepers are being used as stands for the silhouettes.

rifle or ammunition, trying sights, or perhaps different rifles. Though the smaller calibres are allowable, and effective at short ranges, the lightest cartridge effective over the full 500 metres is the 7 × 57 mm Mauser, or equivalent. In the US and Mexico the most common cartridge is the 7.62mm NATO, commercially, the .308 Winchester, with 165 gr. or heavier bullets.

The original course of fire was 20 rounds, five at each distance, followed by jackpot shoots – whoever wanted in, would throw a dollar in the pot, and shoot for it, each man firing one shot at each designated silhouette in order – sheep, turkey, pig and chicken. The man with the most hits took the money and tried to organize another round. However, Americans wanted more shooting and the 40-shot match became standard. From the original two-class system, A and B, the increasing number of competitors brought about the present classification system, based on individual averages in two or more fired 40-shot matches . . . 0 to 10 is Class B; 11 to 16 is A, 17 to 22 is AA and 23 and over is AAA. Awards are made in all four classes at matches, so a competitor shoots against those of his own degree of skill.

Clubs are free to make special categories and awards. A popular one is for metallic-sighted rifles only, and competitors may enter in both open and metallic sights, paying two entry fees

and using two rifles. Classes can be set up for rifles under a specific weight, or for military rifles only, etc. The name of the game is sport without harassing rules. Club and range officials may compete, everyone can shoot. For government, a jury of three competitors of good judgement is chosen by the sponsoring club, to decide on any matter of controversy.

Metallic silhouette shooting must not be considered a rival to conventional competition, but rather a welcome addition to the shooting sports. It has not and does not take competitors from the regular target game. Many shooters fire both. It attracts the vast number of hunters and informal sports-shooters who find that formal target shooting is unable to hold their interest. The spectator appeal, the instant knowledge of hit or miss, the sustained interest of a match not being won until the final shots are fired, the fact that scoring is absolutely without error, the comparatively low-cost equipment – all combine to make this a popular sport wherever it is introduced.

15 BENCH-REST RIFLE SHOOTING

A Heavy Varmint rifle, weight $13\frac{1}{2}$ pounds, during a competition.

SPORT, GAME OR SCIENCE

Bench-rest shooting is the one rifle sport that is not based on military shooting. It is a wonderful, in fact the best, way to introduce a young or new shooter to the pastime. Sight picture, good holding, trigger release, judging conditions – all the important basic requirements for good shooting are clearly seen and recognized.

When one gets too old to 'belly' shoot, or finds it physically difficult to participate in the common shooting sports, one can find solace and a real challenge in the bench-rest game.

Bench-rest shoots are family affairs. Youngsters do well, they tend to have no nerves, good eyes, indifference – all result in good shooting. Mothers and fathers compete, often with the lady of the house exhibiting unusual skill. And grandparents – grandfathers especially – have a good opportunity to instruct and display their knowledge and experience while coaching the youngsters. At bench-rest shoots one sees ten-year-olds, 30-year-olds, and 70-year-olds vying with each other for a medal or a cup.

DEVELOPMENTS

Over the years I have read much about shooting. Interspersed have been short accounts of bench or rest shooting. If memory serves me correctly there was a period in the 1840s to 1850s when it was a popular pastime, using heavy massive guns. Then it more or less died out until the 1890s and early 1900s, when the activity was revitalized, and then died out again prior to World War I.

Present-day rest shooting started in the late 1940s and early 1950s, grew relatively rapidly, and appears to have been fairly static in its development in the past few years. Each period has had similar characteristcs and similar results. For example, in the mid-nineteenth century there were several outstanding gunsmiths and barrel-makers, foremost of whom was Morgan James. There was also an important change in the theory of shape, form and size of bullets, as well as the procedure for forming the new type of bullet.

Not as important perhaps, but important, was the development of better sighting equipment, namely scope sights. In the 1890s and early 1900s Harry Pope, Peterson, Zishang, Schoyen and others proceeded to make rifle barrels that were better than those available in earlier years. Pope also developed a new type and form of bullet to go with his barrels.

So, standards of accuracy in bench-rest shooting went from several inches prior to 1840, to three inches in mid-century, to one inch in 1900, and stayed there until the early 1950s. The revival of the sport at that time led to similar improvements. Clyde Hart, the Harry Pope of modern times, a mason by trade, was not satisfied with the barrels available. He was convinced that better barrels could be made. To make a long story short, he proceeded to develop barrels using modern techniques that established whole new standards of accuracy.

At the same time a shooter from Iceland, an engineer named Jonas Halgrimson, presented the 'expanding up' principle of bullet-making to the shooting world. All of the custom bullet-makers began to use this system. And of course Roy Biehler and Walt Astles made their beautiful sets of dies. These bullet dies with Clyde Hart's barrels, brought the present standards of accuracy to less than a $\frac{1}{4}$ inch.

THE GUNS

Anyone can shoot bench-style with any rifle and develop an impression of the efficiency of that particular firearm. However, if one choses to compete in bench-rest matches, then there are specific rules and gun classifications that one must know and follow.

First comes the bench-rest rifle. This is the unlimited gun. I've seen some that were so heavy it required two men to put them in and on the rests. There are really only two things required here – first, an 18 inch barrel (or longer), and a safely operated firing mechanism. This is the wide open class, home of the 'rail guns', home of the 'return to battery' guns, home of the experimenter.

Theoretically, one would expect to shoot the smallest groups in this class – heavy action, heavy barrel, heavy stock, precision rests front and rear, big high power scopes, no restrictions on bedding methods. It doesn't necessarily work that way.

In the early 1950s the game went in this direction, namely heavy gun, ten shot groups, with wildcat cartridges prevailing: Manciente 'Blue Streak', the Donaldson series (.219 Don. Wasp) for example. Everyone played with their favourite cartridge: recoil, tongue, bullets, old wives' tales, all combined to direct the experimenters towards a small diameter bullet, chiefly the .22 driven at what seemed the ideal 3,000 feet per second.

Fred Huntington made bullet-making dies, and they, although slow, made excellent bullets. The jackets were made from .22 rimfire cases. Then came the man from Iceland, Jonas Halgrimson, with his 'expanding up' principle of bullet-making. This idea was adopted by Roy Beihler and Walt Astles, and the result was the famous B&A dies. Still treasured by those who own them, and combined with modern jackets they produce bullets that are close to ideal.

The big unlimited rifle had its day. An internal fight over mechanical rests versus sandbags, combined with shooting for money, led to a lack of real interest and support. The shooters turned their attention to the lighter guns, particularly the Heavy Varmint IB half pound gun. This is by far the class with the largest number of competitors.

Basically this class is limited to 13½ pounds with fairly conventional stock, three inches or less wide at fore-end, barrel 18 inches or longer. The action may be sleeved and usually is, although many now glue the barrelled action to the stock with epoxy.

The calibres commonly used are .22, 6mm and .308. Cases vary, but most common still is the Remington .222; some are using and winning with the PPC .22, or 6mm using the small primer and Russian case. The latest entry is the Remington BR in 6mm, plagued with case trouble, but one can use the small or large primer. The PPC and Remington BR are very similar in size and shape to the old .219 Donaldson Wasp. The 6 × 47 is a very popular 6mm and is a consistent performer. Some were of the opinion that the PPC was a better cartridge until Gary Anderson of Olympic fame visited the IBS International Championship matches in 1978 and set a new record that should stand for years in his first bench match, using a borrowed 6 × 47.

But, such is bench-rest shooting – the old saying that 'every dog has his day' seems to apply fairly often. The Light Varmint Rifle is another class, and can weigh 10½ pounds inclusive of sights. Otherwise it must meet the requirements of the Heavy Varmint Rifle.

Then there is the Sporter Rifle class that differs from the Light Varmint only in that it must be of a calibre not less than .23 – in other words, it is usually a 6mm or .308. A shooter can use the Sporter Rifle in the Light Varmint class, but not vice-versa, and many do, thus saving the cost of a rifle and still being able to compete without handicapping themselves.

THE COMPETITION PROGRAMME

The rifles mentioned are shot for group size. Namely, the spread of five shots centre to centre in a match. Occasionally some shoots (not registered) are shot for score with these guns. The tournament consists of five 5-shot matches at a hundred yards, and five 5-shot matches at two hundred yards. Both are usually preceded by a warm-up match.

Most shoots involve more than one rifle and the 'top gun' is the one whose aggregates for the two or three guns involved is smallest. I might note that the Heavy Bench gun is commonly a 10-shot group with the two matches resulting in the aggregate winner.

Except for the Heavy gun, where rest rules allow for unrestricted and guiding means and adjustments, both front and rear, matches are shot using soft sandbags both front and rear. There are time limits involved, 12 minutes for 10-shot groups, seven minutes for 5-shot groups.

One other phase of bench shooting that was designed to introduce new shooters to the game is called the Hunting Rifle competition. Theoretically, by using a conventional rifle, or one that might be customized within certain limits, and with a scope of 6-power or less, and 10 pounds maximum weight plus a classification system, the non-competitive handloader, deer-hunter type could be induced to shoot regular bench-rest matches.

This is the second attempt to develop a programme with this goal. The first time was when there was one bench-rest organization, the

National Bench-Rest Shooters Association. Bench-rest shooters have a tendency to see ways to evade or find loopholes in rules, no matter how carefully written. So over a period of time this first attempt resulted in what is now called the Sporter Rifle Class, as used in NBRSA and IBS (International Bench-rest Shooters) competitions.

The Hunter Class, the second attempt to lure new shooters, is gradually following the course of the Sporter Rifle. In the meantime, this class is being shot and is very popular in some areas. It has in fact brought new participants into the sport and so has helped in the slow growth of bench shooting. This class does not shoot for groups, but uses a six-bull target, one sighter and five for score, and a total of 50 possible points per match, with 250 points or five targets as the potential in a tournament.

GADGETS, IDEAS AND THEORIES

A real part of the pleasure of bench-rest shooting is the gathering of gadgets, ideas and theories, each one of which the user feels increases the performance of his gun or guns. In the days of Pope *et al* bullets were shot in order of casting, one case was used and marked so that it was inserted in the chamber in the same position each time, primers were weighed and placed so the anvil was in the same position each shot, bullets were seated at a precise depth. In other words, these procedures were directed at repeating each shot exactly like its preceding shots.

The same theories are applied in the modern game. Time has not changed the train of thought that leads one to apply similar ideas. Knowledge and logic steer development towards the ultra-precise. So, in the modern pastime shooters weigh bullets, and 'mike' bullets for diameter size and length. The industrious spin their bullets and cartridges for concentricity. Many turn the necks of cases on lathe jigs or small hand-turned trimmers. We know that the neck of the case is extremely important, and that most factory cases vary in neck thickness, and that outside turning (not inside neck reaming) is essential. Careful experimenters ream the primer flash holes and trim any rough edges on the inside of the casehole, fire form and trim to length and then proceed to weigh and sort the cases in an attempt to eliminate any and all variations.

Most use straight-line bullet seaters rather than the common seating die used in presses. There are any number of theories in bullet seating, commonly one seats the .30 calibres to seat into the lands, and .6mm's either just clear or just touching the lands, and .22's clear the lands, in other words 'jump' before they encounter the lands. I think that one needs to experiment a bit, trying various seating depths for each gun, and selecting whatever works best. Over a period of time the throat will wear, so seating the bullet out a bit will improve the shooting of the gun as wear occurs.

Most shooters neck-size (about $\frac{1}{8}$ inch) the case only, and constrict the neck so the bullet is held with very light pressure. Some extremists even seat the bullet with their fingers, but generally light pressure is the rule. One should avoid overworking the brass, it shortens the life of the case.

Primers are seated by feel by most shooters, although some use gauges or priming devices so that each primer is set to a precise depth. Very few seat primers with reloading presses. Primers seem to vary considerably from year to year and so the best way to stay up to date is to read match reports in *Precision Shooting* magazine.

All newcomers to the bench game seem to fall into the trap of weighing powder to the grain. If you visit the major matches and observe the experienced shooters you will notice that almost all use commercial measuring dispensers. Some of these have been customized. Many have not. All the popular makes are to be found on the loading benches.

In fact since most shooters load at the matches and will vary the powder according to weather conditions or what is happening at the target, a powder throwing device is essential. A systematic routine operation every time is the important factor, and will give loads that are basically the same with the same dial settings.

A few years back I saved novocaine capsules from my medical practice by the ton, so to speak, for all my friends. They would clean them and use them to store carefully weighed charges, that could be emptied into the case at the match. Some even attempted to control temperature and moisture levels when they weighed and filled the

Using conventional dies and press for reloading ammunition for bench-rest shooting.

capsules. One sees this at the matches occasionally still, but not among the older, more experienced shooters.

When seating a bulleted case to determine seating depth – be careful – use a dummy case without powder or primers. There are several methods in use. One can seat the bullet in the die, then remove and hold the bullet in the flame of a match until it is black with carbon, then chamber the cartridge in the gun with the bolt. Remove and look for the small marks of the lands. In the common press one turn is equal to $\frac{1}{4}$ inch, so, turn the necessary amount to clear, just touch, or to seat into the lands as you wish. Cleaning the bullet with fine steel wool will also work used the same way. Bullets vary, the ogive is not always the same even with commercial makes, so if you change bullets re-check your seating depth.

GUNS PAST AND PRESENT

As I sit and look around my shop I can see a history of the bench-rest stock changes that have occured over the years. In the early 1950s when most of the bench guns were based on Mauser-type actions I can see that full length, action and barrel bedding was the standard. It really was a

lot of fun and a real challenge to work with a small half-round chisel and to check every inch in an attempt to get perfect bedding. Very few could do it well; however, there was the occasional exception like John Warren, the master gunsmith, whose work is still outstanding. I have a heavy bench gun built on a Weber action that is a very large version of the classic stock, perfectly proportioned, full length bedded, and a mate to that gun in the 13 pound (now $13\frac{1}{2}$ pound) Heavy Varmint class full length bedded also. Both guns held range records. Both guns have skeletonized, hand-filed butts, pistol grips, and trigger guards and even though some 'experts' say mahogany can not be checkered, Warren did on both guns. And both guns shot very well for their time, and established range records. I might say the varmint gun is built on a Sako action with the magazine cut filled in with a metal, an early attempt to strengthen the action. These guns deserve a place in a museum.

But even predating this pair are a variety of firearms, customized to improve accuracy. There are Remington Heburns with relined barrels in .22–3,000 calibres by Gebby. There are Manciente Blue Streaks on Winchester HiWalls as well as on Model 70s built by Morgan Cail in .219 Wasps. There is a heavy bench gun with a Charles Hart action – Charles Hart made a few actions, he being the father of Clyde and Robert Hart.

Then I can see the first gun Clyde Hart built for me, a heavy bench gun using a .722 Remington Action. Like all Clyde Hart guns it shot extremely well, and won many matches for me. Then there is a gun built by Clyde Hart using his brother Bob's heavy action that was top gun in the Nationals using sandbags. And, of course, I see the guns I am using today, Remington actions epoxied into Clyde Hart's aluminium sleeves, some are in laminated Clyde Hart walnut locks some in fibreglass stocks, finished to match the colour of the cars I was driving when they were made.

With all these various guns dating from 1840 to the present, an important factor is in the bedding changes that occured with the modifications in the actions.

The bedding of each gun shows the variety of theories developed with each change of gun action. I look at a Morgan James rifle built in 1844. This gun established records. It was shot from a solid front rest attached to the front end of the barrel. Bedding was of no concern here. Then I look at some of my Popes. Some shot within a similar front rest, some shot from a Pope rest, that held the whole gun, some shot from sandbags. The interesting thing is that all of the above guns, when shot on modern rests, shoot best when resting on the barrel rather than the wood or end, when present. The bedding is excellent, but attached to the barrel by screws that affect the barrel vibrations and interfere with accuracy. Well, we have gone from the days when the bedding was checked and corrected the night before a match, and I remember fellows taking guns apart and scraping the bed in the middle of the tournament.

Then 'free floating' barrels became the thing, now it is fairly standard even with hunting rifles. That is, the action and an inch or two of the rear of the barrel fit against the stockwood, the remainder of the barrel does not strike or bear against the stock. This procedure is being used even with the fibreglass stocks. In other words the barrel vibrations are free and not reduced by the stock fore-end.

Of course, the sleeving of actions has solved many problems. Number one, it presents a long (12 inch) round surface to seat against the stock material, be it wood or an epoxy. Number two, it holds both of the scope blocks, thus the block that was on the barrel and susceptible to barrel changes when it heated up with shooting is no longer a problem. It might be of interest to note that the sleeve was invented and patented by a shooter named Owen Bellows, sometime before its value was the accepted thing. I think that if he had been a better mechanic the sleeve would have been used more often and sooner.

The latest system is to glue a short section of the barrel, six inches or less, to the stock with an epoxy resin; thus both the barrel and the action are left free to 'float', that is, neither contact the stock, but rather hang out in the air.

The question now is which is better, the sleeve or the glue job? The sleeve as made by Clyde and Jerry Hart works very well. It is an aluminium tube with cut-outs for loading, the bolt handle and triggers. Onto it goes the action surrounded by epoxy. When it is barrelled the barrel is screwed into the action and does not touch the sleeve. Some gunsmiths have used a sleeve with a flat bottom and parallel vertical sides, but most use the round bottom version and this seems to

be the system accepted and used by most of the shooters. Bedding is quite simple and easy to maintain. It you are building a heavy gun where weight is no problem or even an advantage, a steel rather than an aluminium sleeve is commonly used.

Whether the glue system is better is very debatable. Both systems are used by top shooters, so it is pretty much 'you take your choice'. The gluing is really of the barrel to the stock. Just in front of the recoil lug the stock is gouged out for about six inches then the area is filled with the epoxy and the barrelled action is set in position and allowed to harden. They are difficult to break apart. One can heat up the barrel to 350°F and then a sharp blow with a lead hammer will usually separate the barrel without harm resulting from the heating or the blow, or one can place the whole gun in a deep freeze for a couple of days and then the sharp blow with the lead hammer will result in a separation. Unless the shooter anticipates, and prepares holes in the stock so that the pins that hold the trigger mechanism can be driven out, he is in trouble if he encounters trigger problems.

Since most bench-rest shooters use the 2 ounce trigger built by Remington or Hart, or the new Canjar 'soft pull', trouble can be expected and the need for trigger removal anticipated. So when glue jobs are used, proper preparation of the stock to meet this problem eliminates the headache.

Good gunsmiths can make quarter minute rifles, keeping them cooking requires some knowledge and care. Making them perform to their peak requires good loads, careful holding and reading conditions. Not all groups are small ones, but it's the lack of really bad shots that make for good aggregates, and that is what counts when you enter a tournament.

TRIGGERS AND SCOPES

I have mentioned triggers briefly. From a practical point of view it is essential that one uses either one of the 2 ounce triggers made by Remington or Hart–(it is the same trigger) or the latest 'soft pull' by Canjar. This was designed for international shooting but bench-rest shooters are finding it a fine instrument for their guns. To shoot well a good trigger is extremely important.

As for scopes, there are many good makes, with a lot of variation even in the same make and type. Although there are excellent scopes available today, one of the principle trouble areas in bench-rest shooting is the scope, and it pays to be suspicious of scopes and the mounting system at all times. The wise man will compare one against the other and try to select the brightest one with best resolution. There is a marked difference in scope weights; so often in order to meet the required weight of gun for a particular class this becomes important. The most popular are those with 'Unertl' type mounts in use.

Powers vary from 16 to 36-power, but most shooters seem to settle in with 20 to 25-power. The really high powers are a problem when mirage is present. I have seen days when the target will actually disappear when using a 36-power scope – disconcerting to say the least!

Commonly most shooters will put the mounts on the gun and then using a metal or wooden dowel of the correct size and some grinding compound make sure they are in line. It is surprising to find

mounts so out of line that they will bend a scope when tightened up. Here again weight is a consideration. Often one can gain an ounce or more by selection of a particular mount, and believe me, those ounces are important at weigh-in time at a tournament.

BULLETS AND BARRELS

The fodder one uses in bench-rest shooting, namely the bullet, is available from a variety of sources. There are several commercially-made bullets that meet bench-rest standards, and if one wishes there are a few individuals making bullets by hand who sell them.

If you want to get into bullet-making yourself there are one or two sources for the necessary dies that are of top quality. Occasionally there are ads

Rifles must be cleaned after each relay which will normally be between 7 and 15 rounds.

in *Precision Shooting* magazine for Biehler and Astles dies for sale. This is an interesting pastime that makes for a pleasant evening's work during the winter months.

Although there are a few barrel-makers turning out quality tubes that are for the most part competitive, there is one name that has always appeared when considering barrels and that is Clyde Hart.

Clyde and his son Jerry Hart are the major barrel suppliers to the game. Clyde Hart is really a legend in his own time. Without him bench-rest shooting would not have achieved its present-day standards. The standards he set for himself way back in the 1950s were perfection, and he has maintained those standards through the years. He and Jerry try to make each barrel better than the previous one. They are 'professionals' in the true sense of the word.

They should not be confused with Robert Hart now deceased, Clyde's late brother, and his son Wally, in the business of gunsmithing. Robert and Wally produced gun actions that are excellent pieces of work, rests and other items related to the game. But the famous Hart barrels are made only by Clyde and Jerry Hart.

Clyde, dissatisfied with barrels available in 1950s, decided to make a better one for himself, and in 1951 made his first. If you ask him when he started he will say 'now let's see I cut off my fingers in 1951 – so that was the year.' He has routinely used stainless steel to make bench barrels, except for one batch of about a hundred barrels made of tool steel, so that they could be glued.

There are many old wives' tales about gun barrels. The one I hear most often is that a lapped barrel will wear out faster than one not lapped. Nothing could be further from the truth. Target barrels do not wear out, they burn out. The life of a barrel is related to the nitriding of steel from the heat generated by the firing of the cartridge. And this in turn relates to the load. Generally the so called 'hot loads', will speed up the nitriding of the barrel and thus shorten its accurate life. As a matter of fact every target barrel-maker with whom I have talked laps his barrels.

Design for the patch and armband worn by members of the National Bench-Rest Shooters Association.

THE FUTURE

What has modern bench-rest shooting accomplished over the years, has it affected the shooting game, has it changed the standards of accuracy, has it forced manufacturers to improve their products, has it resulted in new cartridges?

The answer is 'yes' to every question. Certainly, it has changed the shooting game in many ways, big-bore shooters, international shooters, Olympic shooters, smallbore shooters, all have adapted many of the ideas commonly used in bench shooting to improve their guns and scores.

Certainly bench-rest shooting has changed the standards of accuracy. It has reduced the standard from 1 inch to less than $\frac{1}{4}$ inch. It is not uncommon to see groups that measure centre to centre less than $\frac{1}{10}$ of an inch. Think about it!

Bench-rest shooting has certainly resulted in new cartridges. The development of the .308, .243, .244, 6mm, .22-250, .222, .17 just to name a few were all affected by the game.

Manufacturers have also adopted bench-rest practices to improve their products – and they have improved not only the gun but the ammunition, bullets, primers, powders and scopes as well.

Where do we go from here? Who knows? The results in the latest matches show that improvement can still occur. It still is a sport and depends finally on the man or woman behind the gun.

16 AIR WEAPON SHOOTING

THE GROWTH OF THE SPORT

Air weapon shooting is a branch of the sport that has advanced by leaps and bounds during the last decade. This form of organized shooting can look back on a long history; the first Air Gun Association was formed in Britain as early as 1903. The airgun had previously been regarded as being no more than an auxiliary to the shooting sport, a useful way for youngsters to learn the rudiments of the game, or at most, an improved form of 'dry practice'.

The advent of recoilless air weapons dramatically changed all that. Suddenly there was a range of air rifles and air pistols that were capable of performing as accurately and consistently as the best smallbore weapons. The 'toy' image of the airgun vanished overnight, and top marksmen became interested in this form of shooting. The effect was particularly great in the field of pistol shooting, where the lack of accurate and manageable air pistols had been the major cause of stagnation and disinterest.

In 1961 Sweden organized the first Air Rifle International Postal Match, for which the International Shooting Union (UIT) drafted preliminary rules. The range was 10 metres and the targets had a 2 millimetre bull (now 1 millimetre).

Largely due to German initiative (there were some 12000 air rifle clubs in West Germany at that time), air rifle shooting was introduced at the 39th World Championships at Wiesbaden in 1966, the rules being the same as those for the International Postal Match. There were by then some very accurate air weapons being produced, with technical innovations such as the fixed barrel and side-lever cocking, and the results achieved were encouraging. There were eighty entrants for the men's event and eighteen teams. The first world champion was Gerd Kummet of West Germany and the team gold medal went to Switzerland.

The air rifle had now officially arrived, and soon it was to be the turn of the pistol to gain recognition. The International Shooting Union, after pressure from its members, ruled in September 1967 that an air pistol event should be introduced into the programme from 1968. The rules for this competition were introduced in April 1968 together with revised rules for the air rifle, and these rules are in force today.

By the time of the 40th World Championships in Phoenix, Arizona, there were events for both seniors and ladies in air rifle and air pistol, with 218 entries and 49 teams. The first air pistol world champion was Kornél Marosvári of Hungary, and the team event went to the Soviet Union. The first lady champions were Sally Carroll, the local heroine in the pistol, and Tamara Cherkasova of the Soviet Union, the team golds going to the United States and Yugoslavia respectively.

Following this success, the sport took another step forward when the European Shooting Confederation decided to hold their own Air Weapons Championship in Mezibori, Czechoslovakia in February 1971. This was an immediate success, with 209 individuals and 55 teams participating, and it was decided thereafter to make it an annual event.

Thus air weapon shooting became a regular fixture in the shooting calendar and is looked on as the winter event of the shooting sport.

The newest arrival on the air weapons scene is the 'moving target' event, which was officially included in the programme of the European Shooting Confederation in 1978.

The success and steady proliferation of air weapons shooting is easily understandable if one considers that it is a true 'people's sport', as it requires very little in range space, equipment cost or ammunition expenses. Air weapons do not require certificates or licences and are eminently suitable for introducing youngsters to the shooting sport. With proper and sensible application, air weapon shooting can be a 'home sport' – a 10 metre or 6 yards range can be set up in any suitable location at home . . . garage, cellar, spare room, etc. In this sport the participants can put in the amount of training required to keep up with the best in the world, and the lack of ranges and the cost of ammunition no longer limit training schedules.

An Original Model 6 pistol with a selection of targets and pellets. Top left, individually packaged competition pellets and some retrievable darts, useful for practice at short ranges and for aligning sights.

AIR PISTOL SHOOTING

The two basic types of competition for air pistols are the international UIT 10 metre match course and the 6 yard match course. Basically, there is no difference between the two events as far as training and technical requirements are concerned. The shorter distance and the relatively large target of the 6 yard course make this form of air pistol shooting more suitable for the beginner and for those who do not possess the more sophisticated type of recoilless air pistols.

The main event shot at major domestic and international meetings is the UIT Air Pistol course of fire. This event is shot at a distance of 10 metres at the standard UIT air pistol target, which has a 10 ring measuring 12 millimetres, the other rings increasing in size by 8 millimetres. The aiming mark is 60 millimetres in diameter.

Any air or CO_2 pistol of 4.5 millimetres (.177 calibre) may be used, provided that it has open sights, does not exceed 1,500 grammes (53.6 oz) in weight, and fits with all accessories into a box with inside measurements of $420 \times 200 \times 50$ millimetres. The grips may not encircle the hand, though thumb and palm rests are permitted. The trigger pull is a minimum of 500 grammes, weighed with the gun held with the barrel in a vertical position.

The match involves forty shots for record, plus, ten sighting shots. The time allowed is 90 minutes, including sighting shots. Once the match has begun, sighting shots are only allowed between series of ten match shots, which are fired one shot per target.

Similar rules are applied in major competitions on the 6 yard course; however, five shots per target are permitted. Similarly, in Postal competitions there are some variations of the rules with usually more than one shot per target permitted.

There are many good air pistols on the market. The most popular models, though rather expensive, are made by Feinwerkbau of Germany. These pistols have dominated the international scene over the past years. Walther air pistols are also widely used, but the cocking mechanism can be awkward, particularly for women competitors. The cheaper air pistols that do not feature such advanced technical innovations as fixed barrels, side-lever cocking and microsight adjustments are still good value for money and are accurate enough for competitive shooting at 6 yards.

It is surprising that CO_2 pistols do not enjoy greater popularity. In theory, they should be superior to compressed air weapons, as they do not require the effort of mechanical cocking, which can be a problem, as we shall see below. They usually are less bulky and more streamlined. However, in practice these pistols do not come up to expectation and generally lack the supreme accuracy and consistency of the best compressed air weapons. In many countries these weapons are subject to controls similar to those imposed on cartridge weapons.

For the marksman who wants the best, and aims to win major competitions, a recoilless air pistol is a must. When one considers the difference between air weapons and smallbore firearms in particular, the difference in muzzle velocity and the greater stability provided by the recoilless pistols immediately after the shot is released are of paramount importance as far as accuracy and consistency are concerned.

What sets air pistol shooting apart from other forms of pistol shooting (from the technical point of view) is the difference in effect between gunpowder and compressed air as propellents. The muzzle velocity (that is, the speed at which the bullet leaves the barrel) is much slower in air weapons than in conventional firearms. As the pellet spends a longer time in the barrel of an air pistol, an unsteady hold and, in particular, errors in trigger release have a catastrophic effect. When aiming or firing errors are made, the pellet does not leave the barrel until the sideways movement of the muzzle has ended, although the shot has been released much earlier. In contrast, in conventional firearms the bullet leaves the barrel much sooner after the release of the trigger and strikes correspondingly nearer the centre of the target even though the error committed was the same. For this reason the air pistol is a difficult weapon to shoot, and a particular technique must be learned to achieve high scores.

Competitors at the firing line in the 1978 British National Air Weapons Championship held in Cardiff.

TECHNIQUE

The marksman must be physically fit so that he will have body stability, vital capacity and be less likely to 'fade'–to slacken off–in a competition due to physical fatigue. Such fitness can be achieved by exercising, running, swimming, cycling and by taking part in games such as tennis and squash.

You will have to undertake special training to tune the groups of muscles required to achieve the stance and steady hold required in this discipline. For this purpose you can best use your pistol as training apparatus. By holding the pistol firmly, raising it frequently to the aiming position, and holding it steadily in the area of movement (aiming area), you can achieve the special muscle power you need for steady aiming. To increase the effectiveness of these exercises use an additional weight on the arm, or a rubber expander between arm and foot, and exercise your fingers by squeezing a rubber ball, or doing push-ups on the fingertips, pull-ups or any strengthening exercises for the arms.

Correct breathing also has to be learned. It has a significant influence on timing and, together with corresponding muscle power, can help to extend the static phase in the precision stance to the required degree (that is, you can remain on aim steadily for longer). You can achieve good lung capacity by breathing exercises and other forms of physical training.

STANCE

You should position your feet so that you are standing comfortably, with the space between your feet corresponding to the width of your shoulders. The weight of your body should be directed to the balls of the feet; this enables you to lean into the aiming position. Hold your head comfortably with your face towards the target. The stance must allow relaxation of most muscle groups during the aiming process. Muscle tension causes early fatigue and translates into nervous tension.

BREATHING

The movements of the ribcage, diaphragm and shoulder when inhaling cause the arm holding the weapon to waver considerably, so breathing must cease completely during the aiming process. Before lifting your arm to the aiming position, breathe in and out several times to achieve good oxygen concentration in the blood. As you lift your arm to the aiming position, inhale for the last time and release most of the air from your lungs as the aiming position is reached.

AIMING AND FIRING

These two operations must be considered together. If the period taken to hold the sights steady and fire is too long, lack of oxygen or reduced stamina will result in wavering sights.

Keep your eye focused on the foresight. It is impossible for the human eye to focus on both the target and the sights, and if the sights are not kept in focus, even gross errors in sight alignment remain unnoticed and hence uncorrected.

In order to give a good sight picture the sights must be broad and block-shaped. The width of the front sight should be the same as the width of the notch in the rear sight blade (for air pistols 3 to 4 millimetres should be correct). For a good aim, an area two to three rings below the aiming mark is optimal for precision shooting.

Always touch the trigger from the front and squeeze it towards the aiming eye. The trigger finger must not be in contact with the grip or the weapon. Releasing the shot, far from being the end of the firing sequence, is the most difficult part of pistol shooting. As it has to be an integral part of the aiming process, it must be practised until the release is achieved by subconscious effort when the sight picture is correct. The final focusing and steadying of the aim is coordinated with the final pressure on the trigger necessary to release the shot.

Resist the application of 'second pressure' on the trigger. When a shot does not break, the shooter increases the pressure on the trigger to try to facilitate the release of the shot. This, of course, is a conscious effort and will inevitably lead to snatching. The result is a poor shot. It is better to relax, and bring the gun down from aim, and then to recommence the aiming and firing sequence from the start.

The smooth release of the trigger is of paramount importance in the aiming and firing process. As the target is comparatively nearer than in other pistol competitions, an angular error caused by incorrect sight alignment is less severely punished. Also, the sight base of air pistols is nearly as long as that of free pistols and therefore what appears to be a slightly incorrect sight picture, will still be good enough to achieve a hit on the 10 ring, provided the trigger release is perfect. Similarly, holding errors are less severely punished due to the comparatively large size of the 10 ring, allowing a larger than usual area of aim. However, there is simply no margin for error as far as the trigger control is concerned; the slightest overaction on the trigger pull (snatching) will result in a poor shot, as the movement of the muzzle will continue as the bullet travels along the barrel at its low velocity. In order to achieve a really smooth trigger release you must stay on aim longer, even at the expense of some loss of steadiness. It takes a conscious mental effort to be able to accept a not-so-perfect sight picture at the expense of a smooth trigger release.

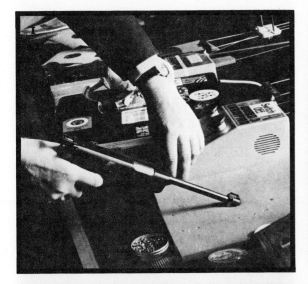

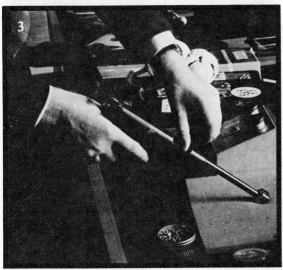

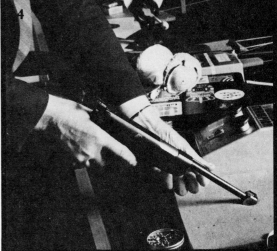

Loading the air pistol.
1. Drawing back the side cocking lever. Note that the muzzle rests on a foam rubber mat to prevent any damage.
2. The lever is drawn right back – the finger of the right hand is well clear of the trigger.
3. The pellet is pressed firmly but squarely into the chamber.
4. The cocking lever is now returned to the closed position.
5. The Feinwerkbau air pistol – these weapons were used by all the winners at the 1976 European Air Rifle and Air Pistol Championships.

A well-fitting 'anatomical' grip, that is, one shaped to the hand, is essential for consistent shooting. As you will have to change targets after each shot and cock the action of your pistol, you must also take up a fresh grip. Unless the grip is made to fit perfectly, you will not be able to take up the same position every time. This will result in a shifting of the shot groups. A palm rest is necessary to counteract the weight of the long barrel. The position of the trigger finger on the trigger must also be constant, otherwise there will be variation in the pressure required for the release of the trigger, resulting in snatching or 'freezing on the trigger'. Naturally, the trigger finger must be free from contact with the grip or frame.

Some shooters prefer to shoot with a barrel sleeve or barrel weights fitted to the pistol. The heavier barrel will mean slower muzzle movement and, therefore, a more 'forgiving' gun. However, the extra weight taxes a shooter's physical powers, and you will have to decide by trial and error the best type of weapon suited to your physical capacity.

FOLLOW-THROUGH

You must practise to achieve a good follow-through, that is, to keep the weapon steadily on aim after the shot has been released. This is essential for good results in all pistol shooting, and in air pistol shooting in particular. Unless the follow-through is planned and practised for each shot, you may lose your concentration; you will relax your grip and focus prematurely and the resulting stray shots will ruin your performance. By observing the sight picture after the release of the shot, you can immediately analyse the faults of your technique and correct them and thus avoid repeating your errors.

Indoor lighting can vary and the shooter will often find himself in difficulties in trying to cope with various light conditions. A yellow tinted lens helps to reduce glare and a diaphragm fitted to the lens can be used to produce a comfortable light level. Too bright a light reflected from the target area can lead to eye fatigue and so to inability to focus clearly. Unwanted reflections from overhead lights can be eliminated by wearing a shooting cap that has a long bill or visor, and side flaps.

UIT CONDITIONS

When shooting under UIT conditions, you must organize yourself and develop a routine. This is essential, as the time limit imposed is less generous than it at first appears. Though 90 minutes seem more than adequate for forty shots, the changing of targets and cocking and loading the pistol after each shot are time-consuming. In fact, you will find yourself occupied with these tasks for over one third of the time allowed! Furthermore, time lost cannot easily be regained, and running short of time in this competition imposes a strong psychological burden on the competitor. As a general 'rule of thumb' you should allow no more than 30 minutes for your sighters and first ten match shots. Thereafter you will have 20 minutes per 10 shots.

It is necessary to take a few short breaks in this match to rebuild concentration. The added physical effort of cocking the gun can add to match fatigue, and this is particularly so with some weapons, which require more strenuous effort by the shooter. A short walk coupled with some gentle loosening exercises should restore the circulation and ease aching muscles.

It is advisable to keep a record of the position of the hits on the targets as the match progresses; otherwise it is difficult to keep a check on the position of the group forming, as only one shot per target is allowed. Due to adaptation of the eyes to the light conditions as the match progresses, there might be some shift in the position of the groups that might necessitate a sight adjustment.

AMMUNITION

There are many good brands of ammunition on the market, some in packs of 500, some individually packed in 50s. Unless they are really fresh, the pellets in the single packs tend to oxidize quickly and this may vary the flight characteristics of the individual pellets to the detriment of accuracy. The packs of 500 are better lubricated and therefore preferred by most top marksmen to the single pack. However, they will have to be inspected before loading in case their flanges are damaged or distorted.

When buying tins of pellets, inspect the tin and if it has been damaged, the pellets inside may be slightly distorted, as they are closely packed. Damaged pellets will give poor groups, as their trajectories will vary.

MAINTENANCE

Air pistols, as a rule, need little maintenance, but it is worth checking on the nylon seals from time to time, as they need replacing even if only slightly worn. Worn seals can cause the air pressure generated in the weapon to vary, and this, in turn, will result in loss of consistency and accuracy of the shots. The sights can work loose after continuous usage; check for tightness before an important shoot.

Right: A duelling target fitted to a turning device. It will face the shooter for a set time and then turn to the edge position.
Below: An Original Model 10 .177 pistol.

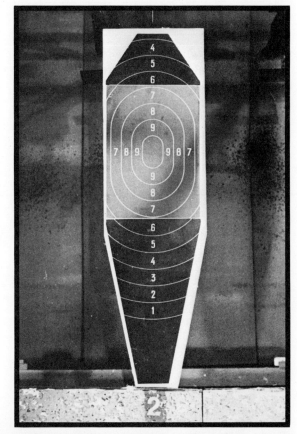

AIR RIFLE SHOOTING

Some years ago when air weapons first came onto the international scene, I was one of the many shooters who frowned. To me 300 metre shooting in three positions is the classic event. It was with this event that all world-class competition started, yet it was gradually being left out of international competition in favour of lesser events, such as the air weapons competition. At that time I visualized the world championships being shot with air weapons, and I thought it would be the death of more than a hundred years of world-class competition. But as a coach I soon came to realize that air weapons have a part to play in the development of a shooter no matter in what calibre or discipline his interest lies. For example, all shooters can use air weapons to train in the winter months when the cold weather makes it difficult to shoot outdoors. Many European countries in which shooting is the national sport, have air weapon clubs that shoot shoulder-to-shoulder matches.

In Britain there is a long-established group of air weapon shooters under the control of the National Air Rifle and Pistol Association; one of their competitions is called the Bell Target. It is shot standing with a rifle at 6 yards. The target is a steel disc with the appropriate lines machined on the face. The bull is a $\frac{3}{8}$ inch diameter hole. If the pellet travels cleanly down the hole it rings a bell, hence the name. You might think that such a competition would be relatively easy until you learn that it is shot in a pub in front of large, noisy and sometimes sarcastic crowds, with the finals being fired shot for shot until one competitor drops a point!

The European Shooting Confederation (ESC), which is a body of the UIT, decided there should be a European championship match for air weapons in February each year. Because air weapons can be shot indoors, the championship can take place anywhere in Europe, no matter what the climate of the host country.

There is a great potential for air weapons. There are a great many places in which they can be shot. Every college, school, and sports centre probably has a gymnasium or hall that could be used for competition throughout the year with entire safety. A thick curtain or blanket hanging loosely will stop an air weapon pellet.

A great number of people have shot an air weapon at one time or another, even if it was only at a fair ground. The weapon used would have been a recoiling type of air weapon.

The easiest way to explain this is to describe very briefly what happens in a cartridge weapon. When the trigger is released, the firing pin moves forward and strikes the base of the cartridge. This itself causes some movement in the weapon and is followed by the explosion within the cartridge, which in turn moves a bullet, large in comparison with the rifle weight, at high velocity up the barrel, causing a violent recoil.

In an air weapon, when the trigger is released, a piston, which itself is a large mass weight, and the spring behind it move forward, compressing air as they go until the air cannot be compressed any further. When this point is reached, the piston rebounds off the cushion of air until the spring again takes over. This process is repeated until the air and the pellet are pushed up the barrel. There is no explosion of powder, and the pellet weight and its velocity are so low compared with the rifle weight as to be of no consequence with regard to recoil.

The manufacturers have solved the recoil problem completely by having two pistons moving in opposite directions, thus cancelling each other's movements. If you watch a top air rifle shooter firing a shot, you will see no perceptible movement of rifle or shooter.

Air target rifles are based on the standard .22 rifle for weight, contour and size. The original idea was to provide an inexpensive form of training for competitors in ladies' and juniors' events. The weapon itself is not cheap, but if you have an engineering mind and some idea of the cost of manufacturing such an article, then you can see that it is value for money. For example, in comparison to a cartridge weapon, an air weapon has many more precision component parts.

Rifle shooting at the British National Air Weapons Championship. The stance is a development of modern competitive shooting. Although it looks ungainly it gives the rifle great stability because the left elbow and the arm which support the rifle can be pressed firmly against the hip.

SIGHTS

Sights on target weapons are, of necessity, accurate, but should be checked for movement from time to time. This is done with a dial indicator, ideally measuring in ten-thousandths of an inch, on a magnetic base stand. Any good gunsmith will do this job for you in a few minutes, and will tell you if the click adjustment is working correctly. It is quite common on a new rear sight to have one click missing when you start to turn the sight in the opposite direction. You can live with this as long as you are aware of it, but any more than two clicks adrift should be put right either with new parts or by adjustment.

The front sight also holds mysteries that some shooters are unaware of. The actual housing that holds the element must not be too large. Generally, the shooter using a top match rifle should use the front sight provided by the maker of the weapon. It is part of the actual sight picture to see a ring of light around the front sight housing, but because of the large eye relief (that is, the distance between eye and sight) employed in the standing position, which can be up to $\frac{1}{8}$ inch, it is easy for the beginner to lose this light around the housing. This must be checked, as it is a most important part of the lining up of the sights. For the trained shooter this task is done by the subconscious mind. The front sight also plays a part in controlling the level of the weapon. It is not uncommon to employ cant in the standing position, that is, laying the rifle over at an angle towards yourself to give a good head position, and better sight line. Whether or not cant is employed, the rifle must be controlled with the aid of a level. The two most common types are a spirit housing or a bar built into the sighting element. I prefer the latter, as it can be related to the subconscious mind to do the job perfectly, but with a spirit level you have to take your eye off the point of concentration (i.e., the sight picture). Look at the spirit level, check that it is correct, and then return to the sight picture. If you cant the rifle and use the element bar as a level, you may have to file the lugs off the element, so that the element can be adjusted to give the angle of cant required on the rifle. The sights themselves should be removed after shooting is finished, and kept in a strong box.

STANCE

Imagine a line from the bull to the firing point. You must stand on this line with both feet so that the line runs just behind the ball of each foot. This means you will be standing at 90° to the target with your left side facing the target (assuming you are a right-handed shooter, of course). Your feet should be in line with your armpits, shoulder-width apart. Putting your feet any further apart will increase the support area, but will put too much weight on the arch of the foot, and force the leg muscles rather than the bones to take the weight of the body and the rifle. Your feet should point naturally and your legs and hips should be relaxed, so that from the waist down the position is as if you were standing talking to someone.

From the waist up you must twist to look toward the target, and lean back to counterbalance the weight of the rifle without moving the hips. This is best achieved by first placing the rifle in the shoulder, then twisting towards the target, introducing the back bend counterbalance of the rifle. The mass weight of the rifle and torso is then dropped onto the hips. It is important that this routine be carried out in the same way for each shot. By twisting the body in this way the same muscles and ligaments are tightened in much the same way as a rope is tightened if twisted in the right direction, making the body more rigid.

Keep your head in as natural a position as possible. It is permissible to roll the head slightly forward, as long as it does not impair the function of the eye in any way. The head must never be tilted sideways, for this will upset your balance.

Adjust the butt plate on the rifle so that the eye can easily see down the sights with a good, consistent cheek pressure on the butt. The cheek pressure must be the same for every shot. Once the head, eye with sight line and cheek pressure have been set up and established, they must remain constant, even if it means that the rifle is canted to achieve this.

The left hand and arm take the weight of the rifle for a right-handed shooter. Ideally, your elbow should rest on your hip, but most men cannot achieve this, so the elbow must be placed on the large stomach muscle to the right of the hip — not too far over or you may get pulse from the heart or the abdominal aorta.

Most women shooters have what I would regard as the classic position. Their build is such that they can get into a good standing position with ease. They have a low centre of gravity, long arms, and large hips, so there is no trouble in resting the elbow on the hip. Their backs are supple, and it is easy for them to get a good back bend, so low that it is possible for some of them to rest the rifle on the flat of the hand.

Your arm from the elbow to the rifle should be slightly forwards of upright, so that the weight of the rifle travels down the almost vertical bone. The arm must not support the rifle by muscle alone or you will push shots up high. The left arm is a bracket that takes the weight of the rifle.

Place your left hand just in front of the trigger guard, and use it to adjust the height of the rifle. The most efficient hand position is the clenched fist, but if this does not give you enough height, open your hand so the weight is taken on bent fingers and thumb. The thumb is usually on the trigger guard. The higher the hand position is, the less efficient it becomes. There are many combinations of hand position, and you should experiment with them, and find one that is comfortable. The height of the rifle must be the first consideration, so that there is a good relaxed sight line on the aiming mark.

Your right hand and arm do little but squeeze the trigger. Use your right hand to hold the pistol grip of the rifle. How tight this grip should be is not too important, but it must be consistent. Place your hand so that the trigger is in the centre of the first pad of the index finger. You must position your whole hand in such a way that the trigger finger can squeeze the trigger straight back, with the wrist in a straight line with the rest of the arm. The trigger must always be squeezed straight back, otherwise shots will be pulled or pushed to the left or right. This applies to all types of shooting. The rest of the arm should be approximately at 45 degrees to the vertical, with the elbow pointing down. If it is too low, it will destroy the pocket the shoulder provides for the butt.

Starting to shoot standing has the big advantage that a shooter learns to accept the wobble associated with the standing position. If shooters first learn to shoot in the prone position, then go on to standing, the shooter is reluctant to accept this wobble, and consequently spends all his efforts trying to make the rifle as still as in the prone position. In his efforts he will hang on too long, and lose all the basic techniques necessary to fine shooting. The standing shooter must accept the wobble, and realize that even grouping within the bull the wobble can be quite large and to get an eight the sight error must be very large indeed.

With air weapons follow-through is most important because barrel time is so slow. Barrel time is the time the pellet is in the barrel after it has been fired. It is possible to spoil a good shot by relaxing your hold too soon, before the shot has had time to leave the barrel. You must endeavour to hold your position and technique until the shot has passed through the target.

Right: The correct grip and support for the air rifle. The weapon shown is fitted with a pistol grip.
Below: The kneeling position. The elbow rests on the knee and the fore end rests on the flattened hand. Care must be taken that there is no wobbling on the right foot.
Below right: The correct stance with feet slightly apart.

COLOUR FILTERS

In addition to the basic rear sight, you should have a good adjustable iris and a colour filter holder. The extremes of light on indoor ranges can vary from near darkness to painful brilliance, and you must be able to cope with them all. The rear sight aperture should be of the iris, not the click-rotating, variety. If you half-click this type of aperture, you are in the white, and in trouble.

The same rule applies to colour filters. At least two European firms produce a very well-made click-rotating set of filters, but the filters are so small that they are optically useless, the colour is almost non-existent, they get scratched when they are revolved, and they are impossible to clean. However, you can get a simple holder for 25 millimetre camera filters. This gives you a vast range of filters in all colours and densities that are optically flat and easily cleaned.

It is difficult for a coach to recommend a colour. The serious shooter should experiment until he finds two or three filters that will help under certain light conditions. There is a standard say-ing where sighting is concerned: You should have a clear front sight, and a fuzzy aiming mark. A serious shooter should not just accept this. With the aid of the iris and colour filters, he can, by experimenting, get very close to having both clear. All uncoated filters reduce light by four percent at every glass-air surface. Light is also lost through the colour in the glass, so at least eight percent of the light passing through the filter is lost, but in this case it is what is required of them.

Two general filters for indoor use are blue and yellow. If the range is lit by incandescent bulbs, then the light given out is yellow, and will be reduced by a blue filter. If the range is lit by fluorescent tubes, the light given off will be in the blue range and will be reduced by a yellow filter. A yellow filter also increases contrast, simply because the eye can distinguish between black and yellow much more easily than it can between black and white, thus making the target look clearer.

Firing the air rifle. The sights are correctly adjusted and the absence of serious recoil permits a light grip.

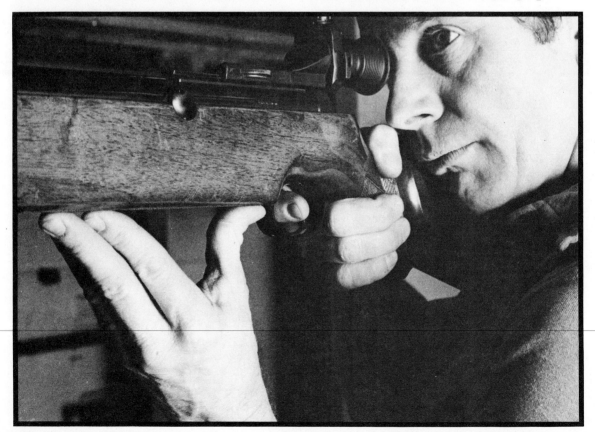

PELLETS

First try to get some idea of which pellets perform best in your particular weapon. This can be done quite simply by shooting groups of ten with various makes using a rest, or with the rifle clamped in some way. Shoot several groups with each make, measure the areas and compare them.

When you have selected a particular match pellet that suits your rifle, there are two more checks you must continually make. The first one is best described using as an example the bullet flight from a cartridge weapon. If you took a file or a knife and cut a piece out of the ogive of a bullet (that is, the complex radius that makes up the nose of the bullet), it would make little difference to its flight and its accuracy, but if you did the same to the tail of the bullet, the accuracy would be destroyed completely. The same principle applies to an air weapon pellet. Always check that the pellets being used are not damaged on the tail, and that the tail is perfectly round. Top manufacturers pack their pellets in special plastic packs so the tail of the pellet is protected, but this also presents a problem. The packs themselves are not air-tight, and after a time the pellets oxidize. A whitish-grey crystal-like surface is produced on the pellet, which destroys the accuracy. Unless your pellets come very quickly from the manufacturer, this is another problem to look for. Pellets sold in tins of 500 give you the best chance of getting fresh pellets, but once opened they must be used fairly quickly.

Always use match grade pellets for their consistent weight. Look at the tails to see that they are not mis-shapen, and see that the whole surface of the pellet has a bright silver look.

CLOTHING

As a coach I recommend a proper leather shooting jacket. It should be made to measure of a non-stretch leather. Any good manufacturer will help you, but ask the opinion of established shooters before buying, Until you have the money for this jacket, a good training top of the tracksuit type is quite useful, as long as it is made of a non-slip material. Never use a prone shooting jacket, which has large pads sewn on the elbows and shoulders; these are useless for standing. A serious shooter should always wear the same amount and type of clothing whenever he shoots.

A pair of shooting boots is very useful for standing shooting. The only contact the shooter has with the firing point are the boots in which he stands, and the normal shoe or boot only touches the ground at the heel, and a very small area under the balls of the feet. Shooting boots have a nice flat sole, giving good contact with no rocking, but they are expensive. Training shoes with flat soles and inside supports are the next best thing. Because the main part of the rifle weight is taken on the left hand, the shooter should protect his hand by wearing a well-padded glove. There are two basic types: the mitt and the glove. The mitt is better if you use a clenched fist to support your rifle, but awkward if you use the fingers to support the rifle. The glove is more versatile. I do not recommend the use of an ordinary glove, as it is too thin and the seams are in the wrong places.

MAINTENANCE

Apart from trigger adjustment, and keeping the exterior clean, all other maintenance should be left to the manufacturers. There are few gunsmiths who understand how air weapons work, and in many cases it is not advisable to send your air weapon for overhaul through the agents.

The manufacturers make a point of asking the user not to oil the weapon. There is a sound reason for this. If air weapons are oiled to excess, a dieselling effect may occur. This is brought about by oil vapour mixing with the air, which explodes on compression. In extreme cases the resulting velocity can be pushed past the speed of sound. The explosion increases the hitting power of the weapon, and there is an air weapon that has a device built in that injects ether into the cylinder of the air rifle just to produce this condition. This rifle is made to take the excessive pressure produced by dieselling, and is sold for its hitting power alone. Apart from the danger dieselling produces in the target weapon, it also produces extremely inconsistent velocities. See also Chapter 4 for more information on the maintenance of air weapons.

Try to avoid mineral oils, which are the worst for producing the dieselling condition. If a part is obviously in need of lubrication, use a *little* silicone-based oil, and wipe away any excess.

17 BLACK POWDER SHOOTING

**Black powder spills from a flask
amid some of the means adopted to
ignite it. Top, a paper cartridge;
right, pyrites and flint; bottom,
a metal-cased centrefire cartridge
from a Martini-Henry rifle; centre,
various percussion caps.**

COLLECTORS AND SHOOTERS

The possession and use of muzzleloading and blackpowder firearms has so much to offer in variety and interest that it is no surprise to learn that its devotees are rapidly increasing in number.

Interest in the sport of modern organized muzzleloading shooting began in the United States in the 1930s, in Britain in the 1950s, and in the 1970s is creating world-wide interest. However, the use of muzzleloading weapons never completely died out in Britain, as many wildfowlers in particular have always preferred to use the larger bore muzzleloading shotgun rather than more modern guns.

Many people collect muzzleloading firearms, and this in turn creates an interest in cleaning them as well as undertaking possible restoration and repair. Some people will be interested only in shooting their muzzleloaders, and may change the weapon quite often until they have found one that exactly suits them and their purpose. It will still be necessary to learn about cleaning and preservation, and to embark on one of the most fascinating aspects of muzzle loading, the preparation of the ammunition. With the breech loader the ammunition is bought as a 'package deal' and while a certain amount of variation in the cartridge loading is possible, it is not possible, even with hand loading the cartridge, to produce the infinite variety possible with a muzzleloader, especially with shotguns.

The historical study of the weapon has produced a steadily increasing array of books, many of great interest and value. As research continues more and more knowledge is made available to shooters and collectors interested in the guns. These books relate to design, special details of lock mechanisms, barrels, breeches, stocks, ammunition and ballistic performance, why this type of weapon evolved and for use by whom, where and how manufactured, from what materials, and possible association with historical events. This does not mean that the use of the muzzleloader as a sporting gun has been neglected; there are now several books on this aspect, but these have mainly dealt with those types of weapons in widest use.

BEGINNING WITH BLACKPOWDER

For newcomers to this fascinating sport it is best, whenever possible, to join an organized club or association. The following countries are known at present to have organizations devoted to black powder shooting: Argentina, Austria, Britain, Canada, Denmark, France, West Germany, Holland, Italy, Japan, South Africa, Spain, Sweden, Switzerland, the United States of America. The differences between shooting organizations in different countries are so great that no specific directions can be given, but most national shooting organizations will know how to contact the groups who are involved in black powder shooting.

The laws regarding the muzzleloaders are so varied that it is essential to consult a shooting organization or someone who is familiar with the local requirements. In some cases the right of possession, even of an original muzzleloader, may be subject to licence. In Britain the possession of an original muzzleloader as a collector's item is unrestricted, but a police-issued Firearms Certificate is required if it is to be shot. Approval or licence may be needed to purchase and possess the black powder used in muzzleloaders; the new substitute for black powder, 'Pyrodex', may be equally affected, although it has been formulated to avoid this. Similarly, it is possible that percussion caps may be subjected to some kind of control. Rifles and pistols may also be the subject of a tight control as to where they may be used. Do not be put off muzzleloading shooting by these obstacles, but it usually takes patience and time to overcome them.

The beginner, however she or he may have learned about muzzleloading, will find the easiest way to join in is to establish contact with a muzzleloaders' group and attend their meetings. It is likely that somewhere in the area there will be a group that suits your particular preference, be it game, clay, target, local, national or international shoots; all these opportunities are available for your enjoyment. If, as is likely, the individual wishes to learn more, help and information are there for the asking.

If this is not possible, then there are books that will provide the information required.

SAFETY

Safety is a matter of the utmost importance and it is recommended that protective glasses be worn for all kinds of shooting. In some organizations it is a condition that all shooters must wear such glasses when taking part in any shooting activity.

It is **never** safe to smoke when handling black powder. Treated with respect black powder is safe and easy to use, but remember that it is easily ignited. Properly made guns, in usable condition, are remarkably safe with black powder and it is difficult to overload them to the point where damage to gun or user occurs. Always remember that there must **never** be a space between the powder and the projectile or shot charge; if this happens, the bullet or shot becomes an obstruction and results in a burst or bulged barrel.

Original – that is, antique – guns must be closely examined before use to be sure that they are sound; professional advice may be needed on this point. When it was made, the gun was proved, but if any alterations have been made, the proof may no longer be valid and reproof may be required. The interpretation of old proof marks may be difficult, and it is a good idea to get a second opinion. It is not good practice to test an old gun by firing it with an overload; all too often the gun is not properly held to control the recoil and is damaged. Get a professional opinion or submit the weapon for reproof, but remember that if it fails at reproof, it may be destroyed; the loss will be partly yours and partly that of those who could have treasured it in the future. If there is any doubt, put the gun back in the cabinet or hang it on the wall. The supply of originals is limited and steadily decreasing in number.

Much has been said about muzzleloading guns that have been found to have an old load of powder and shot in them. It is unusual, but it does happen and it is always wise to carry out a check on any unfamiliar weapon. Take a ramrod or thin piece of dowelling and push it gently down the barrel until it will go no further. Mark the length flush with the muzzle and then withdraw it. Now place the stick on top of the barrel and note where the tip reaches – if the bore is clear, the stick should reach as far as the breech. If it does not, then there is an obstruction and this could well be a load, so treat it with care and seek advice on the best way to withdraw the charge. A firearm cannot fire on its own! The greatest enemies of safety are lack of knowledge, carelessness, and impatience.

ORIGINAL AND REPRODUCTION WEAPONS

Before a decision to purchase any weapon is made, it is essential to appreciate the difference between an original and a reproduction.

'Original' means that the weapon was made when firearms of its type were in general use. 'Reproduction' or 'replica' means that the weapon was made after that type of firearm ceased to be in general use. Basically, the difference is that of antique and modern.

As original weapons became scarcer, the demand increased and prices rose steeply. The result was to create a demand for reproduction weapons which would be cheaper. This market was first catered for in the United States. Soon the market became worldwide, and today it is possible to shoot with weapons that cost much less than the originals now do.

At first the accent was on price. This resulted in reproductions that, while accurate in use, had the amount of handwork reduced to a minimum, thus keeping the cost down. The Italian manufacturers, in particular, were able to supply the demand for a class of weapon aesthetically unsatisfactory but functionally excellent, the accuracy being fully the equal of the original.

Further development has led to the production of a series of more expensive, better quality reproduction rifles, particularly those produced by Parker-Hale Ltd of Birmingham, England. Based on the British .577 Rifle Pattern 1853 and the .451 smallbore muzzleloading rifle, they represent a new approach to the problem in which the accent is on quality and accuracy of reproduction.

**Top: A Rigby .451 long range match rifle.
Bottom: A .577 Enfield carbine, made around 1862, in use today.**

The .577 Rifle Pattern 1853 was probably the best muzzleloading service rifle ever produced and its very wide use and popularity with the troops, both North and South, in the American Civil War is fully documented.

The .451 rifle, although designed as a service weapon, in fact saw greatest use for target shooting. The military type was fitted with superior sights and gradually its range was extended from the 600 yards of the .577 Rifle to 800, 900, 1,000 yards and, finally, 1,200 yards.

Another line of development has been in redesigning older weapons. Sturm Ruger and Company in the United States have produced a totally redesigned percussion revolver using modern materials and techniques. The superiority of this weapon over the original is undoubted, and this has created a problem in competition shooting, which will be considered later.

Similar difficulties occur where the pistol, rifle or shotgun has been completely redesigned and modern sighting systems and other improvements that have been developed or invented since the originals were made have been added. A more accurate and efficient firearm has resulted, but comparability with the original has been lost.

This situation created problems for those who had to make the decisions about competition rules, and the solutions adopted have often been at variance. The national rules of different countries may vary greatly. The differences are usually dictated by the national conditions and developments and by the inheritance of the types of muzzleloaders that evolved in order to meet the former national requirements. Some of these weapons have had a very great effect on the type of competitions that are most popular and most attended. For example, the 'patch ball' rifle predominates in the United States, but attracts very little attention in Europe, although it was a European discovery.

With the forming of the Muzzle Loaders Associations International Committee (MLAIC) a beginning was made to lay down an internationally acceptable set of competition rules. So far these have taken a form more acceptable to Europeans than Americans. One of the principal difficulties is the European preference for the use of original muzzleloading firearms, an approach that would be almost totally impossible to the United States, as the potential supply of originals is inadequate. In time it seems likely that this situation will also apply to Europe and the reproduction will then be used more widely. And although the accent is still on the original in MLAIC conditions, most national organizations are encouraging the use of reproduction weapons by permitting their use in one way or another.

Everyone beginning muzzleloading shooting should be aware of the competition rules to ensure that their choice of weapon does not clash with the conditions governing its future use.

Long range rifle shooting using the back position. The gun is a Rigby .451 percussion rifle, the target 500 yards away, can just be seen through the mist.

MUSKETS

These are smooth-bored, single-barrel firearms that are derived from military weapons. As they originated before a satisfactory system of measurement had been devised, they are usually defined as being of a given 'bore' or 'gauge', which was the number of round balls of lead to the pound. This system found worldwide acceptance and is still in use for shotguns today. For example: 12 gauge = 0.729 inch, 16 gauge = 0.662 inch, 24 gauge = 0.580 inch.

Many muzzleloaders find flintlock muskets, which were replaced as military arms in the 1830s and 1840s, particularly interesting. In view of their age it is not surprising that there is a shortage of them and their price is high. However, there is available a good reproduction of the 'Brown Bess', the British service flintlock musket, which has a more accurately finished bore than the original.

The accuracy potential of muskets is low, and it is usual to limit competition shooting to 50 yards or metres. Competition is normally carried out with powder and ball being loaded separately; the ball can then be much closer to bore diameter and consequently much more accurate. The original weapon was loaded by means of a paper cartridge that contained powder and ball. To ensure an easy fit, the ball was made smaller than the bore and consequently accuracy suffered.

The percussion musket was phased out in the 1850s, and has not attracted a great deal of attention from modern muzzleloaders. As a consequence, there is no reproduction available.

The international competition stipulates that military smooth-bore flintlock muskets shall be shot from the standing position.

Clouds of smoke produced by the Brown Bess .750 smooth bore flintlock musket.

PISTOLS

A few flintlocks have rifled barrels but the vast majority are smooth-bored. They may be single, double or multibarrel. The double barrels may be side by side, or over and under, neither pattern being easy to design due to the size and width of the lock. The most suitable weapon for target practice is the single-barrelled version.

The types most likely to be encountered are the service pistols, which are large in calibre and size, rather clumsy, unduly heavy and not really suitable for target shooting. Slightly shorter overall and of lighter and superior construction are the target and duelling pistols and the pistols carried by officers, all of which are very suitable as target arms.

The medium-sized pistol was sufficiently compact to fit into the large pockets of an overcoat and some of these are suitable for target shooting. The smaller pocket pistol would fit into any reasonable sized pocket, but is really not suitable for anything but close range self-protection.

The MLAIC competition is for an original single shot, smooth-bore flintlock pistol. Reproduction pistols are generally disappointing in quality.

An almost identical classification may be applied to percussion pistols, the difference being that there are proportionately many more with rifled barrels. More target pistols were made, with both smooth-bore and rifled barrels.

The MLAIC competition is for an original single-shot, rifled barrel pistol. Reproduction pistols are usually disappointing; as with flintlock pistols, it is too expensive to reproduce the quality of the originals where so much handwork was employed. Most of the currently manufactured arms show where production problems and costs have changed the original design, and, to the experienced shot, not for the better.

SHOTGUNS

During the nineteenth century the gun industry, particularly in Europe, had access to cheap labour and, consequently, it was possible to have almost any type of shotgun made at very low cost. They were built by hand and it was possible to make even the most eccentric design at a very

reasonable price. It was also possible to build a particular style for a particular market, ranging from the very, very cheap, very poor quality weapon to the plain but very hard-wearing guns used for game shooting for market purposes, to those of the highest quality and most elaborate decoration. Birmingham and Liège manufacturers would produce any style or design at a competitive price and marked in any way the retailer wished. It is not always possible to decide where a gun was made, as sometimes the retailer stipulated that no marks should be put on the guns because that would indicate that they were not manufactured by him.

If one is patient and has access to such places as gun shows and auction houses, sooner or later an original shotgun that is exactly, or almost exactly, what is wanted will turn up. It is then a question of being able to afford it!

In the nineteenth century emigrants poured out of Europe into the thinly populated areas of the world. They needed firearms as much as axes, shovels and ploughs, and having very little money, created a market for the cheap yet serviceable all-purpose firearm. Changes in military firearms brought about by improvements were frequent in the nineteenth century. This resulted in the sale of, first, all smooth-bore flintlock muskets, then smooth-bore percussion muskets, followed by the obsolescence of the larger bore rifled muzzleloaders. With low prices for such arms, the trade bought in quantity and converted each in turn to satisfy this market. Sometimes the antique weapon is easily identified, but in other cases the shotgun musket may have been made of parts from several different weapons and countries and identification may be impossible. They are heavy and clumsy compared with a purpose-built shotgun and because of this are not satisfying weapons to use.

Because of the difficulty of making a reproduction double-barrel shotgun at a commercially acceptable price it has taken much longer for an adequate reproduction to become available. There are far more original shotguns available than any other original firearm. But the supply will become exhausted and in time the reproduction shotgun will be much more widely used. As the potential market increases, so should the availability of quality reproductions, but it is most unlikely that there will ever be more than a very limited range of style and bore available.

Above: Muzzle loaders at the
second International competition,
held at Bisley.
Right: Firing a double-barrel rifle.
Below: The powder can be seen
burning in this photograph of a
double-barrel percussion rifle.

International competition limits the bore size to a maximum of 11 gauge, stipulates the maximum load of powder and shot, and forbids choke boring.

Choke boring, a method of concentrating the shot dispersal, was not used until after muzzle-loaders were obsolete. Currently banned under international rules, its use is a matter that will need to be reconsidered in the future as the sport grows.

So we have single- and double-barrel flintlock shotguns which, except for some made late in the flintlock period, are seldom larger than 16 gauge and are very wide across the locks. Single- and double-barrel percussion shotguns are usually 14 gauge, although later ones tend to be 12 gauge. They were made in a variety of styles, and the barrel weight and length depended on the purpose for which they were required. An adequate reproduction percussion double-barrel shotgun is available, but it might have a choke-bored barrel.

REVOLVERS

Original weapons have survived in large numbers, which has encouraged their use for muzzle-loading shooting. However, the demand exceeded the supply, the price of originals went up, and a reproduction at lower cost became economically possible. In no other field has the reproduction appeared in such quantity, and in such variety of models and quality. Many variations exploit the appeal of the Colt percussion revolver and other types produced during the American Civil War, including several of those made in small numbers by the Confederacy. As well as copies made by other manufacturers, Colt themselves have produced a reproduction of their mid-nineteenth century Navy revolver.

A decreasing number of competitions specify originals. Internationally, there is provision for both original and reproduction competitions, but they are kept separate. A serious problem arises when a good reproduction has had the markings changed so that it is made to appear as an original. Great experience is called for to accurately identify the weapon and a difference of 'expert opinion' may arise. To date there appears to be, on average, a slight superiority in the performance of the reproduction revolver.

PERCUSSION RIFLES

Like shotguns, the range in calibre and variety of percussion rifles is unlimited. In the mid-nineteenth century the calibre of service rifles varied from .41 calibre for the Swiss Federal Rifle to the 12 gauge French Service Rifle. The calibres of sporting rifles varied from .32 calibre rook and rabbit rifles, and some even smaller (pea) rifles in America, to the large bore rifles for use against dangerous game in Africa and India, where the bore could be up to one inch.

During the 1840s and 1850s the military forces of Europe were rearmed with muzzleloading rifles, usually in two distinct stages, each involving a reduction in calibre. By the late 1860s the breech-loading conversions were taking over, which, in turn, were shortly to be replaced by smaller calibre breech-loading rifles. These conversions account for the fact that some muzzle-loading military rifles are so difficult to obtain.

The late 1850s saw the appearance of a new kind of rifle. Sir Joseph Whitworth produced a .451 calibre rifle in which the bullet was $2\frac{1}{2}$ calibres long, in addition to which the bore was a hexagon and the hexagonal bullet a mechanical fit. In fact, the relationship of calibre and bullet length was the important formula; for the first time it was possible to hit what you were aiming at 1,000 yards and beyond, with a rifle of practical military weight and manoeuvrability. The early 1860s saw the development of this principle and the popularizing of rifle shooting in Britain.

The .451 calibre target rifle today is used for medium 300, 500 and 600 yards competition and, preferably with suitable sights, at 900 and 1,000 yards. Demand has outstripped supply and once again the reproduction has come to the rescue. The medium and long range shooter is fortunate in having such a quality firearm available.

In America the patch ball rifle predominates, followed by the .58 and .54 calibre Minie type rifles. In Europe the Minie type rifles, usually .58/.577 calibre, and 'Any' rifles, usually .451/.461 calibre, are the rifles of choice.

Internationally, the accent is still on originals and the range remains 100 metres.

It is not possible to discuss the details of the different techniques for each type of weapon, for much can only be obtained by practice on the range and experimentation with ammunition.

Above: A reproduction Remington
.44 cap and ball revolver.
Right: An original Remington .44.
Below: A big bore sporting gun, the
.577 × 2¾ inch black powder Express
double rifle made by E. M. Reilly.

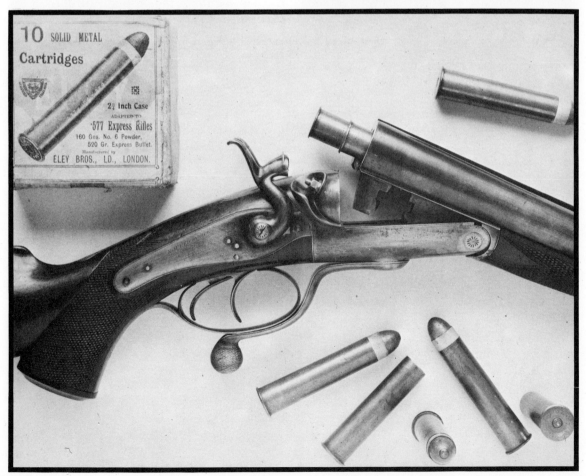

FLINTLOCK RIFLES

Flintlock rifles were usually designed for use with a round ball and fabric or leather patches, but there were some that used short cylindroidal or mechanically fitting bullets. The presence of a touch hole at the breech end of the barrel and the comparatively slow ignition time imposed certain limitations on the pressures that were produced in the barrel, which consequently imposed ballistic limitations. The disconcerting feature about flintlock rifles is their ability to shoot very well one day and, with apparently no change in any factors, indifferently on the next. The flintlock rifle shooter, while always trying to solve this problem, should not be too disappointed if this happens. Most European flintlock rifles are between 16 and 30 bore. The smallbore American rifle is a speciality largely confined to the eastern United States. When the demand for a more powerful rifle arose, for instance to kill the American buffalo, a larger calibre was soon adopted.

The European military flintlock rifle, particularly that of the Germanic states, should not be overlooked. It has a characteristic lock, the principal feature being an extra-heavy mainspring, which ensured that there was almost always a good strong spark from the steel to ignite the powder in the pan. The flintlock musket would frequently misfire for want of this feature. The disadvantage of using such a strong spring was that is slowed up the rate of fire. However, this matter was of much less importance to the rifleman, who was usually employed as a skirmisher and was not expected to maintain a high rate of fire.

The black powder gun at the instant of firing – the cock has swung forward, priming has flashed and the main charge is just beginning to explode.

MATERIALS

Powder

When shooting muzzleloaders only black powder is permissible – with the recent exception of Pyrodex. Nitrogenous or smokeless or semi-smokeless powders must *never* be used, as the mechanical strength of a muzzleloader was not designed to withstand the pressure characteristics of nitrogenous powders.

Black powder is a mechanical mixture of saltpetre, sulphur and charcoal, and is much more difficult and much less safe to make than smokeless powders. The saltpetre and the sulphur can now be refined to almost total purity, and this removes two possible manufacturing variables. The type and condition of the wood from which the charcoal is made are critical factors, as is the time interval between making the charcoal and incorporating it in the mixing mill.

After wet incorporation, a lengthy process and one where economy in time would produce a cheaper product, the water is pressed out of the mill cake. The pieces of cake have to be broken down by corning and then sieved into the various grain sizes required, any larger lumps being returned to the corning process. At the same time as much dust as possible is removed.

In good quality powder, glazing is then carried out by rotating the powder in a barrel until all the grains are polished, a process frequently omitted in modern manufacture. There are few shortcuts that reduce the cost without reducing the quality; the manufacture of high quality black powder is a very exacting process indeed. If black powder is made to burn at a uniform rate, it will produce uniform pressures and, consequently, uniform accuracy.

Do not dry out your powder too much by storing it in an overly warm place, and do not store it in a damp place. If the powder gets damp enough to start to form lumps, the accuracy will be gone even when it has been redried.

Granulation

There is no easy way to identify granule size. It is decided by the number of meshes per inch in a sieve or screen. If the manufacturers were to state the high and low meshes for each type of powder, this would avoid the present confusing method of labelling, which gives no information as to the actual granule size.

During screening the dust and very fine grain are removed first and then, progressively, the coarser granules, those too large being discarded. If, for instance, the powder is sieved into four different granule sizes, the average size of individual granules will be subject to much less variation than if it is sieved into only two screen sizes.

In Britain the usual sizes in the lower grade of powder quality used to be F (the largest) for rifles, FF (medium) for shotguns and FFF (fine) for pistols. In the higher grade of powder the usual sizes were TS6 (the largest) for rifles, TS4 (medium) for shotguns and TS2 (fine) for pistols. Many other types were available, including very coarse grain for punt guns. These have now been reduced to F and FFF, TS6 and TS2.

In the United States the fineness is indicated by the designation F – thus Fg powder is coarse, FFFg is quite fine. Generally, shotguns 12 gauge and smaller, and rifles that do not require a charge greater than 50 granules, will shoot the finer FFFg, FFF or TS2 satisfactorily. The Minie and .451 calibre rifles shoot better with the coarser Fg, F or TS6 powders, as do shotguns of larger bore. This is given as a general guide for the beginner to use safely and comfortably. The finer the granulation, the faster the powder burns and the more rapidly the peak pressure is reached. Most black powder muzzleloaders have long barrels, so coarser-granulated, slower-burning powder (it has plenty of time to burn in a longer barrel) gives a less rapid peak in pressure. This was designed for, and in rifle, shotgun and pistol, produces superior accuracy with diminished recoil.

Flints

Flints of workable size and quality are found in chalk, and were developed from the earliest time. There are other hard stones that fulfil the requirements, but black and amber coloured flints are the best.

Manufactured in a great variety of shapes and sizes, the degree of uniformity of eighteenth and nineteenth century flints is incredible. A high degree of manual skill was required as well as speed in production.

Percussion caps

These were made in two types: cylindrical grooved-sided and the 'Top Hat', or military,

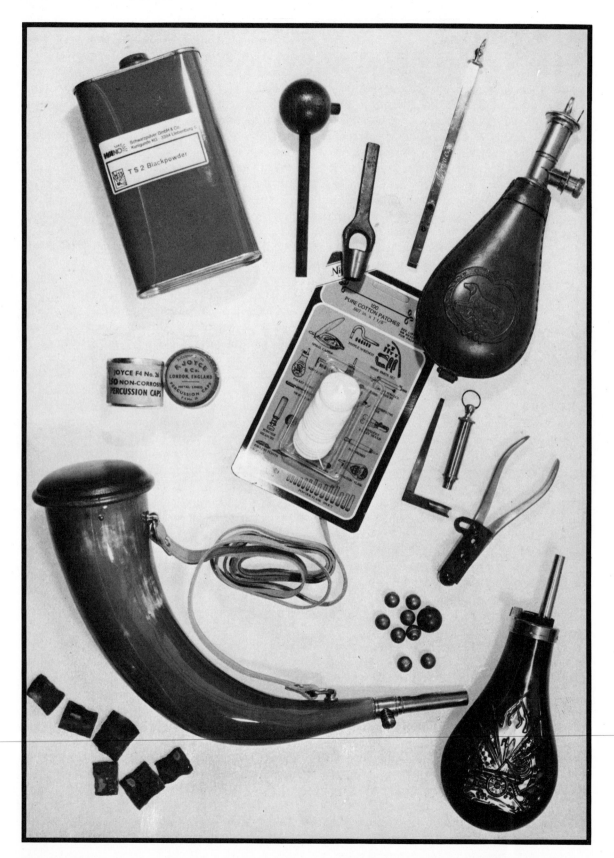

where the sides are 'split'. In both types when the cap is pressed onto the slightly larger nipple, it grips and should not fall off even when an adjacent barrel or chamber is fired.

Once produced in a very wide range of sizes, these have now been so drastically reduced that it may be necessary to fit new nipples to a muzzleloader so that available caps can be used.

Corrosive composition

The cap filling used to contain mercury fulminate and/or potassium chlorate as the principal component. The chlorides formed by the chemical reaction of the explosion attracted water and caused rust and corrosion. The mercury vapour was also a cause of corrosion, but was much less disadvantageous than the chlorides. These caps were reasonably easy to explode without being dangerous to handle and store.

Non-corrosive composition

Corrosion has almost been eliminated by this filling, provided that the arm is properly cleaned after use. The disadvantages of the modern filling are that more composition is needed and it is much less sensitive to percussion than the old corrosive mixtures, so sometimes the lock will need to be 'tuned up' to ensure an adequate blow from the hammer.

There is a device, originally developed at the end of the muzzleloading era in the United States, that uses centrefire cartridge primers. A modernized version is now sold in America. In effect, this obturates the nipple and is more efficient than the ordinary percussion cap because there is far less loss of gas.

Black powder accessories (clockwise from the top): A combined long and short starter, wad punch, cap dispenser, shot flask, nipple primer, nipple key, bullet mould, lead balls, powder flask, powder horn with flints below it, percussion caps, flask of powder. Centre: Cotton patches.

BULLETS

Lead and tin

Pure lead for cast bullets produces the softest possible bullets, but it is very difficult to get good casting. The addition of a small amount of tin is desirable, as it improves the ease of casting.

Minie type bullets

These bullets expand into the rifling, the expansion being caused by a hollow in the base with or without an expanding plug or cup. The bullet is the equivalent of $1\frac{1}{2}$ calibres long. A soft mixture must be used and it is suggested that up to 1 percent tin may be added to the lead.

'Any' rifle

These take the .451/.461 bullets of at least $2\frac{1}{2}$ calibres length. They require a much harder alloy for their casing. In bullets with lubricating grooves, 3 percent tin is satisfactory, but for smooth-sided, paper-patched bullets 5 percent or more tin produces better shooting.

Patched ball

In patched ball rifles the rifling spins the patch rather than the bullet. With shallow grooves and relatively thin patching, the bullet may be up to 4 percent tin. With a larger calibre and deeper grooves, a thicker patching and softer bullet will produce better results.

Mechanical fitting

Brunswick two-groove, Jacobs four-groove or Whitworth hexagonal bullets are a mechanical fit and should be as hard as 'Any' rifle bullets.

Revolver bullets

Round balls can be quite hard, with 4 percent tin or more. These will shoot well in some revolvers, but others will shoot better with a softer alloy. Remember that when fired, the round ball becomes cylindrical for a short section around its equator where it is in contact with the rifling. Elongated bullets should also be hardened. They must not be so hard as to require undue pressure on the rammer lever.

Pistol bullets

The same conditions as for patched ball rifles usually apply to pistols.

Antimony

This metal may also be used as a hardening agent, using approximately half the quantity of tin. It does not produce the same improvement in casting when present only in small amounts.

Shot

This is bought ready-made. Almost all modern shot is lead-hardened by the addition of antimony. The use of plated lead or steel shot is not recommended because it is too hard, particularly for the older barrels, which are not made from steel.

Wads

The use of a good quality, glazed, stiff card wad over the powder is an advantage in all arms except the patched ball and Minie rifles using hollow base bullets. Care must be taken that the wad is not tipped or buckled during loading.

The wad placed on top of the shot in shotguns may be of similar or slightly less stiff card.

A softer card, impregnated with a lubricant, can also be used between the over-powder card and the bullet.

Felt is principally used in shotguns and should be dense for best results. The wad column between the powder and the shot should not be less than two-thirds of the bore diameter. It is often an advantage, if the felt is soft, to put another card wad between the felt and the shot charge.

Because of the high cost of felt many types of materials are now used as substitutes. Probably the most effective are those made from wood fibres; they are very rigid and must be very close to bore diameter. Cork that has been granulated and compressed into sheets from which the wads are cut can also be used, but it is more expensive.

It is an advantage if the shotgun is of such a calibre as to make the use of plastic shot cups possible, but if the bore is rough, it may shave small pieces of plastic from the wad or cup. If these are not removed on discharge, they may cause difficulties if they get into the breech between the nipple and the barrel. It is usually recommended that an ordinary wad column be used with the shot only in a protective plastic cup.

Typical equipment for a shooting session: powder flasks, nipple keys, bullets and a box of grease.

Patching

A cloth containing synthetic yarn is useless, as the synthetic melts when fired and produces erratic shooting. All cloth patching must be thoroughly washed before use to remove the dressing applied in manufacture.

Cotton

Ticking, denim and other thick cotton materials can be used in patched ball rifles and pistols.

Some British and European rifles and pistols were designed to use a thin, fine quality linen, but a thicker, coarser quality was used with military rifles. Great care must be taken to ensure that the linen-type materials contain no synthetics.

Fine quality thin silk was usually confined to use in British and European rifles and pistols, but was occasionally used for patching Minie bullets for target shooting.

Paper is still used, but it must be a high grade bond paper between $1\frac{1}{2}$ and 2 thousandths of an inch thick. Glazed-surface art paper and soft, absorbent paper are totally unsuitable. Except in paper cartridges, the bullet was fired without added lubrication to the patch.

Lubricants

Early lubricants were not petroleum products and when using them it is better to lubricate bullets as close as possible to the time of use, as they often react with lead to give a hard deposit within a few weeks.

Tallow is an effective lubricant but below 40°F tends to be too stiff to melt properly.

Lard is as effective as tallow and is better below 40°F, but melts when the temperature rises above 70°F.

Beeswax has too high a melting point to use on its own, but is very effective when mixed with tallow. A good all-round mixture is four parts tallow to one part beeswax. First melt the tallow in a water bath, then dissolve the beeswax, and stir. The more the beeswax is refined, the harder it becomes. Crude beeswax is brown and may contain remnants of honey comb; fully refined and bleached beeswax is white and hard.

Whale oil

Whale oil is now getting difficult to obtain particularly in its pure form. It is principally used in engineering for quenching tools when they are being heat-treated. It can be used on cloth patch-ing or mixed with beeswax to soften the beeswax and lower the melting point of the mixture. The precise mix depends on personal experience and the degree of refinement of the beeswax. This mix is also a very good all-round lubricant.

Spermaceti

Spermaceti are the solids that separate from whale oil when it is left to stand undisturbed for some weeks. It is now virtually unobtainable, but at one time it was extensively used and was an excellent lubricant. It has a characteristic sweet smell, which serves to distinguish it from tallow, as old specimens look very much alike.

There is now a wide variety of new materials, usually petroleum products, available to fill the need of the patch ball, shotgun and grooved bullet shooter.

The mixtures sold for lubricating bullets when reloading cartridges are not suitable for muzzle-loaders.

For the beginner a four-to-one tallow-beeswax mixture, a suitably thin beeswax-whale oil mixture, or beeswax softened with white petroleum jelly are the best available lubricants.

Mineral grease is frequently used in revolvers, over the bullet, to avoid the risk of igniting adjacent chambers. Most shooters use the kind most readily available.

APPLICATION OF LUBRICANTS

Bullets

The most elementary method is to smear the lubricant on with the fingers, but this is very messy and gives an uneven coating.

A much better way is to warm the bullets to about 100°F and dip them, base first, into melted lubricant and then drain them on a newspaper, base down, until cold. Dipping a cold bullet into melted lubricant tends to give an uneven coating that is thicker at the base.

The bullets can be placed in a tray of melted lubricant of the right depth, and then allowed to cool, after which they are 'punched' out with a piece of tubing of suitable diameter. This takes more time, but it is better to push the tubing over the bullet and then push it out base first with a short wooden rod before racking the bullet in a storage box. The lubricant melts at a temperature considerably below that of boiling water.

Cloth patches

Pre-cut patches may be moistened with oil or soaked in grease, the latter practice being more common with large calibre rifles. Patch ball practice is to place a piece of cloth over the muzzle of the rifle and push the ball into the muzzle carrying the patching with it until it is possible to cut the patch off level with a sharp knife. The patch may be well-moistened with spit, a suitable proprietary lubricant, or the oil or petroleum jelly mixture already mentioned.

Wads

Wads are best lubricated by rolling the edges in lubricant. If some suitable colour is added to the lubricant it is easier to see how much has been applied. It is better not to use too much lubricant on shotgun wads since only a small amount is required.

In using .451/.461 type rifles of the 'Any' class, wads or discs of lubricant may be used between the bullet and the over powder wad.

CLEANING

Modern cleaning rods with jags of appropriate size for the barrel should be used.

About 50 percent of black powder combustion products are solids and water will remove these, particularly if the fouling has started to cake hard, and will dissolve any chlorides that may be present and are likely to give rise to subsequent corrosion. Hot water should be used, and the barrel should be dried and wiped over with an oil that will mix with water and so minimize the effect of any moisture left behind. This type of oil should not be brought into contact with the wood of the stock or butt. The oil used must not have any acid reaction or rusting will occur; some mineral oils, such as paraffin or kerosene, can cause severe after-rusting for this reason. Always check for the appearance of corrosion during the first week after use and cleaning.

A simple powder flask; three-way flask to hold powder, flint and bullets; and a powder horn.

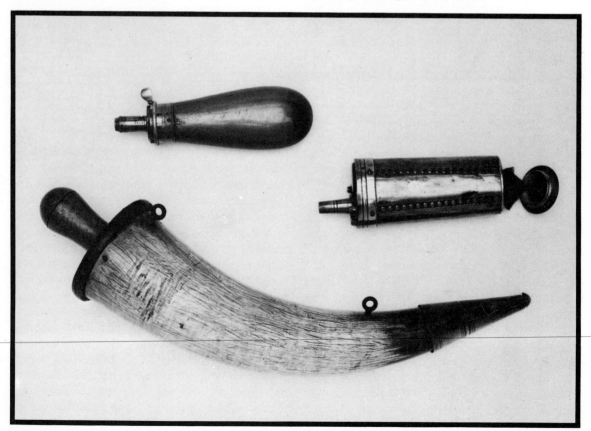

ACCESSORIES

Powder flask and shot pouch

Buy the best possible, with a 'Patent' top in which the cut-off works between two plates. The reproduction Dixon flasks are the best available, and those with the measures designed for use with rifles are a great asset.

A shot pouch with double cut-off measure operated by a rocking lever is most effective.

A funnel is needed for filling the powder flask and shot pouch as well as for loading powder and shot. It is very useful in windy conditions. The funnel must be kept well-cleaned.

Nipple key

It is very nice to have a faithful reproduction, but the essential quality is that it fits the square or parallel flats on the nipple as closely as possible. An all-metal T-shape is often a far more effective tool than the original type.

Nipple or vent pricker

Those made from hard drawn piano or stainless steel wire are preferred, as they must not be too hard or they may break off in the nipple or vent.

Nipple shield

This is a piece of sheet brass or copper with a hole through which the nipple screws to hold the shield in position. It is shaped to prevent escaping gas from eroding the wood of the stock or blowing back towards the shooter.

Screwdrivers

Keep a special set for your guns; one tool for each size of screw head. The original screws have narrow, wedge-shaped slots and the blade will need filing to fit them.

Loading rods

Except in the very small calibres, where a brass rod is best, a loading rod made of tough non-splitting wood of the largest possible diameter is an invaluable accessory. It should have a non-ferrous metal ferrule at the tip and a substantial knob, particularly for use with shotguns.

For rifles the loading rod does not need to be of the same strength. If loading becomes too difficult, something is wrong, and the bore should be checked for fouling or obstruction.

Shooting box

This should be a stout box, as it will have to carry shot or bullets in it, and should have as many compartments as possible to keep the accessories tidy and accessible.

Bullet or wad puller

This must be a tough tool, with a pilot sleeve as close to bore diameter as possible so that it can be used in different sized barrels. On the end of a stout steel rod is a threaded, double female bushing and into this is screwed a toughened tip made like a wood screw. The handle on the rod should be T-shaped and should not revolve. In the unfortunate event of a stuck bullet or wad, lubricate the barrel well with thin oil and then force the screw into the obstruction. It may need a lot of force to remove a stuck bullet and this implement is best made of 'tool steel'.

Score book

Whether your memory is good or bad, it will save you a lot of time and wasted effort to keep a score book, as it provides an instant, accurate recall.

Record weapon, powder type and quantity, shot type and quantity, bullet type, weight and alloy, wads with details, lubricant with details, weather conditions, and, of course, your score.

REPAIR AND RESTORATION

Beware of unskilful cleaning of originals and preserve as much as possible of the original finish. Barrels must not be altered without being resubmitted for proof. Try to restore a weapon in the same style as the original. There are many replacement parts now available, but make sure that they are properly heat-treated.

Removal of breech plugs needs specialized equipment, particularly with double-barrel weapons.

The most common faults in restoration are:
• burred screw slots and scratches from slipping screwdrivers – use properly fitting screwdrivers;
• vice-marks – use adequate padding;
• over-cleaning – do not use anything harder than the metal being cleaned, and use plenty of thin oil.

Beware of chemical cleaners – phosphoric rust removers also remove bluing and browning.

LOADING THE BLACK POWDER WEAPON

The first requirement is to see that the bore, nipple and touch-hole are clean and clear of any obstruction. This is often done on percussion weapons by placing a cap on the nipple and snapping it, but before this is done check that the weapon is empty. With a flintlock, the touch-hole can be cleared with a piece of wire, or a charge of priming can be flashed in the pan.

Now the powder must be poured down the barrel. The size of the charge is a matter of experiment, but it is difficult to overload percussion revolvers; if the ball can be seated in the chamber, then the charge is not too large. For other weapons a little more care is necessary in selecting the charge. Many manufacturers and the relevant specialist works listed in the bibliography will give guidance, but the final decision must be made after carefully controlled experiments. Too much powder will be shown by a firework display of burning powder leaving the barrel with the bullet! Fine-grain powders burn faster and can build up quite high internal pressures, so they should be treated with care and not used in original weapons unless those weapons are in good condition. During the loading procedures the barrel should either be pointing down range in the case of a revolver or, with all other weapons, away from the face and in the air. Fingers should be kept clear of the muzzle or chamber.

PERCUSSION REVOLVERS

The hammer is put to the half-cock position and the weapon is held with the muzzle vertical. The powder is poured into each cylinder from a powder flask or by a measure of some kind. Check visually that each chamber is loaded. Some shooters prefer to insert a wad next, others omit this and place the bullet directly onto the powder. Each chamber will need to be loaded separately. The loading lever fitted to most percussion revolvers is used to seat the bullet firmly on top of the powder. If no lever is fitted, a separate ramrod will be necessary. The bullet should be fractionally wider than the chamber to ensure a really good fit, and this will mean that considerable pressure may be needed to push home the bullet. To prevent any chance of a chain fire (when one shot sets off the next), a layer of grease is often smeared over the end of each chamber. Finally, a cap is placed on each nipple and the weapon is ready for firing.

SINGLE-SHOT PISTOLS, MUSKETS AND RIFLES

The hammer or cock is set to the half-cock position and the nipple or touch-hole checked to ensure that it is clear. The danger with all single-shot weapons is double loading. Unless the shooter is very careful, it is possible to pour two charges down the barrel without realizing it. As it is difficult to check visually, the solution is to develop a set procedure when loading and to stick to it rigidly. Powder flasks, preset measures or small plastic containers holding already measured charges can be used for loading.

The ball for most single-shot weapons is usually smaller than the bore and may need to be patched. The patches can be prepared before the event or the job can be done on the range. A piece of material is held over the muzzle and the bullet placed on the cloth and pushed in with the thumb. Then, with a sharp knife, the material is cut off level with the muzzle, and the bullet and patch are pushed steadily down the barrel. When the bullet is firmly seated, the nipple is capped, or, if the weapon is a flintlock, the pan can be primed with fine-grain powder and the frizzen closed.

One of the critical factors in getting a good performance with a rifle is the size of the patch or wad used in weapons that do not use an expanding bullet, and you must experiment to find exactly the right thickness and type of material.

SHOTGUNS

The procedure is similar to that for rifles. The powder is covered with a fairly thick wad, usually of felt. Lead shot is then poured down the barrel and held in place by another wad. The size of shot

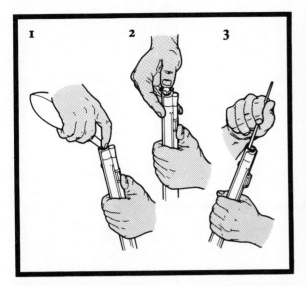

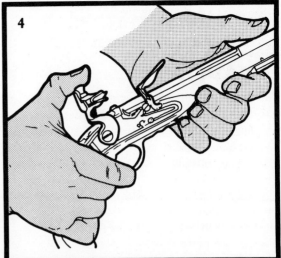

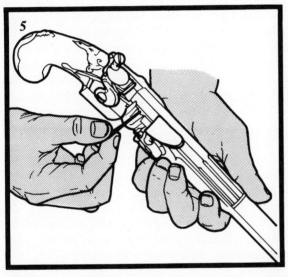

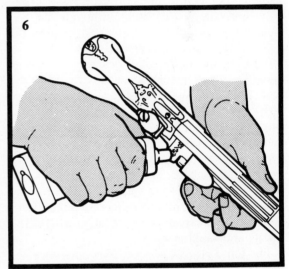

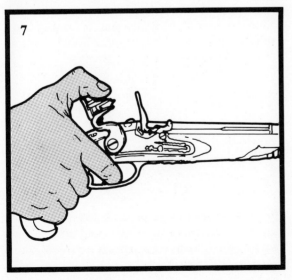

Loading and firing a flintlock.
1. Pouring coarse-grained powder into the muzzle.
2 and 3. A patched ball is inserted and rammed, down on the powder.
4. The flash pan is opened and the gun half-cocked.
5. Carbon must be cleaned from the touch-hole every few shots to avoid a flash-in-the-pan.
6. Priming the pan with fine-grained powder.
7. The final step is to snap the pan cover shut, tilt the gun to the left and tap it lightly so that a few grains of powder enter the touch-hole. When at full cock, the gun is ready.

and charge depend on the type of shooting; again, careful experiments achieve the best results.

FIRING

Muzzleloaders are held, aimed and fired in exactly the same way as cartridge weapons, but the shooter used only to cartridge weapons may find the first occasion on which he fires with black powder is something of a surprise. The first noticeable difference will probably be the recoil. With the very fast-burning modern propellents the recoil is usually a short, sharp kick; the recoil from slower burning black powder tends to be as strong, but less sudden, slower and more sustained.

Next the shooter will probably notice the heavier trigger pull required, although this will depend on whether an antique or a modern reproduction weapon is being used.

Another feature that may surprise the shooter unused to black powder is the hangfire. With the good quality caps available today, the hangfire with a percussion weapon is very slight. It can be quite appreciable with the flintlock, and it is therefore very important that when the weapon is brought into the aiming position it be held very steady and probably for a longer period than would be required for a cartridge weapon. The delay of the hangfire could otherwise be sufficient to allow the weapon to go off target before the bullet has passed the muzzle.

The other big and very obvious difference lies in the amount of smoke. Modern cartridge weapons produce none, but black powder generates clouds of grey-white smoke. The result of a shot is for the world to disappear in a cloud of smoke; it lasts only for a short time, but long enough to be very disconcerting to somebody who is unused to it. It is very useful to be able to see where one's shot is going, particularly when sighting or testing the accuracy of the weapon. This sudden eruption of smoke makes it very difficult, and the services of a friend to spot the impact of the shot will be needed. In certain conditions the dispersal of the smoke can cause problems, for it may drift towards a nearby shooter and cause irritation and coughing. When used indoors, it is most important to ensure that the range is very well ventilated.

Modern propellents produce very little deposit and virtually no fouling. Black powder does both, and in a rifled barrel the cumulative effect of the fouling is very noticeable. Each ball becomes progressively more difficult to push down the barrel. This fouling builds up quicker in hot, dry weather than in damp weather. The dedicated marksman of the mid to late nineteenth century often cleaned out the weapon after each shot. Today few shooters go to this extreme, but it will certainly be necessary to clean the barrel after every few shots. A scour with a phosphor-bronze brush may suffice, but water is really the best cleanser; at worst, a wet piece of four-by-two material should be wrapped around the ramrod or cleaning rod and pushed up and down the barrel several times. It is, of course, better if the barrel can be washed through, but there are obviously practical difficulties in this.

Black powder is not consistent in its quality, and most shooting enthusiasts would probably agree that good quality powder is not easy to acquire. The muzzleloader will soon find that it is very important to assess each fresh supply by a series of test shots.

THE FUTURE

Muzzleloading shooting has a great future. Inevitably, the majority of shooting in the future will be with reproduction weapons, and the production of quality reproductions at reasonable prices will enable the sport to continue. The argument for or against the production of redesigned weapons, in no sense in the spirit of the original, is a difficult one. I feel that we should adhere to tradition – and what a magnificent tradition it is – in what is a traditional sport.

Shooting long range muzzle loading match rifles from the back position (top) and the more common prone position (bottom).

18 CLAY PIGEON SHOOTING

THE BEGINNING

Pigeons had been bred for centuries to provide fresh meat in the wintertime when all other meat had to be salted, and so it was a very short step to consider these birds as targets for competitive shooting. It is generally accepted that the sport of live pigeon shooting had its origins at the Old Hats public house on the Uxbridge Road at Ealing, in those days a village outside London. The public house and the shooting ground attached to it took their name from the fact that the pigeons were placed in holes in the ground and then covered with old hats, which were pulled away with cords to release the birds. Before long another venue the Red House at Battersea, became famous and both these grounds were renowned for the shooting and the betting upon the shooting that went on.

Very soon the hats were replaced by metal boxes or traps into which the pigeons were placed. Upon the pulling of a string or lever the trap was collapsed, releasing the pigeon. Traps were first used at the Hornsea Wood House, to the north of London, and very soon the sport had spread widely. Of course it had to be regulated and two very famous pigeon shooting clubs, the London Gun Club and the Hurlingham Club, both published sets of rules, the latter publishing the last revision of such rules in 1901. It is remarkable how many of those rules have continued to shape the sport today.

The pigeons were bred especially for the sport, being small and fast and retaining the characteristics of the small wild pigeon known as the Blue Rock. The rules were very strict both in regard to the pigeons used and the conduct of both the shooters and the trappers who operated the releasing gear. Some remarkable scores were achieved, the celebrated Victorian shot Captain Bogardus killed 99 pigeons out of 100 in 1880 and scores of 100 ex 100 were recorded in the late 1880s and 1890s.

Monte Carlo became famous for the quality of its pigeon shooting, the ground favouring the pigeons and making the shooting very difficult, matches being won with scores of 12 ex 12. It is rather a strange coincidence that the disapproval of Princess Alexandra, then Princess of Wales, was one of the factors that led to the abolition of live pigeon shooting in Britain and that the disapproval of Princess Grace of Monaco led to the abolition of the sport in Monte Carlo more than 50 years later.

TARGETS

However, shooting at moving but inanimate targets had started long before the Hurlingham Club drew up its last set of live pigeon shooting rules. Glass balls were the targets; plain glass originally but later of coloured glass filled with feathers, thrown from a variety of spring projectors, some simple ones rather like the Roman catapult in miniature, others complicated and capable of throwing more than one glass ball at a time and at varying angles. But even to an ordinary shot, the glass balls were not difficult to hit and so thought was given to producing a target with a skimming flight. This was essentially a disc made of clay and baked, the early ones had a projection or tongue on the rim which was clamped to the throwing arm of the projector or trap as it was still called. It is interesting to note that in these early days of clay target shooting there was a law suit in which one London gunmaker sued another over the use of the words 'clay pigeons', the first one claiming that only his company had the right to call the targets 'clay pigeons'; firstly because they had been the first to use the words and secondly because the defendants' targets were not made of clay but of a mixture of tar and ash, not so far removed from the ingredients of today's targets. These were very similar in appearance to those used today and were in use in the shooting schools which became popular in the 1880s and 1890s. The first mention of a clay pigeon club as such occurred in Botley, Hampshire in 1884. The targets were thrown from traps recognizable as such today and in fact some of these old Victorian machines remained in use as recently as 25 years ago.

Live pigeon shooting was one of the attractions of the season for wealthy visitors to the fashionable resort of Monte Carlo in 1898. The town was famous for the quality of the shooting. The sport continued in this fashion until the middle of this century.

VICTORIAN MARATHONS

There came into being a controlling body known as the Inanimate Bird Shooting Association, which by the turn of the century had changed its name to the Clay Bird Shooting Association and already published a set of rules. These rules only really related to what we now know as Down-the-Line shooting and this followed the general principles of the live pigeon shooting which it was rapidly succeeding. One interesting point is that these early rules provided for the shooter standing not less than 18 yards behind the trap, not 16 yards as now. Some very high scores were being made even in those early days and the remarkable Captain Bogardus crops up again, when, in a marathon match with another famous Victorian shot, Doctor Carver, Bogardus broke 2,103 clays out of 2,500 but was beaten by Carver, who managed 2,227 to win the match. Carver's score included two rounds of 100 ex 100 and in 20 of his 25 rounds he broke over 90 clays.

This was the era of exhibition shooting and professional shots who could attract large crowds to watch them. Marathons were the order of the day and on an earlier occasion the same 'Doc' Carver in a match with a Mr Scott had broken 9,737 glass balls to Scott's 9,735 out of the 9,950 that both had shot at. As early as 1879 Captain Bogardus had shot continuously at glass balls for 7 hours and 20 minutes, breaking 5,500 and missing only 356. This was done with one gun with two pairs of barrels, one 10-bore shooting 1½ ounces of shot in front of 4 drams of black powder and the other pair 12-bore using 1 ounce of shot and 3½ drams of the same powder. It is recorded that he changed the barrels about every 100 targets, to allow them to cool and to clean out the fouling that the black powder left behind. The shot size was the same, size 8, and all I can say is that they were a tough breed in those days!

By Edwardian times the sport of clay target shooting was well established both in Britain and America and also on the Continent. As with so many other sports, the Great War provided a check to the activity but by the early 1920s it was well under way again, still following the pattern of the live pigeon shooting, and being known as Down-the-Line shooting in Britain and Trap

shooting almost everywhere else in the world. It demanded a very similar gun to what used to be known as a 'pigeon gun', fairly heavy and with both barrels carrying quite a lot of choke. This meant that the man with the ordinary game gun was at a disadvantage, as his gun was generally lighter and more open bored. The great majority of guns in use were still of the side-by-side type, but in America the slide action or pump gun had been in use for some years and the so-called 'automatic' gun (really a self-loader) had begun to make its appearance on the line. As American rules called only for single barrel trap shooting, special single barrelled trap shooting models were made, some of them of very high quality.

SKEET

In the mid-1920s a very important development took place. Credit for it is generally given to an American farmer who set up two clay target traps at opposite sides of a circle about 40 yards in diameter and then he and some of his friends amused themselves by walking around the circumference shooting at clay targets released alternately from each trap. The angles were varied in this way, but as the distances involved were never more than about 30 yards, they used the same guns with which they shot the game birds and ground game on the farm. The story goes that because the farmer's neighbour erected some buildings which prevented shooting in one direction, the circle was effectively reduced to a semi-circle, with the shooting positions remaining around the rim of the semi-circle.

The new form of clay shooting soon caught on, especially when it was realised that an ordinary game gun could be used. Rules were drawn up and an American shooting magazine offered a 100 dollar prize for the best suggestion for the new form of the sport and it was won by a lady who came up with the name 'Skeet', from an old Scandinavian word meaning 'shoot'. This was promoted with the aid of the slogan 'The gun game for the game gun' and it came to Britain in the late 1920s and is believed to have first been shot at the Waltham Abbey Gun Club in Essex, which had been established before the First World War.

The layout for skeet. There are two trap houses 40 yards apart, one called the High House, on the left as the shooters stand, and the other the Low House on the right. Targets are thrown alternately, both singles and simultaneous doubles, from the seven shooting stations on the perimeter of the semi-circle as the squad of five (or six) moves around the perimeter shooting in turn, finishing with two singles from the eighth station shown midway between the two trap houses. International Skeet is faster and also subject to a random delay mechanism in the release of targets.

300 yd (274m) safety zone

Below: Shooting skeet at the fourth station.

MODERN DEVELOPMENT

In 1928 the British national body changed its name to the Clay Pigeon Shooting Association, the name it still bears. In the years immediately before 1939 the sport continued to grow, slowly in Britain but much faster in the USA, where the Grand American Handicap, a Trap shooting event, had begun to attract entries numbered in hundreds. The Second World War put a stop to most of the clay shooting but an interesting sidelight was the fact that the RAF trained thousands of airgunners to shoot at moving aircraft with the aid of shotguns and clay targets, the principles being the same for both kinds of moving target, and a number of shooting coaches saw service in the RAF as training instructors.

With the coming of peace, the sport began again, although slowly, and even in the early 1950s the membership of the CPSA was only a few hundreds. With increased leisure and higher incomes, the growth of clay shooting began to accelerate, and more clubs were formed, both for Skeet and Down-the-Line. Sporting shooting began to attract large entries too, the most popular event undoubtedly being the British Sporting Championship, held every spring at Northolt on the outskirts of London. Many Sporting shoots began to be held as part of a larger event with sporting connotations, the most famous being the annual Game Fair promoted by the Country Landowners Association, first held in 1958 and since then an important part of the clay shooting calendar in Britain. The Sporting shoots particularly appealed to the game shot and the rough shooter.

By this time, the older version of the competitive sport, Down-the-Line, had generated a much more difficult form which had become an Olympic event under the name of Olympic Trench shooting, or as it is now known, Olympic Trap. Skeet was now also part of the Olympic Games; a more difficult form of the sport than that shot domestically in the USA and Britain was evolved under the auspices of the International Shooting Union and known as International or ISU Skeet. Competitions in both these disciplines began to make headway in view of the fact that all international events were held under these rules.

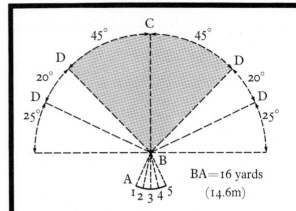

Single Rise shooting.

A	**Firing points 1 to 5, spaced 3 yards apart.**
B	**Trap pivot point.**
C	**50 yard target flight mark.**
D	**Stakes**
DC-DB	**Area within which targets may be thrown.**
BC	**Imaginary centre line.**

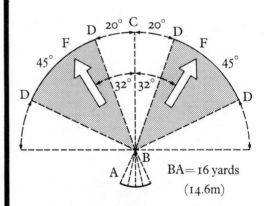

Double Rise shooting.

A	**Firing points 1 to 5, spaced 3 yards apart.**
B	**Trap pivot point.**
C	**50 yard target flight mark.**
D	**Stakes.**
DDB	**Area within which targets may be thrown.**
F	**Most desirable target flight.**
BC	**Imaginary centre line.**

Right: A Down-the-Line championship competition.

300 yd (274m) safety zone

Down-the-Line or Trap. Five shooters take part at one time, and a round consists of 25 targets. Each shooter fires five times from each of the five points shown. The layout can also be used for Double Rise shooting in which two targets are released simultaneously. All targets are moving away from the shooter in a 90° arc. The two smaller diagrams show the details of what is undoubtedly the most popular form of the sport in Britain and the USA.

Olympic trap. There are 15 traps in a trench, three in front of each shooter. Each trap is set at a different angle and the shooters change position five times. The release of targets is controlled by a random circuit and is completely unpredictable. The height of the targets is also varied within certain limits, and their speed is greater than in ordinary trapshooting.

Below: An automatic trap. The trapper releases the clay by pressing the button with his left thumb. The trap can also be fired by remote control.

GUNS

With the increase in all forms of clay shooting, the demand was for special guns for the various forms of competition and so increasing numbers of Skeet and Trap guns were marketed. Because the vast majority of these were designed in the first instance for the American market, where the single sighting plane had long been favoured, they were designed as over-and-under guns or self-loaders. The pump gun was still to be seen on the Trapshooting scene in the United States but as all other forms of the sport demanded a rapid firing of the second shot, it had virtually disappeared everywhere else, as had the side-by-side gun. Regrettably, none of the gunmakers in Britain had foreseen the trend, and so apart from the very few over-and-under guns made to special order at astronomical cost, it was left to the foreign makers to supply what was by now a booming market. In addition to the famous Liege-based company known all over the world by its initials FN, the makers of the over-and-under gun that was the last brainchild of the remarkable genius John Moses Browning, gunmakers in Italy, France, Spain, Germany, America and in some countries behind the Iron Curtain are making and exporting over-and-under guns in Trap and Skeet models. In recent years, Japan, which has coupled the latest in modern technology with first class manual skills from a highly productive work force, has become a major maker and exporter of shotguns, particularly of the over-and-under variety. At least one major American firearms company, Winchester, has its over-and-under guns made in Japan and a number of smaller companies are handling similar guns either under their own name or selling directly with the Japanese name tag. The guns are not particularly cheap but are of very good quality and represent excellent value for money and what is probably the largest manufacturer, B. C. Miroku, now provide a lifetime guarantee with all their guns.

In America the self-loader has a larger share of the market than it does in Britain and as American Trap shooting still only calls for single barrel shooting, at least one famous maker is still producing a single barrelled trap gun.

For Down-the-Line and its allied versions of ABT, Universal Trench and Olympic Trap, where all shooting is done with the gun already mounted in the shoulder, it is virtually essential to have a special Trap model gun, which is of little use for any other kind of shooting. For Sporting shooting one could start with almost any gun that was open-bored and at a pinch one could use the same gun for Skeet. Conversely one could by the same token use a Skeet model for the great majority of Sporting shooting – and even in the field one would not be very disadvantaged with the same gun.

The author shooting ISU Skeet. Note the 'gun down' position.

SPORTING SHOOTING

With the increasing popularity of the Sporting type of shooting, there is now a Browning special Sporting clay shooting over-and-under, different in style and boring from both the Trap and Skeet models and designed especially for Sporting shooting and in particular for what is undoubtedly the most difficult clay shooting of all, the *Parcours de Chasse* or as it is often known, FITASC Sporting, after the controlling body, the *Federation Internationale de Tir aux Armes Sportives de Chasse*. This discipline demands not only a most complicated system of layouts, with traps placed to give a very wide variety of shots, but no less than five different types of clay targets, including the 'Mini', which is less than half the size of the standard target used for Skeet and Trap. It is of necessity very costly to stage, requiring both a large area of land and also a large number of trappers. In spite of that it is becoming more and more popular and in 1978 the 11th European, also the very first World Championship of this event was staged in Yorkshire and attracted a large entry for both events over the week that the shooting lasted. So far it is almost unknown outside Europe.

There is also another well-established variety of competitive clay shooting held under ISU rules and known as Automatic Ball Trap, usually abbreviated to ABT. Although this bears some resemblance to Down-the-Line, in that the targets are all going away from the shooter, it is faster and less predictable than the older sport. This is very popular in France, where one can see numerous signs on the roadside when driving along which simply consist of an arrow pointing down a side road with the words 'Ball Trap' on it. International events are held and a number of British clubs have now installed ABT layouts, which are far cheaper to put in than an Olympic Trap layout.

Universal Trench shooting, is the other kind of shooting sport controlled by FITASC. It could very simply be described as something between ABT and Olympic Trap and possibly because it is more expensive to install than the former and lacks the cachet of the latter, it appears to be less popular than either.

Right: Universal Trench is somewhat similar to Olympic Trench but with only five traps in the trench, set at different angles and heights. In both versions the shooters stand in a straight line, rather than in an arc, as in Down-the-Line.

Below: Automatic Ball Trap. Similar to Down-the-Line in that only one trap is used and the shooters stand in an arc to the rear of the trap, but the targets are faster and oscillate vertically as well as horizontally.

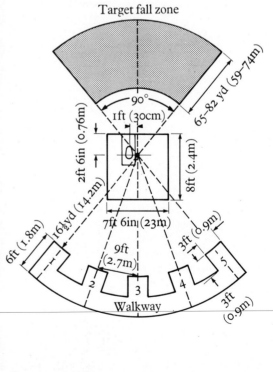

Right: A Universal Trench competition.

Above: Shooting the 'Snipe' stand at a Sporting championship.
Left: Taking a bird on Stand One during a summer Sporting championship.
Below: Shooting the 'Partridge' stand during a Sporting contest.

It is interesting to compare the relative difficulty of all these different kinds of clay shooting and we have an easy method of doing this with the average scores for registered shoots published each year in respect of every member of the CPSA who takes part in such shoots. As I write, the last available year for these is 1977 and a careful study of these, backed up by personal knowledge, reveals that the oldest form of all, Down-the-Line, is by far the easiest. Not only did this version attract by far the most entries in that year but it had far and away the highest average scores. No fewer than 201 people who shot this kind of competition had an *average* score of 95 percent or over, compared with only 24 with an average of 90 percent or over at ABT and a mere six whose score at Olympic Trap was an average of 90 percent or above. Granted that there were far fewer who shot the more difficult varieties, and even fewer Universal Trench shooters produced 14 men with an average of 90 percent or over.

With sporting shooting the position is similar, although not quite so simple. A good sporting layout, with its variety of angles and speeds, will tax even the best of shots and so the average scores are the lowest of any. A further reason is that there are so many kinds of sporting layout that each one tends to be a new experience, whereas in the other disciplines the grounds should all conform to the same standard, although one has only to shoot on some of them to realize that this is not necessarily so! Thus as a general rule anything over 80 percent is a good score and even the best of shots cannot get above the middle 80s as an average.

For FITASC Sporting the performances will show a lower level of scores even than those of ordinary Sporting, although in 1977 Brian Wells, the British winner of the European Championship in both 1977 and 1978, actually had a slightly higher average at the *Parcours de Chasse* than he did for the domestic events but then we are talking of someone who shoots the International version superlatively well and who obviously thrives on tough competition. If only spectators were allowed, this would rank as perhaps the version of our sport with greatest spectator appeal but unfortunately under the rules not only are spectators discouraged but they are actually forbidden. The theory is that each competitor therefore comes to each layout without prior knowledge of what he is up against, not having seen it before. Be that as it may, it effectively denies the public the chance to watch something which is very fascinating visually and would make good television. I feel that although this will never be the cheapest version of clay shooting, it could well become more popular if smaller layouts could be used, thus cheapening the cost, which at the moment is almost prohibitive except for the very keenest and even then they must be prepared to dig deep into their pockets.

Although all clay shooting is beneficial to one's field shooting, ISU Skeet and Sporting shooting, with their 'gun down' position and their greater emphasis on correct gun mounting than the 'gun up' types of shooting will prove of rather more benefit to the game shot or rough shooter, as will the delayed release of the targets which is part of the ISU Skeet. Of course, if you really get the clay fever, you may turn out to be one of those very fortunate few who manage to shoot every kind of clay target with success.

In order to improve the standard of shooting of Great Britain's teams, the CPSA's British International Board has now established a training squad, in which the top shooters in the international disciplines, can come together as a squad, rather than individuals, and thus train together, with the aid of correct coaching and management, and from this squad, international teams will be picked. With the aid of grants of both money and ammunition generously given by leading cartridge manufacturers, this process should cost the members of the squad little or nothing, for the International Board will be responsible for administering the training facilities and will provide what is required. Furthermore, with the aid of grants from the Sports Council, the bulk of the costs of overseas entries can now also be met, international competitors in the past often had to finance such costs to a considerable extent from their own resources, something almost unknown to the shooters from other nations.

So what of the future of the sport as a whole? Over the past few years this sport, which cannot fail to be expensive compared with some others, has seen enormous growth both in the number of events held and in the number of people taking part, and the national body has seen an impressive growth in membership. I think that there are two basic reasons for this. One is that it is part of the trend towards participant sports as distinct from spectator sports and the other is that people are finding that it is one of the few sports without barriers of age or sex. Men, and to a lesser extent women, come into the sport in their early teens and even before and at the other end of the scale there are shooters in their seventies still taking part in clay shooting and still doing well. On both counts clay shooting tends to hold onto its adherents. A further factor is the undoubted sense of friendship and sociability which runs through the sport. Although there are a very few 'prima donnas' among clay shots, and perhaps they have grown in number in recent years, with the vast increase in the value of prizes and prize money to be won, the vast majority of clay shots shoot for the fun of it and, win or lose, are good people to be with. In the almost 30 years that I have been associated with the sport, I have had some tremendous fun and met some wonderful people, some of whom have become great friends. I can recommend anyone who is looking for a sport in which he or she will find fun, friendship and encouragement, to take up clay shooting. The best way to begin is simply to enquire locally (your nearest gunsmith is an obvious place) as to the location of any clubs in your neighbourhood. Find out when they meet and go along, initially as a spectator if you wish. The chance to shoot will undoubtedly present itself and membership may follow if you wish. Once you are in you will find that further opportunities will arise through the contacts you make and of course the shooting press lists shoots usually about two weeks in advance. From then on it is up to you.

Right: Shooting at the tower in a Sporting contest.

Below: Sporting shooting and FITASC Sporting are infinitely variable. Generally, targets are as fast as possible, thrown to simulate the type of shot likely to be met with in the field, and are referred to by such names as 'High Pheasant', 'Bolting Rabbit', 'Snipe' or 'Partridge'. They may vary from clays thrown from a tower, which may be as much as 120 feet high, to special targets which are rolled along the ground to resemble a bolting rabbit. FITASC uses different types of clay target and more traps to increase the challenge. One typical stand, the 'High Pheasant', is shown. This may provide crossing shots or going away shots by varying the position of the shooter.

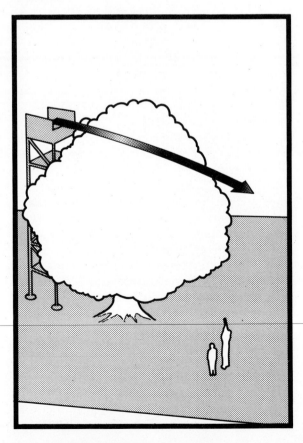

19 GAME SHOOTING AND HUNTING

GAME SHOOTING IN BRITAIN

The term Game shooting covers a wide range of shooting sports in the field, and in its widest sense is a year-round activity. It could be said that the British shooting year begins on 12 August – 'The Glorious Twelfth' – with the opening of the grouse season, followed by partridge shooting and wildfowling on 1 September, and pheasant shooting a month later on 1 October. The official seasons finally end on 20 February with the close of wildfowling, but shooting for sport is carried on throughout the year with rabbits and pigeons the main quarry.

However, there is far more to shooting than the act of firing a gun, and the background to the sport is as important as the sport itself. Partridge and pheasant shooting probably account for more day's sport during the season than any of the others. The methods vary tremendously, from the lone farm worker with his dog and gun walking through the thickets in the hope of flushing a pheasant or two, to the carefully keepered estates, with their formal shoots involving a small number of guns, usually less than ten, waiting for the line of beaters to drive the birds from cover to fly over the waiting line of guns. In each case there will be a close contact with the country-side and its spirit. The lone gun will perhaps see during the quest for his quarry a jay in the wood, or perhaps a family of weasels hunting mice along a dry stone wall, or hear the nightingale sing in the depths of a wood. He may break his hunt for pheasants to stalk a rabbit along a hedgerow, or a hare which is lying motionless in a stubble field. The formal shoot will employ one or more gamekeepers who will be absolutely familiar with the land they are responsible for, and all the birds and mammals and trees and shrubs on it. In order to protect their primary charges, the game birds, during the year they will hunt and trap a wide range of predators ranging from foxes, weasels, stoats, hedgehogs, squirrels and rats on the ground to crows, magpies, jays and jackdaws in the air. They must have an intimate knowledge of all these creatures and their habits and be able to deal with them before damage is inflicted on nesting pheasants and partridges, their eggs or their young.

**Above: Pheasant shooting in autumn.
Opposite: Between drives during a shoot in Hampshire.
Below: Shooting in Riccal Dale, north Yorkshire.**

PHEASANT SHOOTING

The pheasant was introduced to Britain towards the end of the Roman occupation of these islands. It was almost certainly the 'Old English' or black-necked variety, and this is the bird which was generally known in this country until the end of the seventeenth century. Since then a number of other introductions have been made, including the ring-necked or Chinese pheasant, the Mongolian and the Japanese. Cross-breeding has produced fertile hybrids.

The pheasant may be encountered anywhere except on moorland and very high ground, but it prefers land where woodland and copses with sufficient undergrowth for cover alternate with parkland, fields and cultivation.

The pheasant feeds on the ground, with seeds and berries constituting the mainstay of its diet, supplemented by insects, earthworms, slugs, etc., which comprise about a quarter of its intake. The pheasant is generally beneficial to agriculture, but in those areas where large numbers of reared birds have been released, agriculture can suffer unless food is laid down for the over-populated stock. Pheasants nest on the ground, in a wood, copse, hedgerow or reedbed, the nest being a simple hollow scraped in the ground by the hen, usually in a nettlebed or other thick cover. Laying usually begins in April and eight to 15 eggs are incubated for about 24 days by the hen. She also rears the brood alone.

By the time the pheasant shooting season opens (on 1 October) the birds are well grown. The overriding object of driving pheasants is to provide sporting shots that fully test the skill of the guns. This is far more difficult than it sounds, and requires a full knowledge of the ground to be shot and the habits of pheasants in order to be able to place the guns in a position that is likely to fulfill the requirement for the showing of the maximum number of birds, in such a way as to provide testing shots for the guns. This usually involves siting the guns close to a wood or a field of crops that provides shelter and seclusion for the pheasants. The guns are often placed in the bottom of a valley to ensure that the birds fly that much higher over them and consequently provide harder shots, but various other factors must be taken into account before they can be assumed to fly over the guns. Firstly,

pheasants prefer to run or squat tight rather than fly, secondly, they will head for other cover once flying. This cover may be another wood or other holding cover. Once they are on course for their goal they are unlikely to be diverted by the presence of humans beneath them, but rather will be inclined to gain height, thus adding to the sporting qualities of the shoot. Thirdly, they should not be driven against the wind, as they dislike flying into the wind, and are likely to turn before reaching the guns. It will therefore be seen that the selection of the guns' position needs to be made with some care, bearing all these factors in mind. The actual weapons used for pheasant shooting are usually 12-bore shotguns, though occasionally smaller calibres are used, particularly by ladies or by young shots who often use a 20-bore. Most of these 12-bore guns will fire the standard $2\frac{1}{2}$ inch cartridge throwing 1 ounce to $1\frac{1}{8}$ ounce of shot, usually no. 6 or no. 7 shot. These guns are known as game guns, and are traditionally of the side-by-side type. Over-and-under guns and automatics are increasingly seen, though the latter are still unwelcome on many shoots. The guns should wear sober clothing which will not make them stand out against their background, and a tweed jacket is probably most popular. In case of rain a waterproof jacket is worn, usually with waterproof leggings or trousers and rubber boots. A hat is also worn, again usually of tweed, to partially hide the sportsman's face from the oncoming birds.

Once the guns are in position, the line of beaters will advance on the given signal, usually the blast of a horn. The beaters wear normal field clothing and boots and are usually supplied with waterproof trousers or leggings to avoid the discomfort of walking through cover when it is wet. They advance steadily towards the guns, tapping tree trunks and beating thickets with the sticks which they carry. They are often accompanied by close-working dogs, usually spaniels, to assist in flushing birds from heavy cover inaccessible to man. If a large number of birds is flushed, the line may pause momentarily to allow a steady flow of birds over the guns, rather than a large bunch all at once. As the beaters close with the guns, and many birds are left in between, it is important to flush them steadily, rather than causing the last-moment panic which will send too many birds over the guns at once. When the beaters are near the guns, the keeper will judge the moment to end the drive, and will signal this by another blast of his horn, when all firing must cease. The beaters with dogs will then assist in picking up the dead birds, and the dogs will locate and retrieve any wounded birds. The birds will then be tied in pairs, head uppermost in the game cart.

On most modern syndicate shoots the guns are given a brace apiece at the end of the day, the remainder being sold off to dealers to supplement the funds of the shoot. Pheasants retained are hung in a cool place for up to a fortnight before plucking and cooking. During the early part of the season both sexes are shot, though it is generally agreed that hens cook better than cocks, but in January towards the end of the season there may be one or two 'cocks only' days. This is to reduce the population of cocks to hens for the forthcoming breeding season, as pheasants are polygamous and an excess of cocks may harass the hens by continuous fighting, and also the hens may be worried into being infertile.

Right: Cock pheasant.
Below: Pheasant shooting scenes.

PARTRIDGE SHOOTING

There are two types of partridge in Britain, the common, or grey partridge, and the red-legged, or French partridge. The grey partridge is indigenous to these islands, whereas the red-legged was introduced in 1770 to Sudbourne in Suffolk by Lord Hertford.

The grey partridge is slightly smaller than the red-legged, and is most at home on relatively flat areas of mixed arable farmland with plenty of shelter in the form of banks and hedges, and particularly on sandy soils, which do not long remain wet after rain. This type of soil also satisfies another of their needs – grit, which is essential for their diet. Grey partridges may be found outside the breeding season in coveys varying in number from just a few to over 40 birds. Essentially a covey will consist of one or more family units, though a large covey may also contain a few unattached birds. Greys are generally paired off by the end of January, and they begin to nest in late April or early May. The nest will usually consist of a scrape under a hedgerow or on a bank, and the hen will sometimes lay just one egg, then leave the nest with the egg fully exposed. It may be supposed that this is to test the security of the site, but one can only speculate on this point. She will then return and lay the rest of her eggs, up to 14 or 15, and then leave them again for perhaps a day before returning to incubate. Both cock and hen bird will take turns to incubate the eggs, and when the eggs hatch out the cock bird will be in close attendance, brooding the dried chicks while the remainder hatch out. When the whole clutch is hatched, the entire family will head for cover such as a cornfield, where food will be more plentiful and cover from marauders may be found. The chicks feed mainly on insects to begin with, though after a week or so they will begin to pick up tiny seeds, green food and grit though insect matter is of prime importance: without it they die. Reasonable weather too, is important, as they chill easily when damp, or die very quickly on cold nights. An average covey will probably suffer higher casualties during the chicks' first month than during any similar period later.

Generally speaking, partridges are sedentary birds, preferring to stay within a small area, though occasionally a covey will leave one area and travel several miles to another more to its liking. However, in no sense are they migratory. Nobody knows how long partridges will live, though there are recorded instances of birds six and seven years old.

Until they are some four months old, partridge chicks have yellow legs, then gradually they turn grey, though the soles of the feet will remain yellowish. The tips of the first two primary wing-feathers of the young birds are pointed until they are over a year old, when they become rounded. Adult males have chestnut and dark brown splotches on the median wing coverts, while the females have broad bands of dark brown with narrow wavy crossbars of buff which are very noticeable. Both sexes may have the dark reddish-brown horseshoe on the chest, though it may be lacking in some hens. There are many colour variations of the above, varying from very dark to pure white birds.

The French partridge is not a true partridge at all, but rather a francolin, and is found in varying forms in Southern France, Italy, Switzerland, Spain and all over southern Europe through the Middle East as far as Pakistan and India. It is marginally larger than the grey partridge, weighing on average 16 to 18 ounces, as opposed to 12 or 13 ounces. Sexing them is not easy, though adult cock birds have rudimentary spurs which aid the distinction. Young birds can be distinguished by having pale buff edges to the first two primary wing feathers, these first two feathers are also more pointed in the juvenile. Generally, the French partridge is a hardier bird than the grey, and can better tolerate wet, often living well on heavy clay soils which the grey will shun for more sandy and better drained soils. The French partridge is also more of a wanderer than the grey especially in the spring before laying. It can also be more easily tamed, and the writer recalls a covey of about a dozen which inhabited a restaurant in the Turkish hinterland, mingling freely with the tea-drinkers, picking up fallen scraps and sunning themselves by a window.

Top left: Red legged partridge.
Top right: Grey partridge.
Bottom: Shooting partridge on a fine autumn day in the Vale of York.

Partridge always have a tendency to be very reluctant fliers, preferring to run or squat where possible, and even when flying will travel only a short distance, albeit at some speed. Their numbers have been considerably reduced for the same reasons as their indigenous counterparts, namely reduction of habitat through changed farming methods, and the reduction of their insect food supply through the over-use of insecticide crop-sprays.

From the sportsman's point of view the two breeds are very different. The French partridge is slightly larger and faster than the grey, and will take off one after the other when driven, rather than in a single mass of birds, and thus provides a steady stream of birds over the guns rather than a single break of many birds. It flies straighter and higher and in all provides more testing shooting than its native cousin, even though it may be a culinary disaster afterwards.

Partridges are nearly always driven to guns rather than walked-up. This is primarily because of their reluctance to fly, preferring to sit tight or run on the ground, which means that when walked-up they either get up too close to the gun, or will run on some way ahead, and not give the opportunity of a flying shot. It may be said that 90 percent of partridges shot are killed by driving rather than by walking-up. Driving also allows a far larger area to be covered and the birds therein gathered to the guns. Partridge drives are generally much shorter than pheasant or grouse drives, and lend themselves better to the small shoot. Some shoots rich in holding cover will have one drive from the best ground towards an area of beet, turnips, kale or other good holding cover, then hold a second drive at right angles to the first, driving to another field of holding crops. A third will be held at right angles to the second, and a fourth at right angles to the third, returning the birds to the best ground from which they were first flushed. Some of the finest areas in England for partridge shooting are the market-garden areas around Lincolnshire where there are crops in the ground even up until the end of November—cabbages, turnips, sprouts, etc. Of course such areas can be unpleasant to drive when wet and it is essential that beaters are provided with waterproof overtrousers or leggings when beating through standing crops during or after rain.

The positions for the guns should have been decided and clearly pegged out before the drives. There should always be a few extra positions pegged out on each drive to take into account any variation of the wind, and the keeper or the host can arrange which pegs shall be occupied immediately before the shoot. The guns are placed in a line behind a hedge or fence, or, if there are none at the chosen site, butts may be made of hurdles with camouflage of straw or branches. The area before and behind the guns should preferably be grass, stubble or plough, so as to avoid the loss of birds falling in heavy cover. It is quite astonishing how difficult it can be to find a dead partridge lying in even scant cover and dogs are essential when picking up after a drive.

Champion pigeon shooter Major Archie Coats with labrador Juno and the results of a day's shoot in open country.

GROUSE SHOOTING

There can be few forms of bird shooting which are more exciting and testing than driven grouse. The season opens on 12 August and continues through to 10 December, though only heavily-stocked moors will be shot after early November.

The Red Grouse is a native of the British Isles, and may be found on high moorland in several parts of the country, but its strongholds are the highlands of Scotland, particularly on the eastern side, and on the Yorkshire, Derbyshire and Cumbria moors. Its staple diet is the shoots and seed-heads of ling-heather, and the bloom of bell-heather, supplemented by a wide range of other foods which include crowberries, rushes, insects, spiders, slugs, caterpillars, bilberries and cranberries, mosses, fungi and ferns. On the edge of the moor, where the moorland meets cultivated land, grouse will also eat oats, turnip leaves, bramble berries, hawthorn and rowan berries. It is a bird whose life-history was until comparatively recently almost totally unknown, and today there are still large gaps in our knowledge. We do know that the grouse is a very shortlived bird; two out of every three in August are dead before the following August, whether the moor is shot or not. Out of over 1,200 ringed birds recovered in one survey, only 5 percent were older than three years. The cause of their short life may be due to their social system, which is based on autumnal competition for territory.

There are basically two 'social classes' of grouse. Firstly, there are the territorial residents, which hold, and will continue to hold against all comers, their chosen territory, and these birds will form the breeding stock in the following spring. The second group consists of other birds which will be evicted from the territory of the first group. Because this latter group is unable to select suitable ground for feeding, cover and shelter they are likely to be dead by the end of the winter. Thus even if an old bird is not shot during the season, it will have to compete once again for territory by October and if it fails to hold it, it will die. So even on a well-driven moor, a bird which escapes being shot may only live for another month or so before dying. The key to their survival is aggression: if they are sufficiently aggressive they will take a territory with one or more hens each and are virtually guaranteed a further year of life. If they lack sufficient aggression, they will die before they are eleven months old.

Many of the older cocks have returned to hold their nesting territories by mid-September, and they begin to display by early winter, and have often paired by Christmas. Clutches of eggs usually number between 6 and 12, and are laid in April, and are nearly all hatched by the end of May. The weather during the next few weeks is critical to the young chicks, and if there is persistent rain during this period many of the young will die, even though they are very robust. They are able to flutter their wings at a week old, and can fly short distances in under two weeks. Their staple diet at this stage is mainly insects, gradually including more vegetable matter as they grow older. One of the foremost authorities on grouse thinks that the common midge, such a curse to humans in summer and autumn, is a favourite food of the young grouse. They also need quantities of grit, which aids digestion.

A fine specimen of a red grouse on the North Yorkshire Moors.

Grouse can vary greatly in weight: males generally weigh more than females, averaging 20 to 24 ounces, while females may weigh 15 to 20 ounces. One of the curious features of grouse is that during the winter, when feeding conditions are worse, and they require more food to sustain them in adverse weather, they will often weigh more than in summer when conditions are so much better. A female grouse has been recorded as weighing 27 ounces in March.

Grouse shooting, like partridge and pheasant shooting, can be conducted either by walking-up or driving. Very few moors nowadays have regular walking-up, as when grouse are the quarry it is essentially a sport for one or two guns only, usually shooting over pointers, though occasionally a line of guns may be seen. While the bag of walked-up birds is never likely to approach that obtained by driving, it can be very instructive, particularly to the young shot. The places where grouse are to be found, and their behaviour when flushed, may give a novice gun much information and experience which will be useful to him later on when shooting driven birds.

It has been estimated that 90 percent of grouse which are shot are obtained by driving, and it is shooting driven grouse which is probably the most exciting and taxing form of bird shooting in the world. It came into its own during the period 1850 to 1870 for two reasons. The first was the invention and subsequent development of the breechloading gun, which was much quicker to reload than the muzzleloading gun which it superseded; and the second was the development of the railway, which meant that sportsmen could be transported with their guns, dogs and other impedimenta into the heart of the highlands very quickly – a man could board the train in London in the evening and be at his shooting lodge the following evening. By the 1890s shooting parties in the highlands were great social occasions and had their own particular etiquette. These gatherings were probably on the highest plane when they included the Prince and Princess of Wales, and for the ladies necessitated a change of dress at least four times a day. It was not the done thing to appear in the same costume twice in one visit, and the expense involved must have tempered many a sportsman's keenness for his shooting.

Grouse butts are built in a line of eight or more across the side of a hill or along a valley. They are sited some 30 or 40 yards apart, and are usually built of stone, lined with turf inside and out, with extra loose turves which can be removed or added according to the height of the occupant. Each butt is numbered, and having drawn for places, the guns move to their allotted butts with their loader. As most grouse shooting is done with two guns, the loader is an absolute necessity, taking the fired gun from the shooter, reloading it and exchanging it when the other gun has been fired.

The line of beaters will assemble at some distance from the guns, perhaps even a couple of miles, and begin to walk towards the guns, accompanied by dogs which will help to flush the grouse, causing them to fly towards the guns. The grouse will at this time of year be in family groups, and will be flushed in a pack which may number anything from three or four to a hundred. Grouse fly fast, swinging from side to side in flight, usually hugging the ground for some distance before rising up and gaining height. Sometimes they will stay low, and a pack flushed some way from the guns will provide both high and low birds, but all fast and testing, particularly if there is a strong wind. In many places the butts are sited just over a rise, and the shooter will have time only for a very quick shot or two before the birds are over him, a few seconds at the most. In this time he will have to pick his bird, mark its flight, and shoot at it. As the beaters close with the guns more and more birds are flying low, hugging the ground and the shooting becomes more difficult and taxing.

A fair description of a drive has been written by J. K. Stanford, a renowned author who had a deep respect for the challenge of driven grouse: 'Only when the grouse arrive do you realize that they drop completely out of sight in front of you till they cross the rim of the gully a bare twenty yards in front, and you are blind unless a bird is well up in the air. The first grouse, looking as big and black as a Leghorn cockerel, appears straight in front at ground level, jinks at right angles as you raise your gun, and is over your neighbour's head before you can retrieve a hurried miss.

Top: August on the grouse moors of Yorkshire.
Bottom: Shooting over dogs in autumn woodland.

You glimpse another black dot a hundred yards away. He sinks out of sight, then five seconds later bobs up like a jack-in-the-box twenty yards left of where you expected him and is hurtling across you left-handed. You kill two or three birds which give you a fraction more time by being slightly higher, and as you snap at and miss behind a bird which nearly takes your cap off, the rim of the gully seems to vomit grouse at you for thirty seconds, all jinking and swerving right-handed down the wind. These are late October birds and give you no law at all, and the last three crossing the line on a rocket-like curve are so palpably fast that even the professor on your right is swearing audibly.'

There are many other descriptions of driven grouse-shooting, as the grouse not only inspires the best shots to return again and again but to wax lyrical in print on their experiences. Some of the best descriptions are to be found in *The Grouse* by A. J. Stuart-Wortley, published in 1895. One of his descriptions of a drive is particularly exciting, and covers many pages; it gives a wonderful insight into the thrill of the drive, and although written over 80 years ago, is still most instructive to the modern novice. Suffice it to say that few descriptions ever written can match up to the reality of being on the moor, and having to contend with a pack of swerving, swinging and jinking grouse passing over at various heights and varying speeds.

The standard gun used on the grouse moor is an ordinary double-barrelled 12-bore shotgun, often firing light loads of an ounce of shot or even less, and with practically no choke in the barrels. As the average range at which grouse are shot is about 20 yards, there is no need for heavy chokes and heavy loads – if the gun is not pointing in the right direction, no amount of extra shot will make any difference. Many people use a smaller calibre gun for grouse, either a 16-bore or a 20-bore, either because they do not feel confident of being able to swing the bigger gun fast enough to cope with driven grouse, or because they prefer the smaller gun in any case. Ladies, boys and some older sportsmen may be seen with these smaller guns. Another special gun is the 12-bore which fires a 2 inch cartridge (as opposed to the standard $2\frac{1}{2}$ inch cartridge) with a light load, almost the equivalent of the load of a 20-bore gun. This gun is frequently built to weigh a pound less than a normal 12-bore.

WILDFOWLING

Wildfowling has been defined as the sport of shooting those species of wildfowl which may legitimately be shot with smoothbore guns. Within this definition lies a wide variety of different aspects of wildfowling, which may be simply broken down into the different areas in which fowling may take place, ranging from flighting over an inland pond, shooting on the shore, and shooting afloat.

Quarry species in Britain may be divided between duck, geese and waders. Species of duck which may be shot include common pochard, gadwall, wigeon, mallard, pintail, shoveler, teal and tufted duck. Quarry species of geese include whitefront, greylag, pinkfoot, bean geese and Canada geese. Wader species include curlew, bar-tailed godwit, golden and grey plover, common redshank, common and jack snipe.

The shooting season inland for duck, geese and waders except snipe is from 1 September to 31 January. Snipe may be shot from 12 August to 31 January. Below high-water mark of ordinary tides the season for duck and geese is extended to 20 February. In Scotland only these birds may not be shot on a Sunday. Special protection from shooting is extended to all species of swans, shelduck, eider-duck, brent geese and herons.

1. **Canada geese, the commonest of the quarry species.**
2. **Greylag geese on a salt-marsh in the early morning.**
3. **Young ringed plover on the shore, its typical habitat.**
4. **Curlew, a wader species frequently found in upland areas.**
5. **Golden plover well camouflaged on its moorland nest.**
6. **Wintering female teal, the smallest European duck.**
7. **Female tufted duck, a common quarry on inland lakes and ponds.**
8. **Snipe, with its long straight bill and distinctive striped crown.**

1

2

3

5

4

6

7

8

DAILY MIGRATION

Inland shooting usually takes place at dusk or at dawn at a small pond where duck come in to feed at night, though shooting may also take place in moonlight – an especially exciting sport. For this sport it is necessary to have a light cloud cover, with the moonlight faintly penetrating. The flighting duck can be seen as black silhouettes against the softly lit sky, when it is a severe test of wildfowl recognition to identify the bird before shooting. All this must needs take an instant, and yet great care must be taken not to shoot any bird other than those accepted as quarry. Dawn and dusk flighting usually involve the shooter arriving at the site, and concealing himself in a hide or blind. Dawn shooting necessitates the shooter being in position well before the dawn breaks and before the fowl leave their feeding grounds to return to their daytime roosting areas, usually on a large expanse of open water. This daily migration is of the utmost importance, and as all fowling depends on it, it must be clearly understood.

Put in its simplest terms, duck roost and preen during the daytime on large expanses of open water or on sandbanks, flighting inland at dusk to their feeding grounds, which may be on a small flash pond, in a stubble field or even, in autumn, oakwood, when acorns lie plentifully on the ground. Geese on the other hand will flight into their feeding grounds after dawn, returning to their roosting areas at dusk. Both duck and geese use fairly regular flight paths, and it is important for the success of the fowler to know and understand the factors which cause duck or geese to use a particular flight line at a particular time. But it is not as simple as outlined above, for there are several additional influences which alter the flight lines, among them the variations of tide, wind, weather, the moon and the availability of feeding grounds. An early high tide will cause duck to move off their roosting grounds sooner, while a full moon may cause them to stay on until rather later. It may also bring geese off their nightly roost, to feed under the moon. High winds usually encourage wildfowl to move around and this is definitely to the fowlers' advantage, as a near gale will encourage fowl to fly closer to the ground whether they are flying with or against the wind. These factors tend to affect waders far

less, as they do not migrate as duck and geese do. Tides are the major factor affecting them, driving them off the tideline, though high winds may also encourage this.

Clearly, inland goose shooting is the reverse of inland duck shooting, in so far as goose shooting takes place during the day. However, it is generally accepted that geese should not be harassed while on their feeding grounds, which necessitates tackling them on their flight lines at dusk and dawn. Geese, however, are notoriously fickle in their choice of feeding grounds and therefore their choice of flight lines, and successful goose flighting is far more a matter of a lucky choice of flight line than the more predictable interception of the flight lines of duck. Successful goose flighting is better done behind the shoreline, to intercept geese in the morning when leaving their roosting grounds or when returning in the evening.

Guns used for inland flighting vary, but by far the most popular gun is the ordinary 12-bore game gun using normal game cartridges, except that heavier shot is used than for game shooting. For duck, shot sizes used vary between no. 4 and no. 6 shot, while for geese BB to no. 3 are most commonly used. As most shots taken on inland shooting are at comparatively close range, more powerful weapons are not necessary.

Shore shooting, including marsh shooting, often involves the use of heavier weapons, particularly when shooting below the tide line. Here the 12-bore magnum, 10-bore, 8-bore and even 4-bore guns may be used.

Right: Gun and dog wait at sundown by decoys on a quiet Hampshire pool.
Below: White-fronted geese.

SHORE AND MARSH SHOOTING

Tides are the most important factor in shore shooting, but more from their effect on the shooter than on fowl. Tides with the least variation between high and low tide are called neap tides, while those with the highest variation are spring tides. While high spring tides are rather higher than high neap tides, low spring tides are lower than at the neap and uncover areas of the shore or marsh which would be inaccessible during neap tides. The marsh shooter will make a series of hides, usually by cutting out horse-shoe-shaped hollows in the side of the creeks, and retreating from one to the other as the tide flows in and renders each untenable. This form of shooting should be undertaken only by those who know their marsh well, and who are thoroughly conversant with the tides, as many fowlers have been cut off by the tide flowing into a creek behind them.

The marsh gunner should invariably be accompanied by a dog to retrieve his birds, as it is often very difficult to recover birds shot across water or which have fallen into the marsh grasses, except with the aid of a dog. Marsh shooting is usually most successful when birds are compelled by wind or tide to seek fresh quarters. Duck are the usual quarry, and a set of decoys are often used to aid the gunner in drawing the birds. These will be set out in a creek at low tide, and will attract birds seeking fresh grounds after being floated off their roosting grounds by an incoming tide. Storms will cause duck, geese and waders to move about far more frequently than usual, and at these times the discovery of a flight line will give the marsh gunner fine sport.

Shooting on the foreshore is where the larger shoulder guns are more often used. The gunner will follow a retreating tide and dig a 'grave' at a suitable spot before dawn, close to resting geese and under the line he believes they will use when driven off by the next incoming tide at dawn. Or he may conceal himself not far from the low water mark, in a creek or in some other cover, to await the dawn flight. The gunner in his grave will lie on his back, with the geese expected to approach in a direction to the left of where his feet are pointing. This will give him the easiest type of shot. Upon the approach of the geese he will sit up and take his shot. The geese may diverge from the intended line slightly, and the larger-bored guns are more favoured for this type of shooting as a shot may have to be taken at up to 50 yards away. The double-barrelled 8-bore, firing two ounces of heavy shot from each barrel, usually SSG to BB, is probably most favoured for this type of shooting, but the 4-bore is also used, though usually single-barrelled as it may weigh 18 pounds.

The gunner concealed in a creek nearer to the low water mark depends for his quarry largely on wildfowl and waders flying along the shoreline. While the 'grave' gunner's quarry is almost exclusively geese, the tideline gunner may expect to meet any of the quarry species. For this type of shooting also a good retriever is a 'must', as fowl may fall into a partially flooded creek, and unless retrieved by a dog they may be washed away, never to be recovered. The gun most often used for this type of shooting is the 12-bore magnum, throwing $1\frac{5}{8}$ ounce of shot. Some gunners will load a cartridge containing no. 4 shot in one barrel, and heavier shot in the left, thus allowing the correct size of shot to be used for a particular bird shot at. However, most gunners, particularly those using single-barrel repeaters, will use only one size of shot.

The choice of cover when foreshore shooting is of the utmost importance, as wildfowl are among the most wary creatures on earth, and even when flying into driving rain or sleet can be counted on to spot anything unusual on the ground below, flaring away from it, and passing out of range of the gunner careless enough to allow himself to be seen. Hides are often cut in the side of a creek, as on the marsh, and supplemented with netting draped with seaweed or other similar material. And it is quite useless for a gunner to carefully conceal himself if his black and white spaniel is allowed to give the game away. A pile of rocks may be used as cover, and one well-known writer recounts a successful day's sport in a hide made from broken ice floes collected from the water's edge during a particularly cold spell.

**Top left: Wading out in an estuary.
Top right: Setting decoys by
daylight ready for a dusk flight.
Bottom: The end of a successful
dawn shoot.**

SHOOTING AFLOAT

Shooting afloat can be divided into two types, shooting from a moving craft, or from a 'sink'. The latter is quite rarely carried out in British waters, but can be successful. The sink is a small rectangular platform some four feet by three, the centre of which is cut away to allow a tub to be placed in the middle deep enough for the gunner to sit in. The whole device is weighted so that the platform lies awash, and the tub is raised three or four inches from the water-line. Decoys are fitted permanently on the washboard around the tub, and the whole arrangement is towed out by boat to the required position and anchored on a long line, from which a second line rises to the surface. To this second line, a set of decoys is attached, which will lie in a line back to the sink. From the rear of the sink two or three further sets of decoys are laid, the gunner enters and readies himself, while the accompanying boat draws off some considerable distance. The impression is thus given that here is a roosting area on open water and ducks are therefore decoyed to the shooter.

Because of the cumbersome apparatus, and because only a calm day may be used (the extremely small freeboard does not allow any errors to be made) this type of shooting is not as popular in Britain as it is on the Eastern seaboard of the United States.

The other type of shooting afloat is punt-gunning. The gunning punt is specially built for the purpose, being long, narrow and pointed at stem and stern. A punt built for a gunner and a puntsman measures between 21 and 25 feet long, with a beam of about $3\frac{1}{2}$ feet. It is decked over except for the cockpit which measures about 8 feet by $2\frac{1}{2}$ feet. A single punt, for a gunner who is also the puntsman, may measure between 17 feet and 20 feet, also with a beam of some $3\frac{1}{2}$ feet. The cockpit is smaller than in a double punt, and measures about 6 feet by 2 feet. On the punt is mounted the punt gun. This is usually single barrelled, with a bore usually between 1 inch and $1\frac{1}{2}$ inches, though guns are found up to $1\frac{3}{4}$ inch bore, throwing two pounds of shot. The gun is usually seven or eight feet long, and may be mounted on the punt in one of several different ways. The punt may be propelled by rowing or by sail when travelling to and from the gunning

waters, but when setting to fowl the punt is either poled in shallow water, or sculled in deeper water.

The punt gunner's quarry are usually duck which are in estuaries during the day or geese by night, though waders may also be taken. Duck will preen on sandbanks in an estuary, in a secluded sandy bay or on the mudflats, and will be floated off with the incoming tide. The gunner will leave his moorings on the ebb tide, so as to be ready to stalk these ducks on the turn of the tide. The punt, even when loaded with two men, the big gun and other equipment has a very shallow draft which aids the stalk over the shallowest water, and the punt can closely follow the incoming tide to approach the fowl.

When setting to fowl in a double punt the gunner lies on the floor to the left of the gun, while the puntsman lies slightly behind and to the right; supporting himself on his left arm, he sculls or poles the punt with his right arm. This movement should not be seen by the fowl being stalked, as it takes place behind the widest part of the hull. Should the fowlers succeed in closing the gap to within 70 or 80 yards, they will try for a shot, and select a bunch of fowl together. Having fired the gun, the puntsman takes the punt rapidly up to the birds on the water, and any wounded bird will be finished off quickly with a 12-bore gun carried in the punt, which is somewhat inelegantly termed the 'cripple-stopper'.

The reputation of the modern punt gunner as massacring scores of birds at one shot is totally incorrect, though any casual observer looking at the huge gun may be forgiven for assuming this. The truth is that the average kill per shot is nearer five birds than ten, and it is rare for a gunner to get more than two or three shots in a day's gunning.

Most punt-gunning takes place in river estuaries, during the daytime, when ducks are the main quarry. However, occasionally punt gunning may be pursued at night, when geese are the principal quarry, and also on the open sea, with geese and sea ducks being sought. Night gunning is best carried out shortly after moonrise, when fowl are silhouetted on the water, and the gunner approaches from the dark. Geese 'talk' constantly among themselves, and on a still night they may be heard long before they can be seen, which aids the gunner. Some of the best night shooting on British coasts takes place on the Wash, where rafts of geese roost on the vast sandbanks during the hours of darkness and this is also deep-sea gunning, as the Wash is far less sheltered than any estuary. Good seamanship and a good craft are necessary, particularly when a north-easterly is blowing. Punt-gunning is very much a minority sport, even among wildfowlers, as it is expensive, it is restricted to sufficient areas of water, and the prospect of an open small boat in the depths of winter is not everybody's idea of fun. However, to anyone who has tried it, and enjoyed it in spite of the hardships, the inclement weather, and possibly having failed to fire a single shot, there are few more enjoyable and taxing forms of sport.

Most of the shoreline of Britain belongs either to the Crown, or is privately owned, and there are comparatively few places where an intending wildfowler can shoot by right. However, many of the marshes and much of the shore are subject to agreements with local wildfowling clubs, which lease such areas from the owners or from the Crown. These clubs regulate local shooting, remove trespassers from the marsh, encourage the education of other members in wildfowl habits and habitat, and will encourage a voluntary ban on shooting in their area if circumstances arise, such as a long period of icy weather when wild-fowl cannot easily find food and lose condition. Most of these wildfowling clubs are affiliated to WAGBI, the Wildfowlers Association, which offers expert advice to clubs and individual members.

Many clubs rear wildfowl during the summer, these are usually mallard, as they are the easiest to rear and are also the main quarry species. However, many clubs, using the expertise ac-quired through the rearing of mallard, are now rearing some of the breeds which are more difficult to rear, such as gadwall, pochard and teal. In this way they are able to replace some of the wildfowl which are shot each year. In addition, some clubs have sanctuary areas where birds can breed in safety and without disturbance.

Two ways for a solitary hunter to manoeuvre the punt into position, speedily (above) on the Whittlesey Washes in Cambridgeshire, and with stealth (below) off the Essex coast.

DEERSTALKING

**Stalkers 'glassing' the hillside on
Arnisdale Forest above Loch Hourn,
Inverness-shire.**

RED DEER

Whenever the subject of deerstalking is raised, Scotland and its red deer immediately come to mind. In fact deerstalking is carried out throughout the British Isles, and roe deer are probably the quarry far more often than red deer. However, stalking the red deer among the forests and hills of Scotland must surely be the classic type of stalking in Britain. It only became a popular sport a hundred years ago, when it was popularized by the then Prince of Wales, later Edward VII. Before this time the *tainchel* was the method of killing deer, when marksmen with muskets and bows and arrows hid in ambush in a narrow place.

The stalk is the essence of shooting deer in Scotland today. The stalker has to find a herd of deer, select a suitable beast to shoot, and then manoeuvre himself to a killing range, usually less than a hundred yards. If he is a visitor who lacks experience, he will usually be accompanied by a ghillie who knows the deer forest well, and he may also be accompanied by a pony man, leading the pony which will be used to bring the dead deer down to the lodge. The stalker is armed with a high-velocity sporting rifle of a calibre between .240 and .300, though the 7 millimetre and its imperial equivalents, the .270 and .275 are probably the most popular. This last group fires a bullet weighing some 150 grains to 175 grains. Usually the rifle is fitted with a telescopic sight. The confidence inspired by a telescopic sight should not encourage the taking of shots at longer range, though the temptation to do so is clear. It should only be used to improve the accuracy of a shot taken at the correct range. The stalker will also carry a telescope or spyglass.

The term 'deer forest' conjures up visions of wooded glades and rides cut through standing timber. Nothing could be further from the truth; the deer forests of Scotland are in fact heather-clad mountains. They are so-called because once upon a time these slopes and mountains were indeed tree-covered and the trees have disappeared only in the last few centuries. The reasons for this disappearance are complex; tree-felling is only part of the answer, and charcoal burners certainly bear much of the responsibility for the denudation of the forests. Change in the chemical composition of the soil is believed to be the greatest factor responsible.

The visiting stalker will be accommodated at a lodge in the forest, or occasionally at a nearby hotel. Accompanied by a ghillie, he will set off early in the morning to climb high in the mountains, so as to get above the deer which will be lying in the corries, feeding and resting. It can be very important to get this extra height, as deer do not generally suspect danger from above, and are consequently concentrating their attention on the glen. Furthermore, air currents in the glen can play extraordinary tricks, alerting the deer to the presence of an enemy; and finally, it is far easier to slither downhill towards the deer than to make an uphill approach under their alert gaze.

Having reached the heights, the glass is used to survey the glen below, paying particular attention to the corries which may harbour deer. When a herd of deer is located, the glass will be used to select the quarry.

Deciding which animal to shoot is quite a complex question. Firstly, there are animals which are undesirable in the forest. These include hummels (stags without horns), and switches (with four 'points' or less). These should be scarce in a well-managed forest. Secondly, an old stag, weakened with age, should be shot to allow a younger and more vigorous stag to take his harem. Thirdly, mature stags with poor heads can be safely shot, including six-pointers, and heads with weak, narrow beams. Then there are the 'trophy' beasts. Opinion differs as to whether these should be shot, some people prefer to preserve them to improve the breeding stock, and eliminate instead the beasts listed above.

Having picked the quarry, the stalker and the ghillie will choose their route for the stalk. This often involves using a burn as cover if it comes near to the deer. The stalker may withdraw some way, in order to move to one side and locate a better route, or he may decide that to go down on his belly and crawl or slither towards the deer is the best way. By one means and another he will close the gap between himself and the deer to within a hundred yards if possible, before settling down for the shot.

The vast majority of shots taken at red deer in Scotland are taken with the rifleman prone on the ground, though occasionally a sitting or kneeling shot may be taken. Only very rarely can the shooter stand upright for his shot without frightening the deer. For prone shooting, a rest can be made by rolling up a coat or a rifle cover to steady the rifle. When a telescopic sight is used, care must be taken to ensure that the bullet's path from the rifle is not obstructed by heather or rocks which are not noticed through the scope, and which may be as much as three inches above the line of the barrel. In connection with this factor, the back-prone shooting position is seldom used, as any obstruction is likely to be the shooter's foot, with disastrous consequences. On the occasions when a shot is to be taken downhill, the sitting position may be used, where the feet are placed firmly on the ground, and the elbows comfortably on the knees. For all firing positions, the use of a rifle sling will aid the steadiness of the rifle.

The best place for a killing shot depends on several factors, the most important being the position of the deer in relation to the shooter. A lying deer usually presents a limited choice, as the body is usually unseen in the heather, only the head and neck showing above. If the shooter has managed to stalk to within fifty yards or so, a shot striking the base of the head, where the neck joins it, is extremely effective, though good accuracy is called for. If however the shot is wild, there will usually be time for a second shot at the missed or wounded animal, as it must get to its feet before making off. If a standing animal is preferred, a low whistle will attract the attention of the deer, causing it to stand up to locate the source of the whistle.

An animal standing broadside should be shot behind the front shoulder, about halfway between withers and chest. It is better to shoot higher than lower, as the shot will almost certainly find a vital organ, or if high enough, will break the spine. A broadside animal may also be shot at the base of the neck, where it meets the body, about two-thirds of the way up. A shot should never be taken at a running animal unless it has been wounded, when every effort should be made to secure it before it succeeds in escaping. An animal facing away from the shooter may be shot at a range of around fifty yards or so, in the back of the head.

If a wounded stag escapes, it is the absolute duty of the stalker to follow it up and finish it off if possible. Some deer forests maintain deerhounds to track the deer by scent, but today these are few and far between. In the absence of deerhounds, tracking by the stalker and ghillie is necessary. This is usually achieved by following the blood trail and by the ghillie's knowledge.

Below left: A stalk lasting three days pauses on a high outcrop in Inchnadamph Forest, Sutherland. Below right: The spyglass in use, steadied against a walking-stick, in Arnisdale Forest, Inverness-shire.

The ghillie will also be able to decide quickly whether the shot is likely to prove fatal in a short time or not, by observing the type and quantity of blood. This is a complex subject, but basically depends on the type of blood. Bright red blood is arterial, darker blood is venous, pink frothy blood indicates a lung shot, while blood which is dark purple may indicate a liver shot. A stag shot in the upper heart may rush headlong for a short distance before suddenly collapsing in mid-stride. When a shot is likely to prove quickly fatal, the follow-up may be made immediately. However, when a shot is not likely to cause rapid death, the follow-up should not be made immediately but rather after an hour and a half or two hours. This is not as callous as it may seem. When a beast has been wounded and escapes, it will soon seek cover in which to lie up. If it is allowed to rest, it will stiffen up through shock and will be less wary, allowing the stalker to close with it and administer the *coup de grace*. However, if a wounded animal is disturbed too soon, it may run a considerable distance before seeking shelter again, and may thus be lost, to die a lingering death or live as a cripple.

When the stag has been killed the deer pony is brought up while the beast is *gralloched* and bled. The stag should be turned so that it lies with its head downhill. A knife with a 6 inch blade or longer is pushed into the underside of the neck, just above the sternum, and is turned in the body cavity until the blood there is released and pours out. The *gralloch* is the term used for the removal of the stomach and intestine. The deer is rolled onto its back, and the bleeding hole is enlarged by following the line towards the jaw for a few inches, until the oesophagus is exposed. This must be withdrawn, drawing away from the head, and severed as close to the head as possible. The end leading into the body is then tied off with string. Next, the stalker makes a shallow cut, only just skin deep, so as not to slit open the paunch from anus to the lower sternum. He must cut round and remove the penis and scrotum, then reach up to withdraw the oesophagus from the upper abdomen. He cuts round the anus, and withdraws it into the intestinal cavity, then rolls the beast onto one side, and must try to remove the stomach, intestines, liver, kidneys, spleen, all in one piece. The bladder must be found and removed very carefully, ensuring that there is no spillage of urine onto the meat. Finally, the carcass must be checked to ensure that no blood or other matter remains inside, and the stag can be loaded on the pony.

It usually takes two men to safely load the stag onto the pony. Unless the pony is experienced, it should be blindfolded before loading. The stag should be loaded so that it is well balanced, lying on its side with its back towards the pony's head. If the head is not required as a trophy, it should be removed before moving off, as the antlers can catch bushes or rocks, and upset the pony, but as they greatly assist in handling the stag onto the pony, the head should be left on until the loading is completed. If, on the other hand, the head is required, a strap or rope should be passed round the base of the antlers, and the head tied tightly back so that the stag's nose is pressed firmly into its left flank. The pony is then led back to the lodge where the stag is skinned and hung up until it is dry, when it can be butchered.

ROE DEER

Roe deer normally inhabit woodland, though they are occasionally found on some moorland. Their range covers most of the southern counties, and from Lancashire to the north of Scotland, with some pockets in Norfolk and Suffolk. They are absent from Wales, and are now extinct in Ireland. They are believed to have been extinct in southern England by the early nineteenth century, but Scottish animals were reintroduced during the last century, and the animal of today is almost certainly the exclusive descendant of those animals.

Roe deer stand about two feet high at the shoulder, the male weighing some 70 pounds, the more slender female some 15 pounds less. Their winter coat is dark and long, with a white patch on the rump. This moults in the spring, to be replaced by a shorter, more reddish-coloured coat. Only the male has antlers.

The antlers are dropped each year in October or November, and new growth starts almost immediately. The bone thrusts up from the skull to form the new antlers, which are covered in short hair, known as velvet. By the end of February or early March the growth will have been completed and the velvet becomes dry and brittle. The buck will then thrash his antlers against bushes and thickets to remove the velvet, until by mid-May his new antlers are quite clean. He will then keep them until he drops them again in October or November.

The shooting seasons for roe deer are divided into separate buck and doe seasons. Roe are usually shot either by stalking or by shooting from a 'high seat'. The high seat may be a plank secured across two branches of a tree, or it may be a specially-constructed tower with an enclosed and sheltered platform built to cover a glade in the wood, or where two rides cross. Roe deer inhabit heavy woodland, usually lying up in heavy cover during the day and emerging in the late afternoon or evening to feed in the rides or glades, though occasionally they will enter a field of cereal crops where they will both feed and lie up during the day. The technique of the stalker therefore is to be on the ground or in his seat at earliest dawn, or late in the afternoon to cover the dusk period.

During certain seasons an experienced stalker may call the deer to him, for example during the mating season when bucks may be called in by imitating the call of a doe. The stalker will move quietly through a wood, always keeping the breeze in front, and he will stop frequently to look for any sign of movement which will betray the presence of a deer. When one has been located, he will examine it very carefully through binoculars to establish whether it is shootable, and if so, he will proceed to stalk the deer until he is well within range and with a clear shot possible.

The shot is seldom taken lying down when roe-stalking, because of the heavy cover in which the deer live. Perhaps the most common shooting position is the sitting shot, though kneeling shots and standing shots are also often taken. For a standing shot, the rifle may be steadied either by supporting it against a tree, or by supporting it with a stick carried by the stalker.

The correct weapon for roe deer is a rifle. This should have a calibre of between .240 and .300, but anything over .270 should be considered as a dual-purpose weapon which can also be used for stalking red deer. The ideal rifle for roe is probably the .243 Winchester, with bullet weights of 80, 90 and 100 grains, and should have open sights consisting of a wide, shallow V-shaped rear sight, and a large silver or enamel bead fore sight. An alternative rear sight is a large aperture peepsight, but if this is to be used, the rear sight should be removed entirely, and they

should not be used in conjunction. A telescopic sight can be fitted, but should be of fairly low magnification, 4-power at most, with a large object lens for improved image in poor light.

The ideal aiming point for a roe deer, bearing in mind that it will be either in or close to heavy cover, is halfway between the chest and backbone, just behind the foreleg. A bullet here will rake the top of the heart or the aorta, and death will be instantaneous. A shot a few inches lower will also strike the heart and be fatal, but may allow the deer a few seconds, long enough to dash into heavy cover. Another excellent place to place the shot is where the neck meets the body, though this can only be taken when the beast is either broadside on or slightly facing the stalker. A shot here will sever the spine or the carotid artery, causing instantaneous death. If the beast is slightly facing, the bullet may also enter the chest cavity and find the heart. In any case, the animal will drop where it stands.

The real test of a stalker comes if he should have the misfortune to wound the animal. In this case the location of the wound is of prime importance, and can be established in most cases by the signs left behind after the shot, and by following a blood trail. Occasionally stomach contents may be found. These tell their own story, and a long follow-up is almost inevitable. It is most important to use a dog for this work, as the dog on a lead will be able to follow the wounded beast far more quickly than the stalker on his own, and thus hasten a humane death.

After a successful shot, a roe deer is cleaned in much the same way as a red deer and can be placed in a large haversack for carrying off the ground.

Before and during the cleaning, it should be an invariable rule to study the results of the shot. The experience gained from this exercise will in time prove invaluable in placing a shot in an animal standing at an angle to the stalker.

Top left: Roe deer glimpsed in its typical habitat, a forest clearing.
Top right: Group of red deer sighted in open country.
Bottom: A fine red deer stag, the classic quarry for deerstalkers in Scotland.

GAME SHOOTING IN THE UNITED STATES

HUNTERS' PARADISE

Hunters in the United States have been blessed with 'God's plenty', a phrase that John Dryden used to describe Chaucer's *Canterbury Tales*. To do justice to such a vast subject would require an encyclopedic treatment, so I will be very selective in my discussion.

Generally speaking, hunting in the United States can be broken down into four categories: big-game hunting, small-game hunting, varmint shooting, and bird shooting. To give a compendious treatment of each of these I will focus on one species within each category that is uniquely American.

ELK HUNTING

The American elk or Wapiti is for my money the noblest big game animal on the North American continent. Driven from its home on the plains to the alpine regions of the Rocky Mountains by the encroachment of man, the elk is secure in its mountain fastnesses, and is on the increase throughout much of its range. The Big Four elk hunting states are Wyoming, Montana, Colorado, and Idaho, probably in that order of desirability.

The classic elk hunt is a lengthy packstring hunt in a remote wilderness area. This type of hunt was first organized for visiting European nobility such as Sir Samuel Baker in the last quarter of the nineteenth century, and was later organized on many occasions for Teddy Roosevelt. In those days packstring hunts into wilderness areas lasted 30 to 60 days; today they can only last ten days (in the case of elk hunts).

Generally the tented camp is set up in advance of the season. Then the hunters and guides and perhaps some of the other camp personnel ride in just prior to the hunt. The pack-in may be a relatively comfortable ride of eight or ten miles, and again it may be a two-day journey of 50 miles.

The wilderness packstring hunt is one of the world's great hunting experiences, in fact one of life's great experiences. Every time I make a packstring hunt in God's country the whole experience is so rich and so rare that I can hardly believe that it is happening. I am constantly stricken with the thought of how wildly and improbably fortunate I am. Riding out of camp every morning in the thick night, and seeing the coruscation of sparks as shod hooves strike rocks on the trail up ahead, I keep exulting: 'This is the life! This is the life!' And always overhead are 'the wandering stars, to whom is reserved the blackness of darkness forever.' You can have your African safaris; for sheer exhilaration a long wilderness packstring hunt has them beat every time.

There are two classic methods of hunting elk on packstring hunts – bugling and stalking. Bugling is practised only during the rut, from mid-September until early October. A hunter or guide blows through a length of plastic tubing (a bugle) to imitate the high-pitched challenge of a rutting elk. If there are any bull elk within earshot, and if they are sufficiently combative, the hunter may get a response. If he does, the trick is to keep bugling the challenge in such a way that the elk will continue to answer the challenge, will come in closer, and will eventually show itself for a shot. The intervening moments between the first answer and the actual appearance of the elk within shooting range are as thrilling and suspenseful as any in the whole spectrum of hunting.

Opposite and below: The American Elk, or Wapiti, is the noblest big game animal in North America; photographed here in Wyoming.

Stalking elk is practised by surreptitiously approaching – at dawn and at dusk – the alpine parks and meadows where they are known to be feeding; by taking up stands at such places; by watching trails between bedding and feeding areas; by watching the migratory routes leading from summer to winter range when the snows force the elk down out of the high country; and by lots and lots of very thorough glassing.

Bugling is the easier and more productive method, but far more bulls are killed by stalking because the rut is very brief. A man who has taken a mature six by six bull can be proud of the fact that he has taken one of the world's most coveted and prestigious trophies.

Top left: The author with a bull elk shot in the Flattops Wilderness area, Colorado.
Top right: Elk hunting in the White River Wilderness area, Colorado.
Bottom: Elk hunting in the Gallatin National Forest, Montana.
Below: A packstring hunt in the Absaroka Primitive area in Montana.

Appropriate cartridges for hunting elk are, and have long been, a very controversial subject. Generally, however, most experienced hunters will have settled on something like the 25-06, .270 Winchester, .280 Remington, .308 Winchester, 30-06, or 7 millimetre Remington Magnum. The cartridge is not the critical matter. The construction of the bullet and where it is placed are. There seems to be a broad consensus among experienced elk hunters, guides, and outfitters, that the Nosler Partition, the Remington Core-Lokt, the Hornady Interlock, the Speer Grand Slam, and the Bitterroot bullets are the deadliest projectiles for the taking of elk.

The overwhelming majority of elk hunters use bolt-action rifles with telescopic sights, either straight 4-power magnification or one of the variables such as 2- to 7-power or 3- to 9-power. My experience has been that a 4-power scope is perfectly adequate for all elk hunting conditions, and offers the advantages of greater lightness and ruggedness over the larger, heavier, more complex variables. Leupold is the make of scope that will generally be seen riding the rifles of the really knowledgeable and experienced hunters.

WHITETAIL DEER HUNTING

The burgeoning deer herds of the United States and the universality of good deer hunting are a miracle of scientific game management. Today there are an estimated 17 million deer of three species (whitetail, mule, and blacktail) in the United States, whereas at the low ebb of their populations around the turn of the century there were only about a quarter million. Annually over 10 million hunters go afield after deer, and nearly one in four of them is successful. There are several states in each of which over one million licensed hunters go hunting for deer each fall: Pennsylvania, Michigan, and Wisconsin. The state of Alabama has an estimated one million deer, and the legal limit is 68 per hunter per season! Texas, of course, has by far the biggest deer herd in the union–about $3\frac{1}{2}$ million–with a hunter success ratio nearing 100 percent. What's more, an estimated 200,000 deer a year are killed by automobiles.

Whitetail stag with a fine spread of antlers.

Such astounding figures have been made possible by two factors: first, deer, like domestic livestock, are highly amenable to scientific management, and second, whitetail deer (which comprise about 80 percent of the North American herd) thrive in proximity to man. Several carefully controlled studies have shown that as human populations increase in a given area so do the populations of whitetail deer. A recently released study done by the West Virginia Department of Natural Resources predicts confidently that whereas ten years ago hunter success was only about one in ten and is now about one in seven, in a few years it will be one in five–even though numbers of hunters will have increased in the meantime.

Whitetail deer are highly aggressive, adaptive animals. They thrive on the artificial, even unnatural, conditions created by man. Certainly whitetails abounded before the coming of the white man to these shores, but environmental disturbances caused by the white man have enabled their numbers to proliferate far beyond what they were 250 years ago. The foremost of these is extensive cutting of forests, which in turn causes a lush growth of brush at a height easily reached by the deer. When cut-over areas are allowed to reach maturity, the deer simply vanish, there are no foodstuffs for them. This is precisely what is happening in such states as Michigan, Minnesota, and Maine. They were heavily logged over in the last quarter of the nineteenth century, but now their forests are once again reaching maturity. Deer herds, and hunter kills, are in decline there and wildlife biologists are asking that extensive cutting be done.

The second environmental influence by man– forest fires–have some of the same effects as logging. Forest fires in mature, virgin forests, burn cool rather than hot, they kill diseased trees but tend to leave healthy trees unharmed, they make openings in the forest ceiling through which sun can enter to nourish plants on the forest floor, they make germination of some species of trees possible, they kill many insect parasites, and in general have a beneficial effect on forest creatures, especially deer. Controlled burning is now being used as a means of raising declining deer herds in some areas that are grown over with mature timber.

Agriculture is the third great environmental disruption that has enabled whitetail deer herds to increase. This is especially true where cultivated areas adjoin wooded areas. In such areas corn, beans, peas, apples, alfalfa, clover, and hay are staples of the deer's diet.

It can be fairly said that whitetail deer have become dependent on man–not only to provide foodstuffs but also to keep their numbers down to such a level that much crueller agents such as disease and starvation do not have to do the job. Already there is serious over-population of whitetail deer in many areas, but hunters are at the same time demanding ever bigger deer herds. The size of deer herds and the hunter success ratio are sensitive political issues in some states.

The two classic methods of hunting whitetail deer are stand-hunting and still-hunting. Stand-hunting is generally practised during the first two and the last two hours of daylight, when deer are most active. During the rest of the day it is a fruitless technique. When stand-hunting the hunter picks out a spot with a good clear view of an area that offers a high probability of seeing deer. The precise spot should be selected by very careful reconnaissance immediately before the season opens, or the day before the hunter will go afield. Good places to take up a stand are the crossings of one or more well-used trails; places where a well-used trail crosses a stream; and next to fresh scrapings. Scrapings are small patches that bucks scrape clear with their hooves and antlers during the rut, and then urinate on to attract does.

Young whitetail stag.

Whenever he is taking up a stand, the hunter should always position himself upwind of the spot where he expects to see deer, and he should station himself so that the sun will be at his back. This will make it easier for him to see the deer but harder for the deer to see him. Moreover, he should, before seating himself, clear away all twigs and dead leaves that may betray his presence upon the slightest movement, and he should sit with his back against a tree to break up his profile. He should also sit back in deep shadows rather than out in the sunlight. He should also be free of any odours such as alcohol, tobacco, shaving lotion, or soap, although this is a controversial point. Some hunters go so far as to mask their own scent with apple extract or buck scent; others claim that deer are actually stimulated to investigate unfamiliar scents. Finally, the hunter must make himself completely comfortable when taking up a stand. Remember, he must remain *absolutely immobile.*

Much better than a stand on the ground is an elevated stand. This can be either a portable or permanent tree stand, or it can be one of those elaborate, and expensive, permanent high stands with ladders that are unique to Texas deer hunting. An elevated stand offers several advantages over a stand on the ground. First, deer generally do not look for danger from above. This means the hunter has the freedom to move about a bit and be more comfortable, and get his rifle in position without being detected. Second, it gives him a much wider view. Finally, it will in many instances keep his scent above ground level so that even deer approaching from upwind will not scent him.

The second classic technique employed in hunting whitetail deer is still-hunting. Actually, this is a misnomer, because the hunter is not really still. This technique requires pussyfooting along well-used trails very, very slowly, stopping frequently and searching intently for those give-away parts of the deer's anatomy – the flickering tail, that dark Y of the ears, the horizontal back line (which is always out of place in woods or brush), nose, or legs. Seldom will one ever see a whole deer. When still-hunting it is important to stick close to trails. It is noises off trail that alert deer; noises on trail they assume to be made by other deer. Moreover, one must duplicate the speed and rhythm of a deer's movements when still-hunting. This again, is to avert suspicion.

One should hunt uphill in the morning and downhill in the middle part of the day so as to be hunting into the prevailing breezes. When still-hunting it is essential to bend over frequently to look under the brush and cover for the give-away parts of deer anatomy. Bucks especially like to walk with their heads carried low.

The best kinds of days for still-hunting are damp days with a light rain or a light snowfall. The worst days are very warm, sunny days, or very windy days. Proper footwear and clothing are quite important in still-hunting. The usual Vibram-soled boots are too noisy. Much better are crepe-rubber-soled boots, or even basketball shoes or sneakers, weather permitting. Likewise, clothing should be woollen. It is absolutely silent, and it is warm even when soaking wet. Tightly woven synthetics are, by contrast, extremely noisy in brush.

When still-hunting the hunter must never stop in clearings or anywhere else where he may be readily seen. A true master of stealth will always stop in shadows or in front of or behind a sizeable tree to break up his outline. He must, of course, be ready to shoot on an instant's notice; frequently a good still-hunter can jump a buck right out of its bed or walk up to within feet of it. I have on more than one occasion moved close enough to touch a bedded-down buck with my rifle muzzle.

The two other means of deer hunting are driving and rattling, although they are practised much less frequently. The logistics of driving vary greatly according to the lay of the land, and are much too complicated to go into here. Suffice it to say that the idea is to include a large wooded area with standers stationed at likely exit points, and drivers moving *quietly* – not noisily, as is often mistakenly done – towards them. The drivers should move slowly as well as silently. In that manner the deer will also move out slowly, enabling much more slow, deliberate shooting. The deer will seldom go straight ahead of the drivers, but will usually try to sneak out the sides, or double back through the drivers. Sometimes they will actually lie down in thick brush and let the drivers walk right by them.

Hunters pose with a good eating buck taken in West Virginia. Orange clothing is required by law in many states during the deer hunting season.

Rattling is practised mostly in Texas, and only during the rut. A hunter will situate himself in a well-concealed spot, preferably near fresh scrapes, and rattle antlers together in simulation of two bucks fighting. Occasionally he will bang the antlers against brush, or scrape them on the ground. This arouses the curiosity of nearby bucks, which will come out to investigate. In areas of high-density deer populations, such as parts of Texas, this technique can be diabolically effective.

The conventional wisdom has it that the best rifles for hunting whitetail deer are those with plenty of firepower–pumps, lever-actions, and semi-automatics–that churn out ponderous lead slugs at loaf-along velocities. The theory is that in thick brush a heavy, slow-moving bullet is much less likely to be deflected off-course by a twig or branch than is a light bullet propelled at much higher speed. Accordingly the usual calibers recommended are the .35 Remington, the .348 Winchester, .358 Winchester, the new .375 Winchester, the .44 Remington Magnum, and the .444 Marlin. The usual rifles recommended are the Winchester Models 71, 88, and 94; the Marlin Model 336; and the Savage Model 99, all lever actions; the Remington Model 742 Woodsmaster and the Ruger 44 Magnum carbine, both semi-automatics; and the Remington Model 760 Gamemaster, a slide-action.

I am prepared to accept the firepower part of that theory to a limited extent; however I just can't accept that part about the big slow bullets chopping their way unerringly through brush to the point of aim. Extensive testing has shown that no cartridge can be depended upon to drive its bullets consistently through brush to a target on the far side. If anything, the lightweight, high-speed bullets are more effective for this purpose than the heavy, sluggish ones.

The optimal cartridges are the .270 Winchester, the .280 Remington, the 7 × 57, .308 Winchester, and 30-06. In the hands of a skilled rifleman the 6 millimetre cartridges–the .243 Winchester and 6 millimetre Remington–are also deadly performers, but I cannot recommend them at large.

A low-powered scope (2½- or 3-power) or a low-range variable such as the Leupold 1- to 4-power or 1½- to 5-power is ideal sighting equipment for hunting whitetail deer in brushy conditions where ranges are likely to be short and the shooting likely to be fast.

BIG GAME RIFLES

Large-scale American manufacturers such as Remington, Winchester, and Ruger have long been known for turning out accurate, reliable rifles at very affordable prices. The Remington Model 700, the Ruger Model 77 and Number One, and the Winchester Models 70 and 94 enjoy world-wide reputations.

In recent years, however, many American riflemen have become much more sophisticated and demanding. They are now insisting on standards of accuracy, beauty, balance, fit, and finish that no large manufacturer can or will provide. Hence there has sprung up, as suddenly as toadstools on a summer's night, a whole legion of independent craftsmen to satisfy this demand. The rifles they are producing are unquestionably the finest ever produced. Their prices are high, very high, and the waiting time is long, but that seems to deter no one. When one takes delivery of a rifle lovingly crafted by one of these masters, he has, to quote John Keats, 'a thing of beauty' and 'a joy forever'. Most 'bespoke' rifles represent a collaboration among two or more craftsmen, and may require one to two years to complete.

The names of these elite gunmakers are known to cognoscenti of fine firearms around the world. Some of them are: Mark Lee of Northfield, Minnesota, Ken Jantz of Sulphur, Oklahoma and Tom Burgess of Spokane, Washington–all metal-smiths. There are engravers such as Jom Kelso of Preston, Washington and Frank Hendricks of San Antonio, Texas. Al Lind of Tacoma, Washington, Mark Moon of Grand Junction, Colorado and Bill Dowtin of Celina, Texas are all stock-makers. A stock by one of these masters represents a perfect marriage of form and function. Their works embody the wise judgement of Gough Thomas: 'Functional beauty is no mere whimsy, but the last refinement of efficiency.'

Opposite: The bobcat, though a varmint, is a rare and elusive trophy for the experienced hunter.

SMALL GAME HUNTING

The cottontail rabbit is the most sought-after species of small game, but the squirrel is a far more demanding and interesting quarry. The squirrel – and here I include both the fox squirrel and the grey squirrel – is common throughout the eastern United States and many parts of the Midwest. It is found wherever there are sizeable hardwood forests – hickory, oak, walnut, beech, ash – with trees large enough to provide dens.

The squirrel is a most excellent tutor in woodsmanship and a very demanding mentor in the school of rifle marksmanship. (People who hunt them with shotguns I relegate to the outer darkness of pothunters and bumpkins.)

A fox squirrel, whose rapid erratic movements make it demanding quarry for the best rifleman.

To begin with, the hunter must do his homework thoroughly in advance of the season opening. He must search for fresh cuttings (fragments of nut shells); he must listen for squirrels barking; he must try to sight as many squirrels as possible. All this reconnaissance should be done immediately prior to the season. If done too far in advance, the hunter may arrive on opening morning to find that the squirrels have cut out all the nuts and moved on. The hunter should dress in soft, silent camouflage clothing, including a camouflage hat.

The most effective means of hunting squirrels is by taking a series of stands in areas that have plenty of fresh sign. The hunter should sit down with his back against a large tree to break up his outline, and with one or two smaller trees about 2 to 3 feet in front of him to serve as rifle rests. He should remain as nearly invisible as possible, all the while sweeping the treetops and the forest floor with his eyes for those tell-tale bouncing branches or sudden starts of leaves. He must be fully alert to the whirr of squirrel claws against tree trunks, the grating of teeth on nut shells, the methodic rustling in the leaves, the falling of nuts being cut loose by squirrels, and the swishing of leaves high overhead. Acute eyesight is important, but acute hearing is even more important.

Once the squirrel has been sighted, the hunter must immediately begin to prepare for the shot. He must improvise a rest – usually against the side of a tree – and he must consider the acute angle of elevation, especially if the squirrel is in a tall tree nearly overhead. Getting off a shot at a stationary squirrel in the early season – say up until early November in Virginia and West Virginia, where I do most of my squirrel hunting – is extremely difficult, and can try the patience of Job. In the early and middle autumn squirrels are compulsively gathering food for the winter, and move about so nervously that they hardly pause for more than 2 or 3 seconds at a time. Even then they are likely to be wholly or partially hidden by leaves.

It is much more productive, and more satisfying, to hunt them after all the leaves have fallen. Then the hunter can spot the squirrels much farther away, they are moving about in a more leisurely fashion, and their slightest movement in the trees betrays their presence. That is the time of year when the man who is skilful enough to 'thread the needle' – put a bullet in one eye and out the other – comes into his own and shows what shooting is all about.

This supremely exacting sport needs an exceptionally accurate .22 rifle, such as the Anschutz Model 54, the Remington Model 541-S, the Winchester Model 52 Sporter, or the Browning T-Bolt. The scope should be a 4- or 6-power, and should be set parallax-free for the average distance at which the hunter anticipates that he will shoot. Match ammunition is preferable to high-velocity ammunition because of the higher degree of accuracy it offers.

Some hunters prefer an accurate .22 Magnum rifle, such as the Anschutz Model 64 or 1518, because the much flatter trajectory permits easier hits at longer ranges. In this event, the 6-power scope is a better choice than the 4-power. Full metal-cased bullets are the only choice if one uses the .22 Magnum.

Finally, there is the very exclusive school of ultra-long-range squirrel shooting. These men don't take their rifles down off the racks until the trees are completely bare, and they can see a squirrel three football fields away. They would rather shoot one squirrel at a hundred yards plus than a half dozen at half that range. Indeed to squeeze off a shot at a squirrel 150 to 200 yards away and see it pitch head first out of the top of a huge oak and fall and fall and fall, is one of hunting's purest, keenest pleasures. It is also one that very few riflemen are capable of bringing off consistently. It takes, first of all, a supremely good marksman, and then it takes a finely tuned combination of rifle, scope, and handload.

There are two theories as to how one should go about this type of shooting. Both theories begin with a superbly accurate .22 centrefire rifle of sporter weight with an 8-power scope with parallax adjustment, and ammunition handloaded with full metal-cased bullets. At that point the theories diverge. One theory claims that the cartridge must be loaded to a very reduced velocity so as not to damage the meat. The other theory claims that the cartridge should be loaded up to normal velocities. Otherwise one loses the advantages of fine accuracy and flat trajectory that were the reasons for choosing a .22 centrefire in the first place. I am wholly in agreement with the second theory. Of course that high-speed bullet will damage the meat – but the only parts of the squirrel with enough meat to fool with anyway are the hind legs.

Suitable rifles for this kind of shooting are the Remington Models 700 and 788, the Kleinguenther K-16, the Shilen DGA sporter, the Wichita Classic, and the Steyr-Mannlicher Model SL. The preferred cartridge is the .222 Remington, which is the most accurate cartridge yet designed. Such a rig should be capable of placing five shots in a $\frac{1}{2}$ inch circle, centre to centre, at a hundred yards, or much better a $\frac{1}{4}$ inch circle. Remember, when you are trying to 'thread the needle' at 150 to 200 yards there is no margin for error!

A successful squirrel hunter in the woodlands of West Virginia with his freshly-shot bag.

VARMINT HUNTING

Over the years, as bag limits have become penurious and seasons have shrunk, hunters have sought out various non-game species to provide off-season sport. Some such species are foxes, coyotes, bobcats, jackrabbits, and ground squirrels, but without question the Number One Varmint is the groundhog. (I have it on good authority that some benighted souls have at certain times and places called the groundhog a 'woodchuck', but I cannot vouch for the validity of this claim.) Like squirrel hunting, groundhog hunting is a quintessentially American sport. There is nothing quite like it anywhere else in the world. (I should admit at this point that I have enjoyed some very good shooting for high-alpine marmots in the Austrian Alps, but that is a seldom-practised sport there.)

Actually, there is very little 'hunting' involved in groundhog hunting; it is essentially a game of precision long-range marksmanship. The hunters drive slowly through areas where groundhogs are usually found, and stop frequently to make a thorough search with binoculars. The usual areas are fields grown up in hay or legumes, especially if they are adjacent to cornfields or market gardens, and rock walls, railway embankments, old stumps, large boulders, old lumber piles, and abandoned buildings in or near such fields and gardens.

Shots can range from a hundred yards on out to 500 yards, and even farther. Purists, however, seldom shoot at less than 200 to 250 yards. As such, the groundhog is an even more exacting mentor in the post-graduate school of precision rifle marksmanship than the squirrel. For consistent long-range hitting one must be an absolute master at judging wind speed, heat mirage, and distance.

It is a truism among sophisticated riflemen that the portly brown rodent has been the cause for more advances in barrel steel metallurgy, rifling methods, action bedding techniques, bullet making, primer production, and cartridge design than all the shooting matches and shooting wars put together. Groundhog hunting has in turn begotten benchrest shooting, which is a rifle-shooting game dedicated fanatically to the quest of the Holy Grail of rifle accuracy – a perfect, or one-hole group. The groundhog is one of the reasons that Colonel Townsend Whelen's epithet for the USA – 'a nation of riflemen' – still has some meaning.

The typical groundhog-hunting armament is a heavy-barrelled bolt-action rifle chambered for one of the hot .22 centrefire cartridges – the .222, .223, .22-250, or .220 Swift – or one of the 6 millimetre cartridges – the .243 Winchester or 6 millimetre Remington – or perhaps the 25-06. Such a rifle will typically be mounted with an 8-, 10- or 12-power scope with parallax adjustment.

Some of the usual groundhog rifles are the heavy-barrelled Sako Vixen and Forester, Model 70 Winchester, Model 700 Remington, Shilen DGA Varminter, Savage 112-V, Ruger 77V, the Heym SR20, and the Steyr-Mannlicher Models L and SL. However, many groundhog rifles are custom-built for groundhog hunters who are seeking finer accuracy than they can get from a factory-made rifle.

Two other indispensable items of equipment are excellent binoculars, preferably 10-power magnification, and a set of sandbags for resting the rifle over the hood or cab of a vehicle. I have tried many binoculars, but find it hard to beat the Swarovski Habicht 10 × 42s and the Leitz Trinovid 10 × 40s.

Top: A groundhog hunter displays the results of two 250-yard shots in the hayfields of southern Montana. Bottom: The author shooting gopher in Montana. The rifle is a rare Springfield .22, designed for training Army recruits in World War II.

WING SHOOTING

Canada geese flying low over Horizon Marsh, Wisconsin on their way to spend the spring in Canada after wintering down south.

BIRDS AND DOGS

Bird shooting in America has fallen upon evil days. Continuous destruction of habitat, drainage of swamps, construction of dams, clean farming, abandonment of farms, the maturation of second- and third-growth forests, and the use of strong insecticides and herbicides have brought the populations of waterfowl and upland birds down to a pale shadow of what they once were. At the same time the demand for quality bird shooting has been steadily on the increase. Consequently bag limits are parsimonious in the extreme and seasons much abbreviated. On the Atlantic fly-way bag limits have been as low as two ducks per day in recent years. The limit on geese has been the same. Some states allow only two pheasants per day. The limits on ruffed grouse in some states are down to two birds per day – but most hunters will only average that many birds in a season.

A bag of chukar partridge. The chukar, from India, thrives in Idaho, Washington, Oregon and Nevada.

Although certainly not as numerous as it once was, the bobwhite quail has fared better than most species of upland birds and waterfowl. In fact, the bobwhite quail has over the years extended its range considerably. The classic coverts for Mr Bob were long the pride and the exclusive demesnes of the Old South: South Carolina, south Georgia, and northern Florida. In recent years, however, the locus of the best quail shooting has shifted north and west. In their best years, states like Missouri, Texas, Kansas and Oklahoma can boast of shooting as fine as any in the Deep South.

Like squirrel hunting and groundhog hunting, quail hunting is a uniquely American sport. It evolved during the *ancien regime* in Virginia, the Carolinas, Georgia, Florida, Arkansas, and Tennessee. In that day gentlemen followed the dogs on horseback or were transported about in mule-drawn carriages with velvet-upholstered seats. Quail shooting was aristocratic sport par excellence. To its more zealous devotees it became a religion and a way of life. Its high priests have been Havilah Babcock, George Bird Evans, and Nash Buckingham. Together they have created

a small but enduring corpus of classic literature in praise of the glories of hunting Gentleman Bob. No such claim can be made for any other species of North American game bird or animal.

Gentleman Bob is not a quail at all, but a partridge. (In fact, the term quail is a latter-day importation of Yankees and emigres. Unreconstructed Southerners still insist that 'partridge' is the correct word.) Like Brer Rabbit in the Uncle Remus tale, he is dearly in love with the brier patch. And the honeysuckle thicket, too–especially the latter. Put up a covey of bobwhites, and you can bet your Purdey against a gun-shy mutt that if there's a brier patch or honeysuckle thicket within wingshot, they will fly that way. The experienced quail shooter knows this, of course, and always positions himself accordingly. Of course, there are some neatly barbered, carefully control-burned plantations where one is likely to get some open-field shooting, but to shoot there is a privilege reserved for the very few. Generally, bobwhite shooting in the traditional southern coverts is close-in shooting in the thickest kind of tangles.

Dogs and still dogs and yet dogs are what bobwhite shooting is all about – high-stepping pointers and stately setters (English, not Irish, if you please) and even an occasional Gordon. To watch a brace of grand-going pointers quarter back and forth through a quail covert, working well into the wind, honouring and backing each other's points in a stately *pas de deux*, is perfect delight. No serious shooting man can go to his grave in peace until he has seen the grand dog-work of a pair of patrician pointers doing their thing in the thickets of south Georgia.

If bobwhite shooting is all about dogs, it is also all about guns. Bobwhite shooters, it seems to me, take more pleasure in fine fowling-pieces than any other group of bird shooters. As a result of the long-lingering British influence in the South, the side-by-side double gun was up until recent decades *the* gun and the only gun that a Southern gentleman would take afield after quail. I would venture a guess that even today there are more London Best guns and traditional American doubles in the South than in any other part of the nation.

Hunters working through the thickets for quail in West Virginia.

If one were to take a poll of highly experienced quail shooters in the South about what is the ideal quail gun, he would probably come up with a profile something like the following: a double gun (increasingly an over-and-under rather than a side-by-side) in 20-gauge, bored improved cylinder and modified, and stocked to the same dimensions as a skeet gun ($1\frac{1}{2}$ inch drop at comb, $2\frac{1}{2}$ inch drop at heel). Quite a few respondents might prefer no choke at all in the more open barrel. The preferred load would almost certainly be a field load of no. 8s.

If the same poll were taken in the plains states – north Texas, Oklahoma, Kansas, and Nebraska – the profile would be similar except that perhaps the choking might be a bit tighter in the second barrel, and many shooters might assert a preference for a 12-gauge because of the longer shots. (In fact, at the Grand National Quail Shooting Championships, which are held annually near Enid, Oklahoma, no shooter has ever won with anything less than a 12-gauge, and no serious competitor ever enters with anything less than a 12-gauge.) Likewise, I would anticipate a preference for heavy field loads – or even trap loads – in no. $7\frac{1}{2}$.

The French have words that best capture the essence of bobwhite quail hunting: flair and éclat and panache. Bobwhite quail shooting is to the United States what driven grouse shooting is to the United Kingdom. The best commercial quail-shooting resorts – places like Riverview Plantation and Talawahee Plantation in south Georgia – are solidly booked far in advance by shooters who come from the ends of the earth to pay 200 dollars and more a day. I have 'gone to and fro in the earth and walked up and down in it' in search of game birds, but I always return to Gentleman Bob. He is, quite simply, the grandest game bird that North America has to offer.

Opposite: Quail hunting in Missouri. Both dogs are Brittany spaniels, an increasingly popular breed for small game hunting. Below: Hunters setting out for a day of pheasant hunting in eastern Washington State.

20 RANGES: DESIGN AND CONSTRUCTION

PLANNING A RANGE

This chapter is not a definitive survey of ranges, as it is impossible to deal with such an immense subject in a single chapter.

The provision of shooting grounds or ranges for training to maintain a standard of marksmanship for military purposes through sporting activity was a requirement in many countries for centuries. Originally, target shooting was the only form of military training available and many European clubs and associations formed for this purpose are still active today.

From the military viewpoint the introduction of continuous-fire weapons and rapidly changing techniques of warfare brought about the need for shooting grounds capable of simulating active service conditions, rather than providing a traditional target shooting installation. Nevertheless, it is recognized that proficiency in the use of small-arms depends on a thorough understanding of the basic principles of target shooting together with regular practice and competition. Sports shooting, evolving from the military need and fostered by local and national associations, developed in various ways, but not until the founding of the International Shooting Union (UIT) in 1907 was the basis for a series of common events established for sports shooting at international level.

It is desirable when designing ranges to ensure that they conform to the standards laid down in the UIT regulations. In satisfying these requirements, most national practices can also be accommodated. Ideally, target shooting should be conducted outdoors, with the competitors shooting from the comfort of well-designed and protected firing points.

Building a range is an expensive undertaking and, as ranges are rarely commercially viable, a site should be acquired only when a reasonable length of tenure is available. Consultation with the planning authority is essential to determine the zoning proposals for adjoining land, with particular reference to noise pollution, and to obtain, if possible, safeguards against future development that might inhibit use of the range.

Statutory requirements vary from country to country and approval may have to be sought from the military and police as well as from planning and building authorities. The same authority might also be responsible for setting safety standards and issuing a licence or necessary safety certificate before shooting takes place. The formulae for the calculation of safety angles, design of bullet stops, baffles and general protection for ranges also vary. In Britain these matters are the responsibility of the School of Infantry, whose requirements are precisely defined in their advisory leaflets. In the United States the National Rifle Association can be relied upon for advice.

There is no such thing as a completely safe range. Ultimate safety depends upon a number of factors, including the competence of shooters and their supervision, the design standards set by the licensing authority and the quality of construction and maintenance of the range.

**Left: Taking the score at a 25 metre silhouette target installation.
Below: A rifleman at the 300 metre range at Lucerne, Switzerland. Adjustable sunshades are provided at each station.**

OUTDOOR RANGES

In addition to the obvious consideration of the proximity of residential and other development, sites for outdoor ranges should be on level, dry ground facing north or up to 20° east of north. Swampy, excessively undulating ground, hollows and areas of rocky terrain should be avoided. The prospects of finding sites of sufficient area to permit a full danger or impact area unused by, or secure from, the public are remote; and for this reason baffles, embankments and back stops are needed to contain shots in order to satisfy reasonable safety requirements.

Having selected a site, the shooting facilities should be planned. Major schemes for World or Olympic events require extensive facilities, which are carefully defined by the UIT, but at club and county level maximum flexibility of use is particularly important. There are many faces to the sport of shooting. World Olympic event contestants represent the élite, while the real sub-stance of the sport is found at club level in the members who derive satisfaction from competing to a greater or lesser extent in a variety of events or disciplines.

A prudent club administration will promote a programme of practices and competitions to ensure the maximum use of its facilities. Although money will always dictate the extent to which desirable standards can be achieved, it is wise to plan the ideal and realize it in phases as funds permit. There must, however, be no compromise on safety standards.

Care must be exercised in overall design, including such details as floor coverings, dividing screens or blinds, racks, communications and public address systems, target storage, noise insulation, scoreboards, waste target and brass clearing. The firing points and target systems are particularly important.

The 50 metre range at Thun in Switzerland with silhouette targets for pistol shooting. A line of 300 metre targets can be seen in the background.

TARGET SYSTEMS

One aspect of outdoor rifle and pistol ranges that requires labour and can be very time-consuming is marking the targets, particularly rifle targets. Conventional rise and fall targets need to have the score indicated visually and to be marked and patched. In recent years a number of electronic systems have been developed that eliminate the need for markers and patching, and permit the shooter to view his results on a monitor and to receive a print-out on completion of his series. One such system is produced by Saab of Sweden. This is a fully automatic target system and consists of a target with a transmitter and a registration unit. It is intended for shooting at distances between 100 and 300 metres on targets scoring 1 to 10. Immediately after each shot, the registration unit displays the points scored and the position of the hit. At the same time the result is automatically printed on a paper strip, which shows position, points and total points. A hit on a line is recorded as the higher value. The target consists of electrically conductive rubber layers, which are interconnected when the bullet passes through the target. These rubber layers are so elastic that the holes left by the average rifle bullet are less than 1 millimetre in diameter. The target can withstand several thousand shots before replacement. In front of the marksman there is a microphone. When the shot is fired the microphone automatically activates the registration sequence.

Another system is produced by Suis-Ascor of Switzerland. This system is based on the measurement of transit time differences of the sonic boom wave from the bullet. The transit time differences are measured by three acoustic transducers, located below the field of fire.

The 300 metre range at Thun. This photograph shows how a number of different target systems can be accommodated in a well-designed range. The wires for the 50 metre target return system can be seen along the ground.

The target covering consists of a specially developed rubber foil. The measured transit time differences are fed to a computer, which computes the penetration point of the projectile through the target surface, based on geometrical and trigonometrical principles, and converts it into a result displayed on a monitor, both in valuation and position (sixteen sectors). This system is sensitive to scoring 1 to 100, a specific requirement in Switzerland. The target surface is designed as a reverberation chamber in order to eliminate any wind effects. Moreover, in the reverberation chamber the speed of sound is continually measured, as the latter varies depending on humidity and temperature. A process computer is capable of computing the results of thirty-two targets. Integration of electronic data processing, such as transmission and continual updating of results on TV monitors and scores issued at short notice is also possible. A cardboard target for subsequent checking purposes can also be attached quite easily.

For 50 metre smallbore rifle and pistol events scoring is simplified by the use of a target return system, which allows the target to be recalled by the shooter for marking and changing as required. Alternatively, a system consisting of targets on a continuous roll housed in protective cabinets permits the changing of targets as required, but requires collection from the butts.

Turning targets are required for UIT Rapid Fire, Standard Pistol and Centrefire events. These should be in banks of five targets. Many systems are available, and the most efficient are those that are electrically operated. A turning target bank is indispensable for club requirements and permits additional events such as Service and Police Pistol.

The ancillary accommodation of the range should be planned to include offices, locker rooms, stores, magazine, club room with refreshment facilities, washrooms and car parking, as circumstances permit.

The covered 50 metre firing point at Thun. The inclined platforms are for prone rifle shooting. The flaps are folded forwards to bring the rifle shooters' line of sight to the centre line of the targets and avoid shots into the target carrier wires. The flaps can be folded back, as shown, to allow for standing rifle or pistol shooting. The platforms are simple to construct and the arrangement gives the range a much greater flexibility. Both the flaps and the floor of the firing point are covered in a hard-wearing fibre pile carpet.

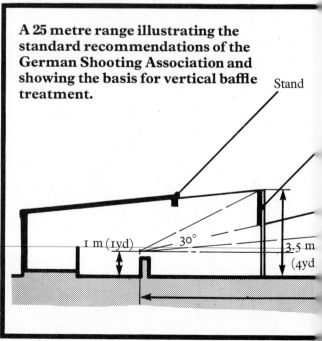

A 25 metre range illustrating the standard recommendations of the German Shooting Association and showing the basis for vertical baffle treatment.

Stand

1 m (1yd)   30°

3.5 m (4yd)

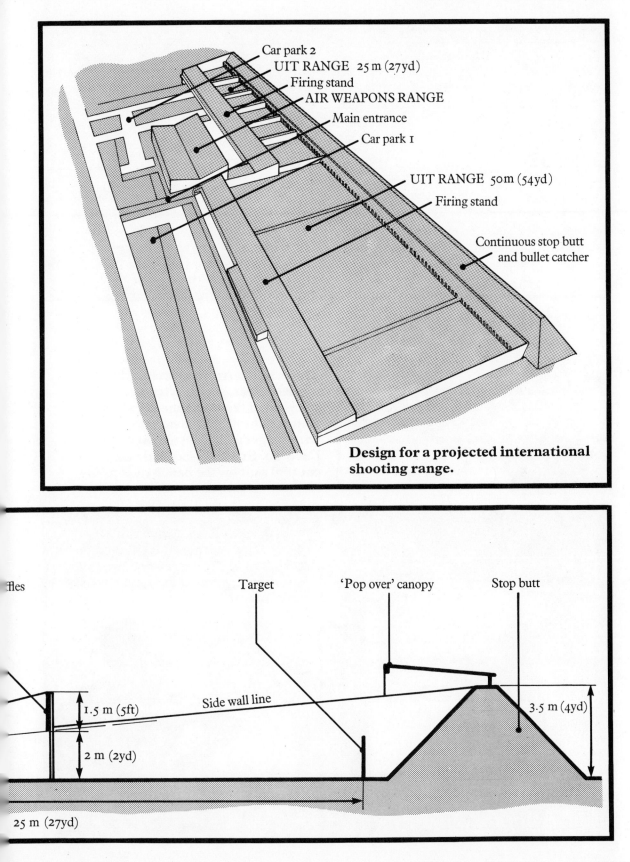

Car park 2
UIT RANGE 25 m (27yd)
Firing stand
AIR WEAPONS RANGE
Main entrance
Car park 1

UIT RANGE 50m (54yd)

Firing stand

Continuous stop butt
and bullet catcher

**Design for a projected international
shooting range.**

fles
Target
'Pop over' canopy
Stop butt

Side wall line

1.5 m (5ft)

3.5 m (4yd)

2 m (2yd)

25 m (27yd)

Above and left: An individual 50 metre target return system suspended from overhead cables. Below: The 50 metre pistol range with target recall system at Lucerne, Switzerland. Note the control unit on the bench next to the shooter on the left.

INDOOR RANGES

The indoor range requires as much care in design as the outdoor range and has many of the same problems. In addition, there are the considerations of artificial lighting and ventilation. The indoor range is usually much smaller and will generally enjoy more use than an outdoor range.

The selection of suitable premises is important. Planning authority requirements may be more stringent in urban areas and the police will have to be consulted with particular reference to security. An indoor range should be located within a well-constructed building. Basement areas of adequate size are often suitable, provided they are relatively free of columns and beams and have adequate access for air ducts to outside air.

The indoor range should be organized into areas to give a minimum of five firing points with a range of 25 metres. The range should have a clear ceiling height of 10 to 12 feet. Economics will usually dictate use for both rifle and pistol shooting, and in this respect some compromise in standards will be necessary. Each firing point should be separated by a screen or blind and provided with a movable table or shelf. A mount for telescopes for pistol shooting is also desirable.

Targets will be located in front of a suitably designed bullet trap, which should be designed to minimize the generation of lead particles and dust, and permit collection of waste lead. (Lead and brass are useful sources of revenue.) Many designs have been produced for bullet traps for indoor ranges, including end-grain timber baulks, absorbent panels, inclined steel plates with sand traps and in recent years, particularly in Europe, steel louvre blind traps. Experience has now shown that the escalator trap design is the most efficient.

A target recall system is essential for an indoor range because it permits greater use of the firing points and accelerates shooting activity. Many systems are available, but not all are suitable for rifle and pistol shooting unless prone rifle activity is conducted from a bench. The overhead monorail system offers the greatest flexibility, particularly with an edge/face turning facility, with various exposure times individually or centrally controlled. A turning target system is as essential to an indoor range as it is to an outdoor range.

The problem of ventilation provokes much discussion and theorizing. It is a fact that the fumes and lead particles generated in indoor ranges by the discharge of firearms, and the chance impact of bullets on target equipment, walls, floors and bullet traps are harmful and must be exhausted efficiently without discomfort or disturbance to shooters. The traditional system of range ventilation is to introduce a full-width air supply behind the firing line, with a similar width exhaust above the bullet trap. An expert in the problem of range ventilation should be consulted during the design stage, particularly when hand-loaded fullbore ammunition will be used. Provided the supply of air is distributed behind and around the shooter, maintaining a pressurized flow effect against carefully located exhausts, the risk from inhalation is reduced.

Indoor range lighting requires careful consideration to give the necessary standards. Sharp contrasts must be avoided and intensities softened through gentle diffusion. Lighting above the firing point should be evenly diffused to allow clear definitions without sharp shadow effects. Dimmer controls are a useful asset. The intensity of illumination should reduce beyond the firing line, increasing to the final level of brightness on the target face. A mixture of different light sources should be avoided, as the quality of light will vary. Tungsten Halogen lamps suitably located and protected are a most efficient source of light for indoor ranges and offer good lamp life if properly installed.

The indoor range will require insulation to reduce sound pollution of adjoining areas and for the comfort of the shooter. Provided the structure is of a substantial nature in brick and concrete, the solution is made easier by allowing surface treatments rather than complete disconnection and isolation. Acoustic treatment should be designed to eliminate much of the sound at source, that is, around the shooter, by the use of wall, floor and ceiling absorbent treatments. Range entry doors should be acoustically treated and made self-closing. The aim of the design should be to isolate the range with no interconnecting ducts or openings that will allow the transmission of noise.

Decoration of the range should be in soft, muted colours, matt finish, avoiding sharp contrasts and glossy surfaces completely. A soft colour, needle-punched fibre carpet may be used for the firing points if funds permit.

Adequate allowance for cupboards and storage areas must be made; this is invariably under-estimated, with consequent disorder. A clean, tidy, well-ordered range, properly lit and decorated is always conducive to a good standard of shooting. Adjoining the range accommodation should be a gun room for the convenience of members and, if regulations permit, a secure locker room.

Club life will revolve around the club room, and this should be designed to provide a comfortable standard for members and their families. A bar or refreshment point is necessary, together with, perhaps, a library and a display of trophies and pictures to illustrate the club's past and present achievements.

The increasing popularity of air weapon shooting indicates the advisability of providing an area for this recognized UIT activity. The basic range design principles apply, but without the problems of ventilation and sound generation.

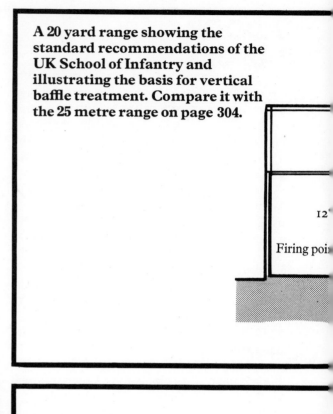

A 20 yard range showing the standard recommendations of the UK School of Infantry and illustrating the basis for vertical baffle treatment. Compare it with the 25 metre range on page 304.

12'

Firing poi

Fire exit

Left: A louvre blind type bullet trap.

Right: Plan of a layout suitable for an indoor club range situated in a basement.

Used targe

Left: An escalator type bullet trap.

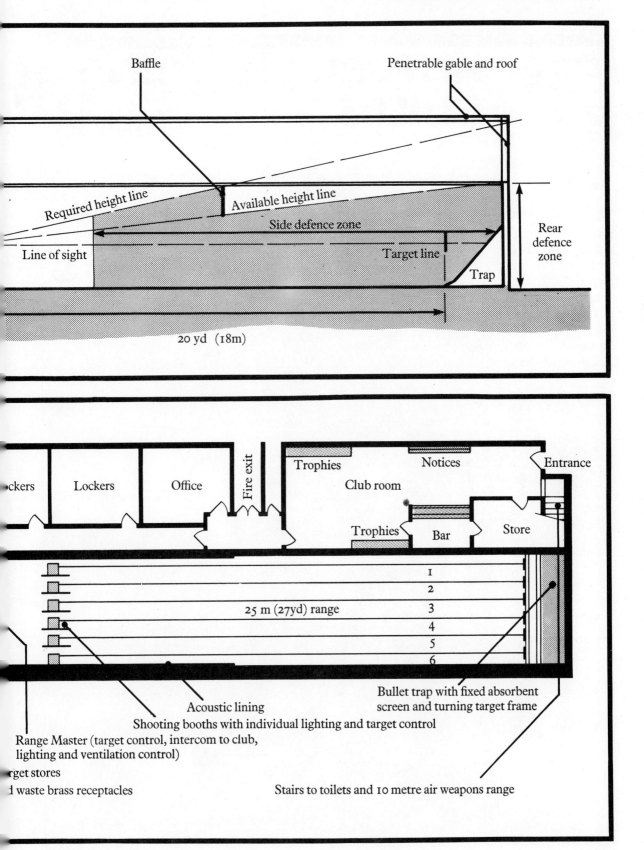

Baffle

Penetrable gable and roof

Required height line

Available height line

Side defence zone

Line of sight

Target line

Rear defence zone

Trap

20 yd (18m)

Lockers

Lockers

Office

Fire exit

Trophies

Notices

Entrance

Club room

Trophies

Bar

Store

I
2
3
4
5
6

25 m (27yd) range

Acoustic lining

Bullet trap with fixed absorbent
screen and turning target frame

Shooting booths with individual lighting and target control

Range Master (target control, intercom to club,
lighting and ventilation control)

rget stores

d waste brass receptacles

Stairs to toilets and 10 metre air weapons range

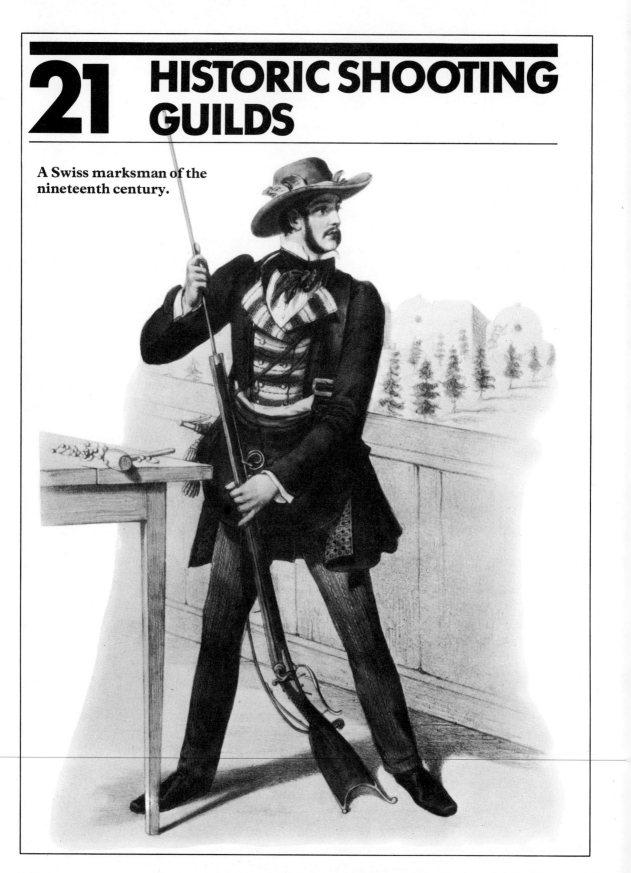

21 HISTORIC SHOOTING GUILDS

A Swiss marksman of the nineteenth century.

MEDIEVAL MARKSMANSHIP

The origins of the European shooting guilds date from the days of the longbow and crossbow, and many of the rules of the early organizations were directly taken over from these gatherings. In many areas, particularly in Germany and Switzerland, shooting societies were originally formed for military reasons. As part of a marksmanship programme for the citizens of walled or fortified cities and towns, men were formed into a local militia to defend the perimeters of the defences in the event of attack or siege. Shooting with the bow or, later, firearms was a part of their rudimentary training, which, certainly in the early years, was taken very seriously. They were not a part of the 'standing army' of the local lord, but an active reserve that held frequent drills during which trials of marksmanship took place.

Until the seventeenth century shooting grounds were often situated in the moat beneath the town walls, or in a convenient angle of the wall itself, which sheltered the targets and provided a natural bullet-trap, at the same time making shooting facilities easily accessible. In later years, with improving firearms and larger participation, the shooting grounds moved further and further from the centre of the population into the surrounding countryside, and elaborate artificial facilities had to be constructed.

By the time that the military and defence elements had become of secondary importance, the institution of target shooting was so firmly established that the transition to a primarily civilian or quasi-military orientation was remarkably smooth. From the very first some form of incentive had been given for the outstanding performance by an individual, and with the growth of target shooting organizations, the giving of prizes developed on an increasingly lavish scale. Where the amenities and facilities had once been of rudimentary and military simplicity, by the time firearms were introduced to the sport the surroundings of shoot meetings had become elaborate and elegantly formalized.

The administrative organization and detailed functioning of a shooting guild formed an important feature of its existence from the beginning. There were rules and regulations governing every conceivable situation and circumstance from the eligibility of young men to join (at least 18 years old, no police record, and a fee) to the social and technical status of retired members. In fact, it is quite clear that the degree of regimentation in almost all *Schützenverein* was a feature not only accepted but much desired by the membership. It created a framework of clearly understood procedures and rituals, the observance of which gave each man responsibilities and privileges consistent with his length of time as a member, his social standing in the community at large, and his skill with arms. There were usually junior or new, intermediate and senior members as well as honorary members. Each of these groups was subdivided into groupings based on the members' skill on the firing line.

All of the larger and most of the smaller shooting guilds had a hall closely resembling the dining room of a tavern; indeed, they were frequently located in a tavern building where a special room would be rented or leased from the owner. The tables and seating arrangements in the hall reflected the status of the members and gave special attention to the current winners in the shooting programme. Here were generally kept the trophies and prizes of the guild, its records and the gifts made to the guild by other guilds or influential officials. Such halls were sacred to the membership and it was considered a great honour to be invited as a guest to a celebration. The guild officials, of which there were many concerned with the running of the club itself and its affiliated smaller units, as well as range officials and organizers usually had offices attached to these halls and a special table for the transaction of business in the hall itself.

Shooting guilds developed from small, local units, several of which would band together to compete against one another within a fixed framework of meetings and regulations, into larger units that then challenged similar organizations farther afield. The national shooting guilds, encompassing all shooting clubs within a country, did not come into existence until the nineteenth century. The definition of 'national' in many instances is open to interpretation. Switzerland, which today retains the strongest links with the historical past in the shooting world, formed its federal shooting guild in 1824, although country-wide contests in which teams from many different towns – but not cantons – had competed against one another had been held as far back as 1452. In Germany, or, more properly, the German states, the first federal organization dates from 1861, with the first country-wide *Schützenfest* coming in the following year, although the Nuremberg shooting guild has existed since at least 1300. A Belgian shooting guild existed from 1791, but the first national meeting did not take place until 1858. Austrian shooting guilds were among the earliest in Europe, but a national organization does not appear until 1880 – an accurate reflection of the very fragmented structure of the various units comprising the Austro-Hungarian Empire. By this time the major interest in shooting was concentrated in the Tyrol and Vorarlberg, which had formed a shooting guild in 1874. Italy found time to organize a national shooting guild in 1882. Sweden–Norway formed a national shooting union in 1861–1862, and Denmark followed suit in 1871. In Holland shooting remained within the purview of the military, but in Luxembourg there was a national society from 1402. The Russian Empire discouraged the private use of precision arms, but Rumania founded a national shooting guild in 1869, and Greece in the following year. In England many small clubs existed for the amusement of 'amateur riflemen' from the time of the threatened invasion by Napoleon in 1805, but the National Rifle Association was not founded until 1860. However, the English organization bore little resemblance to its European counterparts and does not fit into the context of the guild development traced here. Shooting in France, whether with bow, crossbow or firearms, was always closely allied to, and controlled by, the military authorities, and did not develop as a civilian competitive sport until the twentieth century. The French national rifle-shooting society was established in 1864 as the direct result of public enthusiasm over rifle experiments at Chalon, which had received intensive press coverage. A hiatus was created by the Franco–Prussian War, and when the movement redeveloped afterwards it had very much the character and limitations of the English Volunteer movement.

The international aspects of competitive target shooting began far earlier than the national, with towns from various countries competing against each other at festivals that are still recalled for their lavish accommodations and entertainment. At Zürich in 1504 a grand *Schützenfest* was held for both crossbows and firearms, with teams from Augsburg, Frankfurt-am-Main, Innsbruck, Nuremberg, Stuttgart and several Italian cities competing. Zürich and Frankfurt-am-Main were the leading host cities for international shooting events. However, the entire fabric of international shooting competitions was severely torn by the widespread destruction and disruption of the Thirty Years' War, and it was not until the nationalistic resurgence of the nineteenth century that the international side of competitive target shooting was revived to some semblance of the scale of magnificence which it had enjoyed before the 1620s.

Even on a local level the shooting guilds suffered a decline for more than 150 years from the end of the Thirty Years' War in 1648 until the end of the Napoleonic Wars in 1815; some areas were worse affected than others, but certainly the number of guilds and the lavishness of their meetings were sharply curtailed. The motives for this decline also varied. In some regions the local prince feared the existence of an armed and proficient middle-class, while in others there was a more general dislike for military groups and their activities. In still others it was the lack of funds and suitable facilities that prevented the re-establishment of the sport. Opposition probably reached its peak in Austria during the 1780s when Archduke Joseph II forbade shooting guilds. Fortunately, this abolition seems to have ended with the Archduke's death in 1790. The Napoleonic control of a large part of Europe for more than a decade put a further block on the pursuit of shooting for sport, and it was only with the final end of the wars in 1815 that a renewal of interest began to manifest itself. This does not mean that shooting guilds and their activities ceased to exist: far from it, but there were fewer of them, especially in the war-ravaged German states, and their activities, especially on the international scale, were far more limited than they had been earlier.

The stand of the musket shooters at a great Schützenfest held at Zürich in 1504. People travelled for days from as far away as Frankfurt-am-Main and Innsbruck to attend. Well over 200 musketeers and 460 crossbowmen took part in the competitions.

A joyful occasion recorded by the
'Illustrated London News' – the
distribution of the prizes after a
rifle meeting in Vienna in 1868.

SHOOTING FESTIVALS

The best-known aspect of the shooting guilds is their shoot meetings, or shooting festivals. A great deal of the publicity concerning these gala events has centred around the social and entertainment sides, whereas in fact the primary occupation of the competitors was to shoot, and to shoot well in order to gain the valuable and prestigious awards that went to individuals, teams, clubs, guilds, and towns. The expanded nature of the gatherings is largely due to the fact that they were based upon the middle-class membership of the guilds, and the concept of a 'family outing' was strongly rooted, regardless of the region in question. Certain festivals were arranged to honour royalty or local nobility, but the majority catered for their own middle-class members and their families. It was the wives and children, sweethearts and relatives who thronged the entertainment facilities made available while the shooters competed for prizes for personal and community gain. Once the shooting was over, well, that was another matter altogether!

The monotonous and highly standardized paper targets typical of today's target shooting activities give no clue to the amazing diversity of aiming marks formerly employed by the shooting guilds. Many of the concoctions were costly both in ingredients and in construction time. There were live birds, tethered on long strings to the top of Maypoles, turkeys and other larger birds and beasts loosely anchored on the ground with a tiny but vital part of their anatomy visible to the marksman, and a bewildering and ingenious variety of metal, cloth and wooden mechanical targets set to move in unexpected directions. There were also various objects attached to highly decorated backgrounds – in some ways similar to modern fairground shooting booths – and wooden façades painted with hunting, domestic, mythical, and erotic scenes, with targets depicted on the essential aspect of whatever the scene might be. With this array of possibilities to shoot at, scoring procedures were, of course, of an equally variable and complex nature, making comparisons with today's standardized methods impossible. At the international meetings there was somewhat more conformity in the design of targets, presumably to equalize the chances for all shooters. The familiar bullseye (the origins are obvious) was certainly in use at the Zürich conclave of 1504. In fact, the illustrations of this meeting's facilities bear a marked resemblance to modern appurtenances, with the round target and black centres, the marking sheds placed next to the targets, with signalling markers, and scoring personnel seated behind the covered firing points.

The large attendances at these meetings justified the amount of time and money that went into the preparation of targets and shooting facilities, the erection and decoration of entertainment marquees, and the large variety of food and drink. Since a great deal of social prestige was attached to the shooting guilds, they made every effort to provide an outing with which no one – spectators or contestants – could find any fault either during or after the event. Some meetings went on for more than a week. The attendance of more than 1,000 people was not unusual, even in the sixteenth century, and in many instances there were as many as 1,000 competitors. In the fifteenth and sixteenth centuries, when the lavishness of the shooting festivals was at its height, there were dances, tournaments, races, amateur plays, and many types of contests and games, in addition to the shooting and feasting. As late as 1885 the food consumed during the Swiss federal meeting at Berne included 24,000 kilogrammes of beef and veal, 1,000 kilogrammes each of ham and sausages, 8,000 kilogrammes of cheese, 50,000 litres of beer, and 200,000 bottles of wine for the victory dinner alone. The banqueting hall seated 5,000 people.

Prizes formed the main bait for the shooting. The earliest awards were often in the form of domestic livestock. Other items of household use, such as material for clothing and eating utensils, were also common. However, as other talented craftsmen in the community wished to associate themselves with the prestige of the shooting guilds (gunmakers used the meetings to advertise the excellence of their products), prizes became more varied and intrinsically valuable: gold and silver goblets, bowls, plates, salvers, buckles, chains, necklaces, rings, and plaques became the usual prizes, with money as a practical aside. Medals appeared in the seventeenth century, but did not form the majority of prizes until the last half of the nineteenth century, and in many areas they are still given only for secondary achievements in preference to cups and other similar awards.

The distribution of the prizes and the reasons for presenting them were almost as varied as the targets. Until the middle of the nineteenth century, the first prize usually went to the competitor making the greatest number of hits anywhere on the target; the number of bullseyes was of secondary importance until the improvements in the accuracy of the firearms and their ammunition had increased sufficiently to make hitting the centre of the target consistently a feasible proposition. There were many levels of prizes aside from those at the top, and an interesting variety of booby prizes for the lowest score, or the last man to shoot. Prizes were presented between towns, shooting garlands being among the most usual and popular until the Thirty Years' War put an end to this practice and many of the towns themselves. To become the *Schützenkönig*, the king of the shooters, was the most coveted position of any serious target shooter, and the social prestige and prizes that went with this achievement made it well worth struggling for.

With all of the individualism that typified the organization and composition of the shooting guilds, one feature stands out as remarkably uniform: the distance at which events took place was directly related to the overall capabilities of the firearms. Until the nineteenth century the average distance was not more than 150 metres, although longer ranges, up to 300 metres, were certainly in evidence. Few changes were necessary in the location or construction of shooting ranges until the nineteenth century, when the introduction of the metallic cartridge breech-loader and, later, smokeless powder brought sweeping changes to the entire sport.

With the general acceptance of breech-loading rifles, the old form of shooting guild died away. The individualism possible with muzzle-loading arms was largely defeated by the need to use factory-made metallic cartridges in factory-made breech mechanisms. That most personal of all aspects of shooting, the preparation of one's own ammunition, was eliminated. Re-loading did not come into general favour (if indeed it may be said yet to have done so in many countries) until the twentieth century. The potential performance of various cartridges and calibres, rifling twists and barrel lengths robbed the shooter of most of his choice in weapons if he would aspire to the top ranks among marksmen. The local aspects of the shooting guilds suffered because range facilities were now much more difficult to locate with safety and absence of annoyance to the surrounding population, and the number of such ranges that could be authorized by a conscientious local government became fewer and fewer. Emphasis tended, therefore, to be placed increasingly on the national and international events, and shooting as a sport for all became greatly restricted. This, in turn, cut down the number of gunmakers and raised the price of arms beyond the means of many who would otherwise have participated. In addition, today, target shooting is fraught with legal and financial restrictions, and massive social indifference or hostility in many countries where personal protection and a sense of individual accomplishment have been trampled upon by the mores of a highly industrialized and socially anonymous society.

Shooting instruction on a Swiss range. Shooting continues to be a popular sport in Switzerland today; competitions between towns date back to 1542.

22 LAW AND THE GUN

This chapter is a general introduction to a complex subject. Most of us are motorists, and very few of us have an exact and exhaustive knowledge of motoring law. We exist by a combination of common sense and forethought. The same approach may be taken to the law relating to firearms and their use, since many different pieces of legislation and a considerable body of case law are involved. Only a trained legal mind could reasonably be expected to have the opportunity and ability to build up a thorough knowledge of these primary legal sources, but the private citizen who wishes to own or use a firearm should have at least a general knowledge of the subject, for his own good and for the good of others.

This chapter is written mainly for the target shooter, field sportsman and collector. The circumstances of those who must use firearms for non-recreational purposes, such as the gamekeeper, farmer, vet or licensed slaughterer, are treated only in passing.

The reader should bear in mind that the laws relating to firearms have been subjected to widely ranging interpretations over the years, and that in some areas the courts have either established conflicting precedents, or have not as yet been called upon to provide precise interpretations of legislation that is general in its terminology. Because of its nature, this chapter cannot be authoritative, and should be considered as only a guide. Any reader faced with a legal problem concerning firearms or their use should consult the relevant statues and, if necessary, take specialist legal advice.

GUN LAW IN BRITAIN

THE FIREARM: THE LEGAL DEFINITION

According to Section 57(1) of the Firearm Act 1968, a firearm is:

- 'a lethal barrelled weapon of any description from which any shot, bullet or other missile can be discharged, and includes
- any prohibited weapon, whether it is such a lethal weapon as aforesaid or not; and
- any component part of any such lethal or prohibited weapon; and
- any accessory to such a weapon designed or adapted to diminish the noise or flash caused by firing the weapon.'
- Thus a crossbow is not a firearm, but an air gun is, since the ingredient of 'fire' or 'explosion' is required to meet the legal definition.

A 'prohibited weapon' is defined as:

- 'any firearm which is so designed or adapted that, if pressure is applied to the trigger, missiles continue to be discharged until pressure is removed from the trigger or the magazine containing the missiles is empty, or any weapon of whatever description, designed or adapted for the discharge of any noxious liquid, gas or other things; and any ammunition containing, or designed or adapted to contain any such thing.'

All fully-automatic arms are thus prohibited, as are such non-lethal objects as teargas aerosols, tranquilizer dart guns or even antique pepperguns designed to discourage dogs.

Any major component part of a rifle or pistol, such as a barrel, revolver cylinder or action, also requires the relevant certificate for its possession, although in common practice minor parts such as screws, or parts not essential to the firing of the weapon, such as a spare set of pistol grips, are not held to be separately registrable. However, the case of *Watson* v. *Herman* in 1952 established that a telescopic sight is exempt from any separate registration.

Certain types of weapon designed to shoot only blank cartridges, but considered capable of quick and easy conversion to fire bulleted ammunition, for example by boring out a blocked barrel, are legally considered firearms, as are some pyrotechnic devices such as flare pistols.

AIR WEAPONS

Any person aged 17 or over may purchase or possess an air gun, air rifle or air pistol not being of a type declared by the Home Office to be specially dangerous, without any legal formality or licence. The weapon may be used, within the law, without a licence, unless a game licence is required. So far as offences involving firearms are concerned, an air weapon has the same status as any other sort of firearm.

At present specially dangerous air rifles and air guns are defined as those capable of discharging a missile with a kinetic energy exceeding 12ft lbf at the muzzle, or an air pistol capable of discharging a missile with a kinetic energy exceeding 6ft lbf at the muzzle. Such specially dangerous air weapons require a Firearm Certificate for their possession or purchase. Any weapon using a means of propulsion other than air, for instance carbon dioxide, ether or freon, also requires a Firearm Certificate. An air weapon designed only for use underwater (i.e., spear fishing gun) is not considered to be a specially dangerous air weapon, however.

No certificate is necessary to buy or possess air weapon ammunition.

There are restrictions on the possession and use of air weapons by children and young persons, mainly designed to curb vandalism, which are summarized in the later section on children, young persons and firearms.

SHOTGUNS

A shotgun, for the purposes of the Firearms Act 1968, is defined as a smooth-bore gun having a barrel not less than 24 inches long measured from the muzzle to the point at which the charge is exploded, and not being an air gun.

To acquire, possess or use a shotgun, you must have a Shotgun Certificate, unless you can meet one of the criteria for exemption. The only criteria that are likely to be relevant to the private sportsman are as follows:

The carrying of a shotgun belonging to another person, who has a Shotgun Certificate, under instruction from, and for the use of, that other person and for sporting purposes only. This is intended to exempt loaders and ghillies.

Possession in accordance with the terms of a police permit (see below).

The acquisition, possession or use by a person who has been in Great Britain for not more than 30 days in all in the preceding 12 months.

The use of a shotgun at a time and place approved for shooting at artificial targets by the Chief Officer of Police for the area in which that place is situated. Note that many small clay shoots do *not* have formal police approval, and that possession of a weapon before or after such an event is not sanctioned. A gun cannot therefore be borrowed before a shoot, but may only be handed over at the shooting ground itself.

The borrowing of a shotgun from the occupier (who may or may not be the owner) of private premises, and the use of it on these premises in the presence of the occupier.

The holding of an appropriately varied Northern Ireland Firearm Certificate.

A Shotgun Certificate, valid for three years, is issued by the constabulary in the area in which the applicant resides. Unless the applicant already holds a Firearm Certificate, the statements on the application form must be verified by the counter-signature of another person, unrelated to the applicant, who has known him for at least two years, and who is a British subject and a Member of Parliament, Justice of the Peace, minister of religion, doctor, lawyer, bank officer, or person of similar standing. Reasonably wide latitude is given to the definition of 'person of similar standing', especially in remote rural areas.

The Chief Constable is required to issue the Shotgun Certificate unless the applicant is prohibited from possessing a firearm as the result of a court sentence, or cannot be permitted to possess a shotgun without danger to the public safety or the peace. Some police forces attempt to restrict the issue of Shotgun Certificates on other grounds, for example, that the applicant has no land on which to shoot, but such restrictions have no basis in the Firearms Act 1968, and an appeal

against them would almost certainly be successful.

An appeal to the Crown Court may be made against a refusal to grant or renew, or a revocation of, a Shotgun Certificate.

The Shotgun Certificate must be signed in ink by the holder, and any theft or loss of a shotgun in his possession, in Britain, must be reported by the holder to the Chief Officer of Police who granted the certificate. The certificate authorizes the possession of any number of shotguns, and is valid for three years, or six months in the case of a Visitor's Shotgun Certificate, which is intended for people resident outside the United Kingdom. An application for this latter certificate does not require the counter-signature of a British subject.

The possession of a Shotgun Certificate does not exempt the holder from the need to take out a Game Licence (see below) if he intends to shoot game.

Shotgun ammunition may be acquired or possessed without any licence, providing each cartridge contains five or more shot, none of which exceeds 0.36 inch in diameter. Cartridges with larger shot, shot necklaces or single projectiles require an appropriately varied Firearm Certificate for their acquisition or possession.

It should be noted in passing that it is illegal to shoot deer with a shotgun smaller than 12-bore, and with shot smaller than .269 inch diameter. It is also illegal for an authorized person to shoot certain species of protected birds with a shotgun of over $1\frac{3}{4}$ inches diameter at the muzzle.

ANTIQUE FIREARMS AND COLLECTING

As a general principle, no one worries too much about the collecting of antique firearms, except insofar as a fine collection represents a tempting target for the thief. However, most police forces, mindful of public safety, are very unhappy about the accumulation of large numbers of 'modern' firearms in private hands.

The Firearms Act 1968, Section 58(2) states:

'Nothing in this Act relating to firearms shall apply to an antique firearm which is sold, transferred, purchased, acquired or possessed as a curiosity or ornament.'

Until recently, muzzleloaders not of recent manufacture and certain primitive sorts of breechloader that used separate cartridges and percussion caps (known generically as 'capping breechloaders') were considered antique, while breechloaders taking self-contained cartridges were not.

The word 'antique', however, is commonly held to refer to objects at least 100 years old, and this definition is accepted by HM Customs and Excise and widely applied in the antique trade. Since breechloaders capable of firing the ubiquitous .22 short cartridge have been available since 1858, and the Colt .45 Peacemaker was introduced in 1873, it is clear that many arms capable of functioning with modern cartridges could fall within a definition of antiquity based on a 100-year criterion.

As a result, nearly all police forces consider at least centrefire and rimfire weapons to be modern, and to require a certificate for their possession. Many also treat as modern arms using such obsolete self-contained cartridge ignition systems as teat-fire or pinfire. Practices do vary, however, and what is 'antique' in one police area can be 'modern' in another.

The courts have taken an increasingly liberal line, and *Palmer* v. *Parker* in 1974 established that a firearm that was, or could reasonably be considered to be, 100 years old or more is, if kept as a curiosity or ornament, an antique. It may thus be possessed without a certificate. A complex series of subsequent decisions, including *Richard* v. *Curwen*, 1977, have established that, in some circumstances, a firearm may be a good deal less than 100 years old and still meet the definition of an antique, providing, of course, that it is kept as a curiosity or ornament, and that each case would have to be considered on its merits. The greater the age and the degree of mechanical failure of the weapon, the more likely it is to be antique in the eyes of the court.

The police, however, still tend to insist that a Firearm Certificate be issued or varied for any breechloading rifle or pistol using a self-contained cartridge, however old the weapon, or a Shotgun Certificate for any shotgun that conforms to such a definition. Anyone starting a collection of antique breechloaders would be well advised to consult his local police. So far as the collection of modern breechloaders is concerned, the need for the appropriate certificate is not in doubt.

The collecting of old muzzleloaders requires no certificate, and its popularity as a hobby is reflected in the very high prices fine examples command. Nevertheless, the collector should take care to ensure that he retains no black powder, unless he possesses the appropriate permit, and that no arm in his collection has been subjected to restoration involving the replacement of a major part (such as a barrel or revolver cylinder) with a modern substitute, since this would invalidate its antique status.

Air weapons may also be collected without let or hindrance, providing that those whose antique status is questionable do not fall within the definition of 'specially dangerous' air weapons.

SECTION 1 FIREARMS AND AMMUNITION

Section 1 is a term commonly used to group together weapons for which a Firearm Certificate is required for possession or use. These include cartridge rifles, pistols, revolvers, shotguns with barrels less than 24 inches long (which includes many old 'garden guns'), shot pistols, CO_2 powered arms, 'specially dangerous' air weapons (mainly American-made arms operating on the pneumatic principle), muzzleloaders of modern manufacture and such devices as humane killers, flare pistols and, in some constabularies, artillery.

A Firearm Certificate is also required if an antique muzzleloader or capping breechloader is to be fired.

Bulleted cartridges and shotgun ammunition containing less than five shot, or shot exceeding 0.36 inch, also require a Firearm Certificate for possession or use, but blank cartridges of one inch or less in diameter do not.

There are certain exceptions to the requirement of a Firearm Certificate for possession or use, of which the two most likely to concern the sportsman or target shooter are as follows:

The carrying of a firearm belonging to another person, who holds a Firearm Certificate, under instructions from, and for the use of, that other person and for sporting purposes only. This is intended to exempt ghillies, and would not be held to apply to, say, one target shooter relinquishing possession of his target rifle to another shooter for the purpose of easier transport to or from the range.

The possession by a member of a rifle club, miniature rifle club or cadet corps approved by the Home Office (the approval requirement applies to the clubs as well as the corps) of a firearm when engaged as such a member in, or in connection with, drill or target practice. This exemption does not apply to persons who are not members who might be attending such an organization, *except* on a miniature rifle range (whether for a rifle club or otherwise) or a shooting gallery at which no firearms are used other than air weapons not declared to be specially dangerous or miniature rifles not exceeding .23 calibre. This exemption also covers the commercial shooting galleries still found on fairgrounds.

As with Shotgun Certificates, Firearm Certificates are granted by the police authority in whose area the applicant resides, and are valid for three years.

The Firearm Certificate is, however, not so easy or straightforward to obtain as a Shotgun Certificate. The police are required to refuse a Firearm Certificate if the applicant is prohibited from possessing firearms by the Firearms Act, (and it should be noted that, for this purpose, convictions can never be 'spent') or is of unsound mind, or intemperate habits, or is for any reason unfitted to be trusted with a firearm. Persons prohibited by reason of certain sentences or conditions laid down in Section 21 (1) (2) and (3) of the Firearms Act 1968 may apply to the Crown Court for a removal of the prohibition.

The applicant must also provide a good reason to possess the firearm for which he is applying. There are a limited number of generally accepted good reasons, including target shooting, with a rifle or pistol, provided that the applicant is a full member of a Home Office approved club with access to a range suitable for the firearm in question. Vermin destruction or ground game shooting with a rifle would also be acceptable, provided that the opportunity for such use actually existed, and that the land on which the arm would be shot was suitable, and that there would be no threat to public safety. The desire to use a pistol, except perhaps a shot pistol, for vermin destruction or ground game shooting is almost never accepted as a good reason. In most constabularies a very

strong case has to be put up to obtain a Certificate for collecting firearms, especially pistols. Certificates are almost never issued for the purpose of defence of person or property.

A very thorough check will then take place to verify the information on the application form. Enquiries will be made to satisfy the police that an applicant is a fit person to possess a firearm, and that he has no previously undisclosed character defects. The premises in which he wishes to store the weapon may be inspected to establish whether they are sufficiently secure to prevent unauthorized access to the arm. An applicant who lives permanently in a club, hotel or lodging house might well not be permitted to keep his firearm at his place of residence. A check might also be made on other regular occupants of his house. The currency of any membership of an approved rifle club would be investigated, as would the suitability of any land on which the applicant might wish to shoot game.

The police may recommend or stipulate a number of security measures before they will issue a Firearm Certificate, such as the installation of a lockable steel gun cabinet.

If a Firearm Certificate is granted, it will be subject to a number of conditions, four of which are mandatory: The holder must sign the certificate in ink, on receipt; the firearms and ammunition must be kept in a safe place when not in use; any theft or loss of the firearms must be reported by the holder to the police; any change of address must be notified by the holder to the police. On almost all certificates, however, additional conditions are included, usually restricting how and where the firearms may be used. Calibres of ammunition and the maximum quantities that may be purchased and possessed at any one time will also be specified.

A certificate will refer to a specific firearm or firearms. If the holder wishes to acquire additional arms, he will have to apply for a variation for specific types of weapon, say, 'one .22 rifle' or 'one .45 pistol', providing a good reason for each one. Any change in use, or changes in the quantity or type of ammunition would also require a variation.

The grant of a Firearms Certificate attracts a fee, as does a renewal or a variation that increases the number of firearms held. Other variations are free.

Should the grant, renewal or variation of a Firearm Certificate be refused or revoked, an appeal may be made to the Crown Court within 21 days after receipt of the notice of refusal or revocation.

If a Firearm Certificate holder wishes to dispose of a firearm, he may transfer it (with very limited exceptions) only to a registered firearms dealer, or to the holder of an appropriately varied Firearm Certificate. In the latter case the transferor must inform the Chief Officer of Police of the police force that issued the recipient's certificate by recorded delivery or registered post within 48 hours. He may not transfer a firearm or a shotgun to a person whom he knows to be drunk or of unsound mind.

When carrying his firearm, the owner should also carry his Firearm (or Shotgun) Certificate, since any police constable has the right to request the production of a certificate. Failure to meet his request may result in the seizure and detention of the firearm and ammunition.

It is wise to bear in mind that the comprehensive investigations that may take place during the process of grant, renewal or variations of a Firearm Certificate can take time, often several weeks.

POLICE PERMITS

On occasion it may be desirable for a private individual to be allowed to possess (but not to acquire) firearms, for example, to allow the executor of an estate to dispose of firearms legally owned by the deceased. Two forms of permit exist for private individuals, one referring to Section 1 firearms, the other to shotguns. The period of validity is usually very short, a few months at most, and no fee is payable.

PROHIBITED WEAPONS

Since 1968 the issue of an authority to possess prohibited weapons, such as machine guns, has been the function of the Home Office. Except in the rarest circumstances, such an authority is not given to private citizens where fully automatic weapons are concerned. The only reason for an authority to be granted to a private citizen is for the purchase of a tranquillizer dart gun, and even these are granted only very sparingly if a demonstrable need exists.

RELOADING

Until recently, there was no legal restriction over the purchase of reloading components, with the exception of black powder, which required, and still requires, a Black Powder Permit, which may be applied for from the local police. This is not normaliy withheld from anyone who has a legitimate reason to use black powder, for example, a full member of an approved muzzleloading rifle club, but quantities to be held at one time are usually restricted to a few pounds.

Certain types of small-arms primers are no longer on unrestricted sale, mainly because the method of packing them is held to constitute a safety hazard. A Fit Person Certificate, obtainable from the local Criminal Investigation Department, is required for their purchase. Other makes remain freely available.

The reloader for a pistol or rifle should ensure that he does not assemble a greater number of cartridges than his Firearm Certificate permits him to possess at any one time.

INSURANCE

Insurance cover, either against personal accident or for third party cover, is not a legal requirement. Some clubs insist as a condition of membership that each person takes out individual third party cover, and some competitions contain a similar clause in their rules. Such insurance cover is very cheap and, indeed, is frequently included in policies covering the contents of private dwellings.

Shooters are well advised to ensure that they have proper insurance, for their own sake, their family's and the public's.

CHILDREN, YOUNG PERSONS AND FIREARMS

Sections 22, 23 and 24 of the 1968 Act cover restrictions on the acquisition, purchase and use of firearms by the young. These are complex, and confusing, since they represent a consolidation of sections originating in a number of earlier acts.

So far as air weapons and ammunition are concerned, no one under 17 may purchase or hire them, or possess them in a public place, unless either the weapon concerned is an air rifle or air gun (but *not* an air pistol) that is in a securely fastened gun cover so that it may not be fired, or the young person is engaged as a member of an approved rifle club or cadet corps in connection with drill or target practice, or when at a shooting gallery. Children under the age of 14 are further restricted, since they may not possess these items in a public place, and may possess them on private premises only under the supervision of a person aged 21 or over, in which case if a missile is fired beyond these premises, *both* commit an offence.

A person under the age of 17 may not purchase or hire a shotgun or shotgun cartridges. A person under the age of 15 may not have an *assembled* shotgun with him, unless under the supervision of a person aged 21 or over, or when the shotgun is in a securely fastened gun cover so that it cannot be fired. These provisions refer both to public places and private premises.

A person under the age of 17 may not purchase or hire a firearm or ammunition. A person under the age of 14 may not have a firearm or ammunition in his possession, unless in a circumstance where any person would be exempted from the requirements to hold a firearm certificate.

It is thus legally possible for an unaccompanied 14-year-old to be in legal possession of his revolver in a public place, but he would be legally debarred from carrying his shotgun, unless securely cased, or his air pistol in any circumstances whatsoever! In practice, of course, Firearm Certificates for revolvers are not commonly issued to 14-year-olds.

Where required, a person under the age of 17 must hold a Firearm Certificate or Shotgun Certificate, but the firearm and ammunition must be given or lent to him, since he cannot purchase his own.

As far as the possession of an antique firearm as a curiosity or ornament is concerned, young people seem to be in the same position as adults, as they would be when acting as a loader or ghillie for a certificate holder, in accordance with Sections 11 (1) and 22 (2) of the 1968 Act.

RESTRICTIONS ON THE CARRYING OF FIREARMS

Section 19 of the Firearms Act 1968 states that any person who, without lawful authority or reasonable excuse, the proof whereof shall lie on him, has with him in a public place any loaded shotgun or loaded air weapon or any other firearm, whether loaded or not, together with ammunition suitable for use in that firearm commits an offence.

Neither 'lawful authority' nor 'reasonable excuse' is defined by the 1968 Act, but the latter would almost certainly require a specific and fairly immediate reason, such as the transport of the firearm to or from a range, gunsmith or shoot, rather than, for example, the continuous carriage of a sporting rifle in a car in case an unplanned opportunity to use it should occur. Mere possession of a Firearm Certificate, unless specifically varied to give lawful authority, or a Shotgun Certificate, would not be deemed to constitute 'lawful authority' to possess in a public place. A person who has a Firearm Certificate varied in such a manner that it permits *use* of a pistol only for target shooting on approved ranges could not legally *carry* that weapon and ammunition for it except for the purpose of target shooting. A public place includes any highway and any other premises or place to which at the material time the public have or are permitted to have access, whether on payment or otherwise. Besides such places as cinemas, parks and pubs, any form of public transport and even a taxi would be construed as a public place.

Section 20 of the 1968 Act deals with armed trespass. A person commits an offence if, while he has a firearm with him, he enters or is in any building, or enters or is on any land (including land covered with water) without reasonable excuse.

Any person suspected of an offence may be required by a constable to hand over the firearm or ammunition for inspection, and may be searched or detained for search. Any vehicle suspected of being involved in such an offence may be stopped and searched. A suspected person may be arrested without warrant, and any place may be entered by a constable if such an offence is suspected.

Essentially similar provisions relating to 'offensive weapons' are laid down in the Prevention of Crime Act, 1953, and might also be applied, since any object meeting the legal definition of a firearm would also meet the legal definition of an offensive weapon.

PROOF

The proof laws are perhaps the oldest British legislation aimed at a positive form of consumer protection. Since 1813 it has been an offence to sell or offer for sale an unproved arm within the United Kingdom. The proof procedure involves viewing an arm to ensure that there are no obvious flaws that would weaken the gun and the firing of a load much heavier than would usually be used, in order to set up sufficient pressure to create a level of stress that would show up any weakness or flaw in the gun concerned.

There are two proof houses in Britain. The Worshipful Company of Gunmakers of the City of London operates the Proof House at 48 Commercial Road, London E1, and the Guardians of the Birmingham Proof House administer the Gun Barrel Proof House at Banbury Street, Birmingham B5 5RH. Both administer the Gun Barrel Proof Acts of 1868 and 1950, and the Rules of Proof, the most recent of which are those of 1954. Both carry out essentially the same series of tests, but impress with their own pattern of proof-mark those weapons that pass their tests.

The Proof Acts apply to all small-arms, with the exception of air weapons, which, for the purposes of these Acts, are not firearms, and some military small-arms while in military hands. If these military arms are subsequently offered for civilian sale, they must be subjected to proof.

It should be noted that there is no offence in the possession of an unproved arm, and the law specifically allows the importation without subsequent proof of 'any Small Arm ... by any person for his own personal use while it is his own property.' An offence is committed only when a small-arm is sold, exchanged or exported, exposed or kept for sale or exchange or pawned without being fully proved and duly marked.

In practice, no new firearm is offered for sale by commercial dealers unless it has been proved either in this country, or in a foreign proof house whose procedures are accepted by the British Proof Authorities. At present, the *current* proof marks of Austria, Belgium, Czechoslovakia, France, West Germany, Italy, the Republic of Ireland and Spain are recognized. This recognition is reciprocal. It should be noted, however, that some earlier proof marks from these countries are invalid in Britain, and the advice of one of the Proof Houses or a competent gunsmith should be sought if there is doubt about the validity of any proof mark.

Once proved, there is no need to submit the weapon for reproof before disposal, unless the barrels have been enlarged in the bore beyond defined limits or if there has been any material weakening of the barrel or action in other respects. Some indications of weakness are obvious, such as bulges or dents in the barrel, but it should also be noted that, for example, the shortening of a barrel, the installation of an adjustable choke or even the chrome plating of the bore will put a weapon 'out of proof'.

The shooter should also be aware that there are two types of proof: black powder only, and nitro proof for modern smokeless powder. Smokeless powder operates at much higher pressure than black powder, and a weapon that may still have valid black powder proof marks is quite likely to be unsafe with smokeless cartridges. Many shotguns proved before 1925 were subjected only to black powder proof.

A private individual may submit his firearm to one or other of the Proof Houses for proof or reproof. Where reproof is concerned, however, it is wise to have the arm checked over by a gunsmith, and to have any necessary repairs made. The gunsmith will also act as an agent for the reproving process. If the gun fails proof or reproof, it may, in some circumstances, be repaired and resubmitted. If it finally fails reproof, existing proof marks will be defaced, and the weapon may not legally be resold.

Where antiques or collector's items are concerned, either Proof House may, at its discretion, issue a Certificate of Unprovability, which allows the sale or transfer of the weapon if the gun is not for use or cannot be proved, for example, because no ammunition is at present available.

THE FIREARMS OWNER AND THE PRESERVATION OF HIS INTERESTS

This chapter has been written on the basis of the Firearms Act 1968. Since the publication in 1973 of the Green Paper titled 'The Control of Firearms in Great Britain', it has been clear that an intention exists to revise the law relating to firearms. Informed shooting men have seriously doubted whether some measures of control proposed by both Conservative and Labour administrations would have any worthwhile social benefit. These measures would, however, be expensive and time-consuming to administer, and could seriously curtail the pursuit of legitimate shooting sports by law-abiding citizens. The volume of correspondence from members of the public generated by the 1973 Green Paper greatly exceeded any other issue placed before Parliament during this century, and did much to prevent the passage of ill-considered legislation. Such political involvement is time-consuming and regrettable, but the need for it is likely to recur if the proper interests of the shooting public are to be protected. Every shooting man should join the appropriate national and local association, society or club administering his branch of the sport, and every collector should join the Arms and Armour Society or Historical Breechloading Small-arms Association. The Shooters' Rights Association was founded specifically to protect the legal rights of its members, through the courts if necessary, and functions as an advice centre and a clearing house for information on firearms law. The individual shooter and collector should also be prepared to take individual action, when necessary, by writing to his Member of Parliament and stating his point of view on proposed legislation as clearly, calmly and briefly as practicable. Remember that a Member of Parliament is his constituents' representative, but he cannot act effectively on their behalf unless he is aware of their problems.

Grass roots organization of firearms' owners at a parliamentary constituency level is also worthwhile, since an MP is far more likely to react favourably to a single meeting with, or single document prepared by, representatives of his constituency's target shooters, clay pigeon shooters, shooting syndicates, wildfowling clubs and collectors than he is to the daunting prospect of answering individually dozens or hundreds of letters from individual shooting men.

The average shooting man may pay hundreds of pounds for his firearm and accessories, and tens or hundreds of pounds annually on ammunition. A little time, a little money and a little effort spent in becoming aware of his legal position, and in defending it if necessary are small prices for the shooter to pay for the preservation of his sport.

GAME LAW
A BRIEF SUMMARY

Black game, bustard, grouse, partridge and pheasant are always game, and a Game Licence is necessary if you 'take, kill or pursue, or aid or assist in any manner in the taking, killing or pursuing by any means whatever, or use any dog, gun, net or other engine for the purpose of taking any game, or any woodcock, snipe, or any coney (i.e., rabbit) or any deer.' Hares are also included in the general definition of game for licensing purposes.

This requirement is very general in its application. An offence would clearly be committed if a person without a Game Licence allowed his dog to retrieve game birds shot by another.

There are exemptions from the obligation to hold a Game Licence. Beaters and loaders do not require a licence. Deer may be killed on enclosed land (i.e., parks or farms 'enclosed by normal agricultural hedges') by the owner or occupier, or by his direction or permission. Rabbits may be taken or destroyed by the proprietor of any warren, or of any enclosed ground, or by the tenant of any lands (enclosed or not), or by his direction or permission. Hares may be killed, but not at night, by the occupier of enclosed lands, or the owner who has the right to kill hares, or a person authorized by either of them. Only one person may be so authorized, however, and this must be done in writing, on an annual basis. The written authority lapses automatically on the following 1 February, and a copy of the authority must, by law, be registered with the clerk of the local magistrates. Further exceptions also apply by virtue of the Ground Game Act 1880, but the matter is complex and bound up with the exact nature of the ownership or tenancy.

Game Licences are available from post offices and some local authorities. Apart from a Gamekeeper's Licence, to which numerous strictures apply, there are four classes of licence. These are: a £6 licence which must be taken out between 1 August and 31 October, and which expires on 31 July of the following year. This is the *only* one of the four licences that entitles the holder to *sell* game (with certain exceptions relating to rabbits and hares), and then only to a licensed dealer in game. A £4 licence may run either from 1 August or after until 31 October in the same year, or from 1 November or after, expiring on 31 July the next year. An occasional £2 licence is valid for any continuous period of fourteen days.

Besides police officers, there are several groups of people who are legally entitled to ask to see the Game Licence of any person committing any action for which a licence is required. These include the owner, landlord, occupier, lessee or gamekeeper of the land; any officer of certain local authorities, and any person who has himself taken out a Game Licence. If the licence cannot be produced on request, a full name, address and place of issue of the missing licence must be given.

With the exception of deer, wild birds, wild game birds and wild animals cannot be owned while alive. The law only grants the right to take them in defined circumstances.

GAME BIRDS

Close seasons apply to certain classes of game, during which they may not be shot. These dates are inclusive.

> Black game: 11 December to 19 August (except in parts of the West Country, where the close season is extended to 31 August)
> Grouse or red game: 11 December to 11 August
> Bustard or wild turkey: 2 March to 31 August
> Partridge: 2 February to 30 September
> Pheasant: 2 February to 30 September

These birds may not be shot on a Sunday, Christmas day, or at night.

NON-GAME BIRDS

The Protection of Birds Act 1954 relates to all non-game birds and to some birds, such as snipe, which are game for some legal purposes, but not for others. The Act contains three schedules of concern to the shooter. The first lists birds that are either given full protection at all times, or are given special protection during their close season. The second embraces birds that have no close season, and may be taken at any time by any authorized person. These include such sporting quarry as the wood pigeon, stock dove and rook. The third schedule refers to wild birds that may be killed in their open season, and contains various wildfowl, woodcock and snipe.

The Protection of Birds Act also specifies the following close seasons for birds in the third schedule.

> Capercaillie and woodcock: 1 February to 30 September
> Snipe: 1 February to 11 August
> Wild duck and wild geese (in or over any area below high water mark of ordinary spring tides): 21 February to 31 August
> Any other wild bird in the schedule: 1 February to 31 August

The Protection of Birds Act also forbids the taking of birds on a Sunday in many areas of England and Wales. It limits the use of certain types of decoy and artificial lights, and forbids the use of shotguns of a bore greater than $1\frac{3}{4}$ inches at the muzzle, or the use of mechanically propelled vehicles, boats or aircraft for the immediate pursuit of a wild bird for the purpose of driving, killing or taking it. The Act permits the shooting at any time of birds that are neither game nor listed in the first schedule in order to prevent damage to crops, pasture, etc.

WILDFOWL

Most of the seashore and the beds of estuaries and tidal rivers are Crown property, and the public has no general right to shoot there. The Crown may permit the public to shoot in such areas if no damage is likely to be caused. In certain very limited circumstances, however, the right to shoot on the foreshore may lie with a private individual.

DEER

The Deer Act 1963 forbids the killing of deer during the close season or at night, with very limited exceptions relating to sick or injured deer or the protection of crops or pasture.

The close seasons for deer are:

Male red deer, fallow deer and sika deer: 1 May to 31 July

Female red deer, roe deer, fallow deer and sika: 1 March to 31 October

It is illegal to shoot deer with any weapon except either a rifle of .240 inch or larger, with a muzzle energy of 1,700 foot pounds or more, and using a soft-nosed or hollow-nosed bullet, or a shotgun of 12 bore or larger, loaded with shot, none of which is less than .269 inch in diameter. It is also illegal to discharge a firearm from any mechanically propelled vehicle or aircraft, or to use such vehicles or aircraft for driving deer.

SCOTTISH GAME LAW

GAME LICENCES

A game licence is required in Scotland in similar circumstances to those in England and Wales. The law is based on the Game Licences Act, 1860 which applies throughout Great Britain.

SALE OF GAME: PHEASANT, PARTRIDGE, GROUSE AND BLACK GAME

Anybody who has a game licence may sell these birds to anybody licensed to deal in game. A licensed dealer may not buy or sell any game bird after ten days after the expiry of the close game season (except for breeding purposes).

Owing to the introduction of deep freezers it is now legal to possess game out of season.

HARE AND RABBIT

A person does not require a game licence to sell hares and rabbits which he has himself killed or which have been killed by other people on his authority on ground which he occupies.

DEER

Under the Sale of Venison (Scotland) Act, 1968 no person may sell venison without being a registered venison dealer. A registered venison dealer, however, may buy deer from anybody as long as the deer has been lawfully shot.

WILD GEESE

Under the Protection of Wild Birds Act, 1967 it is illegal to sell wild geese at any time of the year.

CLOSE SEASONS: GAME BIRDS

Close seasons for the species of game mentioned under the Game Laws of England and Wales are the same in Scotland except for the partridge, the close season for which ends on 31 August rather than 30 September. Under the Game Act, 1828 it is illegal to shoot any of these birds at night, which is defined as beginning one hour after sunset and ending one hour before sunrise. The close season for ptarmigan, which of course are only found in Scotland, is from 11 December to 11 August. It is legal to shoot ptarmigan at night.

It is generally accepted that shooting game is illegal on Sundays and Christmas Day whether in the close season or not but there does not seem to be a specific legal authority for this view.

HARE AND RABBIT

There is no close season for ground game. It is an offence to shoot ground game at night (as defined above). In England it has been argued that the shooting of hares and rabbits at night is legal in certain circumstances but in Scotland this is not so and people have been successfully prosecuted for it.

DEER

Under the Deer (Scotland) Act, 1959 the close seasons for deer are as follows:

Red Deer Stag	21 October–30 June
Red Deer Hind	16 February–20 October
Roe Buck	21 October–30 April
Roe Doe	1 March–20 October
Fallow Buck	1 May–31 July
Fallow Doe	16 February–20 October
Sika Stag	1 May–31 July
Sika Hind	16 February–20 October

While it is normally illegal to shoot deer during their close season, an occupier of agricultural land or enclosed woodlands may do so if the deer in question is found on any arable land or in a garden or on any land laid down in permanent grass. A person authorized by the occupier of the land could also legally shoot deer in these circumstances.

The situation at night however, is more restricting: it is illegal to shoot deer at night, except, as with the close seasons, where the farmer or forester finds the deer on his land. But in this case the farmer or forester must shoot the deer himself; he cannot authorize anyone else to do it for him.

Despite strong protests from everyone concerned with game and wildlife in Scotland it is still legal to shoot deer with shotguns. However, it should be remembered that this can cause a great amount of suffering to all deer and especially to red deer.

It is always legal for anybody to shoot deer if the object is to prevent unnecessary suffering by that deer or any orphaned deer calf. The Deer Commission also authorizes people to kill deer as part of a controlled cull.

PROTECTION OF BIRDS

With very minor exceptions wild birds are controlled in Scotland in exactly the same way as in England. The close seasons for duck and geese and other wild birds are the same in Scotland as in England.

WILD FOWLING, POACHING AND TRESPASS

In Scotland the foreshore belongs to the Crown. The right of ownership is sometimes bestowed on private individuals but the right of public recreation on the foreshore cannot be prevented either by the individual owners or by the Crown. Accordingly wildfowling is legal if conducted on the foreshore.

It may be difficult for a person to get to the foreshore without crossing private land. Strictly speaking, trespass with a gun is armed trespass and is a criminal offence under the Firearms Act, 1968. In practice prosecutions for armed trespass do not proceed except for poaching or suspected poaching.

Unlike other offences individual landowners may institute private prosecutions for poaching offences. This, however, is likely to be changed in the near future when all prosecutions will be initiated by the Crown.

Trespass is not a criminal offence in Scotland (unless the trespasser camps or lights a fire on private land). This does not prevent a landowner who wishes to prevent such trespass from using just sufficient force to remove a trespasser. If the trespass is persistent the owner can apply for a Court Order (called an 'Interdict') and any infringement of the Interdict would be punishable criminally.

GUN LAW IN THE UNITED STATES

CONSTITUTIONAL RIGHTS

To the British shooter, hedged by restriction, the United States seems a promised land where the gun enthusiast can breathe freely within the law, secure in the knowledge that his avocation is protected by a written constitution.

The American sees it differently. His constitutional battlements resemble the back wall of the Alamo, and each new Congress, each new legislature, convenes like Santa Anna's army beating no quarter on tautly drawn drums. For two decades he has fought a war of attrition, and each turn of the calendar threatens a last stand. Still, the holding action has been largely successful, and could not have been had the Bill of Rights not been there to rally round.

The Second Amendment to the Constitution reads in full: 'A well regulated Militia, being necessary to the security of a free State, the right of the people to keep and bear Arms shall not be infringed.' This has proved vexing to those who wish to outlaw firearms. Their approach is functionally to nullify the Second Amendment by claiming that the founding fathers did not express themselves in clear prose and really did not at all mean what they appear to have said. Thus the President's Commission on Law Enforcement and Administration of Justice (N. de B. Katzenbach, 1965) insisted that: 'The argument that the Second Amendment prohibits state or federal regulation of citizen ownership of firearms has no validity whatsoever. This declaration was supported only by the contention that 'The US Supreme Court and lower federal courts have consistently interpreted this amendment only as a prohibition against federal interference with state militia and not as a guarantee of an individual's right to keep or carry firearms.'

The Supreme Court has ruled in Second Amendment cases on four occasions (*US* v. *Cruikshank, 1876*; *Presser* v. *Illinois, 1886*; *Miller* v. *Texas, 1854*; *US* v. *Miller, 1939*). In the first three instances the court went no further than to say that, like most of the rest of the Bill of Rights, the Second Amendment acted as a limitation on the federal government and not on the states. *US* v. *Miller* (*1939*), which concerned the interstate transport of a sawn-off shotgun, was decided on the grounds of failure on the defendant's part to demonstrate the applicability

of the weapon in question to military use, which could easily have been done, as a lower court subsequently pointed out in *Cases* v. *US (1942)*.

Given the caution of the Supreme Court in this area, it is not surprising that the lower courts have treated it gingerly. In a more recent case, *Burton* v. *Sills (1969)*, the New Jersey Supreme Court, in upholding that state's firearms statute, stated that 'reasonable gun control legislation is clearly within the police power of the state.' But their decision did little more than deny the plaintiff's request that the protections of the Second Amendment be extended via the Fourteenth Amendment to cover state, as well as federal law. There has been a fluster of activity in the lower courts during the past decade, but nothing, it would appear from a perusal of case synopses in *US Code Annotated*, to alter the basic constitutional situation, which bears little resemblance to the interpretation of it given by the Department of Justice and a succession of presidential commissions.

A host of evidence can be brought that a majority in Congress have for two centuries understood the Second Amendment as describing an individual right. Thus the Property Seizure Act of 1941 included an amendment on which the House Committee on Military Affairs elaborated in the following terms:

'The amendment provides in substance that nothing contained in the bill shall be construed to authorize the President to requisition or require the registration of firearms possessed by an individual for his personal protection or sport, the possession of which is not prohibited nor the registration thereof required and that the act shall not impair or infringe the right of an individual to keep and bear arms. It is not contemplated or even inferred that the President, or any executive board, agency, or officer, would trespass upon the right of the people in this respect . . . nor is there any desire or intention on the part of the Congress or the President to impair or infringe the right of the people under Section 2 (Second Amendment) of the Constitution of the United States, which reads, in part, as follows: "the right of the people to keep and bear Arms shall not be infringed." However, in view of the fact that certain totalitarian and dictatorial nations are now engaged in the willful and wholesale destruction of personal rights and liberties, your committee deems it appropriate for the Congress to expressly state that the proposed legislation shall not be construed to impair or infringe the constitutional right of the people to bear arms. . . . There is no disposition on the part of this government to depart from the concepts and principles of personal rights and liberties expressed in our Constitution.'

Moreover, it is widely recognized that the Second Amendment describes, rather than creates, a right to keep and bear arms. The right predated the Constitution and exists without it. It stood as part of the British constitution until well into the twentieth century, was recognized by Blackstone in his *Commentaries* of 1765, and passed from British common law into American common law. Thirty-six state constitutions incorporate a right to keep and bear arms, some of which, like those of Pennsylvania and Vermont, predate the federal constitution and go somewhat beyond its wording in specifying 'that the people have a right to bear arms for the defence of themselves and the state.'

Thus, although those who would outlaw firearms, insisting that the citizen has no right to them, may be both constitutionally and historically wrong, those who proclaim that right have shown little zeal in bringing a test case before the Supreme Court in order to demonstrate it.

The right to keep and bear arms exists; it is part of the Constitution, just as it was in England. But without constant, unrelenting defense, it will be eroded and finally eradicated.

WIDE RANGING STATUTES

Whatever the theoretical extent of his rights, the American shooter or firearms enthusiast is scarcely untrammelled in his exercise of them. It is estimated that there are some 20,000 separate firearms statutes on the books of the United States and its political subdivisions. Whatever the source of this figure, it is accepted and used on both sides of the debate, and it makes little difference if it is five or ten thousand in error one way or another. The point is that the scrupulous shooter has an intimidating task in trying to comply with the law. Those who do not make an effort to inform themselves of the regulations prevailing in their states and localities take a substantial risk.

Machine guns make a good example. We all know what they are. The technical description is straightforward: they are weapons that keep firing so long as the trigger is depressed and there is ammunition in the magazine. Machine guns have been subject to federal control since 1934. In order to own one you must have a licence and pay a $200 transfer tax each time the weapon changes hands. This covers you as far as the federal government is concerned. You may still, however, find yourself in violation of state law or municipal ordinance. Some states and localities recognize the federal licence; others prohibit machine guns altogether. Some require an additional licence from the state adjutant general.

However, if you delve deeper into the statutes, you will find, for example, that the District of Columbia classifies as a 'machine gun' any firearm that shoots automatically *or semi-automatically* more than twelve shots without reloading. This includes, of course, most .22 self-loading plinking and small game rifles with tubular magazines, as well, it would appear, as 9 millimetre pistols such as the Browning High Power and the Smith & Wesson Model 59.

Minnesota, on the other hand, does not classify even a fully automatic weapon as a machine gun unless magazine capacity exceeds 12 rounds. The state does however, classify as a machine gun any full or semi-automatic weapon 'which . . . shall have been changed, altered or modified to increase the magazine capacity from the original design as manufactured by the manufacturers thereof . . . or by the addition, modification or attachment thereto of a device capable of increasing the magazine capacity thereof.' It would appear a close question as to whether an extension magazine, as commonly used in International Practical Shooting Confederation pistol competitions, runs foul of Minnesota's machine gun law.

Several states classify self-loading rifles or carbines of greater than .22 calibre as machine guns if magazine capacity exceeds 18 rounds (Ohio), 14 rounds (Rhode Island) or 16 rounds (Virginia). North Carolina's statute backs onto stage defining what a machine gun is not rather than what it is. Consequently, what it is is never made clear, but the impression left is that a .22 plinker with a tubular magazine is in violation of the state law if the gun's capacity is greater than 16 rounds.

The question of machine gun definition is, as we said, simply an illustration of the density of the legal thicket where one would have expected clarity, if not necessarily legislative uniformity.

A catalogue of absurdities in firearms law, if seriously embarked upon, would fill volumes, and is far beyond the scope of this chapter, as is more than a thumb-nail survey of the *corpus legis* itself.

We will take a very brief and superficial look at the types of law likely to be encountered, and then study federal law a bit more closely.

STATE LAW

There are essentially three strata of firearms law: federal, state, and local. Of these, state law is the most important, for the police power resides in the state. It does not reside in the federal government, and is vested in the municipality only by delegation from the state.

Thus it is, for the most part, state law that governs the sale, purchase, transfer, transport, ownership and use of firearms. The state code or statutes are available for perusal by any citizen at city hall, the county courthouse, and major public libraries. Given the fluidity and complexity of the subject and the extent of misinformation in circulation, reading it yourself is the only way to be sure that you are accurately appraised.

Generally speaking, there are few state restrictions on the purchase of a rifle or shotgun. Several states, notably New Jersey, Illinois and Massachusetts, require a licence called a 'gun owner's identification card' before a shoulder gun may be purchased or possessed.

Restrictions on handguns are stiffer, but still, most states do not require a permit to purchase or possess. However, the prospective purchaser must come equipped with adequate identification, information from which, along with a physical description and the buyer's signature, go into the dealer's federal register for police to consult if they so desire.

Some states (notably Alabama, California, Connecticut, Indiana, Maryland, Pennsylvania, Rhode Island, South Dakota, Tennessee, and Washington) impose a waiting period, ranging from 48 hours to, in the case of Tennessee, 15 days, before the buyer, who has filled out the papers, may receive the gun from the dealer. The state and local police are informed immediately and can, during the waiting period, investigate and take action to block the sale if they have grounds for doing so.

Eight states require the prior issue of either a purchase permit or a gun owner's identification card before a handgun may be bought. These are Hawaii, Illinois, Massachusetts, Michigan, Missouri, New Jersey, New York, and North Carolina.

Regulations concerning carrying handguns, either openly or concealed, in a vehicle or on the person, vary widely from state to state and do not lend themselves to ready summary. Only rarely is concealed carry permitted without a licence. Some states prohibit the practice altogether. Some allow some modes of carry and restrict or prohibit others. There are various licensing systems in various places. Again, the only way to be sure what is required in a specific state is to consult the statutes.

To summarize briefly, most states leave the shotgunner and rifleman well enough alone; some require paper work to one degree or another if you would purchase a handgun to keep in your home or place of business. The laws covering the carrying of handguns are dense and diverse. The necessity for consulting the text of the law itself cannot be repeated too often.

The types of laws we have been discussing will be found in the criminal code. Usually, another volume will contain a thick wad of legislation, supplemented by equally copious administrative regulations, concerning the taking of game. Besides bag limits, seasons, and the issuance of hunting licences, these will specify under what circumstances and *with what weapons* different species may be taken. There may be restrictions on action types, calibres, projectile types, and magazine capacities. Different states have different ideas on the subject. Deer, for example, may only be taken with a rifle in some places, a shotgun in others. Buckshot is prescribed in some areas and proscribed in others. Handgun hunting is permitted in some states and prohibited in others. Again a trip to the statutes is in order, although state fish and game commissions can usually be relied on to give clear and accurate answers to questions in this field.

It is worth mentioning that some states have sweeping anti-poaching statutes, which may, for example, outlaw the transportation of any firearm in a motor vehicle during the hours of darkness during hunting season, violation of which may subject the vehicle and weapon to confiscation and their owner to prosecution. What sort of reception this legislation gets in court, I do not know. But it does exist in some places and one is well advised to be aware of it.

LOCAL LAW

Municipalities in most cases have been content to leave firearms legislation to the state. However, many cities require a licence for dealers in firearms and ammunition, some have restrictions on the discharge of firearms within the corporate limits, and many prohibit the transfer of weapons to, or their ownership by, young people under the age of 21, 18, 16 or 14, as the case may be. Some places permit the mayor to proclaim a state of crisis, inaugurated ordinarily by prohibiting the sale of alcohol. Usually he may also, during this period, prohibit the sale or transfer of firearms and ammunition, but in no case of which we are aware may he call in weapons that are legally held. Such a provision would, in most states, be unconstitutional.

The ordinances are always worth reading. Deer Park, Texas, strenuously prohibits Molotov Cocktails. Fort Worth outlaws the manufacture of cartridges except by private individuals who reload for their own use and not for resale. San Antonio has a similar ordinance, but goes further and requires reloaders to apply for a licence to hold more than 1,000 primers at a time.

Kenilworth, New Jersey, prohibits persons under 16 years of age from owning air guns, sling shots, or bows and arrows, and prohibits their use by anyone. Adults may own a slingshot, but have to take it beyond the city limits to use it. Millburn, New Jersey, takes a darker view, and prohibits fathers from giving their sons of under 18 years 'any machine gun, automatic rifle . . . blackjack . . . bludgeon . . . dagger, dirk, stilletto, bomb or other high explosive.' Millburn also prohibits slingshots. Winfield prohibits the possession of gunpowder, which it lumps into a list alongside nitroglycerine and dynamite. That makes it hard on black powder shooters.

Generally, no one pays much attention to this sort of local statute, but that is the law and there are penalties attached for breaking it.

Some local ordinances cannot be ignored, and New York City, the District of Columbia, Philadelphia and Chicago are regarded as having the most repressive firearms codes in the United States. Washington, DC fell into the hands of gun law advocates who imposed regulations in defiance of both their federal charter and the repeated insistence of Police Chief Jerry V. Wilson that gun laws had nothing to do with crime, and that the only answer was better law enforcement and a more efficient court structure. However, they seem to have been successful, and the National Rifle Association has been obliged to close the underground test range in its headquarters building and move its technical staff out of the District.

In other areas the tide appears to be turning. Sections of the Philadelphia ordinance have been ruled unconstitutional in state courts. In New York City shooters have organized, and the Federation of Greater New York Rifle and Pistol Clubs, Inc. since its formation in 1973 has repeatedly taken the police to court. As a result, the police have been compelled to operate within the law, and the situation is healthier than it has been in the past half-century.

During the summer of 1968 citizens of San Francisco were given from 22 July to 16 August to register all firearms with the police (at a price, of course) or risk six months' imprisonment and a $500 fine. However, the California state legislature passed a pre-emption act nullifying the San Francisco ordinance

FEDERAL LAW

The republic survived splendidly for a century and a half with no federal restrictions on firearms. The remarkable extent of this span of liberalism was due in part to the Second Amendment, and in part to the fact that the federal government had no police power. It still hasn't.

Since the central government has no legitimate police power, the statutes depend for their own legality on being tied either to taxation or to the regulation of interstate commerce. Thus the National Firearms Act of 1934, which regulated machine guns, sawn-off rifles and shotguns and

certain other weapons, was a revenue bill, while the Federal Firearms Act of 1938, which had to do with the licensing of manufacturers and dealers and the prescription of records to be kept by them, was an interstate transport measure.

The 1934 Act and the 1938 Act together composed the body of federal legislation on the subject until 1968 when, in the emotional climate that followed the assassinations of Senator Robert Kennedy and Dr Martin Luther King, a staccato of new statutes was enacted.

Title X of the Civil Rights Act imposes penalties of $10,000 and imprisonment of up to five years on anyone who demonstrates, transports, manufactures or teaches the use of any firearm, explosive or incendiary device for use in rioting or civil disorder.

The Omnibus Crime Control and Safe Streets Act contained two titles of interest. Title VII makes it a federal offence, punishable by $10,000 fine and/or two years' imprisonment, for any person who:
● has been convicted by a court of the United States or of a state or any political subdivision thereof of a felony, or
● has been discharged from the Armed Forces under dishonorable conditions, or
● has been adjudged by a court of the United States or of a state or any political subdivision thereof of being mentally incompetent, or
● having been a citizen of the United States has renounced citizenship, or
● being an alien is illegally or unlawfully in the United States, to own any type of firearm whatsoever capable of firing metallic cartridges. Any person who is knowingly in the employ of an individual meeting one of the above descriptions, and who, in the course of his employment, knowingly receives, possesses, or transports a gun is subject to the same penalties. The President of the United States and the governors of the various states are empowered to grant immunities under this title if they see fit.'

Title IV repealed the Federal Firearms Act of 1938, but incorporated most of its provisions, expanded them, and added new law. Carried over from the 1938 Act was a mass of provisions regulating dealers, prescribing to whom they may sell, and creating offences for the sale, purchase, storage or disposition of weapons that were stolen or from which the manufacturer's serial number had been removed or altered.

The new law in Title IV consisted essentially in the prohibition of mail order sale of handguns, and the restriction of all interstate transactions in firearms and ammunition to federally licensed dealers. There were exceptions for weapons being returned to the manufacturer for repair.

Most of this was further amalgamated into the Gun Control Act of 1968, which is now usually referred to in shorthand as the GCA 68.

One of the vexations of the Act, a minor annoyance in each individual case but of vast cumulative weight, is the requirement that federal forms be completed for each sale of handgun or .22 rimfire ammunition. This amounts to some four billion rounds a year, each as resolutely untraceable as sand or pine needles, and results in the production of tons of paperwork and the consumption of man-years of dealer time.

With two exceptions, a person may purchase a firearm only in his state of residence. The exceptions are, first, that a person may purchase a rifle or shotgun in a state adjoining his own, providing the respective legislatures have passed contiguous state laws authorizing such transactions. At last report, all but five states (Illinois, Florida, New Jersey, Rhode Island and Hawaii) had passed such acts. Secondly, a person hunting or engaging in target shooting outside his own state may, if his rifle or shotgun breaks down, purchase a replacement by presenting to the local dealer a sworn statement attesting his predicament and the name and address of the chief law enforcement officer in his home locality. In no event may a handgun be purchased outside one's state of residence.

These provisions were enacted, it was said, in hope of obstructing criminals who, unable to pass police scrutiny in their home bailiwick, would take advantage of more liberal circumstances elsewhere to arm themselves. Unfortunately, the past several years have seen the development of a vigorous black market in handguns.

For the serious student of firearms the most annoying aspect of the GCA 68, as interpreted by the Treasury Department, has been its outlawing the importation into the United States of hundreds of models and variations of firearms of prime collector interest. The Act limits importation to guns that, in the opinion of the Secretary of the Treasury, are 'generally recognized as particularly suitable for, or readily adaptable to, sporting purposes, excluding surplus military firearms'.

Collector dissatisfaction was inevitable, since the equity of collectors was not taken into consideration in this section of the Act. Still, one must view with awe the bureaucratic colossus that the Treasury has managed to erect on this rather innocuous foundation.

The 'military' side is the simpler. The Treasury considers as 'surplus military firearms', and hence ineligible for importation into the United States, any weapon that has seen military service of any type at any time. Thus target Smith & Wessons, post-1898 Colt single actions, Savage 99 sporting rifles and L. C. Smith double shotguns, which were donated by American sportsmen in 1940 and saw Home Guard service in the Battle of Britain, are, in the eyes of the Treasury, indelibly tainted by the experience and may not re-enter the United States.

Practically every handgun in existence in Europe was pressed into service on one side or the other during World War II. Therefore, virtually the only European handguns that may enter the United States are those of postwar commercial manufacture, ergo, those of the least collector interest. One of the most significant of the postwar designs is the Beretta Model 1951, and its rarest variation is the match target version. However, a match target Model 1951 may not enter the United States, for it was manufactured on special order for the Egyptian army shooting team. Only the military version has been sold commercially, hence only that version qualifies for importation.

The splendid SIG P210 is importable or not depending on the serial number prefix. If there is no prefix, it is importable; if it has an A prefix, it is unimportable. P prefixes are moot, and it may be that they are importable if the P is rollstamped, but not if it is handstamped. D prefixes are a bone of contention.

The 'sporting purpose' clause has been responsible for the erection of an entire new component of federal bureaucracy. A handgun, in order to be 'sporting' in the eyes of the Treasury, must first of all be at least 4 inches high and 6 inches long. If these criteria are satisfied, it must then win a minimum number of 'points' according to federal 'factoring criteria', which are awarded for superficial characteristics of design and construction. Long barrels, tall frames and more weight all garner points, as do striated triggers, adjustable sights and proliferated safeties. Forged aluminium frames earn more points than forged steel, but lose them again on weight.

All this applies only to handguns being imported into the country. However, the Treasury takes a very hard line, and a United States resident who, for example, takes an S & W M19 2½ inch to Britain to compete in Long Range Pistol Championships in Pocket Pistol class may not bring the same gun back home with him: it is too short. Once it leaves the United States, the Treasury revokes its citizenship.

One result of this section of the GCA 68 has been to prohibit the importation by collectors of those weapons of the greatest technical and historical interest in the study of the evolution of the automatic pistol.

Collectors' interests were supposedly catered for in other sections of the Act. Any weapon, for example, manufactured during or prior to 1898 is classified as an antique, and is not subject to federal regulation of any sort. This does not, however, exempt it from state law. A concealed 1873 Colt is very much a concealed weapon. And if a state requires a purchase permit for a handgun, the 1873 may well be subject. It depends on the statute and case law of the state in question.

Other weapons are classified as curios or relics. Literally hundreds of firearms and cartridges, some of them quite recent, have been so designated by the Treasury. This does not, however, mean much. It does not, for example, mean that they may be imported or that they need not be registered, if registration is otherwise required, as is the case with machine guns, penguns, shoulder-stocked cartridge handguns with barrels of less than 16 inches, and so forth. All the curio and relic classification means is that the weapons and cartridges so designated by the Treasury may be exchanged in interstate commerce *between federally licensed collectors*. Thus collectors who register with the federal government legally become dealers in this category of weapon only, and on the restriction that their dealings be only with other licensed collectors. Complete federal transaction records have to be kept, and these are open to Treasury inspection. Most collectors have not felt that the advantages balance the disadvantages.

We mentioned federal registration requirements for certain classes of weapon. Briefly, registration and a $200 transfer tax are required of:

- machine guns (according to accepted technical definition);
- sawn-off or short-barrelled shotguns and rifles, or pistols made from shotguns or rifles. (The legal minimum for a shotgun is 26 inches overall, with 18 inch barrels; for a rifle, 26 inches overall with a 16 inch barrel);
- shoulder-stocked cartridge pistols, if the barrel is less than 16 inches long;
- silencers or sound moderators, whether they work or not;
- destructive devices. These include artillery, mortars, recoilless rifles, bazookas, grenades, land mines, anti-tank rifles, rockets with more than a prescribed charge of propellent or warhead composition, etc.

Registration and a $5 transfer tax are imposed on guns that are classified as 'any other weapon'. These include:

- certain smoothbore pistols, such as the Marble 'Game Getter', originally manufactured to fire shotgun shells;
- penguns, if capable of firing ball ammunition;
- smoothbore shot revolvers.

These provisions were carried into the GCA 68 from the National Firearms Act of 1934, via Title VII of the Omnibus Crime Control and Safe Streets Act of 1968. The GCA 68 is administered by the Bureau of Alcohol, Tobacco and Firearms (BATF), an independent Treasury enforcement agency. Prior to 1968 the present BATF was the Alcohol and Tobacco Tax Division (ATTD) of the Internal Revenue Service. It was a small, tough outfit that spent most of its energy fighting bootleggers. As a sideline, it enforced the National Firearms Act of 1934 and the Federal Firearms Act of 1938 in a calm, evenhanded manner that rarely gave rise to complaint. Unusual for a federal agency, the ATTD claimed it turned a profit for the government; the tax revenues it generated by forcing drinkers to go to legitimate outlets more than covered the agency's annual appropriation. Further to their credit was the number of lives they unquestionably saved each time they raided a still or seized a load of lead-poisoned 'hooch'.

With the passage of GCA 68 the division's name was changed to the Alcohol, Tobacco and Firearms Division (ATFD), and its field strength was doubled. In 1971 the agency was removed from the Inland Revenue Service, and became the present BATF. Today the BATF has more than 2,000 agents, most of them enforcing the GCA 68 and the 1970 Explosives Act.

People had been having second thoughts on the GCA 68 since the ink dried. Even in the emotional atmosphere accompanying its passage, it aroused little enthusiasm outside the gun control circles. It had a majority in the Senate, but in the House it was distinctly a minority measure. Of the 435 Representatives, only 160 had voted for it; 129 voted against and 142 abstained by answering 'present'. Of the 535 members of the two Houses, 230 voted for it, 146 against and the rest abstained. One of the bill's loyal backers was Hubert H. Humphrey, then Vice-President and one of the most popular and respected members of the liberal community. On 20 August 1970 Senator Humphrey wrote:

'In the past, particularly during the emotional period following the tragic deaths of Martin Luther King and Senator Robert Kennedy, many restrictions and limitations were proposed on the use and ownership of guns and ammunition. I supported some of these at that time. Since then, based on reflection and careful consideration of present existing federal legislation and more recent data, I have come to certain other conclusions.'

So had a number of people. At the time of Senator Humphrey's letter, more than 175 members of Congress were on record as favouring a relaxation of the GCA 68. More than a third of them wanted outright repeal, and 113 bills were pending to revoke or relax the 1968 law. None of the bills survived scrutiny by the House Judiciary Committee. Congress did, however, repeatedly vote down firearms registration bills in 1968, and in every succeeding session. Nonetheless, the BATF has announced that it intends to establish, without Congressional sanction, a central computer to record every legal firearms transaction in the United States.

The Bureau estimates that four transactions per gun take place before the first retail sale. If we add used gun to new gun annual turnovers, it appears the computer would be recording some 40,000,000 transactions yearly. Quarterly reports would be required, and the BATF estimates the annual paperwork cost to dealers at $8,000,000.

As crime control goes, the effect will be nil. Under the present system the Bureau has said that they can, with the cooperation of manufacturers and dealers, trace a weapon in twenty-six minutes if necessary. One assumes they mean during business hours.

GLOSSARY

Action

The action is screwed to the stock of a gun and contains all the mechanisms necessary to attach the barrels and to fire the cartridges.

Action body

The steel housing that contains all the moving parts of the action itself.

Automatic

Any gun that continues firing as long as the trigger is pulled. Many guns that are, strictly speaking, self-loading are often referred to as automatics.

Bore

The part of the inside of the barrel which is entirely filled and sealed by the shot and wads when the gun is fired. Commonly used instead of the correct term, gauge, to refer to the size of a shotgun.

Calibre

The measurement of the bore of a rifle, expressed in millimetres or in decimal points of an inch. It is the measurement of the inside diameter of the barrel before rifling, the bullet is made slightly larger for good obturation (*q.v.*).

Cap

The part of the cartridge containing fulminating compounds, which when struck, explode and ignite the powder charge in the cartridge.

Carbine

A shortened rifle. Originally a short-barrelled musket, the name was later given to short-barrelled rifles issued to mounted troops who needed a weapon short enough to fit into a saddle holster without knocking or chafing the horse. It is very popular with modern hunters for deer shooting in woodland and brush.

Cartridge

Shotgun cartridges are graded by the size of their pellets. The smaller the shot, the more pellets in the cartridge and the greater the chance of a hit. Larger shot offers greater penetration at long ranges.

Case hardening

In gun-making the process by which the outside of the action body is hardened by heating it in a furnace together with bone ash. The metal absorbs carbon from the bone ash which hardens the outer layer of steel without reducing the elasticity of the metal inside.

Choke

A constriction left in the muzzle end of a barrel bore during manufacture. The constriction prevents the shot from spreading as much and as soon as it would otherwise have done, thus improving the pattern (*q.v.*). The degree of constriction is strictly measured in thousandths of an inch, from three to 40 thousandths of an inch. Each thousandth is known as one point of choke, thus a gun can be described as having full choke of 40 points, half choke of 20 points. Choke can also be added after manufacture.

Corning

A method of making high quality gunpowder. The milled powder was dampened to a paste and the paste forced through a series of sieves. When dry the powder was composed of small, hard grains of uniform size that burnt faster and did not cake.

Flats

The flat parts machined at the rear of the barrels to fit against the flats of the action.

Gauge

The size of a shotgun bore. Gauge is determined by the number of spherical balls of pure lead of the same diameter as the bore that will make up one pound in weight. For example, a 12-gauge bore will weigh out 12 lead balls to the pound. Bores smaller than 32 are measured in decimals of an inch.

Lever action

Rifle action in which the breech bolt and carrier are operated by a finger-lever trigger guard.

Magnum

A gun that has been specially chambered to fire a load heavier than would be normal with a gun of the same bore.

Minie

A pointed bullet, strictly speaking an aerodynamically stable cylindrical ogive, with a hollow base. Developed by a French officer, Captain C. E. Minie, to solve the problem of fitting a bullet into a rifled barrel without having to ram it home. The Minie bullet is pushed into the bore and the expanding gases of the exploding charge cause the hollow base to expand and fit the grooves of the rifling. The Minie bullet made it possible to reload quickly in battle without having to first wrap the bullet in a greased patch.

Muzzle brake

A means of reducing recoil by fitting to the end of a rifle barrel a device which diverts the escaping gasses at right angles to the barrel through slots in the brake.

Muzzle velocity

The velocity at which the charge leaves the barrel. This is dependent on the progressive nature of the powder used in the charge.

Obturation

Sealing a bore to prevent the gases from the explosion of the cartridge escaping prematurely.

Pattern

The basic value is considered as the number of pellets found inside a 30 inch circle when a 12-bore shotgun, firing a cartridge loaded with $1\frac{1}{16}$ ounce of No. 6 shot and 33 grains of smokeless diamond powder, is fired from a distance of 40 yards. This will vary with the points of choke and composition of the charge.

Pinfire

An early type of cartridge in which the cap was positioned sideways inside the base with a pin above it. The head of the pin protruded through the cartridge case and was driven into the primer to explode the cartridge at a blow from the hammer.

Progressive powders

Powders that are designed to burn in such a way that they produce, as nearly as possible, a constant pressure.

Rimfire

The cap in a rimfire cartridge covers the whole of the base of the cartridge instead of just the centre. The striker therefore does not have to hit the centre of the cartridge to cause it to explode. Rimfire cartridges are now used almost solely in .22 'varmint' model rifles.

Shot

Shot is made from lead with a little antimony or arsenic added to increase the hardness. The spherical shot pellets are made by dropping molten lead down a shot tower into a water tank. Pellets are then polished and graded for size by passing them through a series of screens. The number of pellets in one ounce of shot of any given size is known and is constant.

Trajectory

The curve described by a bullet as it flies through the air. Trajectory must be taken into account when firing a rifle at distances of over 300 yards. At such distances a bullet may drop by between 10 to 30 inches in the course of its flight. A high muzzle velocity will give the flat trajectory desirable in long range shooting.

Wad

Felt, cardboard or plastic discs which hold the shot charge together while it passes up the barrel. Wads are also important for providing obturation (*q.v.*).

FURTHER READING

General

Bearse, R. *Sporting Arms of the World* 1976
Blackmore, H. L. *Hunting Weapons* 1971
Blackmore, H. L. *Royal Sporting Guns at Windsor* 1968
Brander, M. *International Encyclopedia of Shooting* 1972
Burrard, Sir G. *The Modern Shotgun* (3 vols) 1931–1948
Burrell, B. *Combat Weapons* 1973
Burrell, B. *Gun Collectors Guide* 1972
Burrell, B. *Gun Collectors Handbook* 1959
Burrell, B. *Gun Collectors Digest* 1974
Hicks, J. E. *Notes on US Ordnance 1776–1941* 1971
Koller, L. *How to Shoot* 1976
Lavin, J. D. *A History of Spanish Firearms* 1965
Murtz, H. *Exploded Firearms Drawings* 1974
Pullum, B. & Hanenkrat, F. *Position Rifle Shooting* 1973
Purdey, T. D. & J. A. *The Shotgun* 1972
Smith, J. *Smallarms of the World* 1973
Smith, W. & J. *Smallarms of the World* 1962
Smith, W. H. B. *Mauser, Walther and Mannlicher Firearms* 1971
Standl, H. *Pistol Shooting* 1975

Antique firearms

Atkinson, J. *Duelling Pistols* 1964
Bailey, D. W. *British Military Longarms 1715–1815* 1971
Bailey, D. W. *British Military Longarms 1815–1865* 1972
Bailey, D. W. *Percussion Guns and Rifles* 1972
Baxter, D. R. *Superimposed Load Firearms 1360–1869* 1966
Blackmore, H. L. *British Military Firearms 1650–1850* 1969
Blackmore, H. L. *Guns and Rifles of the World* 1965
Blackmore, H. L. *Hunting Weapons* 1971
Blair, C. *Pistols of the World* 1968
Dunlap, J. *American, British and Continental Pepperbox Firearms* 1967
Gluckman, A. *Old US Muskets, Rifles and Carbines* 1965
Hayward, J. *The Art of the Gunmaker* (Vols 1 and 2) 1963 and 1965
Karr, C. L. *Remington Handguns* 1960
Logan, H. *Underhammer Guns* 1960
Neal, W. K. & Back, D. H. *Forsyth & Co. Patent Gunmakers* 1969
Neal, W. K. & Back, D. H. *Great British Gunmakers* 1975
Neal, W. K. & Back, D. H. *The Mantons Gunmakers* 1967
Roads, C. H. *The British Soldiers Firearms 1850–1864* 1964
Rosa, J. *Colonel Colt, London* 1976
Sell, D. W. *Handguns Americana* 1972
Shumaker, P. L. *Colt's Variation of the Old Model Pocket Pistol 1848–1872* 1966
Swayze, N. L. *'51 Colt Navies* 1967
Wilkinson, F. *Antique Firearms* 1978
Wilkinson, F. *The World's Great Guns* 1977

Handguns

Appiano, E. *Revolver e Pistole Automatiche* 1973
Bady, D. *Colt Automatic Pistols* 1973
Cary, L. *The Colt Gun Book* 1973
Chamberlain, P. & Gander, T. *Allied Pistols, Rifles and Grenades* 1976
Chamberlain, P. & Gander, T. *Axis Pistols, Rifles and Grenades* 1976
Chamberlain, W. H. J. & Taylerson, A. W. *Adam's Revolvers* 1976
Graham, R. & Kopec, J. *A Study of the Colt Single Action Army Revolver* 1976
Hoffschmidt, E. J. *Know Your Colt .45 Auto* 1974
Hogg, I. V. *German Pistols and Revolvers 1871–1945* 1971
Hogg, I. V. *Military Pistols and Revolvers* 1970
Hogg, I. V. & Weeks, J. *Military Smallarms of the Twentieth Century* 1973
Hogg, I. V. & Weeks, J. *Pistols of the World* 1978
Jinks, R. *History of Smith & Wesson* 1977
Karr, C. L. & C. R. *Remington Handguns* 1960
Keith, E. *Sixguns* 1961
Leith, F. *Japanese Handguns* 1968

Millard, J. T. *A Handbook on the Primary Identification of Revolvers and Semi-Automatic Pistols* 1974
Nonte, G. *Pistol and Revolver Guide* 1970
Olson, J. *Automatic Pistols of Europe* 1976
Parsons, J. *The Peacemaker and its Rivals* 1950
Pawlas, K. *Pistol Atlas* (Vols 1–8) 1970
Rosa, J. *Colonel Colt, London* 1976
Sell, De W. *Handguns Americana* 1977
Sellers, F. & Smith, S. *American Percussion Revolvers* 1971
Smith, W. H. & J. E. *Book of Pistols and Revolvers* 1968
Sutherland, R. Q. & Wilson, L. *The Book of Colt Firearms* 1971
Taylerson, A. W. et al. *The Revolver 1818–1865* 1968
Taylerson, A. W. *The Revolver 1865–1888* 1966
Taylerson, A. W. *The Revolver 1889–1914* 1970
Tilton, F. G. *Lugers Unlimited* 1965
Walter, J. *Kuger* 1977
Weston, P. B. *Book of Handgunning* 1968
Wilson, R. K. *Textbook of Automatic Pistols* 1975

Police and law enforcement
Bristow, A. *The Search for an Effective Police Handgun* 1973
Greenwood, C. *Police Firearms Training* 1966
Greenwood, C. *Firearms Control* 1972
Roberts, D. & Bristow, A. *Modern Police Firearms* 1969
Weston, P. B. *Combat Shooting for Police* 1960
Williams, M. *The Law Enforcement Book of Weapons, Ammunition and Training Procedure* 1977

Rifles
Blackmore, H. L. *Guns and Rifles of the World* 1965
Corcoran, J. E. *The Target Rifle in Australia 1860–1900* 1975
Haas, F. de. *Bolt Action Rifles* 1971
Pullum, B. & Hanenkrat F. *Position Rifle Shooting* 1973
Reynolds, E. G. *The Lee Enfield Rifle* 1960
Swenson, G. W. *Pictorial History of the Rifle* 1971
Williamson, H. *Winchester, the Gun that Won the West* 1963

Air weapons
Beeman, R. *Airgun Digest* 1977
Hoff, A. *Airguns and Other Pneumatic Arms* 1972
Smith, W. H. B. *Gas, Air and Spring Guns* 1957
Wesley, L. *Air Guns and Air Rifles* 1957
Wolff, E. *Air Guns* 1958

Ammunition
Barnes, F. *Cartridges of the World* 1962
Bartlett, W. *Cartridge Manual* 1959
Hackley, F. W. & Woodin, W. *History of Modern US Military Small Arms Ammunition 1880–1939* (Vol 1) 1967
Lewis, B. *Small Arms and Ammunition in the US Services 1776–1865* 1968
Logan, H. C. *Cartridges* 1959
Suydam, C. *The American Cartridge* 1960

Reloading
J. Amber ed. *Handloaders Digest* 1970
Greenell, D. *ABCs of Reloading* 1974
Naramore, E. *Principles and Practice of Loading Ammunition* 1971
Nonte, G. *Modern Handloading* 1977
Whelan, T. *Why Not Load Your Own* 1957

Military weapons – assault rifles and machine guns
Chamberlain, P. & Gardner, T. *Submachine Guns and Automatic Rifles* 1976
Ellis, J. *The Social History of the Machine Gun* 1975
Hobart, F. W., ed. *Jane's Infantry Weapons* 1975
Hobart, F. W. *Pictorial History of the Machine Gun* 1971
Hobart, F. W. *Pictorial History of the Sub Machine Gun* 1973
Musgrave, D. & Nelson, T. *The World's Assault Rifles* 1967
Musgrave, D. & Smith, O. *German Machine Guns* 1971
Nelson, T. & Lockmore, H. *The World's Sub Machine Pistols* 1978

INDEX

Page numbers in *italic* refer to illustrations

ACKNOWLEDGEMENTS

Numbers in *italics* refer to the position of the picture on the page reading from top to bottom and left to right.

J. A. Bailey/Ardea, London 267 *1*; Bath Press Photo Services 252 bottom, 255; Paul Betschart 173 bottom; R. J. C. Blewitt/Ardea, London 261 top left; Geoffrey Boothroyd 53 bottom, 54 bottom, 155, 164, 165; J. B. & S. Bottomley/Ardea, London 267 *2*; G. K. Brown/Ardea, London 267 *3, 6, 8*; Christ Church College 11; Jim Collins 140, 141, 142, 143, 144, 145, 146; Cooper Bridgeman Library cover *2*, 16, 17 *6*, 21 *4, 6*, 23, 26, 28, 29; Malcolm Cooper 103 *5*, 168, 170, 171; Reg Cox 209, 215; Gerry Cranham cover *4, 5, 7*, 118, 119, 121, 122, 125, 166, 167, 173 top; Werner Curth/Ardea, London 279 *3*; Christopher Dawes 68, 69, 70, 71, 72, 73, 74, 77, 79; Andre Farras/Ardea, London 261 top right, 267 *5*; K. Fink/Ardea, London 284; Paul Forrester 36, 38 *1, 2, 3*, 39, 41 *1, 3, 4*, 42 *2, 3*, 43 *5, 6*, 44 *2, 3*, 45 *1, 4, 5, 6*, 46 *1, 2*, 47 *1, 2, 3, 5*, 48, 49 *1, 2, 3*, 50, 51 *2, 3, 4*, 52 top, 53 *2*, 99, 100, 101 *1, 2, 3*, 102, 103 *1, 2, 3, 4*, 104, 105, 106 *1, 2*, 108, 109, 114, 213 bottom; Elgin Gates 148, 150, 151, 152, 192, 193, 195, 197; Gunshots cover *3, 6, 7*, 15 *4, 5*, 17 *5*, 21 *2, 3, 5*, *7*, 25, 40 centre, 51 top, 58 *2,·3*, 59, 60 *1, 2, 4*, 61 bottom, 64, 65, 91, 98, 113, 116, 133 top and bottom right, 135 bottom, 147, 177, 206, 211, 213 top, 217, 218, 230, 234; Les Hammett 245, 249, 252 top left; Nigel Hinton 126, 128, 129, 131, 133 left, 136, 137, 139; Brian D. Kett 300, 301, 302, 303, 304, 306, 308; Chris Knights/Ardea, London 268, 279 *1*; Lee and Marilyn La Combe 178, 182, 187, 189; A. B. Macnab 54 *1, 2, 3*, 55 *1, 2*, 56, 57 *2, 3*, 232; Mansell Collection 242, 314; John Marchington cover *9*, 256, 271; John L. Morgan 247; Ritchie Moorhead 198, 202, 204;

Muzzle Loaders Association of Great Britain 227 top left; Paul Nicholls 52 *2, 3*, 55 bottom, 57 top, 60 *3*, 61 *1, 2*, 63 top, 93, 94, 95, 96, 97, 101 *4*, 135 top, 191, 223, 224, 225, 227 top right, bottom, 229, 241; Claude Petrone 9; Popperfoto 259 top, 294; Radio Times Hulton Picture Library 24; Sid Roberts/Ardea, London 267 *4, 7*, 279 *2*; Schweizerische Landesbibliothek, Bern 310; John Tarlton cover *1*, 257, 259 bottom, 261 bottom, 262, 265, 269, 273, 274, 276; Richard Vaughan/Ardea, London 263; Victoria and Albert Museum 15 *1, 2, 3, 6*, 17 *3, 4*; T. A. Wilkie 154, 159 bottom, 160, 163; T. Willcock/Ardea, London 285; Stuart Williams cover *8*, 34, 35, 280, 282, 283, 287, 288, 290, 291, 293, 296, 297, 298, 299; Zentralbibliothek, Zúrich 313.

The publisher wishes to thank the following
for their assistance:

Chubbs of Edgware
F. Dyke and Co. Ltd
Holland and Holland
Shooting Magazine
Shooting Times
Ray Ward, Gunsmith
National Rifle Association of America